SHORT STORY WRITING

by Wilson R. Thornley

Wilson R. Thornley has established a reputation as one of the most successful high school teachers of short story writing in the country. Among the many citations his students have received are awards from The National Scholastic Writing Awards Competition, The Atlantic Creative Writing Contest and publication in Scholastic Magazine, Seventeen and Literary Cavalcade.

SHORT STORY WRITING

WILSON R. THORNLEY

BANTAM BOOKS · LONDON
TORONTO · NEW YORK

RLI: $\dfrac{\text{VLM 7 (VLR 4–9)}}{\text{IL 9+}}$

SHORT STORY WRITING
A Bantam Book / November 1976
2nd printing

COPYRIGHT NOTICES AND ACKNOWLEDGMENTS

The copyright notices listed below and on the following page constitute an extension of this copyright page.

Excerpt from "*Two Tramps in Mud Time,*" from The Poetry of Robert Frost, *edited by Edward Connery Lathem; copyright 1936 by Robert Frost; copyright © 1964 by Lesley Frost Ballantine; copyright © 1969 by Holt, Rinehart and Winston. By permission of Holt, Rinehart and Winston and Jonathan Cape Ltd.*

Excerpt from "*Blueberry Bread*" by Olivia Bertagnolli Rackham. By permission of the author.

Excerpt from "*Age of Departure*" by Penny Allred Wright. By permission of the author.

Excerpt from "*Uncle Josh*" by Janet Hurst Gardner. By permission of the author.

To My Wife

Contents

PART I

1

Scene in The Short Story

The art of telling stories through dramatic representation seems so old as to be a natural characteristic of the human mind and spirit. We seem naturally to want to communicate experience, and we have an inbred conviction that our experiences are unique and interesting to others. Reporting our experiences releases us from inner tension, socially and psychologically. The report usually takes the form of a sequential story —something we have accomplished, a problem solved, a conquest attained. Telling it provides a kind of catharsis. It bridges the gap between our inner self and the listener.

Everybody tells stories: the counselor or psychologist illustrates a point or gains rapport with a story; the physician relates a case history; the businessman cites examples, and so on. In school, the student writes narrative themes. These naturally require careful structuring and development. Each student chooses the storytelling method he or she thinks will best serve his purpose. The choosing of a method is equally operative with professional story writers. But this choice and the ability to choose clearly implies a competence in the various possible disciplines. In so brief a treatment as I offer here, it seems wise to analyze just *one* good way to tell a story and to attain competence in that one discipline.

The well structured, true short story form examined here, which submits to the well defined discipline of the art form, has some specific characteristics unique to itself:

Definition of a short story: We should think of a

disciplined short story as a series of reported *scenes* in which a *causative situation* arises which requires a *deciding character* with a *governing characteristic* to try to solve some kind of *problem* along lines of action which he *decides* on as best for his purpose and which suffer *interruptions* or *intensifications* until he comes to the *result* of his final decisions. This condensed definition, with its key words, will be developed throughout the text of the book.

In a short story the reader is concerned with outcomes resulting from decisions made by the deciding character. The short story writer presumes that in the story all decisions and choices must be conditioned. In a story the central figure makes choices conditioned by his past experience which affects outcomes. He attempts to control his natural and human environment to his own desire. His decisions to solve his problem in certain ways pose for the reader the question: "Can the problem be solved under these conditions in this manner?" Answering this question, the writer generates a suspense very different from the interest found in narrative or essay and in the scenes to be found there. The posing of this question in a reported scene becomes the vital element of short story structure. Further, this sort of question invites the reader to participate in working out the solution in cooperation with the deciding character. What happens to him in the scene report happens also to us. Identification becomes more than mere sympathetic understanding. We, for a time, become the deciding character. This sort of identification is not possible nor necessary nor even desirable in a simple narrative, in which no crucial decisions are made and the characters accept what happens in a relatively passive fashion. In a short story such identification and participation are imperative.

If Laurel Ellison had written "So Young to Die," (which you should now read) reprinted in Part Two, as a simple narrative, the reader would be interested in it as an analysis of family relationships, and he would be delighted by the sensory but passive report of scene. He would find sympathy for Linnie and others in like difficulties. He would ponder the implications for himself and be reminded of his own experiences. He would be observant. But he would be relatively detached because the scene would not be directed and given vitality by a decision. Instead, as a short story reported in scenes, he is caught up into Linnie's experience. He does not merely understand her situation, the processes by which her personality is affected, the causes, the resolution. In a radically different way, he goes through the process himself, vicariously. Slowly, as the scenes unfold in the report, he, too, feels the need for acceptance. For the time it takes him to read the story and recover from it, he has so identified himself with Linnie as to become, with her, a little girl needing love. This sort of intense participation through identification is the special quality of the disciplined short story.

Scene the Basic Unit: All we have said so far has been by way of definition and will receive further development in later chapters. But in the beginning it is necessary to make clear the concept of scene as the basic structural unit of composition in a short story. You do not "tell a story"; you do not narrate a sequence of events. Instead, you conceive of the story as happening before you as on a stage (the actors, the settings, the speeches, the stage business, the lighting, and the sound); and you report what you see and hear and otherwise sense in the scenes. When the play requires a change of scene, you report the change. The process is dramatic, not narrative. But a short story is actually not a play. It happens in words, on a printed page. You transpose the stage setting to the imagined scene on paper and communicate with the reader in scene. How is this done? What constitutes a scene report? Let's examine the content of a sample scene.

What Is Scene?: Each of us exists actually in a scene. At any given moment, we operate within a specific context of time and place. Our sensory organs filter our experience of the world around us; we are subject both to the mood with which we initially approach the outside world, and the consequent effect that this world has upon us. The way in which we apprehend the world determines our personal point of view and the way in which we will act within that world.

Right now, as you read this, you are living a little scene, having an experience. How is this happening? What are the component parts of this experience? It is a certain *time,* say an autumn evening after dinner. You are sitting in a reasonably uncomfortable chair at a desk *in a room.* The *study light* is glaring down brightly on this page of print and throwing the rest of the room, if you will glance around you, into relative shadow. The drapes shut out the late evening light. You have a specific *purpose* in this scene: some fellow wrote a guide to short story writing and you intend to study it; you have certain subjective attitudes toward this purpose (the fellow, too, perhaps) which create a *mood* and which you could, if you wished, analyze. These attitudes as well as your physical position relative to the light and the book give you a certain way of seeing. For instance, if you get up and go over to that comfortable couch in the corner and lie down, the scene and your experience will change because the position has changed, though nothing else in the room moved. Test this assertion, if you will, now. So far you have isolated six identifiable elements of this scene that affect your experience: time, place, purpose, position, light, and character.

Now, continue this analysis of scene, extending it to include the functioning of your sensory faculties and their perception of the experience. You *see* this printed page and through it the images and symbols made on your mind by these words with their connotations and associations unique to you. During the glance around a moment ago you perceived all the details of *sight* that identify this place and this time: walls, ceiling, floor, chairs, table, desk, bed, all in minute detail of color and texture with their associations.

You can sniff and *smell* the study, with all the

private identifying odors, subtle, perhaps, but undeniably present and unique so as to make this room
surely yours: fabric, textiles, leather, ink, typewriter
ribbon and oil, lotion, your hands, that candy bar,
and so on: all are part of the experience. If you were
brought into this room blindfolded, could you identify it by the smell alone?

What are you *hearing?* Perhaps your breathing,
and, since it is just after dinner, the inward sounds of
the processes of peristalsis; if the room is quiet, the
faint clicking from the kitchen of dishes being
washed, the muffled monotone of the TV in another
room, the faint movement of the breeze outside, a
dog barking, unidentified sounds from the adjoining
apartment, the quiet turning of these pages. All these
consciously or unconsciously impinge on your hearing organism and become part of this scene experience.

What can you touch? Your clothing, of course, some
of it tight and uncomfortable, the chair you sit in,
this book with its weight and texture and flexibility.
As you moved to the couch a moment ago, you
touched other items. You feel the room temperature,
and all these sensations you react to in some overt
or subtle way.

Can you taste anything? Yes, your mouth and
nasal membranes, perhaps your gum or the candy
bar, the dessert you ate for dinner, or perhaps just
your lipstick or your saliva.

What is being demonstrated here? Simply that you
live in a scene uniquely and individually, that in fact
we all do. No one else in the world can go through
exactly the same actual experience that you have just
analyzed. We do not smell alike, taste alike, see alike,
touch alike, or hear alike. Each person is sensorily
unique, since all experience comes to us through our
individual sensory system. Further, we live constantly in scene, and we move from scene to scene. In
the scene just analyzed we identified eleven elements:
time, place, light, character, point of view, purpose,
and the five senses.

Ideas for Study

1. Report precisely your own sensory perception of a room in your home. Try to report all eleven elements of scene.

2. Blindfold yourself and have a friend lead you into a familiar room. Stand still. Can you identify the room from its odor alone?

3. Stand for one minute in a room and list the sounds you hear, naming the source. Try not to use adjectives.

4. In what ways did the men in Apollo 11 use their sense faculties to explore the moon?

Actual and Imagined Scene: You will observe, in the following scene analyses, that the details are reported in consequential order; that is, one element rises from the preceding element and leads logically to the next; an event rises from the cause and moves toward the result.

This sequence of detail may be determined by the various purposes for the report. Perhaps the mood of the reporter decides the sequential order, as it does in "Blueberry Bread" and in "Uncle Josh." Or perhaps the physical relationship and position of character in the scene may determine the order of detail, as it does in "Age of Departure." Or perhaps the natural order of sense perception will control the sequence, as it does in Ernest Hemingway's "Big Two Hearted River" in the scene on the bridge or in the scene reporting Nick's preparation of his evening meal. Sometimes the physical progress of the reporter through a scene supplies the guide to sequence, as it does in this report of Paul's journey home from school in Conrad Aiken's "Silent Snow Secret Snow":

"On his walk homeward, which was timeless, it pleased him to see . . . the items of mere externality on his way. There were many kinds of bricks in the sidewalks, and laid in many kinds of pattern. The garden walls, too, were various, some of wooden palings, some of plaster, some of stone. Twigs of bushes leaned over the walls; the little hard green winter-buds of lilac, on gray stems, sheathed and fat; other branches very thin and fine and black and desiccated. Dirty sparrows huddled in the bushes, as dull in color as dead fruit left in leafless trees. A single starling creaked on a weather vane. In the gutter, beside a drain, was a scrap of torn and dirty news-paper, caught in a little delta of filth: the word ECZEMA appeared in large capitals, and below it was a letter from Mrs. Amelia D. Grayath, 2100 Pine Street, Fort Worth, Texas, to the effect that after being a sufferer for years she had been cured by Caley's ointment." As the boy moves onward his senses pick up added detail, and it is reported in the sequence of his progress.

In Sarah Orne Jewett's "The White Heron," Sylvia has climbed to the top of the tall tree and Jewett reports the expanse of scene thus: "Sylvia's face was like a pale star, if one had seen it from the ground, when the last thorny bough was past, and she stood trembling and tired but wholly triumphant, high in the tree-top. Yes, there was the sea with the dawning sun making a golden dazzle over it, and toward that glorious east flew two hawks with slow-moving pinions. How low they looked in the air from that height when before one had only seen them far up, and dark against the sky. Their gray feathers were as soft as moths; they seemed only a little way from the tree, and Sylvia felt as if she too could go flying away among the clouds. Westward, the woodlands and farms reached miles and miles into the distance; here and there were church steeples, and white villages; truly it was a vast and awesome world." Here the control over the sequence of detail is exerted by Jewett's need to communicate the effect of the height and distance and detachment and discovery, upon the little girl. The essential idea of consequence in this discussion is that you choose some control over the way you see the scene and let this control govern the con-sequential order of detail in your report.

Thus a scene has many functions in the story: To report sensory experience of time, place, and perception; to analyze and report character and purpose and motive; to fulfill the discipline of story structure; and to delight the reader with its clarity and sensitivity to artistic truth.

To conclude this chapter with another example, let's analyze one scene from James Aldridge's "Bush Boy, Poor Boy," reprinted in Part Three. Paragraphs six and seven will serve to illustrate the elements of scene in a story. We have been told in previous paragraphs of the story that "I" has determined to shoot a fox. In this scene, that is the purpose; "I," the character; Pental Island, the place; day, the time; day, the light; first person subjective, the point of view; and there are the senses of sight, soundlessness, smell, and touch. The mood is one of excitement. Here are all eleven elements except taste arranged in strict consequential order.

Ideas for Study

1. Concentrate on a small experience in your past and report it in a creative scene. Use eleven elements if you can, but do not invent. Be brief.

2. Think of a scene in a story you have read which remains vividly in your mind. Can you see it now? If possible, go back to the story and reread the scene. Identify the scene elements in it.

Some Useful Readings

1. Ghiselin, Brewster, ed., *The Creative Process, A Symposium*. University of California Press, Berkeley, 1952. Mentor, a division of New American Library, has a paperback edition of this book. You ought to own a copy. It is a series of thirty-eight statements on creativity by artists in many fields, including writing and, in my judgment, the best treatment of the subject in print. You should think of it as a basic text, and read it constantly. For a sampling of the book to our purpose read the

contributions by Mozart, D. H. Lawrence, William B. Yeats, Stephen Spender, Dorothy Canfield, Thomas Wolfe, Katherine Anne Porter, and Brewster Ghiselin.

2

Making The Scene Report

The Story Writer's Vocabulary: In the absence of stage props and actors, the writer must report the scenes of his story-drama with no tools except words. What can be said of the vocabulary he uses to transfer experience (character, event, place, lighting, mood, purpose, etc.) to the reader? We have long known that all our knowledge of ourselves and the world outside our skins comes to us through the five senses sometimes assisted by those scientific devices of tele- and microscopes, which extend sense perception in both directions. Awareness of this concept has been sharpened and deepened and extended of late by the electrifying events in space travel. If this is true, the writer who wishes to transmit the experience of the story character in a set of scenes must use words which work at the concrete sensory level of light, sight, touch, taste, and sound.

What sorts of words are most likely to be concrete? We would probably agree at once on nouns and words shaped from nouns. But not all these nouns evoke sensory experience. If you write "labor," you have not named a concrete sensory thing, but an abstraction. "Labor" might refer to the manufacturing of an electronic computer or to the making of a safety pin, to higher mathematics or ditch digging, with a whole range of economic and social implications. If you write "housing," you step down the ladder of abstraction to the building trades and what belongs to them and leave out all the rest. If you write "carpentry," all else is excluded; but you still cannot visualize it. Now, to make an enormous leap down the abstraction ladder: If you say "I saw John drive the 8-penny finishing nail into the door casing," you can point at it, photograph it, see it, hear it, feel it, and given the rest of the context, taste and smell it. The abstraction, "labor," has come to life in a concrete scene experience.

The short story writer can learn a great deal about the use of concrete terms from the work of a poet like Robert Frost. Here is another approach to "labor," from Frost's poem "Two Tramps in Mud Time." After reading this, can you visualize the scene? Do you need to ask whether or not Frost enjoyed his labor?

> Good blocks of oak it was I split,
> As large around as the chopping block;
> And every piece I squarely hit
> Fell splinterless as a cloven rock.
>
> You'd think I never had felt before
> The weight of an ax-head poised aloft.
> The grip on earth of outspread feet,
> The life of muscles rocking soft
> And smooth and moist in vernal heat.

Let's try again, with a different kind of abstraction. If my neighbor says, "Your flowers are beautiful," he leaves out all the sensory scene details which were present to make him offer the judgment. We are standing in bright, early morning sunlight before a bush of brilliantly full-blown American Beauty roses, admiring the color and the softness of texture and the rhythm and grace of the petal, inhaling the fragrance of the rose, aware of the morning coolness. His comment, which includes a subjective judgment, may be appropriate because the scene is before us; our shared experience needs no elaboration into words. But if he wrote the words in the absence of the things, the words would not transfer the experience. Being pure abstractions, they cannot report the sensory scene. We can point to the "roses" and photograph them. We can measure the temperature and test the texture. We cannot photograph "flowers" nor "beautiful."

We do not see a forest as a whole; we see a stand of lodge-pole pine. We cannot see a tree; we see a Lombardy poplar. And the farther down the ladder of abstraction we go to leaves and bark and light and shade and movement and so on, the more sharply do we receive a sense perception of scene. If in describing a leaf we use adjectives like "ugly" or "beautiful," we express a judgment related, not to the leaf, but to ourselves. If, instead, we say "green" or "serrated," we have presented sensory evidence, which can be transmitted to the reader. Good scene writing presents evidence rather than judgment. A story writer reports "things" as he senses them. To do this he uses concrete nouns and "naming" words shaped from those nouns.

Here is a fragment from the notebook of a visiting German student's story. "The first sunbeams slipped out of the cloud layer and gave the mist in the hollow a silver shining, when my brother, Havi, and I went through the high grass in our garden. The morning air was fresh, and every blade of grass gleamed of dewdrops shaped like pearls and glittering like crystal. We reached the wooden hut in which we have our garden equipment, and Havi went in. He came with a scythe, a wooden rake and a thin, grey whetstone. He pricked the stick of the scythe into the soft ground and rolled up his sleeves. 'Fine that you come with me, Sesi,' he said, and started to whet the scythe. The thin whetstone whisked along both sides of the scythe blade, and the tinny, whirring sound tickled my ears. I felt happy."

Can you sense the concrete quality of such verb forms as slipped, shining, shaped, glittering, gardening, pricked, whet (repeated three times), whisked, whirring, tickled? Can you sense the names implied in such adjectives as morning, silver, fresh, wooden (repeated twice), soft, and tinny? Thirty of the seventy words (excluding articles and connectives) are concrete terms. All of this passage is sensory report, except the last adjective. "Happy" is an abstraction drawn from the scene detail but not part of it. Coming at the end, "happy" seems to summarize the concrete words. It generalizes the mood and significance of the scene inductively, as abstractions properly do.

It will be apparent to you that the sharp sensory quality of exact concrete terms in this passage highlights by contrast the blurring of vision produced by clichés. When you read "dewdrops shaped *like pearls*" and "glittering *like crystal*," what happens to your visual perception? We can assume, I am sure, that Senti would not have chosen these stereotypes if she had been reporting the scene in her native German. As it reads now, we have the impression that, far from concentrating on scene to find the exact word which precisely reported the special look of the dewdrops in this morning air, she used the first English words that popped into her mind and thus weakened and dulled the report with the patent insincerity of a cliché. Using a cliché means giving up the search for the precise word. In effect it says to the reader: "You are not worth the effort it takes to find a fresh, exact word; I will use, instead a ready-made rubber stamp." The good writer, from the first declaring a war on the cliché, finds as his best weapon an intense concentration on the unique scene before him. As a secondary defense, some writers build slowly a list of words and phrases they know are liable to be clichés and then simply refuse to use them. One way or another all competent writers avoid the cliché.

Study this opening paragraph from Katherine Anne Porter's story, "Noon Wine":

"The two grubby small boys with tow-colored hair who were digging among the ragweed in the front yard sat back on their heels and said, 'Hello,' when the tall bony man with straw-colored hair turned in at their gate. He did not pause at the gate; it had swung back, conveniently half open, long ago, and was now sunk so firmly on its broken hinges no one thought of trying to close it. He did not even glance at the small boys, much less give them good-day. He just clumped down his big square dusty shoes one after the other steadily, like a man following a plow, as if he knew the place well and knew where he was going and what he would find there. Rounding the right hand corner of the house under the row of chinaberry trees, he walked up to the side porch where Mr. Thompson was pushing a big swing churn back and forth."

Miss Porter does not write "weeds"; but "ragweed"; not "trees," but "chinaberry trees"; and note the concrete verbs: "digging,". "swung back," "sunk," "clumped," "rounding," and so on. In addition to the concrete quality of her words, the unobtrusive metaphor in such expressions as "tow-colored," and "straw-colored," merit your attention.

A prose comparison of two things emphasizes their points of similarity sometimes usefully in a report. A comparison is an expected thing; it discovers nothing we do not already know. Much more startling and revealing is the poetic metaphor, a device by which the reporter discovers an unexpected and surprising similarity in otherwise totally unlike things.

When a writer, working within the complex discipline of the story form and concentrating intently on making the scene report exact and accurate and capable of being transferred to the reader, comes to a detail of some experience which must be so exactly reported that it is not speakable in a prose statement, he often turns to metaphor for accuracy. Porter's choice of the words with their immediate evocation of the comparison of the boy's hair with scutched flax, and of the man's hair with straw, is the essence of the poetic act. In this passage the words focus attention on the exact color of the hair and, by implication, of its texture. How does a metaphor do this?

A good metaphor accurately reduces an abstraction to the concrete level of scene by observing that two things, literally quite different, are unexpectedly and startlingly and accurately alike in one special way. A metaphor is a poetic discovery. It has the parts of a triangle thus: A $\overset{C}{}$ B. In his scene the writer sees that, while A and B are in all other respects dissimilar, yet in one chosen detail, C, they are exactly alike. Miss Porter saw that, while the boy's hair was in all other respects similar to tow, yet in the exact *color and texture,* the hair was precisely like flax fiber after scutching. She saw that, in the precise shade *of yellow,* the man's hair and the otherwise dissimilar straw were exactly alike. Seeing the hair in these ways, we discover her report to be exact and accurate and evocative. You, as a prose writer, will use the poetic device of metaphor to reduce a difficult abstraction to the sensory, concrete terms of your scene report.

Careful selection of words for their connotative meanings will often be useful to you to make your scene report accurate and exact and to increase the depth of insight. The connotative meanings of a word go beyond its literal denotation, or definition, and rise out of association of the word with long established uses. These connotations inevitably cluster round the word and affect your use of the word in reporting exact shades of meaning. A good writer is constantly and acutely aware of the meanings he brings to his report by the connotative associations a reader is likely to attach to words.

For instance, if I write: "That man is a hog," I do not mean that he is literally a pig (which is the denotative meaning); I mean that he is a greedy, filthy glutton, because these connotative associations have grown up round our use of the word.

Think of the different meanings suggested by the two comments if I write of the President: "He has proved to be a great statesman" or "He has proved to be a great politician." Yet the acts and conditions referred to in each sentence may be identical; and the dictionary lists the denotation of these words as synonymous. The Random House Dictionary then offers this caution: "These terms differ particularly in their connotations: Politician is more often derogatory, and Statesman laudatory. Politician suggests the schemes and devices of one who engaged in politics for party or his own advantage. Statesman suggests . . . eminent ability, foresight, and unselfish devotion to the interests of his country. . . ."

Analyze the connotative power of the associations clustered round the word, "crumpled," in this line from

"Noon Wine" in the scene where Mr. Helton is punishing the boys. "Herbert's mouth *crumpled* as if he would cry, but he made no sound."

You will find pages 772-73 of John Ciardi's *How Does a Poem Mean?* a fascinating study of connotations. As a further study take any passage from a genuinely creative writer and test the propositions we have discussed here. In a given paragraph from any short story scene, count the concrete nouns against the adjectives. Test the adjectives and verb forms for their concrete derivations and connotations. Count the judgment adjectives. Observe the uses of abstract terms. Most of all, study how the words which seem exactly right to you rise directly from the scene context. I suggest you start this study with Hemingway's "Big Two Hearted River," Porter's "He," Conrad Aiken's "Silent Snow Secret Snow," or the stories reprinted in Part Three here.

Ideas for Study

1. Review the sections on nouns, adjectives, verbs, and verbals in a good grammar text.

2. Reduce the following abstract nouns to the lowest concrete level you can reach, stepping down the abstraction ladder as the text suggests: livestock, automotive industry, capitalism, love, protest, worship, marine life, bigotry.

3. Starting from each of the following concrete nouns, list words or phrases climbing the abstraction ladder as far into the abstract idea as you can go: a number 12 electric wire, a gasket in an automobile carburetor, a U.S. cent, a strip of bacon, a slice of bread.

4. Beginning with each of the following abstract ideas, descend the abstraction ladder as far into the concrete process as you can go: interior decorating, traveling by air, food processing, writing, merchandising. Concentrate particularly on using concrete verbs and verbals.

The Story Writer's Notebook:

". . . I remember exactly a balcony of a house facing a road, and, the other side of the road, pine trees, beyond which lay the sea. Every morning the sun sprang up, first of all above the horizon of the sea, then it climbed to the tops of the trees and shone on my window. And this memory connects with the sun that shines through my window in London now in spring and early summer. So that the memory is not exactly a memory. It is more like one prong upon which a whole calendar of similar experiences happening throughout the years, collect."

—Stephen Spender, *The Creative Process*

Beginning writers often ask, should I write from memory only, or can I *imagine* an effective scene or story? As the quotation by Stephen Spender suggests, the writing process is often too complex for such a clear distinction. In the work of writing, the imagined scene merges in the mind with the memory of actual experience. It shapes itself as scene or fragment of scene out of glimpses of the past which were vivid actually once, then were dropped into the reservoir of memory. Story writers all seem to have experienced these visualizations of scene out of memory. They agree that such visualizations cannot be willed into consciousness, but they rise unbidden during or after periods of concentration on the story scene. All this clearly suggests that the more experiences a writer can have, provided always that he is sensorily and fully aware of them and that they are natural, human experiences, the more material he will be able to store in memory and submit to the play of imagination as he works on his story scene. Imagination alone will not do; it must be grounded in actual experience out of memory. The trouble is, mainly, not that we do not have experience of story material, but that we are unaware of and untouched by that experience which is constantly around us.

What can you do to help develop this discipline of observation and memory and the mental trick of recall for use in the story scene? One good answer is to keep a writer's notebook. Nearly all fiction writers who discuss their art speak of their own notebook as indispensable. It is a very special sort of notebook, full of recorded sensory scenes. Make an effort to get down briefly, and with little development, the eleven components of a scene that has impressed you, exactly as you experienced it, with complete accuracy and candor. Try to get down your own unique sensory perception of it, and not to be influenced by the distractions of the expected or the established forms of other people's perceptions (another kind of cliché). Of this problem Hemingway said, in *Death in the Afternoon:* "The greatest difficulty, aside from knowing truly what you really felt rather than what you were supposed to feel, was to put down what really happened in action; what the actual things were which produced the emotion you experienced . . . The real thing, the sequence of emotion and fact which made the emotion and which would be as valid in a year or in ten years or, with luck and if you stated it purely enough, always . . ."

Here are some examples of what I mean by the scene subject matter of a writer's notebook, taken from student notebooks available to me:

1. The special fall of light and shadow on fallen leaves in a certain slant of autumn light.

2. The lift and fall of a sprinter's knees running the 220 in practice after school.

3. The feel of tall grass, dry in the autumn, against calf and ankle.

4. The smell of dry sage in a summer rain.

5. The sounds of a tugboat as it berths a freighter at a pier.

6. The psychedelic effect of faces on a crowded street as they come toward me in a steady flow.

7. The smell and shadowy shapes of a deserted stage after a play.

8. The strange illusion of moving forward while watching a stream flowing under a bridge.

9. The change in perspective on seeing a familiar street from the top of a skycraper.

10. The look on the face of a disillusioned child.

11. The sight of a dead sparrow in the frost-hardened rut of a dirt road.

12. A familiar room, bare after the movers have left.

All these fragments of scene reports were later developed, and still later fashioned into finished products and printed in the school literary magazine. They had been tucked away much earlier into a writer's notebook and forgotten, until involuntarily they fused into creative imagination during a period of intense concentration on report of scene in a story.

Sometimes the notebook contains full development into sentence and paragraph. More often the notes simply show lists of words or phrases recording the sensory content of a scene. But they all help to capture the experience and lodge it in memory to be recalled at the right time and place.

In addition to the record of sensory scene, other elements of short story structure belong in the notebook, sometimes independently of scene. Interesting ideas centering about a problem faced by someone, how he solves it or doesn't, his motive, what prevents solution, what finally results—these ideas may not appear in the notebook as scene; but they may later become part of scene in a disciplined story.

A writer also collects striking characters, people known or unknown to him who attract his attention by virtue of some intriguing or interesting gesture or movement, or physical aspect, or idea expressed and so on. These may be reported in the notebook, briefly or in detail, but always in a concrete sensory vocabulary. What people say, how they say it, the exact word and locution, the gesture, facial expression, movement, tone, and volume, all may usefully be recorded, even though disconnected at either end.

As a story writer you are always looking for material. You know you will eventually scene your story about a character facing a problem that he wishes to solve. Thus, causative situations which require decisions interest you. They become apparent around you in real life, in newspapers, in TV.

For example, the following three newspaper excerpts

taken at random report situations which might give rise to problems and suggest solutions:

1. Plain City, January 27: "An eleven-month-old baby girl is reported happy and healthy here after a brush with death. Little Donnell Butler, daughter of Mr. and Mrs. Grant Butler, of 3377 Pioneer Road, was rushed to the McKay Hospital after she choked on candy. Mrs. Butler said that her baby started choking on candy apparently given her by an older brother. The baby had started turning blue . . ." This story would obviously center around the brother and his family relationship, the tensions, his problem, and the dangerous act. It is a situation with most of the story elements present or strongly suggested. The question the brother asks is: "How to get attention, when the baby apparently absorbs all my mother's love."

2. New York, (AP), January 27: "Authorities say a father of four, who was arrested on drug charges, used teams of children to peddle narcotics. District Attorney David Epstein said: 'This man conducts a Fagin-like activity in the sale of drugs . . .'" Here, the situation is extreme and foreign to most persons' experience, but by making one of the children the protagonist, the writer can supply concrete human motivations from memory. Some of the questions suggested were: how to escape the father's domination; how to establish personal self-respect; how to escape arrest; how to "succeed," even when success means peddling drugs.

3. Local press, January 27: "Some 800 Union Pacific Railroad workers walked off their jobs at midnight in Ogden, leaving the rail industry at a standstill in the wake of a nationwide strike." What problems will be faced by the young employee and his family under this stress? What solutions will he find?

These clippings obviously offer ideas for story material. They stimulate invention. They may usefully go into a writer's notebook. If the note can be recorded in the form of a scene or partial scene, so much the better.

It will be apparent from all this that you, as a story writer, work at it all the time. You develop a writer's penchant for sharp observation and awareness, and for storing potential material—sometimes on the spot, more often from immediate memory—in a writer's reservoir, the notebook. I strongly suggest you keep the sort of notebook we have been discussing. It will help you develop: awareness of the world around you; skill in sensory observation, skill in making scene; and a sharper response to experience, and therefore more insight into the meaning of experience.

Ideas for Study

1. With a good friend taste some unfamiliar food. Compare the notebook entries of your taste report. Do the same for touch: stroking a cat, holding an ice cube in your hand, going barefoot.

2. Listen to a record or tape playing one of your favorite pieces of music. Make a list of all the words you can think of to report the sound. Do any of them exactly report your own private perception of the sound? Find one or two of your own words that do fit your private hearing exactly. Put them in your notebook. How would you report the sound of a tuning fork, or traffic, or running water?

3. Study your newspaper and list as many potential story situations as you find. They needn't be spectacular. List some characters with problems.

Some Useful Readings

1. Ciardi, John and Miller Williams, *How Does a Poem Mean?* 2nd Edition. Houghton Mifflin, Boston, 1975. Pages 779 to 795, though directed at poetry, are especially enlightening in a study of the vocabulary of creative writing in the short story. Ciardi treats fully the meaning produced by connotation, association, and emotional response to words.

2. Langer, Suzanne K., *Philosophy in a New Key: A Study in the Symbolism of Reason, Rite and Art.* 3rd Edition. Harvard University Press. This is a profound but readable study of creativity as manifested in various arts. You should study the entire book, but

the first five short chapters deal especially with man's symbol-making propensity. They will help you to understand the creative process with words.

3

Some Scenes Analyzed

Before leaving the preliminary comments on scene as the basis of short story structure, we ought to be even more specific by analyzing some full scenes. The first four scene reports, written by students, originally appeared very sketchily in their notebooks. Then they were developed into full scenes and later used, sometimes much altered, in a full length story.

The comments accompanying each scene report seem to me the best part of this book. I urge you to adopt the following procedure throughout these analyses: first read the text of the scene through, without reading the parallel comments; then, read again each section of the scene and the accompanying comment parallel to it. This means at least two readings of the scene, once for the content and once again for the analysis. Though this procedure makes for slow and painstaking study, your attention to detail here will reflect itself in your own writing.

Scene Analysis:

BLUEBERRY BREAD
by Olivia Bertagnolli

TEXT	COMMENT
1. On Saturday morning, Clara walked to Leo Auff-	1. *Time, Saturday morning; place, top step of the*

man's house on the corner and sat on the top step of the porch where the sunlight pooled and dropped into the narrow slats between the steps. The sun warmed the wind, catching in the leaves of the winter-twisted oak that pushed away from the side of the house.

porch of Leo Auffman's house on the corner of the same block; lighted by the sun—pooling, dropping, warming, catching, wedging, creeping, and reaching (notice these concrete verbs and verbals); six sight details. Note the con-sequence of wind and leaf movement.

2. The light wedged between the bars of the porch rail, creeping along the edge of the porch until it reached the legs of Leo Auffman's wicker chair. Clara loved Leo Auffman almost as much as she loved Mrs. Auffman, with her fat, squat body and her powdered wrinkles that squeezed

2. Light is repeated, and it precedes sight con-sequentially; characters, Clara and Leo. Olivia establishes the point of view; it is through Clara's consciousness that we sense the scene and, therefore, it is Clara with whom we identify ourselves. She gives Clara an identifying characteristic of affection for the Auffmans. We do not (con-sequentially) see Mrs. Auffman till Clara remembers her.

3. out around her neck in rolls, and her blue eyes that lost themselves in chasms of wrinkles when she laughed.

3. She reports Mrs. Auffman, a third character, with detail of sight.

4. No one in the world could make blueberry bread the way Mrs. Auffman could. When the sun had pushed the shadow of the oak tree on to Leo Auffman's shed, Mrs. Auffman brought Clara yellow flaked milk in a heavy enameled cup and blueberry bread wrapped in a red checkered tea cloth.

4. Mrs. Auffman now functions as breadmaker and hostess; light repeated; sight continued, and place, all developed with fifteen concrete details.

5. Filmed bubbles thickened into heavy yellow foam, nibbling against the whiteness of the cup. The larger bubbles burst into rich froth, clinging to the sides of the cup when Clara lifted it to her lips.

5. Notice the use of concrete verbs and verbals again, to report the senses: sight (movement, color, texture); touch (temperature and texture); and taste. Note also the orderly sequence of detail.

6. The cool film glistened on her lips and pooled under her tongue, seeping into her throat; and it was whipping cream, and chunks of smooth yellow cheese hidden in the bottom of her lunch pail; curled cheese on apple pie and white-milk cheese dipped in bee's wax hanging in the fruit cellar. Clara's tongue pushed softly against the roof of her mouth, milk oozing into her throat when she swallowed.

6. Now Olivia reports the senses further in an exploration of both actual impressions and the associations which the impressions evoke: whipping cream, chunks of cheese, apple pie, bee's wax, fruit cellar. Note the use of texture in the last sentence. Clara's character is developed by the choice of detail—these choices would occur only to Clara.

7. Mrs. Auffman unfolded the warm towel with her short fingers. Steam peeled over the curled edges of the basket, and the smell of blueberries spilled over Clara, carrying on the wind. Mrs. Auffman clutched the basket in her brown hands and held the cloth back with her fingers. Clara lifted a firm yellow square from the top. Butter glazed her fingers, and steam dropped from the bottom crust into her hand. She held the crust to her lips, and the steam singed her nose and lips. Fat, yellow squares of sweet bread stuffed with plump

7. Mrs. Auffman reported further; she moves in her appointed purpose to serve the bread. A report of the smell and a qualifying repetition of the wind. From the first paragraph the report of smell moves into a delightful report of taste intensified by touch within the mouth, and temperature and texture and sound in the ears. Sight is reported fully. Thus even so short a sketch is a full scene: light, time, place, character, purpose, point of view, and the five senses—all eleven elements. Notice the metaphoric quality of such words as "fat,"

blueberries, so bloated with thick purple juice that they popped inside her mouth when she bit into the crust; the wrinkled skins burst, pushing out the hot breath and ebony meat of blueberries. Golden crusts against buttered bread and lips: Bread, alive with blots of blue mold spreading through moist curds of air; salted breath, juice-drenched crumbs rolling over her tongue, crunching inside her ears, clinging to her teeth until the sweet frothy milk carried them away.

"bloated," "wrinkled," "golden," "blots," "blue mold." This sort of poetic compression, most useful in short story reporting, occurs throughout the scene. It is accomplished mainly with nouns or verbs or verbals. Olivia uses adjectives sparingly and usually with concrete connotations: narrow, wicker, blue, heavy, yellow, rich, cool, smooth, short, brown, fat, yellow, sweet, plump, thick purple, ebony, golden, olive, moist. She avoids adjectives which make judgments. She doesn't, for example, say the bread is delicious.

In addition to observing Olivia's sensory perception, you can learn a good deal from her about the uses of verb forms. Underline all the verbs and verbals in her sketch. Examine them to find what senses they report and how they move the scene forward. You will notice that Olivia has avoided the careless use of "to be" forms. These become necessary only when the function of the verb is to link or to establish identity or to state an abstraction. They can almost never report scene. She has also avoided the weakness and circumlocution produced by passive verbs.

Note carefully how much detail of Mrs. Auffman's character Olivia develops through the sensory report of scene, of which the character is an element. What do you know, and feel, now, about Mrs. Auffman?

Ask yourself the central questions: "Can I experience the scene she reports? Did the blueberry bread happen, also, to me? To the degree that you can answer "yes," the sketch succeeds in transferring experience.

Ideas for Study

1. Write several sentences using passive verbs. Then rewrite the same content with active verbs. Note the change in emphasis and meaning.

2. Write a report of an actual scene in which eating is the central focus.

Scene Analysis:

Penny Allred's notebook supplied the following scene, later made into a story. In this sketch John is her brother, and the time is the day before he leaves for military service. How does Penny use the concrete details of their hike to convey to you her emotions about his departure?

From AGE OF DEPARTURE
by Penny Allred

TEXT	COMMENT
1. He was up ahead of me on the trail, standing in the bright sunlight; and I could see the sweat darkening his hair along the back of his neck.	*1. In a short paragraph Penny reports character, and some characteristics; place; light; sight; and implications of touch in temperature and moisture.*
2. "Wait a minute," I said, and I sat down on a rock at the side of the trail. "I've got to empty my shoes."	*2. Positioning of characters in place; point of view represented by "I."*
3. John came back making little rock slides with every step. When he got to the rock he stopped and bent down to roll up the cuffs of his Levis. His crew cut was so short and thick on top	*3. Sound here. Notice how the order of the items in the report is governed in consequence by the action; all is in exact time and place sequence. For example, "I" cannot report the crew cut,*

you could hardly stand not to reach out and pat it with the palm of your hand. I almost did, but I decided not to. I knew it would feel like the soft brushes they use on new babies' hair.

4. When he looked up it seemed almost as if I'd never seen him before, as if I hadn't looked at him really. As if I'd never seen his eyes squinting against the sun and making little wrinkles at the corners just tighter than laugh wrinkles, or ever seen his brows drawn together in half a scowl like that, or his teeth white against the tannedness.

5. He picked up a rock, his body moved back with his arm, his white shirt stretched tight, and the rock went up—a black fleck in the blueness. In a second it came crashing down through the oak brush leaves at the bottom of the trail.

6. After that everything was quiet, and the only things moving were the red ants and sometimes a quick, sand-colored lizard.

7. Sometimes I think, "I dreamed I was doing this. Everything looked and smelled just the way it does now, and everything hap-

with its revealing implications of touch, until John bends over. What is the effect of Penny's metaphor in the last sentence?

4. Notice how the objective details of sight evoke and explicate the subjective feelings and give the reader an insight into the character of both John and "I." Here is light repeated effectively, to produce facial expression, and then light again in the contrast of face and teeth. Note carefully the effect of this repetition and the technique of variation in repetition.

5. Movement, and sound and contrasting absence of sound come together, with some parallel microscopic sight detail and light.

7. Smell comes in now, and an interesting subjective reaction in recapitulation which reveals the character of "I." All elements of

pened this way." That's how
it was then. I knew I had
seen John throw a rock just
like that, and after the
crashing down in the leaves,
felt the heat and quietness. I
hadn't dreamed it though. It
really had happened just like
that.

*scene except taste are pres-
ent in this brief report.*

Ideas for Study

1. List Penny's active verbs and note their concrete quality; count the uses of "to be" verbs.

2. Go for a climb, or merely walk around the block,
and report in a scene a one-minute pause. Include
at least ten elements of scene in your report.

Scene Analysis:

*The next passage presents a two-scene report which
was a notebook entry at first and became a short story
later. The full story reports dramatically the experience of a little girl as she watches her uncle decapi-
tate a rooster for the family dinner. In her eyes, the
event takes on the surrealistic quality of a nightmare.
Notice how from the beginning, Janet selected words
connoting more than the simple description of grue-
some details: "bloody," "egg yolk," "smeared,"
"moldy," "spilled," for example, in the first paragraph.*

From UNCLE JOSH
by Janet Hurst

TEXT	COMMENT
1. A bloody, egg-yolk sun dropped on the top of the sandhill, smeared itself over moldy clouds, and spilled purple ocean tide along the edge of the sky.	*1. Scene One: light at first and, by implication, in the details of color, time (sun-down); note here the con-notative force of the words and their effect on mood;*

The little girl leaned against the back door, her body overcast with the shade of the house, and shadows deepened in the folds of her dress.

She looked after Uncle Josh as he scuffed through the leaves, that crackled like dry onion skins, toward the coal shed, his bib overalls hanging loosely from his stiff shoulders. She followed him then, slowly, her hands behind her.

character, with approximate age; Janet gives the point of view to the little girl; we do not see into her consciousness, but we see the scene through her eyes; light persists and changes; place; purpose—to observe and stay close to Josh; sound clear and sharp; sight detail; we not only see Uncle Josh but begin to understand the emotions he causes in the little girl.

What does the report of the girl's hands reveal about character?

2. Uncle Josh's shadow slithered under and over the autumn leaves in front of him, and his right leg dragged along the ground, tugging at the grass and leaving a clear trail through the leaves. His shadow pounced on the coal shed door and loomed up above him one and a half times his own length.

2. Scene Two: a change of place (to the coal shed). Note how the report carefully includes the transition from place (the back door) to place (the coal shed). Light is reiterated and altered. Josh is given a character tag of lameness and deformity; his shadow becomes another sinister being, more than human-sized. Notice "slithered" and "pounced," and "loomed."

3. The little girl shuffled behind him and stared up at him through heavy eyelashes; the door creaked as he yanked it open, turned, and looked down at her. The vein that stood out on his forehead like a purple cord caught some shadows from the sky and rode with them to the two lines that deep-

3. Another glimpse of the girl, sound again, sight; note how Josh comes alive and is revealed both in aspect and in character in the dialog. Why "crunched"? Careful consequence of action here, sharp sight report. The mood of gloom and foreboding is heightened by vocabulary. Notice also the

ened above the bridge of his nose. "Better get in the house, girl," he said, and he crunched over coal, reached up for the ax that hung on the wall, and took it down.

metaphoric report of Josh's facial expression. The point of view does not vary.

4. The blade of the ax glinted in the little girl's eyes, and she shook her head slowly, sideways. Still staring at the blade, she backed out into the leaves; but when the door of the coal shed started to close, she reached out quickly and stopped it.

Dust, silver in a streak of light from a crack in the roof, reached out and pulled the little girl into the shed. The door creaked shut, and she stood there, covered with half darkness.

4. Again the play of light and shadow and careful consequence of detail in the report. Note how effective is a judicious repetition of scene elements, especially light. Why does Janet say that the lighted dust pulled the girl into the shed?

Ideas for Study

1. What is the mood or tone of this report; and how is it produced?
2. Visit a butcher's shop, meat market, barnyard, or meat-processing plant and observe the preparation of meat for eating or sale. Report this in a scene. Count the elements.

Scene Analysis:

It may be well now to examine the expert use of scene by professional writers. The first example is from Richard Wright's symbolic short story, "The Man Who Lived Underground" from the collection Eight Men. In this scene, the man has just let himself down through a manhole into the sewers.

From *EIGHT MEN*
by Richard Wright

TEXT	COMMENT

1. The cover clanged into place, muffling the sights and sounds of the upper world. Knee-deep in the pulsing current, he breathed with aching chest, filling his lungs with the hot stench of yeasty rot.

From the perforations of the manhole cover, delicate

1. Sharp report of sound, announcing place (underground), sight, touch (temperature), smell, point of view, all in two sentences. Note the concrete verbs and verbals: clanged, muffling, pulsing (a metaphor), breathed, aching, filling. Wright evokes smell with both noun and adjective.

2. lances of hazy violet sifted down and wove a mottled pattern upon the surface of the streaking current. His lips parted as a car swept past along the wet pavement overhead, its heavy rumble soon dying out, like the hum of a plane speeding through a dense cloud.

2. Now light, con-sequentially, as the eyes accommodate it in the darkness, reported in metaphor (lances). Report of sound, associated with the character's gesture. Note the concrete metaphoric verbs: "sifted," "streaking," "swept," "dying."

3. The odor of rot had become so general that he no longer smelled it. He got his cigarettes, but discovered that his matches were wet. He searched and found a dry folder in the pocket of his shirt and managed to strike one; it flared weirdly in the wet gloom, glowing greenishly, turning red, orange, then

3. Odor again and its effect. The character's action follows in strict consequence. Now a detailed report of light, including minute particulars of color and effect. Note that the order of light detail is carefully reported as it would be seen in the given situation—no more, no less. Trace throughout the other details Wright uses to establish the character's physical presence within the scene.

4. yellow. He lit a crumpled cigarette; then by the flickering light of the match, he looked for support so he would not have to keep his muscles flexed against the pouring water. His pupils narrowed and he saw to either side of him two steaming walls that rose and curved inward some six feet above his head to form a dripping mouse-colored dome. The bottom of the sewer was a sloping V-trough. To the left, the sewer vanished in ashen fog. To the right was a steep down-curve into which water plunged.

4. Read the passage omitting all adjectives. Is there anything lost? Examine the connotations of such words as "steaming," "mouse-colored," and "ashen." Analyze the effect of the vivid verbs and verbals: "flickering," "pouring," "dripping," "vanished," "plunged." In spite of the nightmarish scene it reports, this vivid passage seems unostentatious, even restrained, because Wright uses words with such precision. The sensory accuracy of the report makes it realistic and believable as well as emotionally powerful.

Ideas for Study

1. The uses of light here deserve special attention. In what specific ways does the report of light affect the scene? Answer the same for smell.

2. Visit some dark, strange place and strike a match. Report the scene. How does the darkness accentuate other senses besides sight?

Scene Analysis:

Here is a scene from a very different writer and from a very different sort of story, set in an English moor landscape.

From FELIX TINGLER
by A.E. Coppard

TEXT	COMMENT
1. . . . Hungry at last and tired, he sat down and	1. *Character, insight (hungry and tired), place,*

leaned against a large ant hill close beside the thick and perfumed furze.

and point of view are established, with details of touch and smell. Time has been reported in a previous paragraph.

2. Here he ate his cake and then lolled, a little drowsy, looking at the few clouds in the sky and listening to the birds.

2. Now come sight, hearing, and light. Taste is implied. A little of "his" character shows in "lolled" and "drowsy."

3. A flock of rooks was moving in straggling flight towards him, a wide flat changing skein, like a curtain of crape. One of the rooks flapped just over him, it had a small round hole right through the feathers of one wing. What was that for?

3. Note this sequence of "zooming in" from the broad to the close, microscopic view. How is metaphor used to evoke the sight of movement? Study the concrete verbs here. Note the indirect report of the character's thoughts. What weight does it provide?

4. Felix was just falling asleep, it was so soft and comfortable there, when a tiny noise, very tiny but sharp and mysterious, went "Ping!" just by his ear, and something stung him lightly in the neck.

4. Detailed report of sound, then touch, made sharper by contrast with the character's sleepiness and sense of comfort. The name of the character appears.

5. He knelt up, a little startled, but he peered steadily under the furze. "Ping!" went something again and stung him in the ball of his eye. It made him blink. He drew back; after staring silently at the furze he said very softly, "Come out!" Nothing came; he beckoned with his forefinger and called aloud with friendliness, "Come on, come out!"

5. Sense report is repeated from a more minute point of view; sound here in the direct dialog, touch, and character insight. Note the phrases accompanying dialog, and the strict consequence of action and observation, as the character moves closer to the source of the "ping."

6. At that moment his nose was almost touching a brown dry sheath of the furze bloom, and right before his eyes the dried flower burst with the faint noise of "Ping!" And he felt the shower of tiny black seeds shooting against his cheek. At once he comprehended the charming mystery of the furze's dispersal of its seeds, and he submitted himself to the fairy-like bombardment with great glee . . .

6. *Gesture, sight, and touch, now in extreme close-up and detail. Coppard concludes the scene with insight into character and setting, broadening the meaning, giving direction and purpose to the scene. In this scene, all eleven elements appear. Did some things happen to you as you read it?*

Ideas for Study

1. How does the detail of the hole in the wing feathers focus attention on the flight? How does Coppard achieve elsewhere the "close-up," microscopic point of view?

2. Some readers might see this passage as a "description of nature" only. What does the scene reveal about Felix's character, and how?

3. Try reporting several scenes from the following list. These reports will be of actual experience, no fiction here at this time. You may cover a very brief time or a limited area, but make the reports as sensorily complete as you can. Use the eleven elements of scene as a checklist against which to measure your report: light, time, place, purpose, character, point of view, smell, hearing, taste, sight, touch. Then submit your report to the class audience, to a friend, or to the editor of your school journal to test it for creative communication. Will they be able from your words to share your experience? Keep these scene reports in a notebook you have set aside for this purpose.

SUGGESTED SUBJECTS FOR SCENE REPORTS:
Drinking a glass of water from a tap.
One minute of traffic at a busy intersection with an

officer directing, or a minute of freeway traffic as seen from an overpass.

A police arrest.

The view from a high building.

A supermarket fresh-fruit or vegetable counter.

The first minute after you enter your living room, arriving home.

A hospital corridor.

Your mother's or father's face or hands.

A heavy machine in action.

A laborer at his work.

The lobby of a large hotel (or small hotel).

One block in a slum section of town.

A running stream.

One minute of dialog. (You may use a tape recorder if you like, but be sure to report the accompanying gestures and expressions and tone.)

Some Useful Readings

1. Hayakawa, Samuel I., *Language in Thought and Action,* 3rd Edition. Harcourt, New York, 1972. Here is an excellent treatment of the objective report. It pays specific attention to the uses of abstract and concrete vocabulary, to tone, to slant, and to the operation of language in a practical world.

4

Dramatic Character Reporting

General Order of Scenes: We have talked about scenes in such detail because they form the basic units of the story. But they do not, of themselves, make a story; and ordinarily one scene has not sufficient space to make a story. Some questions have arisen: How do you arrange the scenes so as to make a well-disciplined short story? What goes into scene besides sensory report to make it a sequential dramatization of events? What controls the order of scenes? What creates suspense? And so on. The next four chapters will furnish some answers. It is useful at this point to remember that a short story is a series of reported scenes, in which a causative situation arises requiring a deciding character with a governing characteristic to try to solve some kind of problem along lines of action which he decides upon as best for his purpose and which suffer interruptions or intensifications until he comes to the end result of his final decisions. The definition supplies its own clues as to the content and sequence of scenes.

A story is made up of three separate and distinct parts. You can make a picture of a story as a series of three stage settings, one or more for each of the three parts of the story, thus:

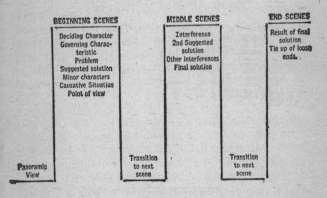

BEGINNING SCENES	MIDDLE SCENES	END SCENES
Deciding Character Governing Characteristic Problem Suggested solution Minor characters Causative Situation Point of view	Interference 2nd Suggested solution Other interferences Final solution	Result of final solution Tie up of loose ends.
Panoramic View	Transition to next scene	Transition to next scene

Of course, these three essential parts may be expanded into as many scenes as are necessary to report the story. But the content of the three story parts, though it may be rearranged within the part, remains as the diagram indicates.

The vocabulary of structure used here will receive full treatment as we proceed through these chapters, but at this point you should see that a writer thinks of a story as being built of three separate parts. Each part accomplishes specific necessary functions in the story, as indicated in the diagram. He keeps the content and purpose of each part separate from those of the other parts. All the story parts occur within a general panoramic view, and transitionary sentences link the parts and the scenes making up each part. Further, the writer thinks of a story as a drama, acted out on stages (scenes) in sequence. We will examine the structure of the story part by part and elaborate the vocabulary of the definition as we use the words.

Deciding Character: According to the implications in our definition of a short story, the deciding character is the individual who is affected by or who tries to decide issues facing him in the solution of his problem and to choose, rationally or subconsciously, or impulsively, a solution. He is the person with whom the reader identifies. He may not be the most important character or the most interesting personality (though he usually is); but unless the point of view (about which we will hear more later) is omniscient, everything that happens in the story comes to the reader through his senses. He takes a point of view which makes it possible for the reader to see into all aspects of the story: he is there and sees the scene, or someone tells him and the reader listens, or, if the point of view is subjective or omniscient, the reader gets inside his skin and knows his motives and what he thinks and feels. This use of the deciding character as the person with whom we identify ourselves provides unity and concentration of purpose and perspective. Thus the deciding character reports every scene; he holds the story together. He makes it possible for the reader not only to see with a single vision but to identify himself emotionally and intellectually with the character. When this is accomplished successfully, the story is completely believable and capable of being experienced because everything that takes place in it takes place in and for the reader, too, as reported in Part Two. "I" is the deciding character in "Grandpa" and in "Feels Like Spring." Linnie is the deciding character in "So Young to Die."

To illustrate further, from the stories printed in Part Three, the deciding character in "Bush Boy, Poor Boy" is "I"; in "Through the Tunnel" it is Jerry; in "Sled" it is Joey; in "Wullie" it is Billie ("I" is a narrator); and in "How Mr. Hogan Robbed a Bank" it is Mr. Hogan.

Ideas for Study

1. Identify the deciding character in some stories familiar to you.

2. List five problems you have actually faced to which you had to decide on a solution. Did your first solution work? Did you decide on a second solution?

The Governing Characteristic: In a piece of writing so brief and so concentrated as a short story, the kind of extended development of changes in character which we associate with the treatment in a novel is usually impossible. Ordinarily, there will be time only for a clear presentation of one governing characteristic. This characteristic may be altered by event, or affected by it, but will remain essentially static. Yet the actions and decisions of the deciding character, to be believable, must correspond to what a reader knows of his total personality. To achieve this reality in a story, the author gives the deciding character a governing characteristic which determines the direction of his choices and decisions. In an early scene, (usually the first scene), he faces his problem, which, though it must be clear to the reader, may not yet be clear to him; the reader watches him *choose* what he *considers* the best *solution* to it and begin *acting on* that decision. The report of this decision demonstrates his governing characteristic in action.

In "Feels Like Spring," Milton Kaplan has the deciding character think: "I'm all alone in New York City, and I guess I'm kind of shy and don't make friends easily." As explicitly as that he states the governing characteristic which controls all of "I's" choices and actions. And just as explicitly he has "I" choose action, as when he thinks: ". . . she'd say quickly, 'Oh, I beg your pardon,' and I'd lift my hat politely and answer, 'That's perfectly all right' and I'd smile . . ."

Another good example of this technique is the dialog in the first fourteen paragraphs of "Sled," Part III, in which the problem, the governing characteristic, and the decision are all sharply apparent during the exchange, not necessarily to the boy, who acts largely on impulse, but to the writer and the reader of the passage.

To keep the governing characteristic always before us, most writers choose some appropriate phrase or word, a gesture perhaps, which will remind us of the governing characteristic. They repeat this character phrase often in well-chosen places. Thus a full paragraph of scene report of character can easily be later re-evoked by a brief, remembered key phrase. Writers usually use such phrases to keep before the reader what structural elements are basic to the story: governing characteristic, scene, and physical appearance, etc. These phrases will be pointed out more fully in the specific comments. But we need here to have the concept of repeated phrases used for repeated evocation.

How is the deciding character presented in a short story? Remember that the basic unit of structure in reporting a short story is the scene, with its eleven elements. One of these elements is character. Reporting character is as simple in concept as this: if your scene includes character, and your report of scene is accurate and complete and to the point, and your visualizations are clear, then of necessity your characters will emerge clearly and pointedly and visually, and the reader will have insight into and empathy for that character. You will have little or no static "description" of character relatively independent of the story structure. The character will act in a scene, will display in the scene by his action and speech and thought, his governing characteristics functioning in the scene as it is reported. He will be identified by a physical characteristic, face, gait, tone, size, age, etc., which clearly identifies him and which is repeated often enough to become familiar. You do not "develop character" in a short story in the sense of reporting complex changes in it as you would do in an essay or novel. You report a character as he occurs in scene, and as the events there affect him.

This is not to say that character is less important to your story than scene or structure. Rather it demonstrates that the way to the handling of a deciding character and his governing characteristic is through faithful scene report. A story moves forward with directness and intensity and all deliberate speed from the first sentence. You do not delay the story for a static description of a character, independent of scene. Rather, a character evolves from the scene of which it is a part.

The scenes in "Bush Boy, Poor Boy," Part III, report two characters, Edgar ("I") and Roy. How does Aldridge evolve these characters from the scene report? In the first five paragraphs he presents the panoramic view. In the first paragraph he tells us that "I" is a boy, poor, living in the "bush," and we know his driving ambition. In the second we learn he is motherless, is no scholar, envies Tom, finds teachers and policemen unfriendly, is a joke to the town boys, is an expert in the "bush" life and a failure in town, and how he envies Tom. In the third paragraph we learn he supports himself by hunting, and we assume his age at between ten and twelve. In paragraph 4 we see again his stubborn determination and discover the physical tag that he goes to school barefoot. With no static description in four paragraphs of the panoramic view, we have a working notion of Edgar, including his age, sex, size, dress, poverty, and his governing characteristics of determination and envy, including his relationship to his peers— all necessary to a clear understanding of the elaboration of character to come in following scenes.

In paragraph 13 we learn that Edgar has problems expressing himself before adults. The next tells us more about the facets of character we have already seen. The governing characteristic has been demonstrated in a minor action. And in paragraph 15 the minor actor, Roy, has been introduced with his tag of age, repeated three times in four sentences. In paragraph 38 we have Edgar's exact age, a necessary bit of information, always most useful in understanding a character. Paragraphs 57 to 70 and paragraph 77 demonstrate in scene action both Edgar's stubborn streak and his kind of shrewdness, both part of his governing characteristic, and also his failure to realize his true psychological situation.

The first fourteen short paragraphs of "Through the Tunnel," Part III, present the two characters. Though the mother seems very minor, she functions to make the situation seem realistic and to elicit from Jerry some revealing comments. We learn of the deciding character, Jerry, his name, age, swimming experience, and his strong but unformed desire for independence from his mother inhibited by his native courtesy to and affection for her. In paragraph 16 we see the desire for independence linked to a "craving that filled his whole body." Thus his governing characteristic comes to light in the report of scene. Paragraph 17 rounds out the character. The governing characteristic is repeatedly tagged in all succeeding scenes. Reference to his mother's white arms gives, by suggestion, the tag of whiteness with all its many connotations to Jerry.

Notice the revelation of age and self-image in paragraph 19: "They were big boys—men to Jerry" and in "He felt . . . proud of himself." And do not miss the insight provided in paragraphs 24 and 30. These help us understand not only Jerry but all boys who have tasted failure.

Study how Lessing uses dialogue to reveal Jerry's intense emotion and preoccupation in one word; "Yes," in paragraph 53.

Notice what a sharp flash of insight into character can be produced in one line: "which now seemed a place for small children," in paragraph 57.

We have seen character revelation and elaboration in scene and dialog. In paragraph 60, first sentence, we see the reporter intrude his own comments on character, breaking the point of view. Which of these techniques seems more effective to you?

Notice how all of this detail of characterization is brought into play at the moment of Jerry's final decision, paragraph 62, second and third sentences. The governing characteristic operates at all decisive moments of the story.

In "Sled," Part III, Joey's governing characteristic is his willingness to deceive. He avoids the outright lie, but acts surreptitiously and deceptively. How are these characteristics elaborated? Notice carefully how the scene is reported. The dialogue of Scene One, paragraphs 1 to 29, shows clearly that his apology is a fraud, his obedience enforced and resentful, his antipathy for his sister deep but controlled for selfish reasons. He is impatient (the buttons). He respects the authority of his mother only superficially and for selfish reasons.

Again in the second scene, paragraphs 36 to 39 show clearly his propensity to deception, together with a kind of arrogance which is inhibited only by fear of authority. All this character elaboration is reported in the dialog and accompanying phrases of scene.

In paragraphs 45 and 46 we are reminded that Joey is only a little boy, with whom we can sympathize in time of stress, but his governing characteristic does not change.

In paragraph 56 of Scene Eight the spoken question, which is really a major decision, though it may have come impulsively with no deliberate attempt to injure, displays sharply Joey's governing characteristic of deceit. The inarticulateness of Joey in the dialogue in paragraphs 61 to 71 further elaborates this. And Joey's lack of reasoned intent does not blur this decision for us.

Even after the events of Scene Eight, which present every opportunity for Joey to have changed his character, he remains essentially true to his governing characteristic in the last two paragraphs of the story. Note that in these paragraphs occurs the only development of character outside of dialogue.

Ideas for Study

1. Invent a short scene which clearly demonstrates some facet of a speaker's character.

2. Invent a short scene in which a character's action demonstrates something about his character.

3. Select a scene from a short story familiar to you in which action demonstrates character.

4. Select a scene in which a decision is made which clearly demonstrates the functioning of a governing characteristic.

5. Select a scene in which a physical tag is repeated effectively.

Minor Characters: As a general rule, if you can report the story with one minor actor, don't use two; if you can do it with two, don't use three. Minor characters must have a necessary part to play in the story structure. According to the part they play, they possess a distinguishing characteristic and a physical tag. This part may be merely to round out a scene and give reality to it, as do the parents in "Wullie," Part III. A minor actor may serve to give insight into and to elucidate the deciding character by dialogue or action, as does the mother in "Through the Tunnel" and as do the mother and sister in "Sled." Or he may function fully in one of the structural elements, as, in "Bush Boy, Poor Boy," Tom Woodley produces the causative situation, and Roy takes part in the interferences and accompanying decisions. He may add reality and humor, as do the townspeople in "How Mr. Hogan Robbed a Bank," Part III. The point is that minor characters never appear in a short story unless they serve a specific, necessary structural or reportorial (scene) function; and their appearance in the story is limited to the performance of that service. When you plan your story, use what minor characters you need, but introduce them into the scene sequence only on specific purpose.

The Problem: Think of the concept of Problem flexibly. The problem in a short story is whatever causes decisions by the deciding character, whether reasoned or involuntary. The problem may involve physical endurance: how to perform the feat of holding one's breath long enough to swim underwater through the tunnel. Or it may be how to develop sufficient skill to catch a twenty-pound cod and shoot a fox. Or the problem may be psychological, as in "Sled": how and whether to deceive. It may be largely an intellectual idea or theme or an investigation into ethics or morality or religion, as in Katherine Anne Porter's "He," Sherwood Anderson's "Unlighted Lamps" and in "Wullie." Or it may be very simply how to rob a bank, or how to get a grandfather to let you ride a horse, as in "Granpa," or how to meet a girl and alleviate loneliness as in "Feels Like Spring." Even in such a lengthy and involved masterpiece of psychology and physical endurance as Stephen Crane's "The Open Boat," the problem is simply how to survive a shipwreck.

The point about Problem is that, though it may be complex and involved or simple and apparent, it must be capable of suggested solution. The deciding character must be able to try to find ways to solve it, to carry out the suggested effort. The decision to act may be simply on impulse without reason, or it may be involuntary or even unconscious or felt blindly. We do not always know clearly why we act, and the deciding character may not know. He may be unaware of his motive. But to the reader and to the writer the decision to act on a suggested solution must be clear. On this point of choice and decision and its effect hang all the elements of suspense in a short story. We ask the question: can the deciding character, given his governing characteristic and the conditions of the problem, solve it along the lines of action he has been impelled to follow? The conditions giving rise to this question have all been clearly reported in the scenes of the *Beginning* of your story. And if the story has been slanted to a theme or idea, this has also been reported in scene. We have mentioned theme earlier. Perhaps a word or two concerning theme or idea may be useful here.

The Story Idea. Most good stories develop either subtly or ostensibly an intellectual idea. It may, in fact, be the writer's reason for writing the story in the first place. But preoccupation with the theme must never override or cloud the reporter's purpose: to record a series of dramatic scenes. The story is never a tract; it is always a play.

To be specific, in "Granpa" the old man says:

"You've found out that there are things in life that people think they want, but when they get 'em, they discover they didn't want 'em at all." All the events of the story support this thesis, but it does not appear anywhere in the story independently of structure. If it did, we would have a tract.

The theme in "Wullie" is not stated as succinctly as it is in "Granpa"; yet it is presented in the scene report throughout. For example: in Billy's reaction to the gun, paragraphs 4 to 15, 32 to 36, 68 to 73, and on thus to the dramatic finale. The theme of everyone's individual responsibility to ensure the humane treatment of animals, is developed fully by scene report, with no outside-of-scene essay on the idea, or even a statement of it.

Once we have made identification with the character, we follow with suspense and participation his blind or rational attempts to solve his problem if he can. And though later interferences (*Middle*) may impede the solution and perhaps require a change in the suggested solution, the problem and the character remain structurally the same and intact throughout the *Middle* and the *End*.

Ideas for Study

1. Select an actual problem which you are facing now. This is for real.
2. Make a full statement of it as it exists.
3. Invent a deciding character, giving him specific limitations.
4. Restate the same essential problem as it might be faced by this imagined character.

5

More of the Beginning

Panoramic View: As each scene exists in its own time and place, so, in the series of scenes called a short story, the scenes exist in a larger time and place. You begin the story by establishing, early in the series, (usually in the first scene), this general setting, called the panoramic view. In this view you provide the general setting in which the succeeding scenes take place. This panoramic view performs the same function as does the TV camera, when it shows first an entire general panorama, then zooms in closer to the immediate subject and shows a sequence of detailed scenes. The panorama will include at least time in general and place in general, and sometimes light, character, and purpose, and some of the senses. Do not ignore it. How and whether you use it will, of course, depend on you and your material and your intent. The panoramic view provides a framework necessary to a clear understanding and perception of entire sequence of scenes.

To illustrate the report of panorama, look at the story "Bush Boy, Poor Boy," in Part Three. The panorama begins with paragraph 2. This is not scene, but narrative. We are given the country (Australia), the province and town (Victoria and St. Helen), which you can locate on any good map of Australia, the river (Murray), the distance up the river from town (three or four miles), and the fact of the Bush, where the story occurs, all of which, if we wish, we can look up for clarity. The time is the era of the Model T. Some of the deciding characters' characteristics and limitations are reported. All the scenes of the ensuing story take on reality and visual clarity from our knowledge of the general panorama in which they occur.

To illustrate further, in Doris Lessing's "Through the Tunnel," the panoramic view is reported in paragraphs 1 to 4. Much less detailed than that in the Aldridge story, the report supplies only the minimum necessary panorama: the place is a foreign seacoast on a resort beach, with a wild, rocky bay juxtaposed to a crowded, sandy beach; the time is summer, and the English boy and his mother are vacationing. To locate the scenes following, this is all we need to know. A panoramic view should supply only the general setting necessary to a comprehension of the succeeding scenes. Preferably, you report it as part of the opening scene, or you may narrate it, if the scene seems ill advised.

Causative Situation: As often as possible, a story ought to, and usually does, open at the causative situation. This is the point at which his problem becomes clear to us and impelling to the deciding character, and demands of him that he try consciously or subconsciously to find a solution to it. It is, of course, apparent to you that you, as a character, are at this moment facing actual problems, some of them perfectly clear to you, others blurred or merely felt vaguely, many of which will eventually arrive at a time when you will be forced to make a decision about solving them: school, family, social life, job, career, neighborhood —all offer problems. Many of them, luckily, need not be solved at all, since they will solve themselves; many can be held off indefinitely. These are not yet ready to become short story material. But a situation may arise for some of these problems which will make a decision imperative; for example, an acceptance into two schools at the same time. Either would present you with a causative situation, requiring decision, and they suddenly turn a merely interesting problem into short story material. In actual life, as in a story, the situation may come on us unaware and not clear, but in a story it must be clear to the reader.

To illustrate the causative situation in action, study

the references to scenes in these stories from Part Three:

In "Bush Boy, Poor Boy" paragraph 2, the final sentence, the arrival of Tom Woodley and his success with the cod and the fox is causative. It requires a decision from "I." In the story "Wullie," paragraph 1, the birthday with the gift of the .22 rifle is causative. It sets off the series of decisions leading to the final result. In the story, "Sled," paragraphs 1 to 3, the snow, coupled with the mother's demand for a humiliating apology, is causative. Perhaps nothing in the sequence would have happened without the snow and the humiliation being juxtaposed at exactly this time. Though the impulse to revenge may not be conscious to Joey, it is clear to us.

The scenes ought to move progressively forward from the first situation. Writers try to avoid the necessity of a flashback scene or a narrative passage. But it is probably better to flash back than to begin too early, before the problem presents itself as causative. Beginning too early before the causative situation arises requires a slow, static process through exposition to the first decision. This, too, is objectionable. Flashbacks are used only to bring in absolutely necessary information, which given earlier would have delayed too long the introduction of the causative situation.

A flashback may be reported in a remembered scene, as it is in Scene Two of "So Young to Die," where Linnie remembers Mart's illness. Or a character may relate the flashback scene. It may otherwise be reported in non-dramatic narrative. While it always impedes the forward movement of the story, it is sometimes preferable to a delayed start.

Point of View: So far we have seen six essential, structural elements which should be reported in the Beginning of the story. One more crucial element of structure must have been established before we can end the Beginning, and begin the Middle with the first interruption. No disciplined short story is possible unless the reader can identify with the deciding character, who attempts to control his own destiny, exercise choice, make determinations. So that for the time it takes to read the story and recover from it, the reader *becomes,* psychologically, the deciding character; and the problem becomes his own.

To achieve this intense participation by the reader, short story structure requires the adoption of and faithful adherence to a point of view which will permit reader identification with the deciding character. He is the actor in the scene through whose consciousness all events of the action, all sensory perception, all decisions, and all results come to the reader. Through this character's eyes, ears, nose, fingertips, the reader *experiences* the story, not merely understands it. This discipline of identification requires that the writer understand the points of view that are available to him, that he choose the one best suited to his purpose, and that he not for an instant shift from that point of view.

The point of view of "So Young to Die" is the one which, for many good reasons, is the most commonly used in short stories. Linnie is the deciding character. All of the story comes to us through her consciousness. It is through her sensory system that we perceive all the scene detail. And, in addition, we use her voice and think her thoughts and share her feelings. Further, we are not aware of anything in the story that she is not aware of. We do not know, for instance, what her sisters or her parents are thinking or doing except by their direct statement or by inference from Linnie's report. We do not know what is going on in a room until Linnie enters it and reports. This point of view is often called, appropriately, the *third person subjective*. Should it be violated for a moment, if, for example, we had observed a scene between the parents and the sisters, before Linnie entered, our hypnotic identification with Linnie would have been interrupted and the tension irreparably lessened. Such a violation of point of view would, like the snap of the hypnotist's fingers, bring us rudely back from Linnie's world of the forlorn little girl into our own world of adult security, and spoil the story.

"Sled," "Through the Tunnel," and "How Mr. Hogan Robbed a Bank" are all reported in the third person subjective point of view. The advantages of this point of view for a full report of inside-and-outside-the-skin analysis of the deciding character and his story are many and obvious. It permits the reporter to remain noncommittal; it allows full exploration of idea, theme, and especially of motive; it offers a variety of means by which the events and scenes of the story can be reported to the reader; it thus encourages that most precious of short story qualities: a complete reader identification with the deciding character; it permits untrammeled and faithful report of dialog; and the third person subjective does all this with much less difficulty for the writer than does any other point of view. For these reasons, most writers adopt it.

The *third person objective* point of view also permits the use of a deciding character. Though it cannot report what is going on inside the character's skin, it has the advantage of being at once completely believable, because the reporter's perception of the external world is limited, like the reader's, and like our real life experience, to actuality, to what the reporter can sense objectively. Since such a report cannot examine the subjective thoughts and feelings of the deciding character, it must supply convincing outward evidence of inward events. The reader, therefore, is probably slightly less than ready to make full identification with the feelings of the deciding character. He cannot participate fully in the decisions, and he cannot be so sure of motive. With story material that requires analysis of motive, of feeling, of subjective reaction, as in the story of psychological insight like Aiken's "Silent Snow Secret Snow," the objective point of view is often inconveniently restrictive. In "So Young to Die," Linnie obviously required subjective analysis, and Laurel wisely chose the third person subjective as the appropriate point of view.

In "Wullie" the point of view is given to a narrator, "I," who, while Adams reports him subjectively, himself narrates Billy in third person objective as we actually see people in real life. We are never told anything about Billy which "I" cannot sense objectively. We induce his feelings, motives, thoughts, solely from the

evidence supplied in "I's" objective report. And part of
the interest in this point of view is like the game we play
when we actually try to penetrate to the mind and
spirit of a real person. This little excerpt from Roger
Martin DuGard's novel *The Thibaults* illustrates the
power of objective reporting to reveal insight without
going inside the skin of the deciding character:

> The first thing Antoine noticed was the lamp which
> a woman in a pink dressing gown was lifting with
> both hands; her ruddy hair, her throat and forehead
> were flooded with the lamplight. Then he observed the
> bed on which the light fell, and the shadowy forms
> bending above it. Dregs of the sunset, filtering through
> the window, merged in the halo of the lamp, and the
> room was bathed in a half-light where all things took
> on the semblance of a dream. Antoine helped M.
> Chasle to a chair and approached the bed. A young
> man wearing pince-nez, with his hat still on, was
> bending forward and slitting up with with a pair of
> scissors the bloodstained garments of the little girl,
> Her face, ringed with matted hair, lay buried in the
> bolster. An old woman on her knees was helping the
> doctor.
> "Is she alive?" Antoine asked.
> The doctor turned, looked at him, and hesitated;
> then mopped his forehead.
> "Yes." His tone lacked assurance.

Besides the objectivity of the point of view here, it
is worth noting the scene detail and the careful process
of con-sequence in the reporting. We get insight into
Antoine by following the scene through his eyes. What,
for instance, is told us by the "mopped his forehead"
gesture about the nature of Antoine? Student writers
usually find the third person objective point of view a
more difficult discipline to manage than any other; but
it is fun to try, and it gives reality and belief to the
reader when it is successful. It offers severe, but not impossible, impediments to identification.

Stories in the *first person subjective* point of view
often tend to be somewhat self-conscious, and often, in
the hands of a beginning writer, sound too much like a

"true confession." Further, the results very often seem improbable and the story lacking in credibility. If the scenes report events which involve the physical safety of the deciding character, it is difficult to ask convincingly: "Can he survive along the lines he has laid down?", when it is already obvious that he has survived to tell the story. Identification, for these reasons, is sometimes difficult, and the reader sometimes finds himself reluctant to participate, as in Mr. Poe's stories of horror. In most of these we are persuaded that the events ought to be horrible, but we refuse to be horrified. Yet in "Granpa" and "Feels Like Spring" the first person subjective seems completely appropriate and useful, and identification seems complete and unembarrassed. This is true because the events and reactions of these stories are subject matter a person might be expected to talk about. They read a little like reminiscences.

The *omniscient author*'s point of view is seldom used in the short story, but is usually reserved for the novel. In this point of view the writer sees all and knows all and enters into all characters and events. There is no single character who, like an X ray, furnishes the reader with eyes and ears. Thus no identification with a single character is possible, and no participation follows. Yet a few very successful stories have used this point of view, one of the best being the justly famous "The Open Boat" by Stephen Crane. However, even in this story, moving and beautifully disciplined as it is, the complete entrapment into experience, the hypnosis, the intense participation through identification, fails. We are fascinated, engaged, sympathetic, moved, but we do not identify. We do not experience the story, rather we observe it happening.

The main points made in this section on point of view are these: First, that the problem of securing reader identification with the deciding character involves a wise choice of point of view, and thus a knowledge of the choices available. You choose the point of view best suited to your purpose. Second, having decided on your point of view, you do not change it even for a sentence or a word, but keep it clear and undeviating to the end. Third, most writers find the third person subjective point of view most useful to their purposes. You must evolve your own best way for each story you write.

Before moving into Chapter Six, we ought to sum up the first five chapters to see how far we have come in the structure of the story: We have reported the panoramic view in which all the scenes of the story will occur; we have noted the causative situation, which precipitates the decisions and solutions; the deciding character, with his physical tags and his governing characteristic has been established, and a point of view has been chosen and identified for him; minor actors with their appropriate characteristics and functions have been introduced; the problem has been clearly defined; the deciding character has made his first decision as to a suggested solution to his problem. We are nearly ready now to consider the structure of the Middle of the short story.

But throughout all this discussion so far, one vital element of short story reporting has been largely absent; that is the use and discipline of dialogue. It is now time we considered it.

The Uses of Dialogue: When two characters come together in a scene they will talk, *unless you have explained their silence.* But in so concentrated a series of scenes as you are writing and as this discipline requires, dialogue must have purpose. A writer uses dialogue to develop insight into character or motive, to report sensory scene without using static description, and to develop the story's structure, that is, the governing characteristic, the decision, the solution, and so on. You will discover that in most good short stories, just as in actuality, a character exposes his personality by his choice and use of words, his idiom, his tone, his face, and his gestures. The situation and the structure must inevitably determine for the writer what words to put into his character's mouth. To illustrate these uses, read paragraphs 25 to 42 of "Bush Boy, Poor Boy," excellent dialogue.

A writer trains his ear to identify the various sounds

of actual dialogue around him. How do people actually carry on a conversation? Exactly what is the idiom peculiar to dialogue? How does the vocabulary of dialogue differ from that of straight narrative? When is the use of dialogue indicated or appropriate? Training yourself so that you can report the dialogue in a scene accurately and with validity requires a good ear, willingness to listen attentively and self-consciously; and it takes practice. Put scenes involving dialogue into your notebook. People all around you are talking. Pay attention to the sounds, throat noises, dialect, idiom, pitch, volume, words, and gestures. All this usually goes too fast for recording, but you can get a good deal of it down in your notebook from memory. The tape recorder is helpful, if you can use it unobtrusively, because you can play it back and study it. Try to catch what people say and do in such situations as on a first meeting, in a serious confrontation, while giving reasons or answers, in anger, in joy, and so on.

But you must be aware that the dialogue you will write into your story will not be actual dialogue, and your story characters will speak, while always in the manner and idiom people use, still they will speak under your conditions and to your purpose, and never at random as in actuality. So you must carefully study the dialogue of fiction, not only the speech, but gestures, movements, facial expressions, tones of voice, which become a part of the speech in accompanying phrases, all helping to effect insight into character, motive, structure and scene.

Accompanying Phrases: Very often in dialogue, the accompanying phrases, which consist of everything that is not part of the actual conversation, can convey as much as the speech itself. Through his description of what goes on inside and around his characters, the author reveals to us both the nature of his characters, and his own overall purpose in the story. In analyzing dialogue, note particularly the placement of the "he said" (or "she said"), or identifying clause. Where does it occur in the speech? How often is it repeated? When does the verb vary from "said" and what are those variations? As an exercise, read the following sentences, and keeping these points in mind, decide which of the passage works best:

1. "This is something you must decide for yourself. I cannot help you. Maybe you need legal advice," she said, thoughtfully.
2. "This is something you must decide for yourself," she said, rearranging the papers thoughtfully. "I can't help you." She looked at him intently. "Maybe you need legal advice."

You can easily demonstrate the uses of accompanying phrases in dialogue by leaving them out of a passage, then juxtaposing the original version and noting the difference in effectiveness. For example, read the speech lines alone in this conversation from Steinbeck's "The Red Pony," where Gitano comes to the farm gate. Without the accompanying phrases, the conversation goes like this (italics mine):

"Do you live here?" *the old man said.*
"Yes," *said Jody.*
"I have come back," *the old man said.* "I am Gitano, and I have come back."
"It's an old man," *he said to his mother.* "It's an old *paisano* man, and he said he's come back."
"What' the matter now?" *she asked.*

The speech lines are recorded here, just as Steinbeck supplied the words. But note what happens to the dialogue when we quote it in full, with the accompanying phrases (italics mine). Analyze them to see what, besides an identification of the speaker, they contribute to character insight and to structure. For example, what scene elements do they add? How do they illuminate character? What part of the story structure (check list) are they contributing? Note carefully the position and nature of the "he said" clause:

The old man drew close to the gate and swung down his sack when he confronted Jody. His lips

*fluttered a little, and a soft impersonal voice came
from between them.*

"Do you live here?"

*Jody was embarrassed. He turned and looked at the
house . . . and toward the barn . . .* "Yes," *he said,
when no help came from either direction.*

"I have come back," *the old man said.* "I am
Gitano, and I have come back."

*Jody could not take all this responsibility. He ran
into the house for help, and the screen door banged
after him. His mother was in the kitchen poking out
the clogged holes of a colander with a hairpin . . .*

"It's an old man," *Jody cried, excitedly.* "It's an
old *paisano* man, and he said he's come back."

*His mother put down the colander and stuck the
hairpin behind the sink board.* "What's the matter
now," *she asked patiently.*

What can be learned of Jody from the phrase, "and
the screen door banged after him?". Or what of the
Old Man from "fluttered a little" and "soft impersonal
voice"? And how is the mother illuminated by the
colander gesture and by the word, "patiently"? The
best way to learn about the uses of dialogue in fiction is
to study it in good writers.

Examples of Dialogue: In "Wullie" the two characters are contrasted expertly in the dialogue from paragraphs three to six; "I," concerned with the gun and
shooting, Billy, with the beauty of the snow. This passage defines the governing characteristics of each boy.
Again note the contrast and the sharpened report of
structure in the ten paragraphs from 13 to 23, especially in paragraphs 15 and 16. Watch the position
of "he said" as near the beginning of the sentence as
possible, and observe the report of movement and scene
in the accompanying phrases. The details of structure
move clearly into play in the dialogue in paragraphs 44
to 61. In this passage the two characters are clearly
exposed; the decision to cure Wullie is plotted; there is
sharp insight into motive. An interesting fact is that
the phrases and the content of what is said, rather than
any distinctive difference in the vocabulary or tone of
the boys' speech, develop the character differences.

In "Through the Tunnel," Doris Lessing limits the dialogue to only ten short paragraphs, mainly at the conclusion of the story. She does this because Jerry and the boys did not understand each other's language and because the sequence of events permitted her to report scenes in which Jerry is alone. Although some stories use no dialogue at all, for instance, Kafka's classic "The Burrow," or Jack London's "To Build a Fire," most stories use dialogue much as we have described it.

This brief discussion of dialogue should make clear several points: First, dialogue, if used at all, should always develop some aspect of structure or scene. Second, the vocabulary, tone, idiom, should be accurate for the situation, the character, and the scene. Third, the accompanying phrases offer the key to the dramatic report of dialogue. And four, the "he said," or identifying clause should be placed at or as near as possible to the beginning of the speech and restrained usually to simple declarative verbs.

What makes writing good is the writer, his revelation of self in his story. The scenes of the story visualized in imagination out of memory as only the individual writer sees them, with detail drawn from the well of sources that come from his own experiences and from reading and thought—this will make his story creative and valuable. His ability to concentrate on scene so that characters come clear, insight is vivid and revealing, action is con-sequential and purposeful—this ability gives point to the short story discipline.

Ideas for Study

1. Report a specific use of the "zoom-in" technique on TV you have observed and describe how it assisted you in the process of viewing subsequent detail.

2. List some actual problems you have faced and invent situations which might precipitate them into short story material.

3. Write as accurately as you can, a short actual exchange of dialogue, reporting all accompanying gestures, facial expressions, vocal tone, body movement.

6

The Middle of the Short Story

Interferences: The Middle of the story presents scenes in which the solution decided upon by the deciding character in the Beginning scenes suffers an interference of some kind which forces the character to reevaluate the situation and to make a new decision for a more effective solution. An interference may be the result of opposing forces, or it may be, but rarely is, an accident. The solutions, however, must always come out of the kind of character you have reported. The decisions may rise from impulse, or blind unawareness, or by deliberate choice of the deciding character, but never from accident.

Accidents are common enough in real life. In actuality they sometimes account for vital decisions and much knowledge and character development. But a story is not life. It is an artistically disciplined representation of life. It has its own limitations, one of these being the necessity of insuring identification by the reader with the deciding character and participation with him in his efforts to solve his problems. This need requires that the deciding character exercise choices, that he try to control his own destiny. But accidents are, by definition, out of control. You do not *decide* to have one, unless it be by suicide. Hence, the only place for accident to function in a story is as an interference to the solution. Here accident becomes a part of the story structure and is legitimate and sometimes useful. It is well to caution against too much use of accident even in this part of structure, however, because it is liable to irritate the reader by appearing more like author meddling than true interference. In any case, if you use an accident, it ought to be explained, as, in "Wullie," Rafe's ability to hit a dog with one throw of the bottle. The suspense of the story lies in the reader's uncertainty about whether the solutions decided upon will eventually solve the problem. And a writer can keep on reporting interferences as long as he thinks he can maintain the suspense and increase the tension. In the Middle you should take care to report the scene detail in strict con-sequential order to insure continuity within the scene and between scenes.

Sometimes the interfering element does not change the suggested solution but merely intensifies the situation and makes more immediate and more pressing the need to solve the problem. Or it may clarify the problem both to the reader and to the deciding character. Whether the Middle scenes report interference or intensification or both, the suspense increases with each interruption, and the reader's concern over the central question heightens. There is a sharp rise in the intensity of the reader's participation and a clarification of his role as partner in the solving of the problem. When the writer reports the final interference or intensification, he has come to the end of the Middle of his structure.

There is little opportunity in the Middle for developing complex changes in character. The writer more adequately sharpens and delineates, and defines and elaborates the governing characteristic, but he seldom radically alters it. He makes sure that the tag of the governing characteristic appears with increasing clarity at all moments of decision. He repeats the physical tag of his character's appearance at all structural points and wherever a clear visual image of the character seems necessary. Where sensory report is indicated to assist in the complete experience of the structure or the character or the idea, he carefully performs the report of sensory scene. He faithfully limits narrative to those transitions between scenes which are necessary for clarity and con-sequence.

Some Examples of Middle: In "Bush Boy, Poor Boy" the problem facing "I" is how to make clear his superiority over Tom Woodley. The first solution is to shoot a fox and catch a codfish. The middle begins at the first interference, the accident of seeing the fox without a gun, reported from paragraphs 6 to 12, with effects continuing much longer. The solution is now altered to include only catching the cod, paragraph 14. The second, major, interference is reported in the scene of the tangled lines and Roy's error, beginning paragraph 105 and on to paragraph 116. The final solution comes in the scenes reported between paragraphs 138 and 148, and at that point the Middle ends. Up to this point we have seen no change in "I's" character, but looking back after the end, we can identify the influences which brought about this change.

In "Through the Tunnel" Jerry's first solution is to join the native boys and promote a friendship, though he cannot speak their language. The Middle begins as this simple solution fails when they "proceeded to forget him" in paragraph 17. The next solution Jerry decides on is to entertain them with clowning, in paragraph 23. This solution fails in miserable embarrassment. His third solution is to find the tunnel in paragraph 31. This solution fails because he is not properly equipped. His fourth solution is to obtain the goggles and try again. From this point on the suggested solution remains the same (to go through the tunnel), and the difficulties are intensified not by a change in solution but by the sensory report of scene to the end of the Middle, which comes clearly with success at paragraph 79. This story will bear careful study as an excellent example of both interference and of intensification and of a sharp increase in intensity brought about by the structure and by faithful report of scene in the Middle.

You will notice that in "Wullie" the minor actor, Rafe, very usefully supplies most of the interruptions and interferences. In "Through the Tunnel" the mother, a minor actor, supplies intensification. In "Bush Boy, Poor Boy" Roy interferes, assists in the solution, and instigates decisions. Thus it is clear that minor actors take sometimes a prominent part in the Middle story structure. As with the deciding character, the minor actor's physical tags are repeated for visual clarity at all points where they function in the structure: Rafe's vicious temper, Roy's age, Mother's delicacy and white skin, and so on. When it is clear to the reader that the deciding character has made his final decision as to the best solution to his problem, you have reached the end of the Middle of the story structure. Some comments on the End will come next.

Ideas for Study

1. Choose one of the problems with its causative situation which you listed in the exercise at the conclusion of Chapter Four. Invent a solution. Invent an interference which is not accidental. Report all this.

7

The End of a Short Story

The End Prepared For: The End section of a story reports the result of the deciding character's final decision on how to solve the problem, which may include a change in the character of the deciding actor. This result, whatever it turns out to be, physical, intellectual, emotional, ought to be and usually, but not always, is inevitable. That is, the reader should have been prepared for it from the first scenes. He ought to be able to say of the result: "Yes, that's right; given the structural components of the story and the decisions made, and the scenes as reported, it could have ended only thus." This requirement of inevitability must be kept in mind during the reports of all decisions, all solutions, all interferences, in each part of the story. The result reported in the End has thus been carefully and progressively prepared for. This does not mean that the end should necessarily be foreseen. Many stories depend on the element of shock or surprise to make the End effective, "Wullie," for instance. But looking back on the story, after the end, the reader should be able to see its inevitability. The End of "Wullie" is inevitable, and we accept it. In "Sled" and "Bush Boy, Poor Boy" an alteration in the character of each boy has been prepared for, and is, in fact, the point of each story.

The writer has one more obligation in the End part, and that is to make sure that all loose ends of scene or structure or character or event have been so neatly tied up that he can say of any unfinished business, as Kipling so often did, "but that's another story." The reader should be satisfied that the present story has come to its appointed end.

Some Endings Examined: In "How Mr. Hogan Robbed a Bank" the End begins with paragraph 26 and ends only twenty-four short paragraphs later. Beginning with paragraph 26, the result of all of Mr. Hogan's decisions unfolds rapidly and is completely reported by the end of paragraph 29. The remaining paragraphs neatly tie up all loose ends.

In "Sled" the End begins with paragraph 61. Everything after that, including Joey's change of attitude in paragraphs 95 to the last, results from the last decision. It is fair to say that this change was intended as perhaps the theme of the story. But it seems not inevitable and is not really necessary to the story. If it is retained because it is the point of the story, then Mr. Adams ought to have been more careful in preparing us for it in the scenes of the Beginning and especially those of the Middle.

In "Bush Boy, Poor Boy" the End begins with paragraph 158. Whatever happens after that will be the result of "I's" final choice. He lets the fox get away when he might have killed it. But this act is now consistent with all we have learned about "I." It has become clear to us during the slow elucidation of his character in the Middle scenes that, while neither his governing characteristic nor the problem has changed, the boy's realization of himself and his situation was slowly dawning into the insight reported in the End result.

If you wish to incorporate character development into your story, you would do well to study how Aldridge reports crucial scenes in terms of increased awareness by the boy of himself and his aspirations. This is a story of no change in aim or intent of structure, but change in self-realization, in awareness, in comprehension of his place in the scheme of things. If the boy had been carrying his rifle on his first encounter with the fox, he certainly would have killed it. The events reported after that: his nightmare, Roy's influence, the fishing episode, the story of Roy's misfortune, and so on, are all reported so sensitively that we observe the changes in the boy (even though we are unaware of their significance); and we are not surprised by the End. Instead, looking back on the story, we are likely to say, "Ah, so this is what it was all about." This is good short story discipline.

Ideas for Study

1. Write an End for the story you projected in the exercises for Chapters Four and Six.

8

The Application of the Discipline

Getting Started: It may be convenient, now, to reduce items we have covered in the foregoing discussion of short story discipline to a compressed, summarizing checklist for planning and revising your short story. The list asks questions on the main problems of structure in an order closely following that of our chapters.

Some writers outline each scene in advance of writing, showing in the plan of scenes each of the structural elements to be reported in each scene, and something of the sensory content of each. Their outline follows the pattern of Beginning, Middle, End, and accounts for structural detail in each part. The actual writing can then proceed with a minimum of organizational difficulty. This is a good, methodical way to get a story started and down on paper while the general ideas are fresh. And it keeps the total story in mind for a long time, with little danger of losing detail and direction during the involved process of writing. Such a checklist as the one offered here will assist in this kind of planning.

Other writers have the general idea and the continuity of the story well in mind. They write detailed scenes in which certain already-foreseen events take place, completing them as units more or less independently of each other and not necessarily in continuity. Then with the individual scenes largely finished, they rearrange and order the scenes into continuity, taking out and putting in as the need rises and the story develops. The checklist assists in such a reordering and in the revision of scene report. Still other writers seem unable to visualize the story as a whole generally or to foresee specific events, or even to know the end in advance. They may have a character in mind which they wish to structure into a deciding character. Or perhaps they have a delightful passage of dialogue that can be worked into a scene. Or a sensory scene opens up before them which they must capture. Or they are taken by an intellectual idea, or a mood or feeling or theme, which they can exploit in a scene. To wait until all this takes shape in the mind as an ordered story would postpone writing indefinitely. In any case, the story begins with writing, and this writer begins by reporting scenes more or less helter-skelter until the story idea begins to take shape in his mind, and the scenes begin to fit into a pattern. Then the rearranging, the inclusion, the rejection of scene follows, guided hopefully by such a checklist.

The main idea for you is to begin writing and keep on writing until you have your story. Do not think of the checklist as a straitjacket. It is intended as a summary of the necessary disciplines described here and a guide to the organization of your scenes. And do not begin revision too soon; you cannot evaluate the story till it is ended. After the story has been written, then the checklist becomes a guide and reminder for the long process of revision and polish which every good writer discovers must be a part of the production of every good short story.

The Checklist

BEGINNING SCENE OR SCENES:

1. Is the deciding character reported in a statement which will be clear to the reader covering:

a. His governing characteristic with its phrases for repetition?
b. His problem?
c. His proposed solution?
d. His physical appearance reported and adequately repeated; age, name?
e. Is the point of view established?
f. Is the panoramic view reported adequately?

2. Do minor characters possess:

a. Characteristics which are clearly stated?
b. Physical appearance adequately reported?
c. A function in the story clearly stated?

3. Does the story begin at the causative situation, and is this situation clearly stated and developed in the report?
4. Is there a beginning of the development of mood and tone?

5. If the theme or idea is important, has it been introduced?

MIDDLE SCENES:

1. Are well-developed intensifications or interferences with the progress of the proposed solutions stated clearly?

2. Do the deciding character's decisions demonstrate clearly to the reader the functioning of his governing characteristic?

3. Has accident been avoided, or explained and used structurally?

4. Is the point of view maintained at all points?

5. Are mood and theme developed?

6. Is the End prepared for?

ENDING SCENE OR SCENES:

1. Are the results of the deciding character's decisions clearly shown?

2. Are the results inevitable or logical?

3. Are all loose ends tied up satisfactorily?

4. Is the idea clearly shown?

OF ALL SCENES:

1. Are all scenes necessary and in the best order? What about flashbacks?

2. Are other scenes needed?

3. Are transitions from scene to scene clear as to time, place, light, etc.? Are scene tags repeated judiciously?

4. Does each scene move the story forward, give insight into character and motive, lead to the final significance?

5. Is each scene adequately reported as to time, place, character, light, purpose, point of view, and the five senses?

DIALOGUE:

1. Is dialogue adequately used to develop and present:

a. structure of the story?
b. scene development?
c. insight into character and motive?

2. Are the phrases accompanying the dialogue effectively used, successfully repeated, and properly positioned?

3. Is the dialogue accurately and properly idiomatic?

In the next part, Part Two, we will analyze three short stories in considerable detail, and comment specifically on the discipline.

PART II

Analyses of and Comments on Three Short Stories

In each analysis, the text of the story has been printed without interruption, with the analysis appearing in a parallel column, the paragraph beginnings of which match the points in the text under discussion. I suggest you read the entire text of the story first to become familiar with the story. Then a second careful reading of both columns, matching the comment to the point in the story, should make the analysis clear, specific, and concrete. Finally, the response to the appended "Ideas for Study" should be made as thoughtfully as possible.

"Granpa" and "So Young to Die" are written by students. "Granpa" was printed in Literary Cavalcade *in May 1960 and reprinted in* Bittersweet *in 1962.*

Story Analysis:

GRANPA
by Jeff Rackham

TEXT	COMMENT
I went to live with my grandparents on their farm in Missouri, just after I turned seven. I suppose at that time my Grandpa was not really old, but he seemed a terribly old man to me. There has never been a man with more wrinkles in his face than Granpa. They were not wrinkles of sorrow or anguish but happy wrinkles. They ran deeply through his cheeks and round his eyes and from the base of his ears down onto his throat and neck. He al-	*The first sentence establishes the point of view as first person subjective, "I" as the deciding character, his age (a most important item in a short story or essay without which nothing else can make true sense), and tentatively the causative situation, that is, the move to Missouri. It also begins the data on the panoramic view, for Missouri is specifically localized. This is a good first sentence. The rest of the paragraph reports the essentials about*

71

ways had a little stubble of whiskers on his chin.

the minor character, Granpa, very important for our interpretation of later scenes. There is a little more than physical appearance. The stubble and wrinkles, when repeated later, evoke this entire image of Granpa. There is development of insight into Grandpa's character with his seeming age and his deliberate neglect of shaving. Strong use of the sense of sight.

He farmed almost sixty acres with horses, not because he was a hard worker but because Granma was. I loved those horses. I watched him round them up in the morning and harness them, and I went to the fields with him and watched them all day long. They were beautiful to me; the largest one was grey and black and her name was Maud, the other black or brownish-black was Billy. Granpa never allowed me close enough to touch them because he said they weren't used to children, but more than anything else in the world I wanted to ride one of them. It didn't especially matter which one, although I think that secretly I liked Maud the best because she stood almost a hand taller than Billy, and her long shaggy mane hung way down over her forehead,

More panoramic view of the total farm, the field. "I loved those horses" introduces "I's" governing characteristic, repeats it, and leads clearly to the problem: "more than anything else in the world I wanted to ride one of them" states the problem succinctly. "I's" first solution is to ask every morning; the first interference is "No, not yet." Jeff uses here the familiar clash of wills and judgments. This paragraph provides some further oblique insight into Granpa in the first-sentence reference to Granma and a full report of the horses which are really minor actors. Maud is labeled, and we watch for later reference and meet it with the delight of recognition. Creatively the panoramic view in the first two paragraphs contains senses of sight and touch (implied)

and Granpa had to push some of it through the cheek strap of the blinders so that she could see. I asked him every morning if I could ride them, and he always said, "No, not yet."

One day toward the end of spring when the plowing was almost finished I went with him to the field and played around the fence and down by the creek, but finally it grew too hot; and I just sat in the shade of the hedge row and watched him and the horses.

I sat with my legs wrapped around the outside of the cool water jug and my back against the rough bark of the hedge row. The heat felt heavy and dense, even in the shade. The sun burned down, making the leaves in the wood on the other side of the field sparkle and flash.

Granpa still wore two pairs of overalls and a heavy wool shirt. He had looped the reins around his neck and pulled his broken straw hat down to his ears.

His great knotted hands gripped both handles of the plow, and he lifted himself into the air and pushed his weight down onto the plow. When he started the horses, he shouted, "Hey-ya!" and slapped the reins across their

and a long list of detail. Structurally, Jeff has reached the end of the Beginning.

Scene One: It begins the Middle of the story: time, (crucial here), place, light, and shade repeated, temperature, character, purpose, point of view. There are sight; touch: "cool water jug," and "rough bark"; smell; all elements but taste.

Note the insight into Granpa developed by his report of clothing.

Notice the sharp accounting for distance and perspective in the point of view as the team circles the field. Note the care with sequence.

backs, then "Gee-a-ther." He made all kinds of shouting noises as the horses plodded along bouncing him behind them. I could hear his cursing even when he trudged out of sight on the other side of the hill.

Two little sweat bees kept buzzing around me, and I swatted at them and finally killed one. I wiped the yellow puss-blood onto my Levis.

The horses appeared again on the other side of the hill, their great shaggy heads bouncing up and down against the crest of the earth. They dropped down into another hollow and I could see only the tops of their heads with their flickering ears and Granpa's hat bobbing along above the ground. Then their heads popped up and they strained back up the rise with Granpa joggling along behind, seeming to hold back as much as he could.

"May black boils seal the womb you came from, Maud!" he shouted. "Hey-ya! Hey-ya!" He stumbled and cursed. "Get in there, Billy."

I think that he wasn't really angry: he just liked to make noise, or maybe in that way he got even with Granma. He went round

The sweat bees help here, sound and touch mainly, but they effectively evoke a hot summer morning by connotation, which helps prepare us for the End.

Note how closely Jeff keeps his eyes on the scene, reporting the action in its time sequence faithfully and briefly, and building carefully to the final decision.

Granpa's shouting evokes distance and nearness. Further insight into Granpa again through the Granma reference, the need for this will be apparent in the final result. The problem and the governing characteristic are both repeated here with increased intensity.

At the end of this scene

and round the field cursing and shouting, and all the time I just sat and dreamed of the chance to ride those horses.

Later in the morning he stopped them, yanked off his hat, took the reins from around his neck, and looped them over the plow handle. He came striding toward me across the furrowed rows of black earth wiping the sweat from his hatband. Sweat had turned his shirt dark across the shoulders.

I jumped up and held the jug for him. He stomped up to me smiling, hot, and dirty.

"Hard work, huh?" he asked, with his Southern slowness.

"Yes," I said, and watched him hold the damp jug to his forehead for a moment. Then he removed the cork with his thumb, and with a motion of his arm, he flipped the jug into the air so that it rested on his elbow, and the water popped and gurgled as he drank. He finished and held it out to me. Water ran down the stubble of his chin. I held the jug with both hands and let the cool water wash around in my mouth and watched him smile at me. When I handed the jug back, I said, "Can I ride the horses today?" I tried to say

we return to the problem faced by "I."

Scene Two: Though place doesn't change, the scene is new because of a new time, new (added) character, and new purpose. It begins with "Later in the morning" and ends with "Just you don't tell your granma": all dialogue and dialogue tag. Jeff makes no attempt to vary the "he said," or identifying clause. He relies on the phrases accompanying dialogue to bring the drama of decision to us.

Note the long, fully developed accompaniment to "Yes," and its meticulous following of sequence of action in which the reader sees Granpa vividly and has considerable insight into "I." This is good reporting. It ends with a clean statement of the problem and its proposed solution. This time the suggestion succeeds, and the story moves into the Ending. Notice here how the senses are reported in dialogue. The accompanying phrases provide ample room for sense reporting: For smell ("hot, and dirty"), sound (voice,

it real casual and adult-like.

He started to smile, but then he frowned as he put the cork in. "Think you can hang on?" he asked.

"Oh, sure" I said, catching my breath and hoping.

"Well," he drawled, and wiped his face with his shirt sleeve.

"Please!" I begged.

"You're still pretty small," he said.

"I'm almost three and a half feet," I said, stretching myself slightly.

He shoved his hands into his back overall pockets and said, "On just one condition."

"O.K.," I said, feeling jittery and excited.

"Just you don't tell your granma," he said, and winked.

And I was off and running across the dirt. As I got closer to the horses they grew larger and larger. They were larger than I ever dreamed. I stopped about three feet from them and stared. They were so tall that I could have walked under them by just ducking my head a bit. They heaved and sighed and shifted and smelled like manure. Maud was all covered with white foam, and her hair was shaggy and falling out. Just as Granpa came up behind me she swung her head around and snorted at me.

"gurgled," etc.) sight, taste ("cool water wash around"), touch ("hold the damp jug to his forehead"), all reported in the phrases. You might learn from Jeff something about concrete verbs and verbals. This scene demonstrates how to use concrete verbs and climactic simple sentences with compound verbs. Take a good look. The scene sadly lacks report of light and change of light.

Scene Three begins the Ending: Jeff has changed slightly the time, place, and position, thus a change of scene; "I" has made his final decision regarding the solution to his problem; the rest is result, thus the Ending section. The vivid report of the team and of Maud in particular is produced by careful observation of a change in the position: "I" is now close up, not away across the fields. All the senses are in play here. Note the repeated phrase for Maud.

Her lips curled back, and she showed her greenish-yellow teeth and snapped them against the bit. I leaped back and Granpa caught me.

She rippled her skin and snorted again. I hung back in Granpa's hands, I wasn't so sure that I wanted to ride her now.

"Ready?" he asked.

"I don't think I'll ride them today," I said, trying to be calm. Maybe he didn't hear me because he caught my waist and lifted me up into the air. I grabbed his hands and shouted, "I don't want to, Granpa. I don't want to!"

"Nonsense!" he said gruffly and started to set me on the horse. I lifted my feet into the air and screamed.

"No, no, no, no, no!" I twisted and jerked and started to cry.

"You wanted to," he hollered, "so you're goin' to." He sat me on the horse, and I could feel the wet lather right through the seat of my pants. "Now hang onto the hames," he said, and placed my hands around the hot metal knobs. The sour-smelling sweat had darkened the bottom of the leather collar. I was terrified, and I was crying and screaming. Maud tossed her head, and I screamed louder. Her hair felt wiry and

The positioning of the speech and the accompanying phrases here is excellent. Notice how they illuminate character, motive, the change in attitudes as the solution progresses, the results of "I" 's decision rising to the cry, "I don't want to, Granpa." This intensification of the feeling from the relatively placid desire in the beginning through the active anticipation in the middle to the acute emotional pressure of the ending produces the desired heightening of suspense in the working out the solution. Note also the adroit use of abrupt break with intensity by the use of some humor: " 'Well, goddamnit, let go!' So I did."

slobbery wet, and it stuck to my arms and hands. I hung on tight and closed my eyes.

"I don't want to, Granpa! I don't want to," I cried. I heard him walk to the plow and snap the reins. "Hey-ya!" he said.

I knew that I was going to die, and I pressed my knees into the horse and dug my fingers into the collar. The horses stepped off and I rose in the air and bounced. I started to scream, then I slipped to one side, and I grabbed and gasped for breath. I couldn't breathe, and I couldn't scream or cry, and I wanted my mother because she would have saved me. Then the horses stopped, and I felt his big thick hands around my waist. He lifted me away from the horse, but I was so terrified that I couldn't let go, and I still held on with all my strength. He pulled and yanked at me, then hollered: "Well, goddamnit, let go." So I did.

He stood me up in the dirt and knelt down facing me, and I opened my eyes. I gasped; my whole body shook and shuddered. The harder I tried not to cry the more tears ran down my face. I looked into his big wrinkled face and saw the grey stubble on his chin and in the groove of wrinkles.

In Scene Four, coming right after the sharp break, the tension subsides more slowly. Note the phrases here which evoke Granpa again and give credibility to "I's" declaration: "I loved this man more than anyone in the world," and all that follows.

The bushy black hair stuck out over his ears, and his lips were smiling slightly, and it was right then that I loved this man more than anyone in the world. He was my father and mother and grandfather and God and no one could ever convince me differently. I tried to stop crying while his eyes looked deeply at me.

"Now you listen," he said, solidly, but kindly, "You've learned something today that many people never learn." He rubbed his rough finger across my cheek and wiped the tear away. "You've found out that there are things in life that people think they want, but when they get 'em, they discover they didn't want 'em at all."

Note how Jeff puts the key sentence, in which he offers the final clear statement of the significance of this story idea, into idiomatic dialogue. This is intellectual insight of a high order. We see not only into Granpa but into the boy and the total experience.

I shivered and gagged on my breath again and looked at him. He stood up and turned me back toward the hedge row and slapped me on the rear. "Now take off," he said.

Scene Five, the final report, ends the story quickly and succinctly with a satisfying tie-up of loose ends.

I started stumbling back over the fresh black dirt still gasping and trying to stop crying. I heard him shout "Hey-ya!" and slap the reins. I turned and looked at him and wiped my eyes. The silver plow cut into the grey crust and rolled over the black earth.

"You granny-scratchin'

black-tongued mule!" he
shouted. "Get in there."

I walked on back to the
hedge row and sat for a
while, thinking.

Ideas for Study

1. Do you judge first person subjective to be the best point of view for "Granpa?" Why? Why not?

2. What is the intellectual significance of "Granpa?" Support your statement.

3. List some items of information Jeff must have been sure of to give this story its tone of authenticity.

4. Make a list of items you know about the character of "I" and Granpa. How were you made aware of these characteristics? How useful is dialogue? How does it illuminate character?

5. What is the best feature of this story? The worst? Why in each case?

Story Analysis:

The first person subjective point of view fitted the purposes which Jeff had in mind for "Granpa." But, as Fred Millett points out clearly in Chapter Three on point of view in Reading Fiction, *there are limitations to the use of "I." In the following short story Laurel Ellison chose to use the third person subjective point of view. In this story, therefore, the reader identifies with Linnie with no limitations on insight and with complete flexibility of scene. As you read "So Young to Die" be aware of the advantages of this third person subjective point of view and decide why it fits Laurel's intent. "So Young to Die" was printed in the May 1957* Literary Cavalcade *and reprinted in* Bittersweet, *1962. Examine the story closely for structure as an art form, for creativity as sensory transfer of significant experience, and for its intellectual values.*

SO YOUNG TO DIE
by Laurel Ellison

TEXT	COMMENT

It was the sounds the mice made playing ball in the roof of the cabin that wakened Linnie. She yawned and began to work her way from the warm eiderdown softness of her nest at the bottom of the bedroll to the cold pillow at the top. Her skin prickled with the cold when she reached the pillow, and the button at the neck of her white flannel nightie was undone again, so Linnie buttoned it up, but it didn't make her any warmer. She reached down, pulled down her nightie and tucked her feet into its warm folds. Then she just lay there.

The bumping had stopped. "I guess even mice have to sleep sometime," she thought. She looked across the room toward the dim forms of her two sisters. Mart sighed and turned in her sleep. Robbie didn't move. Linnie wished the mice would start playing ball again. The cabin was scary when it was so quiet and dark.

She snuggled the top of the bedroll around her neck and lay there. She heard the springs of her parents' big

Scene One presents time, early dawn; place, a cabin bedroom; light, and darkness; and the senses of sound, touch (temperature, texture), and sight. Laurel has already identified all the main characters, given the sisters' names, and established Linnie as the deciding character, and the point of view of the story as third person subjective. She begins to suggest panoramic view with "mice" and "cabin" and "bedroll" and "canvas cover," all of which are associated with camping.

brass bed in the next room squeek. "Everybody but me's asleep." She twisted her head again to see Robbie and Mart. They were just padded lumps of darkness against the monk's cloth curtain on the window. It shone faintly, with the same glow that an egg has when it's held up to the light. She could feel the dampness of the air making the canvas cover of her bedroll clammy and stiff.

Mart didn't cuddle up at the bottom of her bed like Linnie did—any more. She used to, until last July when she had gotten polio and had hardly seemed to have enough strength to breathe, let alone move her small, tanned body. Linnie remembered when the doctor had driven up the mountain to the cabin to examine Martie, and how he'd said in his wheezy voice to Mama, "It's one of the less serious types of polio. Still, I'd like to make some tests." He hadn't looked at Linnie, and he didn't say good-by to her when he wheezed himself out of the door. Nobody even knew she was there.

Of course, Mama had been busy, and Robbie got to help her because she was two years older, but when Daddy had driven up each night in his green Forest

Scene Two is a flashback scene into memory reported within Scene One. Laurel makes the scene do hard work by supplying time, place, minor actor, sight, the sound in the dialogue with its attached phrases. She gives Mart her special characteristic (earlier illness) and Linnie her governing characteristic: (Nobody even knew she was there.)

Scene Three gives the relative ages of the sisters, very important always, and a neat report of Daddy, which also completes the data on panoramic view,

Service pick-up, he'd go right in to see Mart without saying hardly anything to Linnie. Then after dinner he'd write up reports that Linnie knew would go into the box marked LAND MANAGEMENT, CENTRAL UTAH. She wished Daddy would stop looking so tired and being so cross, that Robbie would stop acting so smart, and that Mama would let her in to see Mart.

Now Mart was better, but they still paid more attention to her. Linnie began to wonder if they even loved her any more. Nothing had ever happened to her to make them feel sorry for her.

Suddenly, Linnie sat straight up in bed. "I'm going to die," she said. The cold made her shiver, but she sat up anyway. "Dying is more important than having polio, and I'm going to die bravely." She said it twice but it didn't sound brave because her teeth were beginning to chatter.

even to the exact geography. Robbie is given her characteristic ("smart"); and the governing characteristic of the clearly emerging deciding character is repeated. Part of Scene One remains still in memory (flashback), but the necessary information leading to the causative situation is supplied.

This is transition to the present. It also clearly restates the governing characteristic ("Linnie began to wonder . . ."); the causative situation ("Nothing had ever happened . . ."); and the problem (how to be noticed); and it prepares for the suggested solution. This is a good, hard-working paragraph. Though it is narrative, it exists within Scene One.

Scene Four: With sharp report of sound and touch, Laurel here states flatly the suggested solution: " 'I'm going to die.' " This is good scening. It makes this one basic point of structure clearly and succinctly, and it comes immediately after the statement of problem. From this point on we are held in suspense, wondering whether the deciding character can solve her problem along the line laid

*down. Will the suggested
solution work? In these first
four short scenes the point
of view, governing characteristic, causative situation,
problem and suggested solution have come quickly and
neatly in that order. In addition Laurel gave the
characters with their characteristics, and the panoramic
view to give reality and
perspective to all succeeding scenes. Scene Four
marks clearly the end of
the beginning of the story.
Also in this scene she establishes the tone of the story
by juxtaposing " 'I'm go-
ing to die bravely' " against
"her teeth were beginning
to chatter." She repeats
carefully throughout this
technique of placing side by
side the childlike tragedy
against the ludicrous, to
create the tone of good-
humored, adult recognition
of and indulgence of childish trouble.*

She lay down in bed
again. She could see the
people at her funeral. They
were all crying and saying,
"She was so young to die.
She wasn't even ten-and-a-
half." Linnie could even see
the beautiful little girl lying
in a coffin made of cut glass
and silk and lace. There
was a sweet, gentle smile on
the white, little face; and
it was framed by a cloud of

*Scene Five: The middle
of the story begins here
with a "dream" scene re-
ported with sound and sight
and with strong suggestion
of light. The adjective pile-
ups here sound childish, as
they should. All the detail
develops Linnie's problem,
her suggested solution, and
her governing characteristic.*

shining auburn (not red) hair. Her mother came up and looked sadly at her daughter's smile and said, "She died so bravely," and her father had to hand her mother a dry hankie.

"I'd better write them a note," Linnie thought, "and tell them to put my 'Album of Horses' and 'Thee, Hannah' and 'King of the Wind' in my arms instead of flowers." She tried to make a hot, salty tear trickle down her face, but she couldn't cry, and her face began to ache from trying.

It was beginning to be light outside, although the cabin was still quite dark, Linnie could see the shadows that the rough place on the logs of the cabin walls made against the one below it. The whole inside of the cabin was painted gray, right over the logs. She liked them gray, because it made the red-and-yellow plaid of her coverlet show up more in the day. The bouquet of lupines and wild geraniums she had put in her window yesterday drooped from the edges of their bottle, silhouetted against the pale curtain.

Linnie wished Mart would wake up and talk to her. Maybe the mice knew. Maybe that was why they'd

Scene Six returns clearly to the present in the first six words of transition. Here Laurel attends to the changes in light and time and adds detail to the panoramic view. She uses sight skillfully, but she (sadly) omits the sense of smell. The governing characteristic and the solution are again repeated, for development.

Scene Seven is a transition scene, changing place and purpose, and reporting touch, sound, and sight.

stopped playing. Nobody plays when a person is going to die.

Linnie got out of bed and felt around for her red-and-white sneakers under the bed. They felt clammy and were colder, even, than the painted wood floor. She climbed up onto her squeaky old army cot again to put them on. Then she pulled the cheviot from the foot of the cot.

She slid off the bed, went over to the metal double bed, where Mart and Rob were sleeping, crawled over Mart to wake her up and sat down next to the wall. She patted Mart's tanned face, and Mart's brown eyes flickered open like the gas lantern's flame—and then closed. "Mart," Linnie whispered, "I'm going to die!"

"Everybody does, Linnie," Mart whispered back. "Do you want to climb in bed?"

"No," Linnie said.

"Be quiet. You'll wake up Robbie." Mart's brown Dutch boy cut didn't even look messed up, Linnie thought.

"Listen. Robbie broke her arm. Daddy's teeth got pulled out by that drunk dentist. Mama got pneumonia when she was little, and you got polio, and

In Scene Eight all the points of structure so far used are further developed. Note Laurel's use of the braid as repeated development of the deciding character's personality and her use of Mart, a minor character, to develop the story tone. Mart's age is established. Pay attention to Laurel's carefully reported sequence of action in her verbs and her transition. All the senses except taste are used here.

you're a year littler than me, see?" Linnie was pulling her right braid hard. She felt cold, now, and she unsnapped the side of Mart's double bedroll and climbed inside to warm herself. "Nothing bad's ever happened to me yet." Her eyes filled up with tears that made her braid look like a blur of orange watercolor. "See, God's been saving me up for the very worst of all, and what is worse than dying?"

Mart's eyes widened. "I'll bet you're right. I never thought of that." She lowered her voice and stared at Linnie. "When do you think you'll die, Lin?"

Linnie wiped her eyes with the sheet. "Today, maybe. Maybe now!"

"Well, let's go to sleep, then. We can't stop you." Mart snuggled down and put her arm around Linnie.

"No. I'll be back in a minute." Linnie climbed back out of bed, tiptoed across the floor, pulled the gray, wooden door open, and stepped out onto the strip of cement that ran along the east side of the cabin.

The sun hadn't come over the top of the sky line yet. She shook out the cheviot, wrapped it around her, and twitched her head to release

This is transition. Here is a good place to note the way Laurel has been using concrete verbs. "Climbed," "tiptoed," "pulled," "stepped," "ran," all evoke sensory impressions. So far in the story she has used the abstract "to be" forms only twenty-three times. Be aware of her verbs. They work without strain or ostentation.

her braids from under it. Then she started up the path to the latrine.

Small, rough stones looking like bit-off, hardened pieces of Mama's raisin pudding rolled under the soles of her sneakers and into the damp foxtails under the currant bushes. She pulled off some of the fuzzy, red currants that were still left and ate them one at a time. They were sweet and full of little seed grains. For the first time, Linnie looked down the mountain.

The whole valley was clotted with a mass of white and gray clouds; little wisps of pink-white vapor slipped along, close to the ground. Linnie didn't need to go to the latrine any more. She climbed up the three steps of the stile, pulled off the cheviot, dropped it on one of the steps, and ran down the other three.

She ran through the wet grasses to the middle of the field and stood there for a minute, then, forgetting she was going to die, spread her arms out straight and whirled. She whirled around as fast as she could in the mist, until her nightie was wet below her knees and stuck to her legs instead of whirling out as she twirled. She began to laugh, and she tossed her braids back over

Scene Nine supplies a transition in time, place, light, and purpose to the next scene which is intensely communicative, and very important for its empathy with Linnie.

Scene Ten: Knowing that the value of her story lies in its insight into the mind and spirit and sensory world of this little ten-year-old, Laurel has developed this scene fully. All senses are at work; all the elements of scene are invoked, the light and change of light, for instance, is reported six times. She keeps the tone; note the effect of the reference to the currants, for example. This

her shoulder and started to catch at the slowly-moving clouds around her. "I've never tried picking clouds," she thought.

Then she remembered— and stopped laughing. "And I guess I will never get to do it again." She turned and walked back up to the path. "It's too cold, yet, to be going without a wrap." She scolded herself, and climbed over the stile to get the cheviot and wrap it around her.

Then she sat down on the top step and looked down on the clouds in the fields and out across Philadelphia Flat. "Maybe that's what heaven's like," she thought, pulling the wet flannel away from her legs. The wet had made the little violet sprigs on her nightie go purple.

"Maybe," she said out loud, "maybe I'm in heaven now and don't know it." She hunched down on the splintery step and looked around her. She was beginning to feel really cold. Every summer when they came up here Mama called this place heaven. But this wasn't the right place, Linnie decided. In heaven they wouldn't have any flies at all, not even in the latrines. She straightened up and felt better.

Down at the foot of the stile a little yellow prim-

is a good place to call attention to Laurel's use of symbols. The closing of the yellow petals of the evening primrose becomes a fine symbolism of both little Linnie and the central idea of the death wish. Do you know enough psychology to define the meaning of such other apt symbols as "the warm eiderdown softness of her nest" in the first paragraph or, in Scene Seven, the wilted lupines and wild geraniums?

Note the verbs in this scene and study their sensory effect. Note the care with idiom in such things as ". . . the little violet sprigs on her nightie go purple," and note the accurate and minute observation.

Structurally Laurel has rounded out the death wish, Linnie's suggested solution, and given it reality and believability by accurate reporting.

rose was almost shriveled up for the day. Linnie watched it until the delicate yellow petals had formed a small, soft cone. "Now it's dead," she thought, "it only bloomed one night, and it's dead." She pulled her braid over her shoulder and chewed sadly on the tip. It tasted like Woodbury's shampoo and watery vinegar.

A quiet breeze had started to blow at the little wisps of clouds, and now they started to scuttle away toward the pale-green cabin. She stood up, wrapped the cheviot around her, and went a little way into the field. She held out her right arm toward the moving clouds. "I am a pioneer woman at my cabin," she said gravely. "I face a horrible death with bravery." Her eyes filled with tears. "Even pioneer women cried," she thought, and started across the stile and down the path, stopping to pick some more currants. "I may never eat wild currants again," she said, and went across the bridge and into the cabin.

She took off her wet nightie and spread it over the bottom of the double bed. Then she took off her red sneakers. She crawled over Mart and curled up

Scene Eleven is transition, returning from the moving experience of Scene Ten to the previous symbol of childish security in Scene Eleven.

beside her in the warm
bedroll.

At about ten o'clock that
morning, Linnie was sitting
outside the cabin on the
wood-cutting block while
Mama braided her hair,
when old Tim Mortenson
rode up on his bay horse,
Rachel. He wanted to use
the Forest Service telephone
that hung in an iron box
outside the cabin. Mama
had brushed Linnie's hair
until it was electric and was
flying around her face. The
sun shining on it made it
look like delicate threads of
spun copper. She wondered
if in heaven they made you
wear a cloth to hide your
hair like in the Bible. If
they did, maybe she would
go down into hell and see if
they made you wear one
there.

The sunshine silvered
Rachel's forelock, the hair
on her nose, and the long
stubble on Tim's tanned
face, intent as he cranked
the handle of the telephone
making three raspy short,
and two long rings, and
shouted into it. When he
hung up the receiver and
clanged the metal door of
the box shut, Mama invited
him to come in and eat
some of the newly-baked
cookies. She didn't offer him
any hot coffee, because Tim
was a very strict Mormon.

*Scene Twelve: Changes
of time, light, and character all reinforce Linnie's
problem and solution, but
no change in the problem
nor in the essential decision.
The succeeding scenes are
meant to increase this tension and maintain our suspense.*

*Notice that dialogue has
been used to develop either
character or structure or
scene. In Scene Eight it
builds chiefly structure; in
Scene Ten it permits insight
into the character and motivation of the deciding
character; in Scene Twelve
notice how Mart's "Boy,"
offers insight into Mart and
by contrast into Linnie and
her problem. Notice also
how the dialogue reveals
both scene and character.
The essential thing to remember about dialogue is
that the words spoken and
their accompanying phrases
must both function in some
part of the structure.*

Tim chuckled from down in his plaid flannel shirt and raised his eyebrows at Linnie. "How'd you kiddies like to ride Rachel for a while?"

"Boy," Mart yelled from the doorway of the kitchen, "boy, we'd sure like to!"

Linnie let Mart and Robbie ride Rachel that morning. If she should fall off, she might die. Instead she sat down by Robin, Tim's best sheep dog, and looked for little sparkles on top of the mare's-tail clouds, in case the sun was shining on golden harps or something, in heaven. But she didn't see anything except two red-tailed hawks wheeling a lonely pattern in the sky.

That afternoon, Mama, Robbie, and Mart went down the mountain to do some shopping. Linnie stayed at home. Almost anything can happen to you in a car, especially on a narrow, winding road.

The scene is continued in place but there is a transition in time and some intensification of the problem.

She thought maybe she ought to say good-by to the mice, so she waited until the car had gone. Then she pushed through the tall grasses at the south end of the cabin and boosted herself under the eaves. She peeked in and whispered, "Good-by, mice." She couldn't see anything moving. She waited. Those mice weren't even paying at-

Scene Thirteen, transition in time. Note the intensifying repetitions.

tention; They didn't care if she died.

When Mama and the girls came back from town, they brought Daddy with them. And there was Robbie sitting right next to him and acting so smart. Linnie wished she'd gone down the mountain with them. Then maybe she'd have gotten to sit next to Daddy.

After dinner, Daddy brought out his guitar, and they sat around the campfire and sang. Linnie loved this, and she leaned back against Daddy's legs while he played. She watched the flames leap upward and spit out little showers of sparks when they reached the blackness. They lit up Mama's face and made her hair shine as she sang, gazing all the while at the blinking coals on the outside edge of the fire.

Beyond the warm circle, the night was clear. The stars seemed very close and very white. Linnie turned away from the fire to let her face cool and to warm her back. She shivered as a cold breeze blew past her and made the two tall, green-black spruce trees sigh and whisper to each other. She could smell the raw greenness of bruised grasses and the hot incense of the pine in the fire.

Mart's eyes sparkled as

Scene Fourteen evokes rich experience with all the scene elements; the sensory report of lighting and touch and smell are especially effective, where intimacy is to be evoked. Laurel selects the sensory detail carefully to build tension and repeat the essentials of structure. This scene ends the middle of the story. What follows, as the End of the story, should report the results of Linnie's decision to solve her problem in her own way.

she sang. Linnie wondered if her own eyes sparkled. Maybe that was why Daddy liked Mart better. Daddy loved to sing Mexican songs, and now he sang about El Quelele, Linnie's favorite;

Papa White Hawk is dead,
Aye, yi, yi, yi.
He died at three in the morning.
And the baby white hawks,
Aye, yi, yi, yi.
Cry them to death in their woe.

Linnie's eyes filled with tears, and she could feel her nose going red. Everybody always talked about dying. She got up, kissed Mama good night, and then kissed Daddy. He set down his guitar and hugged her too tight. He set her down and kissed her on her sunburned nose. She was afraid maybe she would cry, so she said, "Good night, Daddy," and went into the cabin.

She undressed in the dark and got into her flannel nightie. She could still feel Daddy's short, rough whiskers against her cheek.

She was in bed when Mart opened the door stealthily and slipped in. Robin followed her.

"I told her about you dying," Mart whispered.

"Yeah, and you sure are a dim bulb," Robbie whis-

Scene Fifteen: If Linnie's governing characteristic is a sense of insecurity and neglect, if her problem is how to be noticed and cared for, and if her solution is to die and thus be made much of and cried over, the reader would expect to see the result (either success or failure) of the decision in this scene. Laurel has not made the results quite clear. The

pered. "Dying is the best thing that can happen to you."

"Jesus said so . . ." Mart interrupted.

"So," Robbie went on, "That's a best, not a worst to happen to somebody. And besides, you're still a baby. Nothing's hardly had time to happen to you yet. Besides, God doesn't save up people to let the worst happen to them. You only die because He likes you so much that He wants you to live closer to Him."

Linnie pulled her braid hard. Robbie was going so fast that Linnie couldn't interrupt until she stopped for breath.

"So that maybe you could go over to his house and visit Him sometimes?" Linnie whispered.

"Sure, stooge," Mart whispered back. Linnie bit the tip of her braid. It tasted like Woodbury's shampoo and watery vinegar. Suddenly she giggled. Robbie and Mart giggled, too.

After her sisters had gone to bed, Linnie was almost asleep when she was awakened by scatchings and scurryings, then a bump. She smiled and curled up again in her nest at the bottom of her bedroll. The mice were playing ball again.

dialogue of the last scene seems to report failure since there is no evidence that the parents demonstrated their love for Linnie to her satisfaction. But instead of having increased fears of insecurity, she allows her sisters to persuade her in the dialogue that her whole idea involved in the death wish was incorrect for her purposes; and she accepts the verdict happily and returns to her "nest," her problem not solved, but her frame of mind improved. This ties up the loose ends, but does not show a clear-cut result of the decision. Laurel may have felt an impending descent into sentimentality in the camp-fire scene and, wishing to avoid it, avoided also the happy direct result of decision. My own feeling is that the well-developed tone would have sustained a much closer adherence to structure. Perhaps Laurel should have reworked the last section of the scene and disciplined herself to structure.

Whatever you decide about the ending, you have seen an eventful day in the life of an insecure ten-year-old reported in fifteen scenes which moved forward in sequence to a preconceived significance. They held life in suspension, as does all good literature,

*while you realized some
aspect of its significance.*

Ideas for Study

1. Write a short paragraph identifying the panoramic view of this story. Be sure you stick to the text.

2. State Linnie's governing characteristic. What is her problem?

3. What is the tone of voice of this story?

4. What is the effect on tone of the adjective "couples" in the first paragraph of the middle: "She lay down in bed again. She could see . . ."?

5. What part of structure is "pulling her right braid hard"?

6. What is the meaning of the "nest" and of the "lupine" symbols? How do these meanings help tell the story?

7. Why is the "Tim Mortenson" episode necessary? Why not?

8. What is your judgment about the Ending of this story?

Story Analysis:

Let's have one more look, this time at a professional writer's work, before you try your hand at writing a short story. Kaplan's "Feels Like Spring" appeared first in The American Family *in 1952.*

FEELS LIKE SPRING
by Milton Kaplan

TEXT	COMMENT
I stop at the corner drugstore for breakfast of doughnuts and coffee. I eat fast because I'm a little late, and then I race to the subway station and gallop down the steps to catch	*In Scene One Kaplan establishes "I" as the deciding character, the point of view as first person subjective, and the governing characteristic of loneliness: "We're strangers"—this will*

my usual train. I hold on to the strap and make believe I'm reading my newspaper, but I keep glancing at the people crowded in around me. They're the same ones I see every day. They know me and I know them, but we don't smile. We're strangers thrown together accidentally.

I listen to them talk about their friends, and I wish I had someone to talk to, someone to break the monotony of the long subway ride.

As we approach the 175th Street station, I begin to get tense again. She usually gets into the train at that station. She slips in gracefully, not pushing or shoving like the rest, and she squeezes into a little space, clinging to the pole and holding on to an office envelope that probably contains her lunch. She never carries a newspaper or a book; I guess there isn't much sense in trying to read when you're mashed in like that.

There's a fresh outdoor look about her, and I figure she must live in New Jersey. The Jersey crowd gets in at that stop. She has a sweet face with that scrubbed look that doesn't need powder or rouge. She never wears make-up except for lipstick. And her wavy hair is nat-

be repeated. Panoramic view comes with "subway station." There are time, place, character, (no light, sadly), taste, smell, touch, and a first reference to the problem.

Here Kaplan states the problem succinctly: "I wish I had someone to talk to."

He presents the causative situation in a short sentence and repeats it later, with some insight into the deciding character. The minor character is reported briefly and given a characteristic: "graceful" "squeezes into a little space," "fresh outdoor look." The detail of the lunch in her envelope provides subtle insight. Note the care with which Kaplan reports details of "She": twenty separate concrete terms in ten sentences. Note how these are repeated. Far from static, this description moves the story forward to the result, sets up the first decision, provides clear insight into the governing characteristic and the problem.

ural, just a nice light brown, like the color of poplar leaves when they turn in the fall. And all she does is hold on to the pole and think her own thoughts, her eyes clear-blue warm.

I always like to watch her, but I have to be careful. I'm afraid she'd get sore and move away if she catches me at it, and then I won't have anyone, because she's my only real friend, even if she doesn't know it. I'm all alone in New York City, and I guess I'm kind of shy and don't make friends easily. The fellows in the bank are all right, but they have their own lives to lead, and besides, I can't ask anyone to come up to a furnished room; so they go their way and I go mine.

The city is getting me. It's too big and noisy—too many people for a fellow who's all by himself. I can't seem to get used to it. I'm used to the quiet of a small New Hampshire farm but there isn't any future on a New Hampshire farm any more; so after I was discharged from the Navy, I applied for this position in the bank and I got it. I suppose it's a good break but I'm kind of lonesome.

This paragraph states the characteristic of the minor character, and pairs it with the repeated characteristic in the deciding character. The problem is elaborated in a full paragraph of subjective report in which is reported, in addition, some details of insight, and the first proposed solution resulting from a decision.

As the development continues with some background of panoramic view which also helps develop into the deciding character, we have at the end of this paragraph all the essentials of the beginning of the story: Deciding character— his point of view, his governing characteristic, repeated phrases of character, the causative situation, the problem and the first suggested solution with its built-in interferences: "She's my only real friend, even if she doesn't know it." The next paragraph begins the middle.

As I ride along, swaying to the motion of the car, I like to imagine that I'm friends with her. Sometimes I'm even tempted to smile at her, not in a fresh way, but just friendly-like, and say something like "Nice morning, isn't it?" But I'm scared. She might think I'm one of those wise guys and she'd freeze up and look right through me as if I didn't exist, and then the next morning she wouldn't be there any more and I'd have no one to think about. I keep dreaming that maybe some day I'll get to know her. You know, in a casual way.

The middle of this story presents a sequence of "dream" scenes, beginning: "I like to imagine," a little like the sequences in Thurber's classic of its sort, "The Secret Life of Walter Mitty." "I's" first solution, interfered with by the girl's indifference, changes now to the second solution: to dream the "real" friend. This paragraph starts a new scene in the story, Scene Two, with a new (dreamed) time and purpose. The paragraph also provides the transition into the dream scenes. Note that these are not flashbacks for information occurring before the situation arose. These scenes move the solution and decisions forward to the end.

Like maybe she'd be coming through the door and someone pushed her and she brushes against me and she'd say quickly, "Oh, I beg your pardon," and I'd lift my hat politely and answer, "That's perfectly all right," and I'd smile to show her that I meant it, and then she'd smile back at me and say, "Nice day, isn't it?" and I'd say "Feels like spring." And we wouldn't say anything more but when she'd be ready to get off at

Scene Three, new time, and intensified purpose. Be aware of the gradual rise in the level of intensity through the following scenes to the final emergence from the dream. This very necessary intensification of scene is developed by a clear use of repetition, and the careful selection of concrete details in the scene report. Dialogue is most effectively important here; study the speech and notice the accompanying phrases. They

34th Street, she'd wave her fingers a little at me and say, "Good-bye," and I'd tip my hat again.

The next morning when she'd come in, she'd see me and say, "Hello," or maybe, "Good morning," and I'd answer and add something like "Violets ought to be coming up soon"—something like that to show her I really knew a little bit about spring. No wisecracks because I wouldn't want her to think that I was one of those smooth-talking guys who pick up girls in the subway.

After a while, we'd get a little friendlier and start talking about things like the weather or the news, and one day she'd say, "Isn't it funny? Here we are talking every day and we don't even know each other's names." And I'd stand up straight and tip my hat and say "I'd like you to meet Mr. Thomas Pearse," and she'd say very seriously, "How do you do, Mr. Pearse. I want you to meet Miss Elizabeth Altemose." She'd be wearing those clean white gloves girls wear in the spring, and we'd shake hands and then we'd break out laughing and the other people around us would smile because people in the subway are so close

are very skillfully effective. Kaplan's use of the tenses seems flawless to me.

Scene Four. Study how "Violets ought to be," etc., and the accompanying phrases reveal character. How much can be realized about "I" from this simple disclosure?

Kaplan develops Scene Five fully to increase tension. Running through seven short paragraphs of dialogue, it moves the story forward according to a preconceived program of solutions decided earlier. At this point, answer some questions: why the persiflage about introduction? What is the effect of "clean white gloves"? (She might have been bare-handed). What insight into "I" is given by "I'd stand up straight and tip my hat"? One of the delights of this sort of subjective report is the recognition of self. We all daydream more or less constantly, projecting images of ourselves into dream situations. Perhaps we all skirt,

to you that they can't help sharing a little of your life.

"Thomas," she'd say, as if she were trying out the sound of it.

"What?" I'd ask.

"I can't possibly call you Thomas," she'd say, "It's so formal."

"My friends call me Tommy," I'd tell her.

"And mine call me Betty."

And that's the way it would be. Maybe after a while I'd mention the name of a good movie that was playing at the Music Hall and suggest that if she weren't doing anything in particular—

And she would come right out with, "Oh, I'd love it!" I'd knock off a little earlier and meet her where she worked and we would go out to dinner somewhere. I'd ask some of the men at the bank for the name of a good restaurant. And I would talk to her and tell her about New Hampshire and maybe mention how lonesome I got, and if it's a really nice place and it's quiet and cozy, maybe I'd tell her how shy I was, and she'd be listening with shining eyes and she'd clasp her hands and lean over the table until I could smell the fragrance of her hair and she'd whisper, "I'm shy, too." Then we'd both lean

more or less closely, the borderline of schizophrenia. Observe, too, the light-hearted tone here, poignant but not solemn, which the careful selection of detail produces, and which lends credence to the scene. Near the end of this scene is a tentative (dream) result of the solutions.

Scene Six reports a change of time and place. Senses work actively here. Note the use of smell and touch, both most intimate.

back and smile secretly, and we'd eat without saying much because, after all, what's there to say after that?

We'd go to the Music Hall and I'd get reserved seats and we'd sit there relaxed, enjoying the movie. Some time during the picture, in an exciting part, maybe her hand would brush against mine, or maybe I'd be shifting my position and my hand would touch hers accidentally, but she wouldn't take it away and I'd hold it, and there I'd be in the middle of eight million people, but I wouldn't be alone any more; I'd be out with my girl friend.

And afterwards I'd take her home. She wouldn't want me to travel all the way out. "I live in New Jersey," she'd say. "It's very nice of you to offer to take me home but I couldn't ask you to make a long trip like that. Don't worry, I'll be all right." But I'd take her arm and say, "Come on. I want to take you home. I like New Jersey." And we'd take the bus across the George Washington Bridge with the Hudson River flowing dark and mysterious below us, and then we'd be in New Jersey and we'd see the

Scene Seven brings the tension in the dream sequence to a climax with a full sense report which clearly states the (dream) solution: "I'd be out with my girl friend." The following narrative paragraph concludes the dream sequence of decision and solution and marks the end of the middle of the story. The reader is ready, now, to see how all this planning in the dream world succeeds. Arrival at 175th Street station begins the End.

lights of small homes and we'd stop in one of those little towns, Englewood, Leonia, Ridgewood—I looked them up on a map, wondering which one was hers—and she'd invite me in, but I'd say it was too late and then she'd turn to me and say, "Then you must promise to come for dinner this Sunday," and I'd promise and then—

The train is slowing down and the people are bracing themselves automatically for the stop. It's the 175th Street station. There's a big crowd waiting to get in. I look out anxiously for her, but I don't see her anywhere and my heart sinks, and just then I catch a glimpse of her, way over at the side. She's wearing a new hat with little flowers on it. The door opens and the people start pushing in. She's caught in the rush and there's nothing she can do about it. She bangs into me and she grabs the strap I'm holding and hangs on to it for dear life.

"I beg your pardon," she gasps.

My hands are pinned down and I can't tip my hat but I answer politely, "That's all right."

The doors close and the train begins to move. She has to hold on to my strap;

Scene Eight, "The train is slowing down," a clear scene repetition, returns us to the actual present. The repetition of the street station number tumbles the reader out of dream into reality and increases the tension: "Will it work," he says, "will the dream solution succeed?" This is the eighth and final scene. Everything that happens in this scene does so because it has been prepared for. It is believable because the reader has been conditioned, structurally, to believe it. The result of the series of decisions is clear success. All loose ends are accounted for. And the reader has progressed through a series of scenes to a significant realization of life, to a clarification, too, as one of our greatest tellers of stories, Robert Frost, puts it: "a momentary stay against confusion."

there isn't any other place
for her.

"Nice day, isn't it?" she
says.

The train swings around
a turn and the wheels
squealing on the rails sound
like the birds singing in
New Hampshire. My heart
is pounding like mad.

"Feels like spring," I say.

Ideas for Study

1. Explain the difference between a "flashback" and
the "dream scenes" in this story.

2. List the phrases and ideas repeated in order to
raise the level of intensity in the story. Show how at
least one of them operates.

3. Select five accompanying phrases of the dialogue
and show how they give insight into "I." List other instances of character development.

4. How does the item of the map of New Jersey give
insight?

Your assignment for Part Two: Write a disciplined
short story. Your world: family, home, work, school,
social contacts, your reading experience, the whole reservoir of sources available to you out of memory, brims
over with people in causative situations deciding on
solutions to their problems, and you are part of that
world. Communicate it in a disciplined report.

Some Useful Readings

1. Anderson, Sherwood, *Winesburg, Ohio.* 2nd Edition. Viking Press, New York, 1960.

2. Brondfield, Jerome K., ed., *Bittersweet.* Scholastic
Press, New York, 1973. This collection of high school
prizewinners demonstrates the high quality of work

done by young writers when they discipline their work into an art form.

3. Stegner, Wallace and Mary, eds., *Great American Short Stories*. Dell, New York, 1976. This is an excellent collection. Some of the stories referred to in Part One are here. Read especially "Silent Snow Secret Snow" and "He."

4. Updike, John, *Pigeon Feathers and Other Stories*. Knopf, New York, 1962. Paperback: Fawcett, New York, 1971.

PART III

Five Short Stories for Reading and Analysis

Preliminary Note: Part Three suggests that a beginning writer can learn how to write short stories by exercising rigid self-criticism in the writing of stories and, by reading competently written stories and analyzing them to discover technique, form, content, and so on. Part Three offers some help in finding good stories for analysis by reprinting five carefully selected stories, and by accompanying each with a set of questions and directions which should start and guide some analysis. The exercises are aimed at answering a central question: "What can you learn about writing your own short stories from reading and analyzing this one?" They are addressed to the learning writer, not to the literary critic nor to the student who reads for literary scholarship or appreciation.

A story derives from the writer's perceptive observation and careful report of scene and from structural discipline. A story represents an artistic observation and reformulation of life, reported within the discipline of short story structure. It is no exaggeration to say that you, as a character, and all about you, are at this moment facing actual problems, many of which will eventually arrive at a time when you will have to make decisions about solving them. School, family, social life, job, career, neighborhood, all offer problems. Many of them need, luckily, not be solved or can be held off indefinitely. But some of them will soon become *causative,* will demand solutions. All these are the raw material of short stories; all contain the central story idea: how to live in your own world in spite of family; whether to tell a lie or not; how to rise above the smug provincialism of your neighborhood; how to prevent cruelty to an animal; how and whether to test your own physical stamina, to prove yourself; or how to rob a bank. These are some of the story ideas which lie inside the scene reports and structural disciplines of the stories in Part Three. The stories all around you can become apparent to you if you will concentrate on creative observation and keep an eye out to structural disciplines. Story ideas are all about you in the raw material of life, but they do not come ready-made into stories. You have to discipline them, reformulate them, report them into the artistic performance of the short story.

I hope that reading these five stories, following the directions, and answering the questions in the guide to analysis, and going beyond this into individual analysis of further aspects of the story will be interesting work. I am sure it will improve your own writing of stories, which is our purpose.

The paragraphs of each story have been numbered for easy and accurate reference in working out the analyses. I urge you to be painstaking, to take time for careful study. My feeling is that it is better to analyze one story completely and correctly than to work on five of them superficially.

BUSH BOY, POOR BOY
by James Aldridge

"Bush Boy, Poor Boy" can demonstrate for you a good many points about how to make a short story. The question you pose yourself is always: "What can I learn about writing my own story by reading and analyzing this one?" I hope you keep this question in mind as you try to answer my questions and follow my directions on the pages following the story.

You may find useful some notes about the author, James Aldridge. He was born in Victoria, Australia, and grew up there and on the Isle of Man. A glance at Webster's Geographical Dictionary and at a map of Australia will show you how the Murray River borders northern Victoria and runs nearly 1,200 miles into the Darling River. It is navigable to Albury. Perhaps on some maps you might find "the town of St. Helen"; on mine it doesn't show. You might investigate the special connotations of the word "bush" in Australian geography.

"Bush Boy, Poor Boy" was copyrighted in 1951 and printed in Harper's Magazine.

I have numbered the paragraphs for easy specific reference, but you may need to number the specific line in the paragraph for exact analysis. I suggest you read the story through once for the initial experience, then reread as you analyze. Make use throughout of your checklist and definitions supplied in Chapter Eight.

1. Once there were two things that were worthwhile doing in life. One was to shoot a fox, the other to catch a twenty-pound cod. At one time these achievements were so important to me that I abandoned everything else in life to pursue them. Why, I couldn't exactly say, but the reason began somewhere in the difference between myself—a bush boy and a poor boy, and young Tom Woodley who was a town boy and a rich boy. There it began; but in the way of life, it became something quite different to me in the effort to achievement.

2. I lived with my father, a woodcutter, on the Murray River, three or four miles outside the town of St. Helen, Victoria. The truth is, I didn't know much about anything except the bush, whereas young Tom Woodley was a clever boy with everything he touched: school, playing sport, church-going, and being liked by everybody in the town, and that included the teachers and the policeman. Where Tom was the best of everything, I was the worst of it, except in the bush. Every boy in town had something he could laugh at me about, but once they came out of the town and along the river, I could beat them all: that is, until young Tom Woodley came out to the river in his father's Model-T Ford on a picnic and within an hour had shot a fox with a .22 rifle and pulled in a fifteen-pound Murray cod on a line.

3. These were things that I, a bush boy, had never achieved. I had caught amazing quantities of fish, and I had caught a Murray cod of ten pounds, but never anything larger. When I could get the ammunition, I had shot large numbers of rabbits; in fact, I almost lived by selling rabbit skins, yet I had never once been able to get a fox in range.

4. With Tom Woodley I knew it had been luck, but that didn't do me any good because I knew that I had

nothing to stand up to now, nothing at all; and I stopped going into the town altogether; in fact, I even stopped going to school, and I stayed in the bush, determined to catch a twenty-pound cod and shoot a fox before facing the laughter of the boys in shoes and the joking of men behind counters.

5. The fox was the more difficult proposition, and yet the day came when I was to stand near enough to a fox to club it to death, if only I had been big enough to do it.

6. It was really an accident. For once I was not hunting or fishing, but looking for mushrooms. I was on Pental Island, which was covered with lagoons and swamps and dry patches and clumps, and as I was walking through a shallow pool, I came out on a small dry rise with one clumpy bush on it. I was picking mushrooms under the bush when I saw the fox. He had smelled me, but there was nowhere for him to go. He was more afraid of the water than he was of me. He backed away from the bush, and I backed away from him. The dry land we shared was only about thirty feet square, and he was less than ten yards away; but here I was without a gun and there was the fox, standing with his tail up and his teeth bared, but not making a sound.

7. I stepped slowly back into the water. I couldn't do anything without a gun and I knew it would take me an hour to get home: I had to swim a river and then go over a mile through the bush. Even so, I knew foxes; and I knew that this one was terrified of the water and would die before he would move into it. So I put down the mushrooms I had collected in a sugar bag, and got through the pool and started to run for home.

8. At home I had a .22 rifle, but the very reason I didn't have it with me was my lack of ammunition; and as I ran I begged myself to think of a place where I could find just one shell: no more. As I ran I thought of the .22 shell I had lost last year in the woodpile. That was no good. I had tried a dozen times before to find it. I could not borrow any, and there weren't any shells in all the drawers in the house: I had searched them time and time before. I was running for nothing, but I

didn't stop. I ran through the high grass and came to the river. I jumped off the point and swam across the deep hole and waded the rest. Then I ran up the high bank, through the willow trees, and made for home.

9. I got home and started to hunt in the woodpile, raking up the chips with my hands and feet, still panting and puffing from the run. I couldn't find that .22 in the dust and the chips of a year ago, so I went desperately into the house. I looked in the chamber of my rifle, but it was empty: I had known, but I had hoped. Then I knew there was only one thing to do. My father was away cutting wood, so I went into his room and got the .303 that hung on the wall. It was so big that I could hardly carry it, but I lifted it down. It had a clip of three shells in the magazine. It was clean, but it hadn't been fired for years. My father wouldn't even fire it himself, and the shells were in it in case of emergency. I took it down and carried it outside. This was the worst thing I could do. I was not allowed to touch this gun, not to touch it at all. But I didn't care now.

10. I put the heavy .303 over my shoulder like a log and started to run back with it. I was tired already, and I was half-walking before I had gone far. Still, I kept running in spasms, I walked and ran, and when I got to the river I nearly sank trying to keep the gun out of water. I couldn't hold it up, and it was well dipped by the time I got across.

11. I covered the distance from the river to the lagoon very slowly. I was starting to shake inside, puffing in and out; but I managed to run the last hundred yards to the swamp and the pool. I looked across the twenty-five yards of water to the island, and at the same time I pulled back the bolt of the .303 and put a shell in the chamber. Then I waded across to kill my fox.

12. But the fox had gone. I kicked the bush and looked into it, looking for a hole or a warren, but there was nothing at all, except a few droppings and a feather. He had gone and that was that. I could understand how he had been caught on the dry land in the first place: a quick break in the lagoon had obvious-

ly flooded the land around him as he slept on the rise; that was clear enough; but I couldn't see how he could get off, knowing his terror of water. I started to hunt on the other dry patches, and then on the whole dry land. It was hopeless. So I went home with my mushrooms and the .303.

13. I got a hiding with a harness strap for taking the .303, because I couldn't give any explanation of why I had taken it. I did not try to tell the truth: I simply made up a long story about chasing a wild pig. My father said there were no wild pigs in the whole country. I knew that, too, but I got the hiding anyway.

14. I went back looking for that fox the next day and thereafter. I kept looking; and though I was eventually looking for any fox, it was always the same fox to me. I kept looking and hunting, even though I had no ammunition. Then one night I wept for a couple of hours in bed for the mystery and the difficulty of it all, and the next day I went back to fishing for a twenty-pound cod.

15. There were a number of places along the Little Murray River which were good for cod, and I knew them all. The best was at old Roy Carmichael's. Roy had a house which he had built of a boiler. Outside (near the river) there was a gate he had taken from some old church, but there wasn't any fence. On the gate there was a latch that said IN and OUT. Roy always put it on the right one if he was in or out. He had built mud steps down to the water's edge, and as the river rose in winter and went down in summer, Roy would mark the height on the steps with an iron peg. I used this peg to hold my rod as I fished for cod, and old Roy himself came down to get some water just as I was putting a mussel on a hook.

16. "Why don't you use worms?" he asked me.

17. "I've used up just about every worm in the countryside," I told him.

18. "What about the Council's pig yard?" old Roy asked.

19. "I can't go up there," I said. "I got caught digging under the stone floor."

20. Roy was thin and old. He had a gray mustache

that dropped right over his mouth. Sometimes he laughed for no reason at all, and he laughed now.

21. "How is your father, Edgar?" he bellowed at me.

22. "He went into town to sell some wood," I told him.

23. "How do you like it when they laugh at him in town?" Roy said.

24. I didn't know what to say to that, so I asked him why he lived in the boiler.

25. "I lived over it for twenty years," he said. "Now I live in it. That's the best boiler that ever went into a river boat. They don't make them like it any more. If she hadn't hit the Point, the old Rang Dang would be going yet, with that boiler still inside her."

26. I knew all about it. The old Rang Dang was a paddle steamer that had tried to come up the Little Murray. It had hit low ground at the Point and sunk. Old Roy had been the captain of it. He had waited around to try and get the Rang Dang up from bottom, but the boat had fallen apart, so he had only saved the boiler. He had stayed right there and lived in the boiler. That was a long time ago. I had asked him once why he didn't get another boat. He had picked up a dead sunflower and thrown it at me, so I hadn't asked him again. My father, Edgar Allan, had told me that he couldn't get another boat anywhere after that. They, I suppose whoever owned the boat, said he was drunk when he hit the Point. After that Roy never drank, just to prove that he had not been drunk at the time.

27. "You know that's a two-inch boiler," he said to me now.

28. "It looks thick enough," I said.

29. "It hasn't got a flaked spot in it. Come on up. I'll show you."

30. I had been through this before, but I hooked my rod under a stone and went up with him. He passed the gate and put it to IN. He opened the heavy metal fire-door and bent down to get inside. The boiler was filled with a number of things, mostly made from old petrol tins. It had a floor of wood and there were all sorts of clocks with bodies made of tins. There were flower pots in tins with curled-over edges, a cut-out tin

was set in a fireplace, and the bed was made of kerosene tins framed together. Everything was painted red. On one side, he had taken out a whole plate so that he could get into the extension he had built. You could still see all the holes where the pipes had been.

31. Old Roy gave me a sledge hammer. "Go on," he said. "Hit it. Hit it anywhere you like."

32. I didn't like doing it. When I hit, everything fell down from the shelves. He insisted.

33. "Hit it anywhere!"

34. I found a clear spot, gripped my bare feet on the floor, and swung the sledge hammer as best I could, upward. It bounced off the iron side, and everything rattled down.

35. "Harder!" Roy shouted. "Anywhere!"

36. I hit the side harder this time, in the same place.

37. "How old are you?" old Roy said. He was angry.

38. "Eleven," I told him.

39. "Can't you hit harder than that?"

40. "There's no room," I said.

41. "There has to be room," he said. "What happens if you're looking for a flaked spot and you don't hit hard enough? A head of steam hits it and the whole lot blows to smithereens. Give it to me. Look."

42. Old Roy swung the hammer up onto the plate. The whole place shook and the tins rattled. He hit it again in another place. Everything fell down and clattered about. Roy kicked everything aside and walked to the back and hit it there. He kept hitting it until he was too tired to do it any more.

43. "You see," he said. "Not a flake." He was shaking; he was an old man.

44. "What about everything on the floor?" I pointed to the mess.

45. "Junk!" he said. "The only thing worthwhile around here is the boiler."

46. We went out then and back to the mud steps.

47. "What are you fishing for?" he asked me.

48. "A big cod," I told him. "Twenty-pounder."

49. "You used to fish for bream."

50. "I know, but I'm after a big cod." And I told Roy about Tom Woodley and the fox and the cod.

51. "Have you been getting any cod lately?" I asked.

52. "No. Perch. That's all there is in this river. Yellow-bellies."

53. "Fish are fish," I said.

54. "Why don't you go over to the Big Murray?"

55. "The river is still too high to swim."

56. "I'll take you over in the boat."

57. "No thanks," I said very quickly. Roy had taken me over once before, saying he would pick me up when I came back, if I shouted to him. I had come back and shouted, and he hadn't come. He had forgotten all about me. The river had been too high and fast to swim, so I had stayed on Pental Island all night, getting a hiding when I went home the next day.

58. "I'll come over with you," he said. "I'm getting sick of the taste of perch."

59. "All right," I said.

60. Roy went to get some lines and the oars to his boat. His boat was always tied up here at the steps. He had built it himself, and it was the best small-boat on the river.

61. Roy came down and looked at my rod and said: "What do you want a rod for? A line is better for cod: they are like elephants: they catch themselves."

62. "I like a rod," I said. I liked to fish with a rod. If I caught that twenty-pounder I wanted to catch it on a rod.

63. "Leave it behind," Roy said.

64. "It's all right. I want to take it."

65. Roy shouted: "Whatever-your-name-is, leave that rod behind!"

66. I stood there and didn't get into the boat.

67. "Are you coming or aren't you?" Roy shouted. He was red in the face.

68. "If I can bring the rod."

69. "Get in," he said. "Get in. Bring the rod. What do I care? You're like the rest of them. You can laugh at me! Get in. Do you hear me!"

70. He was shouting at the top of his voice, and he shouted and swore all the way over. As we went across we were carried downstream by the current, but Roy knew exactly where it would take him. He had another

set of steps on the Pental Island side of the river, and we landed right on them.

71. Pental Island was between the two rivers, the Big Murray and the Little Murray. The Little Murray came out of the Big Murray twenty miles upstream, it wandered about, then it came back to the big river just below Roy's place. There was a clump of gums where the two rivers joined, and that was where we were going now.

72. On the way I told him about the fox on the dry spit of land. I asked him what he thought had happened to it.

73. "Did you ever see a fox chased by a snake?" he said.

74. "No," I said.

75. "That's it," Roy said. "That's it, Edgar. He was scared off by a snake."

76. "If he wasn't scared off by me, he wasn't scared off by a snake."

77. "I tell you it was a snake." Roy got angry again. "They are more afraid of snakes than of you," he said. I didn't believe it.

78. At the timber we walked straight through to the deep hole under a hanging gum. Cod were always in the deep holes. Bream were on sandbanks. Perch were in backwaters. Fishing for perch you used a float; but for cod and bream you fished on the bottom, and used two hooks above the sinker.

79. "You can take the dead tree," Roy said. This was the best place. I thanked him, but it did not mean anything because wherever I fished, he would cast his line near mine and then come around by me and talk. He didn't believe that noise scared off the fish.

80. "Have you ever seen a fish with ears?" he used to say. When I said, "No," he would say, "Well how the devil can they hear? If they could hear they could talk, or bark. Have you ever heard them talk?"

81. "No," I would say, "but I've heard them bark."

82. "You're a liar, Edgar," he would say. "How can a fish bark? It hasn't any ears."

83. Now I walked out on the dead tree and sat on a fork. Half of the dead tree was in the water. I could

drop the line straight down into the hole; but I like to cast a bit. I baited with mussels, let about a yard of line hang on the end of the rod, put my thumb on the wooden reel, and swung the rod. The sinker flew out, taking the line; and it plunked down right where I wanted it. Roy undid a heavy cord line from a stick, baited it, and whirled it over his head and threw it. The bolt which acted as a sinker plunked down very near mine: too near. I jumped, because I believe noise frightens fish.

84. We sat quietly for a while, and I held the line lightly, waiting for bites. Then Roy got up and walked over to the tree and came out on it.

85. "Why don't you go to school?" he said to me.

86. "It is too far away," I said.

87. "School is never too far away," he said. "You could walk."

88. "It takes too long," I said. "Two hours."

89. "What are two hours! Can you read and write?"

90. "Yes," I said. I could read very little. I could hardly write. Most people thought I would say "No" when they asked me that, but I didn't like saying "No."

91. "That's not enough," Roy Carmichael said. "You have to know about figures and some history."

92. "I know," I said. "I would like to know about them."

93. "Yes. You ought to go to Castle Donnington school."

94. "I used to go," I told him, "but Miss Gillespie sent me home."

95. "What for?" Roy was angry straight away.

96. "She said I was pretty dirty; and I didn't have any books. It wasn't any good having them. I used to swim the river to save time, and I accidentally dropped the books in the river near the Point one day. They were no good when I got them up. It's funny she thought I was dirty: I had to swim the river every day."

97. "What does it matter if you're dirty? What's the matter with dirt? You know who the only clean people are? The drapers and butchers. The ones in the bank, and the dentists. You know who the best boys are at that school, Edgar?" he said.

98. "No," I said thinking about the fish.

99. "The little bleeders of the drapers and the butchers. Do you know what they grow up to be?"

100. "No," I said.

101. "Drapers and butchers. I've watched them. They are the ones for schools. The dirty faces can go to Hades. You can go to Hades. If I was a boy I could go to Hades. I am the only man alive who can take a boat up the Little Murray, but I could go to Hades. The ones that can sell a pair of drawers and keep their necks clean, they're the ones. If I had a boat, I would teach you to take it up the Little Murray. I'm the only man alive that can do it. What does your father do, Edgar?"

102. Roy knew what he did, but I told him: "He carts wood," I said.

103. "Is that a reason for a town to belittle a man?" Roy said.

104. I didn't care about that. I was getting small bites, nibbles. I could imagine the fish just pulling on the side of the bait, tearing it away without touching the hook, so I waited. Then it all happened.

105. "Look at your line," I said to Roy.

106. He looked over to the bank, and the willow springer to which he had tied his line had been pulled clean out of the bank, and was tight in the water. Before he could leave me, I felt a big pull—a tremendous pull—on my own rod, and I jerked it up to hook the fish; but the rod bent and nearly broke, and I knew I had my big one.

107. "You've hooked my line," Roy shouted in my ear. "You'll lose my fish."

108. "It's on mine," I cried back as I held onto the rod, almost falling into the water, just hanging on.

109. "No," Roy said. "You've hooked my line. Give me the rod."

110. He was dancing up and down, his face was red, and his hair was aloft. "You'll lose my line, you're pulling it in. You'll lose the fish."

111. I didn't have time to look around at Roy's line. I was trying to hang onto the fish that had hold of mine, and at the same time keep Roy from taking my rod away from me.

112. "What's the matter with you!" Roy said, and got a good grip on my rod. "Let it go, will you? I'll break it on your back."

113. The fish pulled, the rod bent, Roy and I held onto it.

114. Then Roy swung his arm and knocked me clean off the log into the shallow water behind, and by the time I got out he was reeling in the fish and walking back to the bank to land it. I ran over and tried to get the rod back, but he pushed me away and landed the fish.

115. It was a Murray cod all right, and it was more than twenty pounds. It was fat and gasping and kicking as Roy whipped it right up the bank away from the water. I ran up to get hold of the line. I could see already who had caught it.

116. "It was on my hook, it was on my line," I cried at Roy, and I was really crying. "You caught my fish." It had been Roy's line that had tangled with mine: it was his that had ruined this catch. "You caught my fish," was all I could shout at him.

117. "What's the matter with you?" Roy said, and I thought he was going to hit me again. "I got the fish out, didn't I? You would have let it go, you would have fallen in the hole, you would have lost it."

118. "You got my fish," I said. "That's the fish I've been waiting to catch."

119. "Well, you caught it," Roy said and put his foot on the cod to take out the hook.

120. "I didn't catch it," I said, "You did!"

121. "It was on your line," he said. He was laughing now.

122. "What's the good of that! You pulled it in. You caught it. You took it away from me. You caught my fish."

123. "Well, you can have it," Roy said.

124. "I don't want it. I just wanted to catch it."

125. "Well, you caught it. You can say you caught it. I won't deny it."

126. "That's no good," I cried. "Tom Woodley caught his fifteen-pounder. You should have let me catch this one." I was not exactly howling, but I was

practically screaming at Roy, because I knew that I would have little or no chance of ever again catching another big one.

127. Roy was sorry and said: "Never mind, Edgar."

128. I swore then, round and long.

129. Roy got mad again and threw a clod at me.

130. "You stole my fish," I said from a distance, to insult.

131. "Take your fish!" he shouted.

132. "I don't want it," I said, and then I ran.

133. I tried to get Roy's boat out and back across the river, but I beached it on some shallows and Roy caught me and took it over and laughed at me all the way across. Then he held onto me, on the other side, and I said I'd never get a fish like that and never get a fox. Never again. I was finished now, and Roy knew it, and he hung onto me and told me he would let the world know I had caught that fish; and moreover he would help me get that fox. He had ammunition and a fox whistle, and if I came back tomorrow he would hunt a fox and maybe fish again. Then he let me go.

134. "Don't you want your rod?" he called after me as I went.

135. "Keep it," I shouted back, and swore at him again.

136. He threw it at me, and I ran away cursing and shouting, leaving my rod, and leaving the big Murray cod that should have been mine.

137. That cod was mine, and I knew it. Yet not having it, and not having caught it, the thing began to overwhelm me. It was always on my mind, from the moment I lost it, and before long it had become something that I had but could never have: something I had achieved yet could never achieve. The puzzle and mystery of this was even worse than the mystery of the disappearing fox, and if I'd wept a little in bewilderment over that, this time I had nightmares that made terror of incidents I had long since forgotten. All of them were puzzles, and all of them were repetitions of the same feeling: to have wanted something so much, to have almost had it, and then to have lost it at the moment of success. It made me sick, and it seemed that I was

never in peace again. More and more the necessity of killing that fox became a way to solve these things and give me back a day without thought and a night without terror. That fox was the fulfillment somehow, and I knew I had to achieve it or be miserable forever.

138. Then late in summer Roy gave me my chance. He found me one day on Pental Island, and after he had boxed my ears for taking a revenge shot at his fox terrier, he began to laugh at me.

139. "Are you still bawling and howling about that fish?" he said to me.

140. I hadn't forgiven him even then for that fish. He had certainly told the town I had caught it (a twenty-eight-pounder), and he had thus half-saved me from Tom Woodley and the town boys; but I hadn't forgiven him because I knew I hadn't caught it, and because my sudden nightmare and its life-puzzle wouldn't let me go, and I blamed him for that, too. I wouldn't talk to him about that fish, but he laughed and didn't care, so I didn't care, and I told him I would call the next day and get my rod back.

141. "Do you still want that fox, Edgar?" he asked me.

142. "Yes, but I want to get it myself," I told him.

143. "Don't be such a moaner," he said. "And if you do want a fox, you come down here tomorrow morning before daybreak and I'll show you where you can get one."

144. "Where is he?" I asked Roy. I didn't trust him now.

145. "You come down tomorrow morning and I'll show you," he shouted.

146. "You'll show me where it is, and then you'll shoot it yourself," I said.

147. "You holy little beggar boy," he called me with a red face. He seemed very upset, and I was sorry. "You come down here tomorrow morning before light and I'll take you over and get you that fox! D'you hear!"

148. "All right," I said, because he seemed desperate about it.

149. I don't think I slept at all that night, because

I knew that Roy would really show me a fox, and within shooting range. By now, hunting the fox had become habit, even though it was still the most vital thing in my life—the one solution and the one satisfaction to the puzzle and inconsistency of each day and each thing. I just didn't know where I stood these days, and more and more all things had become a puzzle to me because of the loss of that cod. Perhaps it was my own doing now, because I could always set off on a blind and hopeless route of thought by asking a few questions about myself, and then about anything: a worm, a gatepost, a hinge, a piece of wood. All I had to do was look at anything and ask myself what it was and where it came from and what had brought it to this state and where would it go, and all the nightmare of the lost Murray cod would return. Yet on this night I knew it would end, because tomorrow I would hunt that fox, shoot it, achieve the simple aim, finish this whole puzzle, and go back to normal again. That was tomorrow.

150. I was over at Roy's long before light, and I had to kick on the boiler door to wake him up. He told me to go away and leave him in peace, but I kept on kicking the door and he finally got up. He gave me a piece of cold meat to eat, and we rowed across to Pental Island. Roy knew Pental Island even better than I did, because he had trap-line all over it, and he covered it almost every day. We emptied a few of his traps as we went, and he had me carrying the rabbits on my shoulder as he walked ahead.

151. "Don't make so much noise," he said to me as we climbed a little hill. The rabbits were hitting my back, and their bellies were making a rolling and rumbling sound. "Drop those things and keep quiet," he said in a whisper.

152. Roy didn't creep, as I would in hunting. He walked upright, but he walked very carefully and slowly, stopping absolutely still from time to time and then moving on again. I moved behind him, doing what he did, and holding my .22 loaded and ready. When we reached the dry red top of the hill, which was bare and round, Roy lay down carefully and put his head over the top. It was still dark, but light was breaking the sky.

153. "Down there," Roy whispered and pointed to a clump of three or four sphinx bushes, "is a fox warren. That old fox is sleeping there now."

154. "I can't see him," I said.

155. "Of course you can't," Roy growled between his teeth. "He'll be coming out when the sun comes up. Can you hit him from here?"

156. It was about fifty feet down to the clump, and if the fox wasn't running I knew I could hit him. "Leave him to me," I said because I didn't want Roy to interfere. He had a .22 himself, and he held it ready for use.

157. "Well, keep your mouth closed and your feet still," Roy said, "and wait; and when you see him come right out, let him have it."

158. We waited, and I had a feeling now that this was all right. It was simple enough to be lying here, it was simple enough for anything in life at all. The sun would rise, the fox would come out, I would shoot, and life would again be normal. I had never felt so sure and relaxed in my whole life before, and I looked at Roy and cocked a grin. I was forgiving him the cod.

159. "Keep your eye on that bush," Roy whispered angrily.

160. I watched the bush and watched the horizon. The sky became pink, the mist rose, the crows flew high, and the kookaburras laughed; and then came the sun; and a little after the sun came the fox.

161. He was old and red. He had white feet, a white tip on his tail, and alert ears. He came out of a hole near the bush and put his head around quickly and lifted his nose up and crouched. Then he walked a few feet as if the ground was hot right under him. He turned around and looked straight up at the hill; and then he sat on his tail and licked his paw, and I had my rifle up to my face.

162. My .22 was old and the sight was off, so I sighted below and to the left of his head. It was easy and sure. The chance was here, the world was assured, and just as he licked the side of his jaws, I was easing on the trigger.

163. Yet I didn't fire. Whatever the reason, what-

ever the restraint, I didn't want to kill that fox and I
didn't intend to. I held the sight and kept my cheek on
the gun and the finger on the trigger and thought to
myself that all I must do is give it a pull and that fox
would be dead, and I would be alive.

164. "Go on," Roy said as if he would kill me himself for being a fool.

165. "I don't want him," I said and put down the
gun.

166. "Shoot!" he said right in my ear.

167. "I don't want him!" I said aloud and the fox
heard and was gone like a shot. Roy stood up and I
could see his .22 follow the fox for the first few seconds.
Then he fired. I was still lying down, but I saw the old
red fox go tumbling over; but I didn't care. At the same
moment another one came leaping out of the warren
and went running away, full of life.

168. "Why didn't you shoot!" Roy cried as he re-
loaded his gun.

169. "I don't know," I said. I really didn't know.

170. "Are you sick or something?"

171. I shook my head. I thought for a moment that
I would like to stay on this hill forever.

172. Roy looked hard at me and laughed for no
reason and forgot about the fox and sat down on the
side of the hill.

173. "How old are you, boy?" he asked.

174. "Twelve now," I told him, still waiting for his
temper.

175. "Twelve," he said slowly. "Do you know how
old I was when I lost the Rang Dang, lost my boat,
lost everything, and never got it back?"

176. I didn't know and I didn't care.

177. "Fifty-two," he said. "Fifty-two."

178. I had no idea what he was talking about except
that he had lost something and never got it back. For
my part I only knew that I was quietly happy again
without knowing why.

179. If I had hoped to solve the puzzle of life by
killing a fox for the loss of the cod, I knew I was
wrong. Life was life, somehow, and that fox had been
too alive for me to shoot. The fish didn't matter, the fox

didn't matter, Tom Woodley and the town boys didn't matter; and though I had spared one life to learn so much, I had killed five or six rabbits by the time we went home.

180. Yes, life was life; but I had it licked.

Guide to Analysis

A. SCENES

1. There are twelve scenes and seven narrative transitional sections. Can you bracket each of those scenes and narrative sections? Remember: a scene exists in a *particular* time and place, etc.

2. Select the scene you can "realize" most fully and elaborate the eleven components. Go as far with this exercise as you like.

3. What paragraphs comprise the essential panoramic view?

4. What can you learn about the handling and the uses of panoramic view within scene in paragraphs 70 and 71?

5. Explain fully how specific names of things give authenticity to this story. For examples, examine paragraphs 41 to 78.

6. Is this production of authenticity equally true of "drapers" and "bleeders" in paragraphs 97 to 101?

B. STRUCTURE

1. What specific elements of structure does Aldridge supply in the first paragraph? In the entire panoramic view? How many times has he tagged the problem in the panoramic view?

2. Why did he write the last sentence in paragraph 1?

3. Describe the point of view in this story. In what sentence is this duplicity of tone first made clear? Did you note any deviation from this point of view? How does the tone help to produce the humor? Where?

4. Here is a rough outline of the story structure. Indicate, after each part, the sentence (using numbers of paragraph and sentence) which first indicates that structural part:

I. The causative situation:

II. The deciding character:

 a. his governing characteristic:

 b. his problem:

  his *first* solution:

   the *first* interference:

  his *second* solution:

   the *second* interference:

  his *third* solution:

   the *third* interference:

III. The result:

5. How many times (count) did Aldridge repeat the basic characteristic and the problem?

6. At what exact points can you mark the end of the Beginning; the end of the Middle?

7. How can Aldridge defend his "result"?

 a. Is it prepared for? (specific lines)

 b. Does it result from: the governing characteristic? (specific lines) the solution suggested?

8. Why are paragraphs 6 to 8 of Scene One necessary?

9. Why are the materials in the long transitional narratives of paragraphs 8, 10, and 11 not reported in scene?

10. Why does the story require the boiler episodes of Scenes Six and Seven, paragraphs 26 to 45?

11. What insights into the boy do we get in the narrative of paragraphs 133 to 137 and in 149?

12. What can you learn in these paragraphs about transition (as distinguished from scene report) in carrying out the story structure?

C. DIALOGUE

1. Study the dialogue in Scene Ten (for example), paragraphs 79 to 132. Some critics have called this dialogue "naturalistic," as different from "artistic" or "realistic." What characteristics here would you label "natural"?

2. Read Roy's dialogue in paragraphs 173 to 177.

What insight into his character is supplied here? Point out specific spots in the story which have prepared us to accept this insight near the end. State Roy's governing characteristics.

3. What insight into the boy do we get in the narrative of paragraphs 133 to 137? Why did Aldridge use narrative here instead of scene report?

4. Explain the consequent order of dialogue tags as used by Aldridge. A good example might be the passages from paragraphs 153 to 157.

D. THE STORY IDEA

1. How is this story a significant clarification of life?

2. The story idea is summed up in paragraphs 167 to the end. State it.

3. Show the specific lines which tag the story idea from paragraphs 1 to 167.

WULLIE
by Howell White

Howell White has been an engineer, a technical writer, a purchasing agent, and a part-time writer of fiction. "Wullie," which appeared in Cosmopolitan *in 1958, won the Maggie Award that year.*

The point of view in "Wullie" is interesting for several reasons. "I," though he is the teller of the tale, is not the deciding actor. He is simply the reporter. The events merely happen before him, and he reports them using the third person objective point of view. But the fact that this is an eye-witness report insures credibility. Further, we can get more than ordinary insight into Billy (the deciding actor) because Joe knows him intimately. In a way, Joe's obtuseness sharpens our own insight. Study how this is accomplished; for example, in Scene One, paragraph 16, the question is revealing of both Joe and Billy.

The story has a very strong ending, brought about partly by the final dramatic act and partly by skillfully intensified scene report through the Middle of the story. This skill in building intensity is worth careful study.

1. It is almost too good to be true to wake up on a Saturday morning—no school—with a shiny new .22 rifle propped against the bed, and with the ground white with the first snow. When you're twelve, happiness comes in big chunks.

2. I carried the gun downstairs and held it in my lap while Mom brought me ham and eggs as if I were a king. When you're twelve you're too old for a regular birthday party with cake and ice cream and girls in party dresses; but the day was mine, and I knew just what I wanted to do with it. In fact, I already had something cooked up with Billy Ryan. As soon as I finished breakfast, I phoned him.

3. "I got it, Billy," I told him. "It's a beauty."

4. "That's nice, Joe," he said. "Did you see the snow?"

5. "Oh, sure," I said. "We're going to the quarry, remember? And I'll teach you how to shoot."

6. "Say! It'll be beautiful with all the snow."

7. I was a little disappointed that Billy was more excited about the snow than about my new .22. Billy was my best friend, but I couldn't always figure him out.

8. Billy had moved to Woodfield the previous summer from some place in Arizona. His Dad worked for a big company with plants and offices all over the country, and he was always being transferred. Besides Arizona, Billy had lived in California, Kansas, Chicago, and in Atlanta, Georgia.

9. It was quite a contrast to my life. I'd never lived anywhere but Woodfield, and neither had my parents. My dad owned the department store on Main Street—the one with the big red and gold sign that looked like a five and ten.

10. It was only a short walk from Billy's house, and he was over in ten minutes flat. That was just enough time for Mom to make some sandwiches. We put the sandwiches in our pockets; Mom patted us on the back; and we were off. I carried the gun, muzzle down, under my arm the way Dad had shown me.

11. We swung off up the main road, not saying much, just covering ground until we got to the old Peabody farm. We turned off the road, scrambled down the bank

and then climbed over the old stone wall into the pasture. Here we picked up the old road that led to the granite quarry.

12. There wasn't too much snow, so walking was easy; and there wasn't a cloud in the whole blue sky. The air was cold, stinging in the nostrils, but the big yellow sun kept us warm. On the open fields the snow was so bright that if you looked at it too long, little red and green specks would start dancing in front of your eyes.

13. "Hey, look!" Billy cried in sudden excitement. "A fox!"

14. I brought up the gun in a hurry. "Where?" I asked.

15. "Oh, no!" Billy said. "Don't shoot anything."

16. "What good's a gun if you don't use it?"

17. "Oh—please! I don't want you to shoot anything." He was looking at me, eyes wide open, kind of half scared. "Please!" he said again.

18. "All right." I dropped the gun. "Didn't see him anyway."

19. "I didn't see a fox," Billy said, "just his tracks. Look!" He pointed to the snow. I saw nothing to get excited about.

20. "He stopped here for a while. Maybe he saw something. Yes!" Billy was ranging in the snow. "Over here, a rabbit. We can reconstruct the crime." Billy took a long step, careful to avoid the tracks. "The fox jumped . . . the rabbit made two hops . . . and the fox caught him, here! See, there's fresh blood in the snow."

21. "Let me see."

22. "Come on, let's see where he went!" Billy was off like a tracking dog. We followed the trail in the snow for half a mile and then lost it in the pines by the old Indian well.

23. "Well," Billy said, "I guess Mr. Fox will have his meal in peace. Now—where do we go from here?"

24. We would have to walk a good mile to the quarry if we went back the way we had come, but there was a shortcut that would take us past Rafe Jones's place. Rafe might not even be there. And if he was, we could probably sneak by without being seen.

25. As we went along, I told Billy about Rafe. Ever since his wife died, he had lived alone in a shacky old farmhouse that was falling down around his ears. He kept some chickens, and made enough from them to keep himself in canned goods and have enough left over to get drunk every Saturday.

26. Nobody liked Rafe. He was a really mean person. Just about the meanest thing he ever did was back when he still had his egg route, and he set out to cure the Bements' little dog of chasing his truck. Nobody could blame the dog for chasing that beat-up truck of his; it rattled and clanked and moaned and groaned and it smelled of chickens and Rafe. Well, even though the Bements were just about Rafe's best customers, he stopped the truck in the road before he turned into their place, and he tied a burlap sack to each of the front wheels. Then he drove, flip-flap, flip-flap, down the long drive. Skippy, the little terrier, made one dash at the flapping sack, sunk his teeth in it, and then was spun off violently as Rafe stepped on the gas. Rafe Jones was mean, clear through.

27. When we came in sight of his place I was relieved that his old truck was not in the yard. Rafe was probably in town, starting to tank up. The old place hadn't changed much since I'd seen it last. The roof sagged a little more; a couple more windows were broken, maybe. The same old cans, bottles, and bits of garbage lay around the front door. There was one new thing . . . a big sign nailed to the maple tree next to the chicken house: KEEP OFF—BAD DOG. And there was the dog, chained to a trolley that ran between two trees, across the front of the chicken house.

28. He was the ugliest dog I'd ever seen. The minute he caught our scent he put his head down, his hackles went up, and he charged toward us with his blue lips pulled back from yellow teeth. When he reached the end of the trolley, the chain caught him and snapped him to his hind feet. He stood there, fighting the chain and snarling.

29. He was a big brute, of no particular breed, but he must have had some mastiff in him, and maybe some

German shepherd. His coat was rough, shaggy, kind of a dirty orange-brown in color, with some bare pink spots on his haunches where the skin showed. He had flapping ears and a mangy sickle tail that drooped down between his legs.

30. The dog fell back. Then, tongue flecked with foam, he charged again. The chain jangled as it came straight, and the overhead trolley squeaked against the eyebolts.

31. "Let's get out of here," I said. "I don't want to be around when that thing breaks."

32. I started on, but Billy did not move. He was standing facing the dog. Without turning, Billy said softly, "Go on, if you want to. I'm going to make friends."

33. "Don't be crazy. That dog's mean. You read that sign?"

34. Billy never turned. "Be quiet," he said to me. "Go or stay—but don't make a sound."

35. I stayed, my heart in my throat. Billy stood, not moving, for ten, maybe fifteen minutes. The dog was now tired out. He stood there, head drooping, hackles raised. Billy talked to him in a sort of croon. I couldn't hear the words, just the tone. Then Billy moved a step closer to him. The dog snarled deep in his throat. Billy wheedled softly. The snarl died. Billy took another step forward, and another, and the dog eyed him. Billy reached out his hand, holding out the back of it. He was near enough so the dog could have sprung at him. It was comforting to have my gun along.

36. But the dog didn't jump him. Instead he started to sniff the back of Billy's hand. Billy let him sniff all he wanted, and all the time Billy was crooning to him. Next thing I knew he was in close. The dog had his nose to Billy's trousers, sniffing. Every once in a while Billy took a slow step toward him. When he reached an overturned bucket, he sat down. The dog stood near him, head down, hackles still up. Billy's hand slowly went out to the dog's shoulders and Billy began to stroke the angry hairs, talking, talking all the time. Gradually the angry hairs lay down.

37. Then everything seemed to happen at once. Rafe's truck rattled past me and skidded to a stop by the maple tree. Rafe jumped out, shouting, "What the hell's goin' on?"

38. The dog turned on Billy, slashing with yellow teeth. Billy jumped from the bucket and ran beyond the reach of the chain. The dog charged at Billy but the choking leather collar snapped him upright, and he stood clawing the air.

39. Rafe's face was splotchy red. "Get off'n my place!" he shouted over the dog's raging. "And don't come back."

40. He took a bottle from his pocket and tipped it to his lips to drain it. "Aw, shut up," he shouted at the dog, and hurled the bottle. It was a wild shot but lucky. The heavy bottle caught the dog on the head. He did not yelp.

41. We took off, I tell you.

42. I had always liked the quarry in the wintertime. The straight, granite walls curved like a cup; they reflected and held the sun's heat like an oven.

43. I found some old cans and set up targets against the granite wall. Between Billy and me, we shot up two boxes of cartridges. Then we took off our coats to feel the sun while we ate. I stretched out on a rock. "This is the life."

44. Billy sat up, frowning. "What are we going to do about Wullie?" he asked.

45. "Wullie?"

46. "Red Wull. Rafe's dog."

47. "How'd you find out his name?"

48. Billy laughed. "Oh, I don't know what his name is. That's just what I called him. He seemed to understand."

49. "Oh," I said, "I get it now. Wullie, like Adam McAdam's Red Wull, the killer in Bob, Son of Battle."

50. "No!" Billy was fierce. "He wasn't a real killer. He just never had a chance."

51. "I never thought of it that way. I always thought that he was the bad 'un."

52. "There aren't any bad ones," said Billy. "Did you see those sores on Wullie?"

53. "On his back? Looked like mange."

54. "I don't mean those. Around his neck where the collar is, it's all raw and open. There's pus in it."

55. "I didn't get close enough. Say—let me see your hand." I had forgotten about Billy's hand until that moment.

56. Billy opened his hand. There were two scratches on his palm. "It's nothing. I sucked it clean."

57. "Better put something on it."

58. "Oh, yes. Say—" Billy was suddenly excited. "I'm coming back tomorrow. We've got some wonderful salve, penicillin stuff. I'll put that on Wullie's sores."

59. "We can't come back."

60. He looked scornful. "You don't have to, if you're afraid."

61. "I'm not afraid," I said loudly. But I was lying.

62. We shot up a couple more boxes of cartridges. By then the sun was dropping so we started home.

63. We didn't talk after we'd decided to come back to see Wullie again. And there was no talking Billy out of it. Billy didn't even notice the tracks in the snow on the way home. He just slogged along, thinking about Wullie.

64. We had just come into the cedars near the swamp, when a rabbit popped up twenty feet away. He had broken his freeze behind a clump of dry grass, and he went skittering across the path. Almost without thinking, I took off the safety and threw the gun to my shoulder and fired.

65. What a shot! The rabbit gave one jump, about five feet in the air, then fell down and lay there kicking. I could hardly believe it. A running rabbit, going across the field—with a .22! Wait till I tell Dad, I thought.

66. "Did you see that, Billy?" I shouted.

67. Billy had seen, all right. Not even stopping to find out if I was going to fire again, he ran ahead of me up to the rabbit. When I got there he had the rabbit in his arms and he was cuddling it as if it were a puppy.

68. "You promised you wouldn't, Joe; you promised you wouldn't!" Billy was staring at me, his eyes angry.

69. "Aw, it's only a rabbit." I had to kid him out of this. "Mighty good eating too."

70. "Oh, no!" Billy said. "Oh, no!"

71. I took the rabbit from him.

72. "Come on," I said. "Come to my house and I'll show you how to skin it. The skin comes right off, just like a sweater. Then Mom'll fix it for supper and you can stay. . . ."

73. "No, no, no!" Before I knew it, Billy was off, half running up the hill through the cedars.

74. I took the rabbit home and skinned it, but it wasn't the fun it should have been. Mom fixed it for supper—I knew she would, since it was my birthday. I wanted to surprise Dad, and tell him about my lucky shot after Mom brought the rabbit to the table. But that didn't turn out so well, either. Dad lifted the covered dish (Mom had made it into a fricassee) and poked at the cut-up pieces with a serving spoon. Then he said, looking at me with a straight face, "Umm, it's been a long time since I've tasted stewed cat."

75. It was kind of hard to eat any after that. Dad and his corny jokes! What a birthday!

76. Sunday, after dinner, I was fooling around with the rabbit skin, scraping it and putting it on a frame to dry, when I saw Billy coming up the road. I covered the skin with an old sack to get it out of sight.

77. "Hi, Joe!" Billy called. He wasn't still angry about my shooting the rabbit. "See what I got for Wullie."

78. He held out a big brown bag so I could see inside. It was full of table scraps. There was a slice of ham, hardly eaten. Mom would never have thrown out a piece of meat like that.

79. "And now look at this," Billy said, and fished in his jacket pocket, bringing out a tube and a small bottle. "Penicillin and vitamins. We'll fix old Wullie up, all right."

80. Billy was like to bust with excitement. "Come on!" Then, kind of doubtful, "You want to come, don't you?"

81. "Sure," I said. "Of course I want to come. Just let me tell Mom we're going."

82. I went into the house and up to my room to get the gun. I picked it up. Sure was a sweet little rifle. But we probably wouldn't have any time for the quarry today. Besides, cartridges were kind of expensive, with two of us shooting.

83. It was only about a half-hour's walk to Rafe Jones's place the way I took Billy that day. "How come you know so much about dogs?" I said. "Thought you never had one."

84. "Never did. Dad says no dog till we settle somewhere."

85. "You could take him with you when you move."

86. "Oh, no, it wouldn't be fair: keeping him cooped up all the time. But if I lived where you do, Joe . . . Boy, oh, boy!"

87. "Yeah," I said. "I been thinking about a dog." I had been going to say a rabbit dog, but changed it.

88. We came out on the shoulder of the hill and looked down on the hollow where Rafe's place was. The dog—Wullie—was lying down, kind of listless. The beat-up old truck was sitting there under the maple tree.

89. "Aw, that's too bad," I said, but I felt kind of relieved. "Rafe's there." I turned back.

90. "Where you going?"

91. "We can't see Wullie when Rafe's there. You heard him."

92. "Sure I heard." Billy was scornful. "And I'm going to ask his permission to feed his dog. You don't have to come."

93. "Oh, I'll come," I said, but I wasn't too happy about it.

94. I followed Billy into the hollow. Wullie saw us coming and started to charge at us the way he had the day before. Billy didn't go to Wullie. Instead, he marched straight up to the front door, knocked, and knocked again. Then he peered through the dirty glass pane.

95. "He's there all right," Billy said. "Asleep."

96. "Drunk."

97. "All right, come on. He won't bother us any."

98. We went back toward the chicken house and

Wullie charged, snarling. Billy did just what he'd done the day before. He stood perfectly still until Wullie got tired, then held out the back of his hand for Wullie to sniff. It didn't take long for Billy to get to the overturned bucket. I guess Wullie smelled the food. Before Billy gave it to him he poured on some of the vitamin stuff from the little bottle, then spread the meat on the bag. Wullie wolfed the food in about two seconds. All the while Billy kept talking to him in that wheedling sing-song.

99. When Wullie had licked the paper clean he came to Billy, sniffing for more. Billy had the tube of penicillin ready. He squeezed two inches of it on his fingers. He let his hand slide up to the sore place under the collar.

100. Wullie's head snapped around with a snarl. Billy held still and didn't take his hand away, and Wullie didn't bite. Then Billy's fingers found the sore place again and began to rub in the ointment. All the while, Billy kept on talking. Wullie stood with his head down, letting Billy take care of him. His old sickle tail hung straight down between his legs. That dog couldn't even wag his tail.

101. "Now ain't that a real purty pitcher!" At the sound of Rafe's voice, Wullie snarled at Billy—but didn't bite. Rafe was at the end of the runway, weaving a little until he put his hand against the old maple. Neither of us had seen him.

102. "Thought I told you kids to stay off'n my place," Rafe said. "You deaf, or just plain ornery?"

103. Billy stood up, slowly, to face him. "I tried to ask your permission, sir."

104. Rafe blinked at the "sir," but Billy wasn't trying to be funny. "Well you ain't got it, fancy boy," Rafe said. "I don't want that dog gentled. He's there for just one reason: to keep out chicken thieves and little sneaks."

105. Billy, very slowly, left the run.

106. "I was only trying to help him," Billy said.

107. I could see the next thought flash into Rafe's mind.

108. "That's a valuable dog," Rafe said. "I'll sell him to you for . . . ten bucks."

109. "I don't have any place to keep a dog," Billy said.

110. Rafe's sly smile was wiped off his face. He took a step toward Billy and raised an arm. "Then git, the both of you, and don't come back!"

111. Rafe turned and walked disgustedly to Wullie, who was standing, head down, hackles bristling. Rafe lifted a booted foot and kicked Wullie in the belly. Wullie ki-yied.

112. Rafe swung his arm toward us. "Get'em, you mutt!"

113. Wullie charged until the chain bit into his neck. We heard his snarls even after we were out of sight.

114. At school on Monday Billy told me that his father had got the word last night: they had to move again. "Gee, that's too bad, Billy," I said. "I sure hate to see you go. I'll miss you a lot."

115. "I like it here. You sure are lucky, Joe."

116. "Oh, I don't know." Billy was the lucky one, I thought.

117. "We have to leave as soon as we can," Billy said. "Say—you want to come with me after school? I want to say goodbye to old Wullie."

118. "Gee, Billy, I don't know. Do you think . . ."

119. "Why don't you bring your gun along? We can stop in the quarry afterwards. I'll buy the cartridges."

120. "You don't have to buy'em." Billy always seemed to have money. I told you he was the lucky one.

121. "I want to buy'em," said Billy. "And I think I'll get old Wullie some real grub, too."

122. "Okay, Billy," I said. It'd be fun at the quarry.

123. As soon as school was out we stopped at the hardware store for cartridges, and Billy stopped off for meat. He bought a big knuckle bone for twenty-five cents, and then he got two pounds of ground round for a dollar seventy-five. That was better than we ate at home. Mom always bought chuck for hamburger. I stopped in at the house to pick up the gun, and we were off. It felt good to walk with a gun under my arm.

124. When we got to Rafe's place, I was relieved to see his truck wasn't in the yard. Old Wullie started the same old snarling charge, but he didn't keep it up more than about ten seconds when Billy held out the back of his hand. I stood around outside the runway, keeping my eyes and ears open for Rafe's truck. I sure didn't want to tangle with him again.

125 Billy went right in and sat on the bucket and gave Wullie the meat. Wullie just seemed to inhale it. Then Billy gave him the knuckle bone and Wullie lay down and held it between his big forepaws, and worked on it with his yellow teeth. All the time Billy was talking to him in that way he had.

126. Then Billy got up and came to where I was standing.

127. "Let me have your gun a minute," he said, and took it from my hand. He reached into his pocket for the new box of cartridges and loaded the gun.

128. He carried the gun with him and went back to sit on the bucket. Wullie rolled his eyes and made a noise deep in his throat, the way a dog does when he's enjoying a bone.

129. Then Billy put the muzzle of the gun behind Wullie's ear and pulled the trigger. With the shot, Wullie sighed and rolled on his side. The sickle tail flipped twice in the dust.

130. That's the only time we ever saw it wag.

131. Then Billy was sitting in the dirt holding Wullie's head in his lap, with a trickle of blood spreading on his pants. And then Billy leaned down and kissed the dirty old head.

132. Pretty soon he got up, picked up the gun and brought it to me. He reached into his inside pocket and took out a new ten-dollar bill. He looked around, kind of blindly, for a stone. He went back to Wullie and put the ten-dollar bill on his ribs, and weighted it carefully with the stone.

133. As we started off, we heard the rattle and groan of Rafe's truck coming up the road, but we never looked back.

Guide to Analysis

A. SCENES:

1. There are fourteen scenes, four narrative sections (the first one relatively long, from paragraph 1 through paragraph 11), and five short transitions. Bracket and label each of these scenes, and narrative and transitional passages.

2. Analyze the structural content of the first narrative section. Why is the second narrative section (paragraphs 23 through 26) necessary?

3. Find in Scenes Two, Four, Eleven, and Twelve the specific preparations for the end result.

4. Paragraphs 119 through 121 are necessary as con-sequential action in preparation for the result. Do they "give away" the end too early for you? Why? Why not? In answering these questions, stay within the report.

5. In Scene Three, paragraph 40, a drunken Rafe throws a bottle and hits Wullie neatly in the head. Do you believe this? Why? Why not? Confine your reasoning to the report.

6. Analyze, as examples of detail, the sensory report in Scenes One, Two, and Eleven.

B. STRUCTURE:

1. This is Billy's story; he decides; his decisions bring about the Middle and the End. Joe is the observing reporter. He is subjective, reporting his own inside-the-skin reactions as well as what he sees. But he reports Billy objectively. We do not get inside Billy's skin. Thus Billy's story is reported from the third person objective point of view, and there are no violations. Joe is an interesting character, and the events impinge on him and affect him (as we shall see in later questions), but it is Billy's story we must analyze for structure (fill in the outline):

I. The causative situation:

II. The deciding character:

  a. his governing characteristic:

  b. his problem:

    his first solution:

       its intensification:

    his second solution:

       its intensifications (there are at least three):

    his third solution:

III. The result:

  a. for Billy:

  b. for Joe:

2. Identify the three parts of the story.

3. Are paragraphs 77 and 80 in Scene Eight violations of the objective point of view?

4. We never see Billy fire the rifle till the last scene, and we do not see Joe teach Billy how to shoot as he had promised. Why? Has Mr. White slipped up in his con-sequential action report? Are you satisfied with this handling?

5. Study Billy's lines in the dialogue of Scene Six, paragraphs 68 through 73. Do they make Billy seem effeminate? Why? Why not? Be specific.

6. Is the result inevitable? Support your judgment fully.

7. What are the advantages of the point of view used in this story? What are some disadvantages?

C. CHARACTER:

1. Indicate throughout the story those sentences tagging Billy's governing characteristic. What else do we know about his character?

2. What does paragraph 16 indicate about Joe? What do paragraphs 75 and 76 indicate about Joe's character?

3. Which boy has more courage?

4. Why should the narrator (Joe) be made less admirable than the deciding actor (Billy)?

D. STORY IDEA:

1. State the story idea in a sentence and support your judgment with specific reference to the scenes.

THROUGH THE TUNNEL
by Doris Lessing

"Through the Tunnel" by Doris Lessing appeared first in The New Yorker *in 1955. Miss Lessing was born in Persia, grew up in South Africa, and is now an English citizen, publishing in New York and London. Her stories possess a subtle insight and penetration, both qualities demonstrated in this story of the age-old human desire for physical test of stamina. Why do people do impossible things at incalculable risk? Men climb mountains, they say, "because the mountain is there."*

1. Going to the shore on the first morning of the holiday, the young English boy stopped at a turning of the path and looked down at a wild and rocky bay, and then over to the crowded beach he knew so well from other years. His mother walked on in front of him, carrying a bright striped bag in one hand. Her other arm, swinging loose, was very white in the sun.

2. The boy watched that white, naked arm, and turned his eyes, which had a frown behind them, toward the bay and back again to his mother. When she felt he was not with her, she swung around.

3. "Oh, there you are, Jerry!" she said. She looked impatient, then smiled. "Why, darling, would you rather not come with me? Would you rather—" she frowned, conscientiously worrying over what amusements he might secretly be longing for which she had been too busy to imagine.

4. He was very familiar with that anxious, apologetic smile. Contrition sent him running after her. And yet, as he ran, he looked back over his shoulder at the wild bay; and all morning, as he played on the safe beach, he was thinking of it.

5. Next morning when it was time for the routine of swimming and sunbathing, his mother said, "Are you tired of the usual beach, Jerry? Would you like to go somewhere else?"

6. "Oh, no!" he said quickly, smiling at her out of that unfailing impulse of contrition—a sort of chivalry. Yet, walking down the path with her, he blurted out, "I'd like to go and have a look at those rocks down there."

7. She gave the idea her attention. It was a wild-looking place, and there was no one there, but she said, "Of course, Jerry. When you've had enough, come to the big beach. Or just go straight back to the villa, if you like."

8. She walked away, that bare arm, now slightly reddened from yesterday's sun, swinging. And he almost ran after her again, feeling it unbearable that she should go by herself, but he did not.

9. She was thinking. Of course he's old enough to be safe without me. Have I been keeping him too close? He mustn't feel he ought to be with me. I must be careful.

10. He was an only child, eleven years old. She was a widow. She was determined to be neither possessive nor lacking in devotion. She went worrying off to her beach.

11. As for Jerry, once he saw that his mother had gained her beach, he began the steep descent to the bay. From where he was, high up among red-brown rocks, it was a scoop of moving bluish green fringed with white.

12. As he went lower, he saw that it spread among small promontories and inlets of rough, sharp rock, and the crisping, lapping surface showed stains of purple and darker blue. Finally, as he ran sliding and scraping down the last few yards, he saw an edge of white surf, and the shallow, luminous movement of water over white sand, and, beyond that, a solid, heavy blue.

13. He ran straight into the water and began swimming. He was a good swimmer. He went out fast over the gleaming sand, over a middle region where rocks lay like discolored monsters under the surface, and then he was in the real sea—a warm sea where irregular cold currents from the deep water shocked his limbs.

14. When he was so far out that he could look back not only on the little bay but past the promontory that was between it and the big beach, he floated on the buoyant surface and looked for his mother. There she was, a speck of yellow under an umbrella that looked like a slice of orange peel. He swam back to shore, relieved at being sure she was there, but all at once very lonely.

15. On the edge of a small cape that marked the side of the bay away from the promontory was a loose scatter of rocks. Above them, some boys were stripping off their clothes. They came running, naked, down to the rocks.

16. The English boy swam toward them, and kept his distance at a stone's throw. They were of that coast, all of them burned smooth dark brown, and speaking a language he did not understand. To be with them, of them, was a craving that filled his whole body. He swam a little closer; they turned and watched him with narrowed, alert dark eyes.

17. Then one smiled and waved. It was enough. In a minute, he had swum in and was on the rocks beside them, smiling with a desperate, nervous supplication. They shouted cheerful greetings at him, and then, as he preserved his nervous, uncomprehending smile, they understood that he was a foreigner strayed from his own beach, and they proceeded to forget him. But he was happy. He was with them.

18. They began diving again and again from a high point into a well of blue sea between rough, pointed rocks. After they had dived and come up, they swam around, hauled themselves up, and waited their turn to dive again.

19. They were big boys—men to Jerry. He dived, and they watched him and when he swam around to take his place, they made way for him. He felt he was accepted, and he dived again, carefully, proud of himself.

20. Soon the biggest of the boys poised himself, shot down into the water, and did not come up. The others stood about watching. Jerry, after waiting for the sleek

brown head to appear, let out a yell of warning; they looked at him idly and turned their eyes back toward the water.

21. After a long time, the boy came up on the other side of a big dark rock, letting the air out of his lungs in a sputtering gasp and a shout of triumph. Immediately, the rest of them dived in. One moment, the morning seemed full of chattering boys; the next, the air and the surface of the water were empty. But through the heavy blue, dark shapes could be seen moving and groping.

22. Jerry dived, shot past the school of underwater swimmers, saw a black wall of rock looming at him, touched it, and bobbed up at once to the surface, where the wall was a low barrier he could see across. There was no one visible; under him, in the water, the dim shapes of the swimmers had disappeared. Then one, and then another of the boys came up on the far side of the barrier of rock, and he understood that they had swum through some gap or hole in it. He plunged down again.

23. He could see nothing through the stinging salt water but the blank rock. When he came up, the boys were all on the diving rock, preparing to attempt the feat again. And now, in a panic of failure, he yelled up, in English, "Look at me! Look!" and he began splashing and kicking in the water like a foolish dog.

24. They looked down gravely, frowning. He knew the frown. At moments of failure, when he clowned to claim his mother's attention, it was with just this grave embarrassed inspection that she rewarded him.

25. Through his hot shame, feeling the pleading grin on his face like a scar that he could never remove, he looked up at the group of big brown boys on the rock and shouted "Bonjour! Merci! Au revoir! Monsieur, monsieur!" while he hooked his fingers round his ears and waggled them.

26. Water surged into his mouth; he choked, sank, came up. The rock, lately weighted with the boys, seemed to rear up out of the water as their weight was removed. They were flying down past him, now, into the water; the air was full of falling bodies. Then the

rock was empty in the hot sunlight. He counted, one, two, three. . . .

27. At fifty, he was terrified. They must all be drowning beneath him, in the watery caves of the rock! At a hundred, he stared around him at the empty hillside, wondering if he should yell for help.

28. He counted faster, faster, to hurry them up, to bring them to the surface quickly, to drown them quickly—anything rather than the terror of counting on and on into the blue emptiness of the morning. And then, at a hundred and sixty, the water beyond the rock was full of boys blowing like brown whales. They swam back to the shore without a look at him.

29. He climbed back to the diving rock and sat down, feeling the hot roughness of it under his thighs. The boys were gathering up their bits of clothing and running off along the shore to another promontory.

30. They were leaving to get away from him. He cried openly, fists in his eyes. There was no one to see him, and he cried himself out.

31. It seemed to him that a long time had passed and he swam out to where he could see his mother. Yes, she was still there, a yellow spot under an orange umbrella. He swam back to the big rock, climbed up, and dived into the blue pool among the fanged and angry boulders. Down he went, until he touched the wall of rock again. But the salt was so painful in his eyes that he could not see.

32. He came to the surface, swam to shore and went back to the villa to wait for his mother. Soon she walked slowly up the path, swinging her striped bag, the flushed, naked arm dangling beside her. "I want some swimming goggles," he panted, defiant and beseeching.

33. She gave him a patient, inquisitive look as she said casually, "Well, of course, darling."

34. But now, now now! He must have them this minute, and no other time. He nagged and pestered until she went with him to a shop. As soon as she had bought the goggles, he grabbed them from her hand as if she were going to claim them for herself, and was off, running down the steep path to the bay.

35. Jerry swam out to the big barrier rock, adjusted the goggles, and dived. The impact of the water broke the rubber-enclosed vacuum, and the goggles came loose.

36. He understood that he must swim down to the base of the rock from the surface of the water. He fixed the goggles tight and firm, filled his lungs, and floated, face down on the water.

37. Now he could see. It was as if he had eyes of a different kind—fish-eyes that showed everything clear and delicate and wavering in the bright water.

38. Under him, six or seven feet down, was a floor of perfectly clean, shining white sand, rippled firm and hard by the tides. Two grayish shapes steered there, like long, rounded pieces of wood or slate.

39. They were fish. He saw them nose toward each other, poise motionless, make a dart forward, swerve off, and come around again. It was like a water dance.

40. A few inches above them, the water sparkled as if sequins were dropping through it. Fish again—myriads of minute fish, the length of his fingernail, were drifting through the water, and in a moment he could feel the innumerable tiny touches of them, against his limbs. It was like swimming in flaked silver.

41. The great rock the big boys had swum through rose sheer out of the white sand, black, tufted lightly with greenish weed. He could see no gap in it. He swam down to its base.

42. Again and again he rose, took a big chestful of air, and went down. Again and again he groped over the surface of the rock, feeling it, almost hugging it in the desperate need to find the entrance.

43. And then, once, while he was clinging to the black wall, his knees came up and he shot his feet out forward and they met no obstacle. He had found the hole.

44. He gained the surface, clambered about the stones that littered the barrier rock until he found a big one, and with this in his arms, let himself down over the side of the rock. He dropped, with the weight, to the sandy floor.

45. Clinging tight to the anchor of the stone, he lay on his side and looked in under the dark shelf at the place where his feet had gone. He could see the hole.

46. It was an irregular, dark gap, but he could not see deep into it. He let go of his anchor, clung with his hands to the edges of the hole, and tried to push himself in.

47. He got his head in, found his shoulders jammed, moved them in sidewise, and was inside as far as his waist. He could see nothing ahead.

48. Something soft and clammy touched his mouth. He saw a dark frond moving against the grayish rock, and panic filled him. He thought of octopuses, or clinging weed.

49. He pushed himself out backward and caught a glimpse, as he retreated, of a harmless tentacle of seaweed drifting in the mouth of the tunnel. But it was enough.

50. He reached the sunlight, swam to shore, and lay on the diving rock. He looked down into the blue well of water. He knew he must find his way through that cave, or hole, or tunnel, and out the other side.

51. First, he thought, he must learn to control his breathing. He let himself down into the water with another big stone in his arms, so that he could lie effortlessly on the bottom.

52. One, two, three. He counted steadily. He could hear the movement of blood in his head. Fifty-one, fifty-two. . . .

53. His chest was hurting. He let go of the rock and went up into the air. He saw that the sun was low. He rushed to the villa and found his mother at her supper. She said only, "Did you enjoy yourself?" and he said, "Yes."

54. All night, the boy dreamed of the water-filled cave in the rock, and as soon as breakfast was over he went to the bay.

55. That night, his nose bled badly. For hours he had been underwater, learning to hold his breath, and now he felt weak and dizzy. His mother said, "I shouldn't overdo things, darling, if I were you."

56. That day and the next, Jerry exercised his lungs as if everything, the whole of his life, all that he would become, depended upon it. Again his nose bled at night, and his mother insisted on his coming with her the next day.

57. It was a torment to him to waste a day of his careful self-training, but he stayed with her on that other beach, which now seemed a place for small children, a place where his mother might lie safe in the sun. It was not his beach.

58. He did not ask for permission, on the following day, to go to his beach. He went, before his mother could consider the complicated rights and wrongs of the matter.

59. A day's rest, he discovered, had improved his count by ten. The big boys had made the passage while he counted a hundred and sixty. He had been counting fast, in his fright. Probably now, if he tried, he could get through that long tunnel, but he was not going to try yet.

60. A curious, most unchildlike persistence, a controlled impatience, made him wait. In the meantime, he lay underwater on the white sand, littered now by stones he had brought down from the upper air, and studied the entrance to the tunnel. He knew every jut and corner of it, as far as it was possible to see. It was as if he already felt its sharpness about his shoulders.

61. He sat by the clock in the villa, when his mother was not near, and checked his time. He was incredulous and then proud to find he could hold his breath without strain for two minutes. The words "two minutes," authorized by the clock, brought the adventure that was so necessary to him close.

62. In another four days, his mother said casually one morning, they must go home. On the day before they left, he would do it. He would do it if it killed him, he said defiantly to himself. But two days before they were to leave—a day of triumph when he increased his count by fifteen—his nose bled so badly that he turned dizzy and had to lie limply over the big rock like a bit of seaweed, watching the thick red blood

flow onto the rock and trickle slowly down to the sea. He was frightened.

63. Supposing he turned dizzy in the tunnel? Supposing he died there, trapped? Supposing—his head went around in the hot sun, and he almost gave up. He thought he would return to the house and lie down, and next summer, perhaps, when he had another year's growth in him—then he would go through the hole.

64. But even after he had made the decision, or thought he had, he found himself sitting up on the rock and looking down into the water, and he knew that now, this moment, when his nose had only just stopped bleeding, when his head was still sore and throbbing—this was the moment when he would try. If he did not do it now, he never would.

65. He was trembling with fear that he would not go, and he was trembling with horror at that long, long tunnel under the rock, under the sea. Even in the open sunlight, the barrier rock seemed very wide and very heavy; tons of rock pressed down on where he would go. If he died there, he would lie until one day—perhaps not before next year—those big boys would swim into it and find it blocked.

66. He put on his goggles, fitted them tight, tested the vacuum. His hands were shaking. Then he chose the biggest stone he could carry and slipped over the edge of the rock until half of him was in the cool, enclosing water and half in the hot sun.

67. He looked up once at the empty sky, filled his lungs once, twice, and then sank fast to the bottom with the stone. He let it go and began to count. He took the edges of the hole in his hands and drew himself into it, wriggling his shoulders in sidewise as he remembered he must.

68. Soon he was clear inside. He was in a small rock-bound hole filled with yellowish-gray water. The water was pushing him up against the roof. The roof was sharp and pained his back. He pulled himself along with his hands—fast, fast—and used his legs as levers.

69. His head knocked against something; a sharp pain dizzied him. Fifty, fifty-one, fifty-two . . . . He

was without light, and the water seemed to press upon him with the weight of rock. Seventy-one, seventy-two. . . . There was no strain on his lungs. He felt like an inflated balloon, his lungs were so light and easy, but his head was pulsing.

70. He was being continually pressed against the sharp roof, which felt slimy as well as sharp. Again he thought of octopuses, and wondered if the tunnel might be filled with weed that could tangle him. He gave himself a panicky, convulsive kick forward, ducked his head, and swam.

71. His feet and hands moved freely, as if in open water. The hole must have widened out. He thought he must be swimming fast, and he was frightened of banging his head if the tunnel narrowed.

72. A hundred, a hundred and one. . . . The water paled. Victory filled him. His lungs were beginning to hurt. A few more strokes and he would be out. He was counting wildly; he said a hundred and fifteen, and then, a long time later, a hundred and fifteen again. The water was a clear jewel-green all around him. Then he saw, above his head, a crack running up through the rock. Sunlight was falling through it, showing the clean dark rock of the tunnel, a single mussel shell, and darkness ahead.

73. He was at the end of what he could do. He looked up at the crack as if it were filled with air and not water, as if he could put his mouth to it to draw in air. A hundred and fifteen, he heard himself say inside his head—but he had said that long ago.

74. He must go on into the blackness ahead, or he would drown. His head was swelling, his lungs cracking. A hundred and fifteen, a hundred and fifteen pounded through his head, and he feebly clutched at rocks in the dark, pulling himself forward, leaving the brief space of sunlit water behind.

75. He felt he was dying. He was no longer quite conscious. He struggled on in the darkness between lapses into unconsciousness. An immense, swelling pain filled his head, and then the darkness cracked with an explosion of green light. His hands, groping for-

ward, met nothing, and his feet, kicking back, propelled him out into the open sea.

76. He drifted to the surface, his face turned up to the air. He was gasping like a fish. He felt he would sink now and drown; he could not swim the few feet back to the rock. Then he was clutching it and pulling himself up onto it.

77. He lay face down, gasping. He could see nothing but a red-veined, clotted dark. His eyes must have burst, he thought; they were full of blood. He tore off his goggles and a gout of blood went into the sea. His nose was bleeding, and the blood had filled the goggles.

78. He scooped up handfuls of water from the cool, salty sea, to splash on his face, and did not know whether it was blood or salt water he tasted. After a time, his heart quieted, his eyes cleared, and he sat up.

79. He could see the local boys diving and playing half a mile away. He did not want them. He wanted nothing but to get back home and lie down.

80. In a short while, Jerry swam to shore and climbed slowly up the path to the villa. He flung himself on his bed and slept, waking at the sound of feet on the path outside. His mother was coming back. He rushed to the bathroom, thinking she must not see his face with bloodstains, or tearstains, on it. He came out of the bathroom and met her as she walked into the villa.

81. "Have a nice morning?" she asked, laying her hand on his warm brown shoulder a moment.

82. "Oh, yes, thank you," he said.

83. "You look a bit pale." And then, sharp and anxious, "How did you bang your head?"

84. "Oh, just banged it," he told her.

85. She looked at him closely. He was strained. His eyes were glazed-looking. She was worried. And then she said to herself, "Oh, don't fuss! Nothing can happen. He can swim like a fish."

86. They sat down to lunch together.

87. "Mummy," he said. "I can stay under water for two minutes—three minutes, at least." It came bursting out of him.

88. "Can you, darling?" she said. "Well, I shouldn't

overdo it. I don't think you ought to swim any more today."

89. She was ready for a battle of wills, but he gave in at once. It was no longer of the least importance to go to the bay.

Guide to Analysis

A. SCENES:

1. This story is presented in sixteen scenes, with three sections of narrative and two passages of transition. Bracket the scenes exactly and indicate the other passages. Remember, a scene occurs in a particular time and place and with a particular character.

2. Compare the sensory development of scene in this story with that in "Bush Boy, Poor Boy" or "Sled." What effect does scene development have on story interest? On story idea? On the story significance?

3. Scene Thirteen is progressive, that is, we move through the tunnel so that "place" seems to change. What holds the scene in one place? Why is this scene not a transition from one end of the tunnel to the other? What is the essential difference between the narrative section following Scene Eleven and the progression in Scene Thirteen?

4. In Scene Thirteen, underline the words dealing with light.

5. Would you say that "Through the Tunnel" is well scened? Explain.

B. STRUCTURE:

1. List the fragments which present the panoramic view. Is this part of structure sufficiently well presented for you? Why?

2. Place the story on this structural outline and indicate the sentences which first present each part of structure.

I. The causative situation:

II. The deciding character:

    a. his governing characteristic:

  b. his problem:

     his first solution decided:

       the first interference:

     his second solution decided:

       the second interference:

     his third solution decided:

III. The result:

3. Is the result inevitable? Justify your judgment with specific sentences.

4. Indicate the end of the Beginning and the end of the Middle.

5. Describe the point of view here. Do you find violations? Are these violations justified by the effect produced? What would be lost to the story from a strict adherence to Jerry's point of view? What would have been gained?

6. Count the number of tags of Jerry's governing characteristic; of the mother-son relationship.

7. Jerry's central problem is complicated by his relationship to his mother and to the boys. How does this enrich the story significance? Such complication could have been easily avoided. Would you have done so? Defend your judgment.

8. Do you think the decision in paragraph 64, coming after the tentative decision in the preceding two paragraphs, is realistic and believable? Defend your judgment specifically.

9. What insights into Jerry do you get in the long narrative passage between paragraphs 49 and 62? Why are these insights necessary? Justify the use of narrative here in place of scene.

C. DIALOGUE:

1. In this story the dialogue is limited to only the first two scenes and the last scene, with fragments in the narrative sections. There are at least three good reasons. Can you see these reasons?

2. What effect on the story comes from the absence of dialogue in all but three scenes?

3. How does the dialogue illuminate the mother's character? What can you learn of her from what she says?

D. THE STORY IDEA:

1. State the idea of this story in one sentence.

2. Where, specifically, do you find the idea presented in the scenes and narrative sections? Where implied by action? By dialogue?

3. Why did Jerry cry in Scene Nine? Do you believe this? Why?

4. Why was it "no longer of the least importance" to Jerry "to go to the bay"? Have you been sufficiently prepared for this ending? Where?

SLED

by Thomas E. Adams

Stories are made of actual life processes rearranged to fit the requirements of an artistic discipline. "Sled" perfectly illustrates this use of the commonplace. It is a story which, partly by brilliant report of sensory scene, reports the episode of a boy, whose pride has been injured by his sister and who "gets back" at her by letting her ride a broken sled and by blaming her for the break. How simple? But how movingly true. The scene reports here will pay you for careful analysis.

"Sled" appeared first in Sewanee Review *in 1961 and won the O'Henry Award in 1962, four years after Adams had graduated from LaSalle College, Philadelphia, Pennsylvania.*

1. All the adventure of the night and snow lay before him: if only he could get out of the house.

2. "You can't go out," his mother said, "until you learn how to act like a gentleman. Now apologize to your sister."

3. He stared across the table at his sister.

4. "Go on," his mother said.

5. His sister was watching her plate. He could detect the trace of a smile at the corners of her mouth.

6. "I won't! She's laughing at me!" He saw the smile grow more pronounced. "Besides, she is a liar!"

7. His sister did not even bother to look up, and he felt from looking at her that he had said exactly what she had wanted him to say. He grew irritated at his stupidity.

8. "That settles it," his mother said calmly, without turning from the stove. "No outs for you."

9. He stared at his hands, his mind in a panic. He could feel the smile on his sister's face. His hand fumbled with the fork on his plate. "No," he said meekly, prodding a piece of meat with the fork. "I'll apologize."

10. His sister looked up at him innocently.

11. "Well?" said his mother. "Go on."

12. He took a deep breath. "I'm . . ." He met his sister's gaze. "I'm sorry!" But it came out too loudly, he knew.

13. "He is not," his sister said.

14. He clenched his teeth and pinched his legs with his fingers. "I am too," he said. It sounded good, he knew; and it was half over. He had control now, and he relaxed a bit and even said further: "I'm sorry I called you a liar."

15. "That's better," his mother said. "You two should love each other. Not always be fighting."

16. He paused strategically for a long moment.

17. "Can I go out now?"

18. "Yes," his mother said.

19. He rose from the table glaring at his sister with a broad grin, calling her a liar with his eyes.

20. His hand plucked his jacket from the couch and swirled it around his back. The buttons refused to fit through the holes, so he let them go in despair. He sat down just long enough to pull on his shiny black rubbers. Finally he put on his gloves. Then with four proud strides he arrived at the door and reached for the knob.

21. "Put your hat on," his mother said without looking at him.

22. His face toward the door, screwed and tightened with disgust. "Aw, Ma."

23. "Put it on."

24. "Aw, Ma, it's not that cold."

25. "Put it on."

26. "Honest, Ma, it's not that cold out."

27. "Are you going to put your hat on, or are you going to stay and help with the dishes?"

28. He sighed. "All right," he said. "I'll put it on."

29. The door to the kitchen closed on his back and he was alone in the cold gloom of the shed. Pale light streamed through the frosted window and fell against the wall where the sled stood. The dark cold room was silent, and he was free. He moved into the shaft of light and stopped, when from the kitchen he heard the muffled murmur of his mother's voice, as if she were far away. He listened. The murmuring hushed and he was alone again.

30. The sled. It was leaning against the wall, its varnished wood glistening in the moonlight. He moved closer to it and saw his shadow block the light, and he heard the cold cracking of the loose linoleum beneath his feet.

31. He picked it up. He felt the smooth wood slippery in his gloved hands. The thin steel runners shone blue in the light, as he moved one finger along the polished surface to erase any dust. He shifted the sled in his hands and stood getting the feel of its weight the way he had seen his brother hold a rifle. He gripped the sled tightly, aware of the strength in his arms; and he felt proud to be strong and alone and far away with the sled in the dark cold silent room.

32. The sled was small and light. But strong. And when he ran with it, he ran very quickly, quicker than anyone, because it was very light and small and not bulky like other sleds. And when he ran with it, he carried it as if it were part of him, as if he carried nothing in his arms. He set the rear end on the floor, now, and let the sled lean against him, his hands on the steering bar. He pushed down on the bar and the thin runners curved gracefully because they were made of shiny blue flexible steel; and with them he could turn sharply in the snow, sharper than anyone. It was the best sled. It was his.

33. He felt a slight chill in the cold room, and in the moonlight he saw his breath in vapor rising like cigarette smoke before his eyes. His body shivered with excitement as he moved hurriedly but noiselessly to the door. He flung it open; and the snow blue and sparkling, and the shadows deep and mysterious, the air silent and cold; all awaited him.

34. "Joey!" From the kitchen came his mother's voice. He turned toward the kitchen door and refused to answer.

35. "Joseph!"

36. "What!" His tone was arrogant, and a chill of fear rushed through his mind.

37. There was a long awful silence.

38. "Don't you forget to be home by seven o'clock." She hadn't noticed, and his fear was gone.

39. "All right!" He answered, ashamed of his fear. He stepped across the threshold and closed the door. Then he removed the hat and dropped it in the snow beside the porch.

40. He plodded down the alley, thrilling in the cold white silence—the snow was thick. The gate creaked as he pushed it open, holding and guiding the sled through the portal. The street was white, and shiny were the icy tracks of automobiles in the lamplight above. While between him and the light the black branches of trees ticked softly, in the slight wind. In the gutters stood enormous heaps of snow, pale and dark in the shadows, stretching away from him like a string of mountains. He moved out of the shadows, between two piles of snow, and into the center of the street; where he stood for a moment gazing down the white road that gradually grew darker until it melted into the gloom at the far end.

41. Then he started to trot slowly down the street. Slowly, slowly gaining speed without losing balance. Faster he went now, watching the snow glide beneath his shiny black rubbers. Faster and faster, but stiffly, don't slip. Don't fall, don't fall: now! And his body plunged downward and the sled whacked in the quiet and the white close to his eyes was flying beneath him as he felt the thrill of gliding alone along a shadowy

street, with only the ski-sound of the sled in the packed snow. Then before his eyes the moving snow gradually slowed. And stopped. And he heard only the low sound of the wind and his breath.

42. Up again and start the trot. He moved to the beating sound of his feet along the ground. His breath came heavily and quickly, and matched the rhythm of his pumping legs, straining to carry the weight of his body without the balance of his arms. He reached a wild dangerous breakneck speed, and his leg muscles swelled and ached from the tension, and the fear of falling too early filled his mind; and down he let his body go. The white road rushed to meet him; he was off again, guiding the sled obliquely across the street toward a huge pile of snow near a driveway.

43. Squinting his eyes into the biting wind, he calculated when he would turn to avoid crashing. The pile, framed against the darkness of the sky, glistened white and shiny. It loomed larger and larger before him. He steered the sled sharply, bending the bar; and the snow flew as the sled churned sideways, and he heard suddenly a cold metallic snap. He and the sled went tumbling over in the hard wet snow. He rolled with it and the steering bar jarred his forehead. Then the dark sky and snow stopped turning, and all he felt was the cold air stinging the bump on his forehead.

44. The runner had snapped; the sled was broken. He stared at the shiny smooth runner and touched the jagged edge with his fingers. He sat in the middle of the driveway, the sled cradled in his lap, running his fingers up and down the thin runner until he came to the jagged edge where it had broken.

45. With his fingers he took the two broken edges and fitted them back into place. They stuck together with only a thin crooked line to indicate the split. But it was like putting a broken cup together. He stared at it, and wished it would be all right and felt like crying.

46. He got up and walked slowly back down to the street to his house. He sat down between the back bumper of a parked car and a pile of snow. Cradling the sled across his legs, he put the two edges together again and stared at them. He felt a thickness in his

throat, and he swallowed hard to remove it, but it did not go away.

47. He leaned back, resting his head against the snowpile. Through his wet eyelids he saw the lamplight shimmering brightly against the sky. He closed his eyes and saw again the shiny graceful curve of the runner. But it was broken now. He had bent it too far; too far. With his hand he rubbed his neck, then his eyes, then his neck again. He felt the snow coming wet through his pants. As he shifted to a new position, he heard the creaking of a gate. He turned toward the sound.

48. His sister was walking away from his house. He watched her move slowly across the street and into the grocery store. Through the plate-glass window he saw her talking with the storekeeper. He stared down at the runner. With his gloves off, he ran his fingers along the cold smooth surface and felt the thin breakline. He got up, brushed the snow off the seat of his pants, and walked to the gate to wait for his sister.

49. He saw her take a package from the man and come out of the store. She walked carefully on the smooth white, her figure dark in its own shadow as she passed beneath the streetlight, the package in her arm. When she reached the curb on his side, he rested his arms on the nose of the sled and exhaled a deep breath nervously. He pretended to be staring in the opposite direction.

50. When he heard her feet crunching softly in the snow, he turned: "Hi," he said.

51. "Hi," she said and she paused for a moment. "Good sledding?"

52. "Uh-huh," he said. "Just right. Snow's packed nice and hard. Hardly any slush at all." He paused. "I'm just resting a bit now."

53. She nodded. "I just went for some milk."

54. His fingers moved slowly down the runner and touched the joined edges.

55. "Well . . ." she said, about to leave.

56. His fingers trembled slightly, and he felt his heart begin to beat rapidly: "Do you want to take a flop?" In the still night air he heard with surprise the calm sound of his voice.

57. Her face came suddenly alive. "Can I? I mean, will you let me? Really?"

58. "Sure," he said. "Go ahead." And he handed her the sled very carefully. She gave him the package.

59. He put the bag under his arm and watched her move out of the shadows of the trees and into the light. She started to trot slowly, awkwardly, bearing the sled. She passed directly beneath the light and then she slipped and slowed to regain her balance. The sled looked large and heavy in her arms, and seeing her awkwardness, he realized, she would be hurt badly in the fall. She was moving away again, out of the reach of the streetlight, and into the gray haze farther down the road.

60. He moved to the curb, holding the bag tightly under his arm, hearing his heart pounding in his ears. He wanted to stop her, and he opened his mouth as if to call her; but no sound came. It was too late: her dark figure was already starting the fall, putting the sled beneath her. Whack! And her head dipped with the front end jutting the ground, and the back of the sled and her legs rose like a seesaw and down they came with another muffled sound. The street was quiet, except for a low whimper that filled his ears.

61. He saw her figure rise slowly and move toward him. He walked out to meet her beneath the light. She held the sled loosely in one hand, the broken runner, dangling, reflecting light as she moved.

62. She sobbed and looking up he saw bright tears falling down her cheeks, and a thin line of blood trickling down her chin. In the corner of her mouth near the red swelling of her lip, a little bubble of spit shone with the blood in the light.

63. He felt that he should say something but he did not speak.

64. "I'm . . . I'm sorry," she said and the bubble broke. "I'm sorry I . . . your sled." She looked down at the sled. "It'll never be the same."

65. "It'll be all right," he said. He felt that he ought to do something but he did not move. "I can get it soldered. Don't worry about it." But he saw from her

expression that she thought he was only trying to make her feel better.

66. "No," she said, shaking her head emphatically. "No, it won't! It'll always have that weak spot now." She began to cry very hard. "I'm sorry."

67. He made an awkward gesture of forgiveness with his hand. "Don't cry," he said.

68. She kept crying.

69. "It wasn't your fault," he said.

70. "Yes, it was," she said. "Oh, yes, it was."

71. "No!" he said. "No, it wasn't!" But she didn't seem to hear him, and he felt his words were useless. He sighed wearily with defeat, not knowing what to say next. He saw her glance up at him as if to see whether he were still watching her, then she quickly lowered her gaze and said with despair and anguish: "Oh . . . girls are so stupid!"

72. There was no sound. She was no longer crying. She was looking at the ground: waiting. His ears heard nothing; they felt only the cold silent air.

73. "No, they aren't," he said half-heartedly. And he heard her breathing again. He felt he had been forced to say that. In her shining eyes he saw an expression he did not understand. He wished she would go to the house. But seeing the tears on her cheeks and the blood on her chin, he immediately regretted the thought.

74. She wiped her chin with her sleeve, and he winced, feeling rough cloth on an open cut. "Don't do that." His hand moved to his back pocket. "Use my handkerchief."

75. She waited.

76. The pocket was empty. "I haven't got one," he said.

77. Staring directly at him, she patted gingerly the swollen part of her lip with the tips of her fingers.

78. He moved closer to her. "Let me see," he said. With his hands he grasped her head and tilted it so that the light fell directly on the cut.

79. "It's not too bad," she said calmly. And as she said it she looked straight into his eyes, and he felt she

was perfectly at ease; while standing that close to her, he felt clumsy and out of place.

80. In his hands her head was small and fragile, and her hair was soft and warm; he felt the rapid pulsing of the vein in her temple; his ears grew hot with shame.

81. "Maybe I better go inside and wash it off?" she asked.

82. With his finger he wiped the blood from her chin. "Yes," he said, feeling relieved. "You go inside and wash it off." He took the sled and gave her the package.

83. He stared at the ground as they walked to the gate in silence. When they reached the curb he became aware that she was watching him.

84. "You've got a nasty bump on your forehead," she said.

85. "Yes," he said. "I fell."

86. "Let me put some snow on it," she said, reaching to the ground.

87. He caught her wrist and held it gently. "No," he said.

88. He saw her about to object: "It's all right. You go inside and take care of your lip." He said it softly but with his grip and his eyes he told her more firmly.

89. "All right," she said after a moment, and he released his hold. "But don't forget to put your hat on."

90. He stared at her.

91. "I mean, before you go back in the house."

92. They both smiled.

93. "Thanks for reminding me," he said, and he dropped the sled in the snow and hurried to hold the gate open for her.

94. She hesitated, then smiled proudly as he beckoned her into the alley.

95. He watched her walk away from him down the dark alley in the gray snow. Her small figure swayed awkwardly as she stepped carefully in the deep snow, so as not to get her feet too wet. Her head was bowed and her shoulders hunched and he humbly felt her weakness. And he felt her cold. And he felt the snow running cold down her boots around her ankles. And though she wasn't crying now, he could still hear her

low sobbing, and he saw her shining eyes and the tears falling and she trying to stop them and they fell even faster. And he wished he had never gone sledding. He wished that he had never even come out of the house tonight.

96. The back door closed. He turned and moved about nervously kicking at the ground. At the edge of the curb he dug his hands deep into the cold wet snow. He came up with a handful and absently began shaping and smoothing it. He stopped abruptly and dropped it at his feet.

97. He did not hear it fall. He was looking up at the dark sky but he did not see it. He put his cold hands in his back pockets but he did not feel them. He was wishing that he were some time a long time away from now and somewhere a long way away from here.

98. In the corner of his eye something suddenly dimmed. Across the street in the grocery store the light was out: it was seven o'clock.

Guide to Analysis

A. SCENES:

1. Bracket and number the scenes and transitions. I count ten scenes and four short transitions. Do you agree? Though you remember that a scene exists in a particular time and place, you must observe that the place in Scene Three is *the street*. And Scenes Four and Five take place on the sled, a different place from the street. Thus, Scene One runs from paragraph 1 through paragraph 28; Scene Two runs from paragraph 29 through the third sentence in paragraph 39; Scene Three runs from the third sentence in paragraph 40 through paragraph 40; and the Fourth Scene runs through paragraph 41. Complete the identification of scenes and transitions.

2. The first scene is a good, hard-working scene. List all the structural information given to us in this one scene.

3. Why does Adams report Scene Two in such a wealth of sensory detail?

4. All but the first scene are reported in the dark of night. How does Adams light his scenes? Underline all reports of light.

5. What is the effect of not using names in this story? We hear "Joey" only once.

6. Analyze completely the sensory elements of Scene Two and Scene Ten.

B. STRUCTURE:

1. Account fully for the absence of panoramic view in "Sled."

2. Fill in the following outline of structure. Observe that the story is duple: the major physical episodes of the sled, the sister, and the brother-sister relationship; and minor psychological story of the boy's mind and spirit.

   I. The causative situation:

  II. The deciding character:

      the minor characters:

    a. his governing characteristics:

      his minor characteristics:

    b. his problem:

      his minor problem:

        his first solution:

          first interference:

        his second solution:

          second interference (major and minor)

        his third solution:

          third interference:

        his fourth solution:

  III. The result:

      major:

      minor:

3. Describe the point of view used here. Observe the fact that it is never violated. How, specifically, does

this strict adherence to one point of view affect you?

4. Is the accident to the sled believable? What makes it so?

5. Are the results (minor and major) inevitable?

6. Oral communication breaks down between the two children. Are you prepared for this? Where, specifically?

7. Why are the last three paragraphs (final scene) necessary?

C. DIALOGUE:

1. Study the "he said" clauses in the dialogue. What words are used besides "said"? Underline the dialogue *tags* which contribute to an understanding of character; of structure.

2. Can you find any dialogue not used for structural purposes?

3. List the bits of dialogue that illuminate character.

4. What are the uses of the dialogue in paragraphs 21 through 28?

D. CHARACTER:

1. Make a complete analysis of Joey's character supporting yourself by lines from the scenes.

2. Make a prediction of Joey's adult character and support your judgment.

3. Which tells you most about Joey's character, the dialogue or the scene report?

HOW MR. HOGAN ROBBED A BANK
by John Steinbeck

This Steinbeck story, which first appeared in The Atlantic Monthly *in March 1956, is rich in lessons for the writer. You will want to examine for example, his choice of a long, beginning, narrative passage before the first scene report, in this case, a flashback coming before the causative situation has been introduced. How effective is this method? Does it have dangers or limitations? Note too, how Steinbeck uses consequent detail. No move is omitted; no act is related out of order; no unnecessary action is reported. Of additional interest is Steinbeck's manipulation of the third person subjective point of view, with subtle variations from that point of*

*view. How does he accomplish these variations? Why,
and to what effect?*

*The tone is lighthearted, a good-humored bantering
brand of satire. How does Steinback use understatement to intensify humor? Does he manage to maintain
the tone throughout, without deflecting attention from
the plot?*

1. On the Saturday before Labor Day, 1955, at
9:04½ A.M., Mr. Hogan robbed a bank. He was forty-
two years old, married, and the father of a boy and
a girl, named John and Joan, twelve and thirteen re-
spectively. Mrs. Hogan's name was Joan and Mr. Hogan's was John, but since they called themselves Papa
and Mama that left their names free for the children,
who were considered very smart for their ages, each
having jumped a grade in school. The Hogans lived at
215 East Maple Street, in a brown-shingled house
with white trim—there are two. 215 is the one across
from the street light and it is the one with the big tree
in the yard, either oak or elm—the biggest tree in the
whole street, maybe in the whole town.

2. John and Joan were in bed at the time of the
robbery, for it was Saturday. At 9:10 A.M. Mrs. Hogan was making the cup of tea she always had. Mr.
Hogan went to work early. Mrs. Hogan drank her tea
slowly, scalding hot, and read her fortune in the tea
leaves. There was a cloud and a five-pointed star with
two short.points in the bottom of the cup, but that was
at 9:12 and the robbery was all over by then.

3. The way Mr. Hogan went about robbing the bank
was very interesting. He gave it a great deal of thought
and had for a long time, but he did not discuss it with
anyone. He just read his newspaper and kept his own
counsel. But he worked it out to his own satisfaction
that people went to too much trouble robbing banks
and that got them in a mess. The simpler the better,
he always thought. People went in for too much hulla-
baloo and hanky-panky. If you didn't do that, if you
left hanky-panky out, robbing a bank would be a relatively sound venture—barring accidents, of course, of

an improbable kind, but then they could happen to a man crossing the street or anything. Since Mr. Hogan's method worked fine, it proved that his thinking was sound. He often considered writing a little booklet on his technique when the how-to rage was running so high. He figured out the first sentence, which went: "To successfully rob a bank, forget all about hanky-panky."

4. Mr. Hogan was not just a clerk at Fettucci's grocery store. He was more like the manager. Mr. Hogan was in charge, even hired and fired the boy who delivered groceries after school. He even put in orders with the salesmen, sometimes when Mr. Fettucci was right in the store, too, maybe talking to a customer. "You do it, John," he would say and he would nod at the customer, "John knows the ropes. Been with me—how long you been with me, John?"

5. "Sixteen years."

6. "Sixteen years. Knows the business as good as me. John, why he even banks the money."

7. And so he did. Whenever he had a moment, Mr. Hogan went into the storeroom on the alley, took off his apron, put on his necktie and coat, and went back through the store to the cash register. The checks and bills would be ready for him inside the bankbook with a rubber band around it. Then he went next door and stood at the teller's window and handed the checks and bankbook through to Mr. Cup and passed the time of day with him, too. Then, when the bankbook was handed back, he checked the entry, put the rubber band around it, and walked next door to Fettucci's grocery and put the bankbook in the cash register, continued on to the storeroom, removed his coat and tie, put on his apron, and went back into the store ready for business. If there was no line at the teller's window, the whole thing didn't take more than five minutes, even passing the time of day.

8. Mr. Hogan was a man who noticed things, and when it came to robbing the bank, this trait stood him in good stead. He had noticed, for instance, where the big bills were kept right in the drawer under the counter, and he had noticed also what days there were likely to be more than other days. Thursday was payday at

the American Can Company's local plant, for instance, so there would be more then. Some Fridays people drew more money to tide them over the weekend. But it was even Steven, maybe not a thousand dollars difference, between Thursdays and Fridays and Saturday mornings. Saturdays were not terribly good because people didn't come to get money that early in the morning, and the bank closed at noon. But he thought it over and came to the conclusion that the Saturday before a long weekend in the summer would be the best of all. People going on trips, vacations, people with relatives visiting, and the bank closed Monday. He thought it out and looked, and sure enough the Saturday morning before Labor Day the cash drawer had twice as much money in it—he saw it when Mr. Cup pulled out the drawer.

9. Mr. Hogan thought about it during all that year, not all the time, of course, but when he had some moments. It was a busy year too. That was the year John and Joan had the mumps and Mrs. Hogan got her teeth pulled and was fitted for a denture. That was the year when Mr. Hogan was Master of the Lodge, with all the time that takes. Larry Shield died that year —he was Mrs. Hogan's brother and was buried from the Hogan house at 215 East Maple. Larry was a bachelor and had a room in the Pine Tree House and he played pool nearly every night. He worked at the Silver Diner but that closed at nine and so Larry would go to Louie's and play pool for an hour. Therefore, it was a surprise when he left enough so that after funeral expenses there were twelve hundred dollars left. And even more surprising that he left a will in Mrs. Hogan's favor, but his double-barreled twelve-gauge shotgun he left to John Hogan, Jr. Mr. Hogan was pleased, although he never hunted. He put the shotgun away in the back of the closet in the bathroom, where he kept his things, to keep it for young John. He didn't want children handling guns and he never bought any shells. It was some of that twelve hundred that got Mrs. Hogan her dentures. Also, she bought a bicycle for John and a doll buggy and walking-talking doll for Joan —a doll with three changes of dresses and a little suit-

case, complete with play make-up. Mr. Hogan thought it might spoil the children, but it didn't seem to. They made just as good marks in school and John even got a job delivering papers. It was a very busy year. Both John and Joan wanted to enter the W. R. Hearst National "I Love America" Contest and Mr. Hogan thought it was almost too much, but they promised to do the work during their summer vacation, so he finally agreed.

10. During that year, no one noticed any difference in Mr. Hogan. It was true, he was thinking about robbing the bank, but he only thought about it in the evening when there was neither a Lodge meeting nor a movie they wanted to go to, so it did not become an obsession and people noticed no change in him.

11. He had studied everything so carefully that the approach of Labor Day did not catch him unprepared or nervous. It was hot that summer and the hot spells were longer than usual. Saturday was the end of two weeks heat without a break and people were irritated with it and anxious to get out of town, although the country was just as hot. They didn't think of that. The children were excited because the "I Love America" Essay Contest was due to be concluded and the winners announced, and the first prize was an all-expense-paid two days trip to Washington, D.C., with every fixing—hotel room, three meals a day, and side trips in a limousine—not only for the winner, but for an accompanying chaperone; visit to the White House —shake hands with the President—everything. Mr. Hogan thought they were getting their hopes too high and he said so.

12. "You've got to be prepared to lose," he told his children. "There're probably thousands and thousands entered. You get your hopes up and it might spoil the whole autumn. Now I don't want any long faces in this house after the contest is over."

13. "I was against it from the start," he told Mrs. Hogan. That was the morning she saw the Washington Monument in her teacup, but she didn't tell anybody about that except Ruth Tyler, Bob Tyler's wife. Ruthie brought over her cards and read them in the Hogan

kitchen, but she didn't find a journey. She did tell Mrs.
Hogan that the cards were often wrong. The cards had
said Mrs. Winkle was going on a trip to Europe and
the next week Mrs. Winkle got a fishbone in her throat
and choked to death. Ruthie, just thinking out loud,
wondered if there was any connection between the
fishbone and the ocean voyage to Europe. "You've got
to interpret them right." Ruthie did say she saw money
coming to the Hogans.

14. "Oh, I got that already from poor Larry," Mrs.
Hogan explained.

15. "I must have got the past and future cards
mixed," said Ruthie. "You've got to interpret them
right."

16. Saturday dawned a blaster. The early morning
weather report on the radio said "Continued hot and
humid, light scattered rain Sunday night and Monday."
Mrs. Hogan said, "Wouldn't you know? Labor Day."
And Mr. Hogan said, "I'm sure glad we didn't plan
anything." He finished his egg and mopped the plate
with his toast. Mrs. Hogan said, "Did I put coffee on
the list?" He took the paper from his handkerchief
pocket and consulted it. "Yes, coffee, it's here."

17. "I had a crazy idea I forgot to write it down,"
said Mrs. Hogan. "Ruth and I are going to Altar
Guild this afternoon. It's at Mrs. Alfred Drake's. You
know, they just came to town. I can't wait to see their
furniture."

18. "They trade with us," said Mr. Hogan. "Opened
an account last week. Are the milk bottles ready?"

19. "On the porch."

20. Mr. Hogan looked at his watch just before he
picked up the bottles and it was five minutes to eight.
He was about to go down the stairs, when he turned
and looked back through the opened door at Mrs. Hogan. She said, "Want something, Papa?"

21. "No," he said. "No," and he walked down the
steps.

22. He went down to the corner and turned right on
Spooner, and Spooner runs into Main Street in two
blocks, and right across from where it runs in, there is
Fettucci's and the bank around the corner and the

alley beside the bank. Mr. Hogan picked up a handbill
in front of Fettucci's and unlocked the door. He went
through to the storeroom, opened the door to the alley,
and looked out. A cat tried to force its way in, but
Mr. Hogan blocked it with his foot and leg and closed
the door. He took off his coat and put on his long
apron, tied the strings in a bowknot behind his back.
Then he got the broom from behind the counter and
swept out behind the counters and scooped the sweep-
ings into a dustpan; and, going through the storeroom,
he opened the door to the alley. The cat had gone
away. He emptied the dustpan into a garbage can and
tapped it smartly to dislodge a piece of lettuce leaf.
Then he went back to the store and worked for a while
on the order sheet. Mrs. Clooney came in for a half a
pound of bacon. She said it was hot and Mr. Hogan
agreed. "Summers are getting hotter," he said.

23. "I think so myself," said Mrs. Clooney. "How's
Mrs. standing up?"

24. "Just fine," said Mr. Hogan. "She's going to Altar Guild."

25. "So am I. I just can't wait to see their furniture,"
said Mrs. Clooney, and she went out.

26. Mr. Hogan put a five-pound hunk of bacon on
the slicer and stripped off the pieces and laid them on
wax paper and then he put the wax-paper-covered
squares in the cooler cabinet. At ten minutes to nine,
Mr. Hogan went to a shelf. He pushed a spaghetti box
aside and took down a cereal box, which he emptied
in the little closet toilet. Then, with a banana knife, he
cut out the Mickey Mouse mask that was on the back.
The rest of the box he took to the toilet and tore up the
cardboard and flushed it down. He went into the store
then and yanked a piece of string loose and tied the
ends through the side holes of the mask and then he
looked at his watch—a large silver Hamilton with black
hands. It was two minutes to nine.

27. Perhaps the next four minutes were his only
time of nervousness at all. At one minute to nine, he
took the broom and went out to sweep the sidewalk
and he swept it very rapidly—was sweeping it, in fact,
when Mr. Warner unlocked the bank door. He said

good morning to Mr. Warner and a few seconds later the bank staff of four emerged from the coffee shop. Mr. Hogan saw them across the street and he waved at them and they waved back. He finished the sidewalk and went back in the store. He laid his watch on the little step of the cash register. He sighed very deeply, more like a deep breath than a sigh. He knew that Mr. Warner would have the safe open now and he would be carrying the cash trays to the teller's window. Mr. Hogan looked at the watch on the cash register step. Mr. Kenworthy paused in the store entrance, then shook his head vaguely and walked on and Mr. Hogan let out his breath gradually. His left hand went behind his back and pulled the bowknot on his apron, and then the black hand on his watch crept up on the four-minute mark and covered it.

28. Mr. Hogan opened the charge account drawer and took out the store pistol, a silver-colored Iver Johnson .38. He moved quickly to the storeroom, slipped off his apron, put on his coat, and stuck the revolver in his side pocket. The Mickey Mouse mask he shoved up under his coat where it didn't show. He opened the alley door and looked up and down and stepped quickly out, leaving the door slightly ajar. It is sixty feet to where the alley enters Main Street, and there he paused and looked up and down and then he turned his head toward the center of the street as he passed the bank window. At the bank's swinging door, he took out the mask from under his coat and put it on. Mr. Warner was just entering his office and his back was to the door. The top of Will Cup's head was visible through the teller's grill.

29. Mr. Hogan moved quickly and quietly around the end of the counter and into the teller's cage. He had the revolver in his right hand now. When Will Cup turned his head and saw the revolver, he froze. Mr. Hogan slipped his toe under the trigger of the floor alarm and he motioned Will Cup to the floor with the revolver and Will went down quick. Then Mr. Hogan opened the cash drawer and with two quick movements he piled the large bills from the tray together. He made a whipping motion to Will on the floor, to

indicate that he should turn over and face the wall, and Will did. Then Mr. Hogan stepped back around the counter. At the door of the bank, he took off the mask, and as he passed the window he turned his head toward the middle of the street. He moved into the alley, walked quickly to the storeroom, and entered. The cat had got in. It watched him from a pile of canned goods cartons. Mr. Hogan went to the toilet closet and tore up the mask and flushed it. He took off his coat and put on his apron. He looked out into the store and then moved to the cash register. The revolver went back into the charge account drawer. He punched No Sale and, lifting the top drawer, distributed the stolen money underneath the top tray and then pulled the tray forward and closed the register, and only then did he look at his watch and it was 9:07½.

30. He was trying to get the cat out of the storeroom when the commotion boiled out of the bank. He took his broom and went out on the sidewalk. He heard all about it and offered his opinion when it was asked for. He said he didn't think the fellow could get away— where could he get to? Still, with the holiday coming up—

31. It was an exciting day. Mr. Fettucci was as proud as though it were his bank. The sirens sounded around town for hours. Hundreds of holiday travelers had to stop at the roadblocks set up all around the edge of town and several sneaky-looking men had their cars searched.

32. Mrs. Hogan heard about it over the phone and she dressed earlier than she would have ordinarily and came to the store on her way to Altar Guild. She hoped Mr. Hogan would have seen or heard something new, but he hadn't. "I don't see how the fellow can get away," he said.

33. Mrs. Hogan was so excited, she forgot her own news. She only remembered when she got to Mrs. Drake's house, but she asked permission and phoned the store the first moment she could. "I forgot to tell you. John's won honorable mention."

34. "What?"

35. "In the 'I Love America' Contest."

36. "What did he win?"

37. "Honorable mention."

38. "Fine. Fine—Anything come with it?"

39. "Why, he'll get his picture and his name all over the country. Radio too. Maybe even television. They've already asked for a photograph of him."

40. "Fine," said Mr. Hogan. "I hope it don't spoil him." He put up the receiver and said to Mr. Fettucci, "I guess we've got a celebrity in the family."

41. Fettucci stayed open until nine on Saturdays. Mr. Hogan ate a few snacks from cold cuts, but not much, because Mrs. Hogan always kept his supper warming.

42. It was 9:05, or :06, or :07 when he got back to the brown-shingle house at 215 East Maple. He went in through the front door and out to the kitchen where the family was waiting for him.

43. "Got to wash up," he said, and went up to the bathroom. He turned the key in the bathroom door and then he flushed the toilet and turned on the water in the basin and tub while he counted the money. Eight thousand three hundred and twenty dollars. From the top shelf of the storage closet in the bathroom, he took down the big leather case that held his Knight Templar's uniform. The plumed hat lay there on its form. The white ostrich feather was a little yellow and needed changing. Mr. Hogan lifted out the hat and pried the form up from the bottom of the case. He put the money in the form and then he thought again and removed two bills and shoved them in his side pocket. Then he put the form back over the money and laid the hat on top and closed the case and shoved it back on the top shelf. Finally he washed his hands and turned off the water in the tub and the basin.

44. In the kitchen, Mrs. Hogan and the children faced him, beaming. "Guess what some young man's going on?"

45. "What?" asked Mr. Hogan.

46. "Radio," said John. "Monday night. Eight o'clock."

47. "I guess we got a celebrity in the family," said Mr. Hogan.

48. Mrs. Hogan said, "I just hope some young lady hasn't got her nose out of joint."

49. Mr. Hogan pulled up to the table and stretched his legs. "Mama, I guess I got a fine family," he said. He reached in his pocket and took out two five-dollar bills. He handed one to John. "That's for winning," he said. He poked the other bill at Joan. "And that's for being a good sport. One celebrity and one good sport. What a fine family!" He rubbed his hands together and lifted the lid of the covered dish. "Kidneys," he said. "Fine."

50. And that's how Mr. Hogan did it.

Guide to Analysis

A. SCENES:

1. The first eleven paragraphs are narrated by the teller of the story. Scene One includes paragraph 12 and the first sentences of paragraph 13. Scene Two includes the rest of paragraph 13 and all of 14 and 15. Bracket the twelve scenes which make up this story, and the four transitions. Paragraphs 29 through 41 are again narrated.

2. How much time does this story cover?

3. Offer some good reasons for the extended narrative sections.

4. Order the first eleven paragraphs into tentative scenes. What would each scene contain? Why didn't Steinbeck do this?

5. Why did Steinbeck have Mrs. Hogan forget to tell Mr. Hogan the news and then call him from Mrs. Drake's home (paragraphs 32 through 39)?

6. Make a careful comparison between the scene element content in this story and that in "Sled." Why are Steinbeck's scenes so lacking in the eleven elements, light for instance?

7. Part of Steinbeck's skill with scene derives from his power to suggest strongly the scene elements not reported overtly. Examine Scene Three, for example, and indicate words that suggest scene elements without actually stating them in a report.

8. Would you call these true scenes on our terms?

B. STRUCTURE:

1. Go through the story and indicate all violations of the strictly third person objective point of view. Try to think out why Steinbeck permitted these violations.

2. What effect do these violations have on the story?

3. Can you identify with Hogan? If not, what prevents identification?

4. In Scene Seven, paragraph 7, would it improve the story to omit the sentence: "He knew that Mr. Warner would have the safe open now and he would be carrying the cash trays to the teller's window"? Support your judgment.

5. Place the story on this structural outline:

   I. The causative situation

  II. The deciding character

     a. his governing characteristic:

     b. his problem:

        his first solution:

          the first interference:

        his second solution:

          the intensifications (list all)

  III. The result:

6. Was the result inevitable?

7. Can you find a flaw in the report of Mr. Hogan's procedure?

8. Illustrate Mr. Hogan's obedience to his own dictum: ". . . forget all about hanky-panky."

9. How well does Steinbeck handle panoramic view?

C. DIALOGUE:

1. Steinbeck uses very little dialogue here. In the first narrative passage, what technique substitutes for dialogue, yet has much the same effect as true dialogue?

2. Point out instances of humor in the dialogue.

D. HUMOR:

1. Usually satire has a serious intent, to cause some social action which may lead to improved social mores. Is there any such intent here? Support your argument

2. Analyze one passage which you find humorous. What makes it funny? What is the quality of this humor?

3. Would you call this an important story of similar dimension to "Wullie?"

Dick, Jane, and Spot. Reconsidered.

A look at education as it really is.

☐ A PARENT'S GUIDE TO CHILDREN'S READING Nancy Larrick	2108	$1.95
☐ THE NAKED CHILDREN Daniel Fader	2328	$1.75
☐ BEING WITH CHILDREN Phillip Lopate	2886	$1.95
☐ HALF THE HOUSE Herbert Kohl	6409	$1.95
☐ THE WAY IT SPOZED TO BE James Herndon	6572	$ .95
☐ DEATH AT AN EARLY AGE Jonathan Kozol	6738	$1.50
☐ THE ANGEL INSIDE WENT SOUR Esther P. Rothman	7171	$1.25
☐ OPEN EDUCATION: A SOURCEBOOK FOR PARENTS AND TEACHERS Ewald Nyquist & Gene Hawes, eds.	7535	$1.95
☐ READING, HOW TO Herbert Kohl	8329	$1.95
☐ TEACHER Sylvia Ashton-Warner	8627	$1.50
☐ GETTING READY: THE EDUCATION OF A WHITE FAMILY IN INNER CITY SCHOOLS Lois Mark Stalvey	8722	$1.95
☐ HOW TO SURVIVE IN YOUR NATIVE LAND James Herndon	10452	$1.50

Buy them at your local bookstore or use this handy coupon for ordering:

READ TOMORROW'S LITERATURE—TODAY

The best of today's writing bound for tomorrow's classics.

START A COLLECTION

With Bantam's fiction anthologies, you can begin almost anywhere. Choose from science fiction, classic literature, modern short stories, mythology, and more—all by both new and established writers in America and around the world.

☐	THE MARTIAN CHRONICLES Ray Bradbury	2440 •	$1.75
☐	50 GREAT HORROR STORIES John Canning, ed.	2851 •	$1.95
☐	THE NICK ADAMS STORIES Ernest Hemingway	2860 •	$1.95
☐	BIG CITY STORIES Tom & Susan Cahill, eds.	2945 •	$1.95
☐	HEROES, GODS AND MONSTERS OF THE GREEK MYTHS Bernard Evslin	6328 •	$1.25
☐	THE WORLD'S BEST SHORT SHORT STORIES Roger B. Goodman, ed.	6382 •	$ .95
☐	TEN MODERN AMERICAN SHORT STORIES David A. Sohn, ed.	10161 •	$1.25
☐	TIMELESS STORIES FOR TODAY AND TOMORROW Ray Bradbury, ed.	10249 •	$1.50
☐	THE BALLAD OF THE SAD CAFE AND OTHER STORIES Carson McCullers	10252 •	$1.50
☐	50 GREAT SHORT STORIES Milton Crane, ed.	10315 •	$1.95
☐	TWENTY GRAND SHORT STORIES Ernestine Taggard, ed.	10326 •	$1.50
☐	50 GREAT AMERICAN SHORT STORIES Milton Crane, ed.	10362 •	$1.95
☐	75 SHORT MASTERPIECES: Stories from the World's Literature Roger B. Goodman, ed.	10721 •	$1.50

Buy them at your local bookstore or use this handy coupon for ordering:

Bantam Book Catalog

Here's your up-to-the-minute listing of every book currently available from Bantam.

This easy-to-use catalog is divided into categories and contains over 1400 titles by your favorite authors.

So don't delay—take advantage of this special opportunity to increase your reading pleasure.

Just send us your name and address and 25¢ (to help defray postage and handling costs).

BANTAM BOOKS, INC.
Dept. FC, 414 East Golf Road, Des Plaines, Ill. 60016

Mr./Mrs./Miss_____
(please print)

Address_____

City_____State_____Zip_____

Do you know someone who enjoys books? Just give us their names and addresses and we'll send them a catalog too!

Mr./Mrs./Miss_____

Address_____

City_____State_____Zip_____

Mr./Mrs./Miss_____

Address_____

City_____State_____Zip_____

FC—6/77

BAD
THINGS

TAMARA
THORNE

ZEBRA BOOKS
KENSINGTON PUBLISHING CORP.
http://www.kensingtonbooks.com

ZEBRA BOOKS are published by

Kensington Publishing Corp.
119 West 40th Street
New York, NY 10018

All Kensington titles, imprints, and distributed lines are available at special quantity discounts for bulk purchases for sales promotion, premiums, fund-raising, educational, or institutional use.

Special book excerpts or customized printings can also be created to fit specific needs. For details, write or phone the office of the Kensington Special Sales Manager: Attn.: Special Sales Department. Kensington Publishing Corp., 119 West 40th Street, New York, NY 10018. Phone: 1-800-221-2647.

Zebra and the Z logo Reg. U.S. Pat. & TM Off.

ISBN-13: 978-1-4201-3256-4
ISBN-10: 1-4201-3256-3

First Pinnacle Books Mass-Market Paperback Printing: March 2002
First Zebra Books Mass-Market Paperback Printing: September 2013

10 9 8 7 6 5 4 3 2

Previously published under the title *Panic* by Pocket Books.

Printed in the United States of America

For Kenny Curry—
the best big brother in the world

ACKNOWLEDGMENTS

First, thank you to Lawrence Morris, O.D., for sharing his knowledge and invaluable speculations on the nature of vision. Also, thank you, Kevin Shrock, M.D., for patiently answering all my bizarre medical questions.

Grateful appreciation goes to Kay McCauley and the Pimlico Agency and to my terrific editors, John Scognamiglio and Dana Isaacson.

Special thanks go to Nigel and Dave, experts on feline psychology, and to Robert, Quinn, and Doug for all that good stuff—you guys are the best!

BIG JACK

Winter cold, winter dreary
Winter leaves
No sap, no fool
Winter bones
No need to panic
Big Jack sleeps,
The little ones too.

March buds, April flowers
May blood
So green, so new
Spring veins pump
And children panic
Big Jack wakes,
The little ones too.

Summer heat, summer passion
Summer nights
So hot, so hungry
Dark desires
The children cower
Big Jack stands
The little ones too.

Autumn red, autumn brittle
Autumn cravings
So harsh, so clear
Child, run
Before he gets you
Big Jack walks,
The little ones too.

1

October 1, 1972

Wrapped in panic, smothered in fear, Ricky Piper trembled on the threshold of the shadowy hallway and steeled himself for the long journey to the living room. He would have preferred to remain with his mother and their housekeeper, Carmen, in the bright, yellow kitchen, but she'd given him permission to watch cartoons. If he didn't do it, she'd know he was afraid again. That was the last thing he wanted.

Swallowing hard, telling himself to walk slowly, he stepped onto the forest green carpeting. His resolve lasted all of two seconds before his screaming nerves made him sprint down the hall. First he passed the dark, silent dining room, then the wall of linen closets, and finally he bolted beneath the stern disapproval of a collection of Piper ancestors, framed and watching him from the corridor walls.

Ricky arrived in the front room, heart thumping, head dizzy from holding his breath. Exhaling, he wished that his mom and dad weren't so nuts about wasting electricity. Though he knew there was nothing scary *in* the house, he just couldn't stop expecting that something was going to jump out of the dark and grab him.

The air in the living room seemed thick and murky. The last dregs of afternoon sunlight seeped in between the ragged shadows cast by the towering oak outside the picture window. Not wanting to look out the window, Ricky walked backward toward the chair and reading lamp by the front door. With the sureness of long habit, he reached under the lampshade and turned the switch, holding his breath again until the friendly golden light relieved the gray gloom. Then, still without looking, he reached behind the chair and felt for the drapery cords. Finding the right one, he tugged, listening to the soothing whisper of fabric and metal until the gentle snick told him the drapes had closed on the outside world.

If it were his house, Ricky told himself as he crossed to the television cabinet and turned the set on, the curtains would stay closed *all* the time.

Felix the Cat slowly came into focus. He was using his bag of tricks to foil the Professor and Rockbottom. Ricky didn't like Felix's voice, but he sure wished he had his bag of tricks. If he did, he'd use it to get rid of the greenjacks: the little ones *and* the big one, all of them. It wasn't really the dark he was afraid of, but the jacks, who only came out at night. If he had a magic bag of tricks, he'd make it always daytime and he'd make all the grass and bushes and trees—especially the old oak—disappear too, so there would be nowhere for the greenjacks to hide. If he could do that, he wouldn't have to be scared anymore. He and his brother would be safe.

Robin, who was outside right now with Grandfather Piper, wasn't afraid of the greenjacks, but he didn't have the sight and was unaware of the danger. Ricky worried a lot about Robin because he'd just giggle when he warned him to be careful outside, even on Halloween, the worst night of the year. That was when Big Jack came out. Not only could anyone see him if he wanted them to, but he could actually snatch anybody he wanted, snatch them and take them away. But Robin wouldn't believe it. He thought Grandfather's stories were fairy tales like Hansel and Gretel or Goldilocks and the Three Bears.

Recently Robin had started teasing Ricky by making believe that he could see the jacks and even talk to them. He did all the things he knew scared Ricky, too, like climbing in the oak tree.

Because of his brother, and because he knew his parents were starting to worry about his "overactive imagination," as they called it, Ricky had started making believe too. He pretended, even to his twin, that he'd never seen a greenjack, but had been playing a game of pretend all along. It was the hardest thing he'd ever done in his entire seven years.

Like fingers, oak twigs tapped on the window glass. Shivering, Ricky hunched into a ball in the safe glow of the television set and lost himself in the cartoons.

"Richard Piper, you're going to get x-rayed to death sitting that close to that damnable machine; that is, if you don't go blind and kill all your brain cells first!"

"Grandfather!" Startled, Ricky twisted around and saw the old man, who must have come in through the kitchen door. He stood in the hall doorway, frowning disapproval. Robin, snug in the crook of his arm, grinned and extricated his abbreviated body from the old man's arms, swinging like a monkey, slipping down his grandfather's legs as if they were tree trunks. He twisted just before he reached the dark green carpet and dropped nimbly onto his hands.

"Watch this!" he commanded. He tested his balance, then began to walk on his hands, then run, toward his brother, his little legless body held straight up in the air over his head.

Reaching Ricky, he flipped himself over and came to a rest on his buttocks. "I bet you can't do that."

Ricky didn't think he could. He was almost four feet tall, a perfect boy from his head to his toes, and Robin was his identical twin except that he'd been born without legs, which made him about two feet shorter. He had a bottom and a weenie, just like Ricky, but then he just ended, in smooth curves of white skin.

"Try it!" Robin goaded.

Ricky planted his hands on the carpet and began to lower his head.

Grandfather asked, "Why is that set on, Richard?"

"Sorry," he mumbled, turning it off. His grandfather hated the television, and Ricky was just glad that the old man lived in the little cottage in the citrus orchard behind the big house. If he were here all the time, he'd never let anyone turn the TV on.

The old man's gaze was stern under his bushy white eyebrows. "Did your mother tell you you could watch that thing?"

He hesitated, knowing that if he told the truth, Grandfather would lecture his mom. "No, sir."

"You turned it on without asking permission?"

Robin grabbed his hand and squeezed it. "Yes, sir," Ricky replied, braver because of his brother's silent support.

For a moment the old man stared holes through him, and Ricky tried to shrink into the carpet, his stomach doing flip-flops as he wondered what his grandfather was going to say next.

But suddenly Grandfather Piper's face broke into a rare smile. "Well, you've got a little spunk hidden in there somewhere after all! Good for you, boy. Maybe you're finally growing some balls!"

Ricky, amazed and confused, smiled tentatively. *Why would he want to grow balls? You bought them at the toy store.*

Robin giggled.

"But I still don't want that cursed thing on when I'm in this house. You're seven years old, you have to exercise your brains *and* your body. Is that understood?"

"Yes, sir."

"Damn house feels like a cave," the old man said, then, to Ricky's horror, he opened the drapes. Dusk had gathered outside, and Ricky looked away quickly. "That's better," Grandfather said, looking from boy to boy with false sternness. "Do you two want to hear a story?"

"Please!" Robin cried happily.

"Please!" Ricky echoed, nearly as enthusiastic. Though the stories frightened him, he always wanted to hear them because he'd decided that the more he knew about the green-jacks, the safer he would be.

"Alrighty, boys. I'll tell you about *my* great-grandfather. That would be your great-great-great-grandfather, Thomas McEnery Piper. He was blessed with the sight, as the men of the Piper clan sometimes are . . ." Grandfather's midnight blue eyes sparkled as he looked from boy to boy. "Or perhaps he was cursed. I don't know, because I don't have the sight. What about you, Robin? You see the greenjacks, don't you, boy?"

"Sure!" Robin cried. The word bubbled through his delighted laughter.

"Well, what do you say, boy? Is the sight a blessing or a curse?"

"A blessing!"

Grandfather turned to Ricky. "And what do you say, Richard? A blessing or a curse?"

Ricky looked at his Keds and shrugged. "I dunno. I don't see them."

Robin made a silly face. "Liar, liar, pants on fire!"

"Robin," Grandfather admonished sternly. He turned back to Ricky, his voice getting that gentle sound that adults often took with him, as if they were afraid he might break. "If you could see them, Rick, what would it be?"

He looked up and stared the old man right in the eye. "A curse, Grandfather. It would be a curse."

Grandfather Piper's eyes bored into his for a long time, then he shook his head slowly. "I swear, boy, sometimes you're enough to make me think there's truth in those old stories. Sometimes I think *you* really do have the sight."

"No, sir." Ricky wanted to cry as he told the lie. "I just pretend."

"I see." The old man paused, giving Ricky one last long look before clearing his throat. "Well then, boys, let's get on with it. Thomas Piper had the sight, for better or worse, and tonight I believe I'll tell you about the first time the greenjacks almost nabbed him. He wasn't much older than the two of you. Have I told you boys this story before?"

"No," they lied in unison. It was Grandfather's most-told tale and Ricky's favorite.

"Come on, then, let's sit." The old man turned and walked slowly toward his favorite recliner, which sat next to the huge fireplace, directly across the room from the picture window. Robin hurried ahead, showing off his new handstand trick. When he reached the chair, he bunched his powerful biceps and propelled himself up onto the chair arm in the blink of an eye. Then, grinning at Ricky, he did his spider imitation, bugging his eyes and flexing his elbows so that he moved up and down, like a spider on its web. The sight made Ricky snicker. Robin could always crack him up.

Grandfather eased into the recliner and waited while Robin situated his small body in the crook of his arm. Then Ricky climbed onto his knee.

"Ready?" Grandfather asked.

"Ready!" the boys chorused.

"Thomas McEnery Piper lived in the family home in Glenkerrie, a village in the Scottish Highlands, west of Inverness. Just like here in Santo Verde, Glenkerrie was renowned for the way the trees and flowers and crops grew. Do you know why?"

"Greenjacks!" Robin cried.

Despite himself, Ricky glanced up at the picture window. The wind plucked one faded leaf, then another, from the old oak tree. It was still almost a month until Halloween, but most of the leaves still clung to the twigs and branches. His mom had told him yesterday that it would probably be November before the tree was only a skeleton again. He wished it were over with—a month, especially this month, took forever to go by.

"That's right, the jacks," Grandfather said. "And do you know *why* they lived there?"

"Because we did!"

"That's right, Robin. They chose that place because it was the Piper ancestral home. Greenjacks and Pipers have lived there for centuries. All over the world there are bits of land where trees and grass grow far better than they should, and these are the places of the jacks—and of people who, like some of the Pipers, see them."

Grandfather rambled on. Every story began with the same introduction, and you had to wait through it to get to the good stuff. Recently the old man had added something new that Ricky thought was really interesting: science. Grandfather said it was probably a gene that made you see the jacks and that about a fourth of all the male Pipers had that gene. When Ricky had asked his father about it, though, he'd just snorted and said that he'd believe it when he read it in *Scientific American.*

Grandfather was up to the part about greenjacks and trolls being second cousins once removed when Ricky saw a jack approach the window. At twilight it was barely visible, a small, smooth creature made of a vague glow that grew brighter as night took the sky. It reached the window, and he saw the suggestion of a gleefully cruel face peering through the glass. Ricky squirmed nervously, and Grandfather gave him a stern glance without losing the rhythm of his story.

Greenjacks, Ricky knew, were small, never more than two feet tall unless they melted together. If they did that, they lost their shifting, semihuman form, but this one looked normal, so Ricky wondered how it could be tall enough to peek in a window two and a half feet from the ground. (Ricky had measured it.) Shivering, he looked away.

"Greenjacks attach themselves to families like us because there's always a chance that they can trick someone possessing the sight into giving up his body. Sometimes a sighted man will even agree to trade bodies with one of them. The jacks' bodies aren't physical like ours are, and that means they can't taste or smell or feel anything in the material world, any more than a scientist can enter the world of the amoebae he studies under his microscope." Grandfather's smile made a million little wrinkles around his eyes. "Just like people, greenjacks always want what they don't have, and so they crave physical sensation very, very much." He paused dramatically. "They lust for it and will do anything to get it—make promises, lie, even try to scare you to death. And on Halloween . . . on Halloween they get together to make Big Jack out of tree limbs and plants. On that one night their power is so great that they can enter Big Jack and bring him to life. And that night, because Big Jack is physically real, they can use him to—" Grandpa snapped his fingers—"snatch little boys like you! Just. Like. That!"

Robin giggled again, and Ricky stole another peek at the window. A second face had appeared, human yet not, liquid and solid and air all at once, ever-changing, ever-shifting. Once, Ricky had tried to draw a picture of one. It came out looking smooth and gray-green, with huge glittery black eyes and a small mouth.

Though the drawing wasn't exactly right, the jacks sure didn't look much like trolls to Ricky. Trolls were squished and wrinkly and sort of cute. At least troll dolls were. Green-jacks *seemed* small-bodied and long-limbed, even when they weren't. Sometimes they looked more like little whirlwinds, but they always seemed old and bad and not at all cute.

One of them waved at Ricky. A glimmer of a lipless mouth twisted into a nasty smile.

Ricky . . . Ricky . . . Icky Ricky . . .

Their voices wafted in through the frames and vents of the house like a fluttering of leaves on a breeze. He heard them inside his head. *Ricky, come out and play, Icky Ricky.*

"Oouh!" Ricky jumped as something poked him in the thigh. Robin was staring at him.

Grandfather harrumphed. "Richard, what's wrong?"

He hesitated. "Robin punched me."

"Robin?"

"He wasn't listening," his brother said impishly. "I think he's looking for greenjacks."

"Well, Rick?" Grandfather asked patiently, "Do you see any?"

Before he could frame an answer, Robin said, "Ricky, I fixed it so they could see in. I pushed dirt up under the windows."

Speechless, Ricky stared at him.

Grandfather chuckled. "Very inventive of you, Robin."

"There's a whole pack of them out there!" Robin volunteered. "They're playing leapfrog."

"Good for them, but they're going to have to play by themselves," Grandfather added firmly, "if you want to hear the rest of the story. Ready to pay attention?"

"Okay." He stifled a giggle.

Satisfied, Grandfather went on, "Since it seems that you two can see the jacks"—here he gave them a wink showing that he was just playing along—"you can see for yourselves that greenjacks are very sociable creatures, and that's why they only want to be in human bodies capable of seeing and communicating with their own kind. Which is why they wanted Thomas."

Ricky . . . Icky Ricky . . . Come. out and play, hey, play . . .

Shut up! Ricky thought.

"Young Thomas knew that the little greenjacks couldn't hurt him, so he wasn't afraid, not even at night when they're most active. Early on, the little jacks tried to talk him into trading bodies with one of them. They told him he could run and play all the time and that he'd never have to do what his mother told him, or mind his manners at all, but Thomas was smart and he wouldn't do it, no matter what they offered him. When they finally stopped trying to tempt him, he was even more careful because he knew they'd try to trick him out of his body.

"And try they did. Spring and summer and fall, they tried all sorts of tricks, and one night, when he was nine years old, his vigilance slipped, and the greenjacks almost got him.

"Young Thomas was a smart boy, a brave and kind boy, but he was no more perfect than any other boy, and one afternoon, about four o'clock, he did a very foolish thing. He decided to walk along the top of a wall, even though his mother told him not to. And can you guess what happened?"

"He fell!" Robin said immediately.

Grandfather nodded. "That's right. It was a very tall wall, and he landed on his head and lost consciousness. Greenjacks can get you if you're knocked out or almost dead, of course. Unconsciousness is good because they can force you out of your body and lock you in one of theirs, but almost dead is better because you can't put up any kind of fight at all. They're in, you're out.

"Young Thomas fell on the wrong side of the wall, and when he didn't come in with the milk—did I mention he was supposed to be in the barn milking the cow, not walking on walls?—his mother and father called him and called him. When he didn't answer, they went to look for him.

"They found him just as the sun was setting. He still lay on the ground, unconscious, and though his parents couldn't see them, they knew that the greenjacks would be out. Afraid, they looked at one another, then his father picked Thomas up and carried him in, and they sat by his bed and waited to see if he would still be their son. Or if he was a changeling."

Grandfather leaned forward, frowning dramatically. "Thomas's parents prayed they weren't too late, but his father held a sword in his hand, ready to run the body through if his son had become a changeling."

"He would have killed his own son?" Robin asked, just as he always did.

"Yes, he would have. It's happened before and it will happen again," Grandfather added menacingly. "Once a jack possesses your body, nothing but a mortal wound will make it leave. Only then will it flee for its own immortal body, and only then is the poor human changeling's soul released—either to go to whatever lies on the other side, or, for the less fortunate, to return to its original body if it's not quite dead yet."

Ricky had goose bumps. The story thrilled and scared him. He could feel the greenjacks outside staring at the back of his head.

Sicky Ricky, icky Ricky, Ricky, Ricky . . .

Words were their toys, and they rhymed on and on. Ricky could hardly stand the shrill voices in his head.

"Fortunately," Grandfather continued, "when he woke

up, he was still Thomas. Do you know how his parents could tell?"

"How?" Ricky asked.

"He answered the questions his parents asked him correctly, something a jack changeling couldn't do so quickly. Also, he wasn't clumsy, like he wasn't used to his body. Finally, his eyes were still Piper eyes, midnight blue, like ours. Sometimes, not always, when a greenjack takes a human body, the irises turn darker, like the color of a greenjack's soul. Thomas remembered nothing of his accident, except for hearing the voices of the jacks as they surrounded him, and he promised never to climb the wall or do any other forbidden things again." The old man cleared his throat. "Years later, Big Jack almost got him on Halloween night, but that's another story for another night. I think it's almost dinnertime. Something smells good."

As Grandfather's voice ground to a halt, Ricky saw that the little jacks were no longer at the window. The two, and a half dozen more, were cavorting in the grass under the oak tree.

"Ricky?" Robin asked softly. "Are they there?"

Ricky looked at his brother. Sometimes, after they were in bed with the lights out, Robin would still admit to him that he maybe believed in greenjacks even though he couldn't see them. "Yeah, sure," Ricky said lightly. "They're there."

It was weird to look at his twin, to see a boy just like him except for not having the jack-seeing gene and not having a complete body. There were other differences too. Robin was brave like Thomas Piper, and Ricky was a coward.

"Ricky?" Robin said suddenly. There was no mischief in his voice, only a sort of hopefulness.

"What?"

"They're out there right now, aren't they?"

Ricky nodded.

"Grandfather?"

"Yes, Robin?" The old man smiled benignly, just as he always did after he told one of his stories.

"If I traded bodies with a greenjack, could I have legs too? Like Ricky's?"

Grandfather's eyes looked like dark pools of water as he pushed a chestnut curl from Robin's forehead. "I wish it were so, but it's not. Remember, when you dance with the devil, you become a devil yourself."

The boy nodded gravely, and Ricky could feel his brother's unhappiness and longing as if it were his own. It hurt. Robin was almost never sad. Most of the time he took pride in what he could do, and Ricky knew that was part of the reason he liked to show off so much with all his handstands and acrobatics. He could even run almost as fast on his hands as Ricky could on foot. Impulsively he leaned over and hugged his twin. "I'd share my legs with you if I could."

Robin hugged him back hard, then pulled away and gave him a small tentative smile that quickly evolved into his typical mischievous grin. "It's a good thing you can't share your legs, Ricky, 'cause you need 'em a lot worse than I do!"

"Bite me!" Ricky said, and giggled uncontrollably. Robin looked shocked, then he burst into laughter.

"Richard!" Grandfather intoned.

Ricky silenced instantly.

"Where did you learn that kind of language?"

"From you."

"Me? I don't think—"

"You said it to that Jobber's Witness yesterday when he wouldn't go away. Remember, just before you slammed the door in his—"

"Jehovah's," Grandfather interrupted. "Listen here, young man, promise me you'll forget you heard that, because if you say it around your mother, she'll fill your mouth with Ivory Soap." His sternness dissolved "And mine, too."

"I promise," Ricky said. His gaze drifted back to the window, his nervousness returning as he watched the greenjacks dance and whirl and tumble. Occasionally two or three of them would melt together to briefly form other shapes: a ghostly whirlwind of iridescence that looked sometimes like leaves, sometimes like butterflies, a small tempest of flickering greens, golds, and reds that never quite left the ground. The jacks were earth creatures, tied to the land, and they couldn't leave it except for that one night a year when they made Big Jack. Big Jack could climb trees and cross water and he could snatch people, but at least he couldn't leave nature and come indoors. The only unsafe place inside the house was the dirt-floored root cellar, and Ricky never, never ventured down there.

He shivered as several jacks suddenly merged into a tall ghostly blob that bore resemblance to Big Jack, as if they could read his mind and were performing just for him.

Ricky . . . Ricky . . . Icky Ricky, come out and play . . .

He shivered. Maybe they *could* read his thoughts. Maybe they were, right this minute.

"Look how the leaves are blowing out there," Grandfather said as he gently dislodged Ricky from his knee. He rose, carrying Robin, and walked to the window. "Quite a little tornado going under the oak. Couple of 'em."

"You see them?" Ricky asked before he realized that Grandfather was talking about the real leaves that blew around in the evening wind.

"Of course I do. My eyes are as good as ever." He shot a serious look at Ricky. "It's said that the greenjacks love to play in the falling leaves. Do you see them, Richard?"

"Uh, no." Then he saw the expectant look on his brother's face. "Oh, yeah, I see a couple now," he said, making sure he sounded like he was just playing along.

"What are the jacks doing, Ricky?" Robin asked, the longing back in his voice.

"They're dancing."

"In the leaves?"

"No, Robin," he said solemnly. "They *are* the leaves."

2

October 31, 1972

Cackling autumn leaves scuttled across the wide wooden steps of the old front porch. The night wind kissed the door-frame and whispered through the wire mesh, bringing with it the acrid spice of burning pumpkin and a last lingering trace of cold rainwater.

Ricky Piper sat in his father's easy chair and nervously rubbed his fingers over the nubby gold upholstery. It was a test of will, sitting here, but Carmen had reassured him that it would be good medicine for him to try it since there was no way the jacks could get in the house. The only thing separating the chair from the open front door was a maple end table holding a big basket of Halloween treats, candy corn and Tootsie Pops.

Ricky . . . Icky Ricky . . . Ricky . . .

No! Go away! He curled into a ball, hugging his legs within the circle of his arms, ducking his head so that his ears were muffled between his knees, so that all he could see was the vague greenish glow of the phosphorescent paint his mom had brushed on his skeleton costume.

He hated the costume because it reminded him of Big Jack.

And tonight was Big Jack's night, when anyone could see him and anyone could be snatched. Once, Ricky had asked

Grandfather how the little jacks chose which ones of them would be part of the monster, but the old man didn't know and guessed they drew straws. The rest of the little ones would be out, too, tonight, more frighteningly clear than on any other night of the year.

Last Halloween was the first time Ricky had ever seen Big Jack. He caught a glimpse of the creature from his bedroom window as it shambled around under the oak. It looked like a cross between a skeleton and a tree. He woke up Robin, but by the time his twin got to the window, Big Jack had disappeared. Later, near midnight, Ricky saw him again, this time crouched in the high branches of the oak tree right outside his bedroom window. He looked like part of the tree until he moved. Ricky screamed, but Big Jack was gone before anyone else could see him, and his parents thought he was having another nightmare about Grandfather Piper.

The old man had died last year, only two days after telling that last story about Thomas McEnery Piper. He'd had a heart attack during dinner, and an ambulance came and took him away. Ricky never saw him again, except at the funeral, where he'd looked like a big wax doll with rouge on his cheeks and powder on his face. Right after that, Ricky began having dreams in which Grandfather Piper, lying in his coffin, opened his eyes and looked at him. His eyes weren't blue anymore, but black, even the white part, all black. He'd open his mouth and say, "Icky Ricky, play with me!"

He'd had the nightmare several times before Halloween and he'd woke up screaming, so when he saw Big Jack, he let them think he'd had another dream about Grandfather. That was the smartest thing to do.

Even now, Ricky sometimes still woke screaming from the nightmares—about Big Jack, not Grandfather—and he wished his dad would cut down the oak tree. He couldn't bear to look at the leafy shadows the moonlight cast across the twin beds and the cowboy wallpaper on their bedroom walls, even though he knew there was nothing there except, perhaps, on Halloween night.

Tonight.

They were out there: in the night, in the wind.

Ricky . . . Ricky . . . Ricky . . .

But they couldn't get him, not here in the house. He knew it because Carmen had reassured him of it over and over. They couldn't even come up on the porch, she said, and he knew from his own experience that she was right about that, too. He was safe, but it didn't matter: He was still afraid.

He wished he could be more like his ancestor Thomas in Grandfather's stories. Thomas wasn't afraid; he could walk among the greenjacks at night and ignore them, not a cowardly bone in his body. He was so brave that when he was fifteen (a foolish age, Grandfather used to point out) he tried to kill Big Jack himself, but he'd failed. Grandfather would never tell them more than that, but had promised that he would when the twins were older.

Now he'd never know what had happened to Thomas. Ricky's dad had never been interested in the stories and didn't know them, so the tales had died with Grandfather Piper.

The wind sighed, exhaling smoke-scented breath through the tree limbs, mingling its song with the voices that called his name. The jack voices sounded a little like leaves rustling in a whistling wind, and when he used to make the mistake of asking if anyone else could hear them, they'd laugh and say that's what they were—leaves. Or they'd shake their heads and give one another knowing looks and say, "What an imagination you have, Ricky Piper."

When he was six and a half, he'd tried very hard to stop talking about the greenjacks, and he'd managed pretty well until Grandfather's death. Last year, because of the dream and because he'd actually seen Big Jack, he'd begun talking about them again, and hadn't stopped until he overheard his folks discussing him and saying that maybe they should have him talk to a doctor. After that, he never said another word to them or to Robin. He felt so alone that sometimes he cried, but at least he had Carmen. Though she always promised him she'd never leave, he was always afraid he'd wake up one morning and she'd be gone, especially since she'd met her boyfriend, Hector. Ricky didn't think he could stand it here without her.

He loved his parents very much, but they just didn't understand like Carmen did. His dad and mom both thought the greenjack stories were fairy tales. As for Robin, he got that wishful look on his face, like he wanted to believe, less and less frequently now.

He glanced up at the portrait of Grandfather Piper hanging on the wall behind the recliner and wished he hadn't died. Not only did he miss him, but sometimes it seemed like the old man knew he could see them.

Though Carmen didn't exactly believe, she once told him that one of her uncles back in Mexico was a *brujo* doctor and that he said he could see things, just as Ricky could. When Ricky asked her if she believed her uncle, she only said that she believed that anything was possible.

So even if she didn't quite believe, at least she never teased him or said he was too old for fairy tales. Instead, she helped him learn how to act as if he weren't afraid, and she always protected him on Halloween, either by playing along when he pretended to be sick like last year, or by taking him out before dark to trick-or-treat. Right now he could hear her and Mom talking and laughing in the kitchen while they washed the dinner dishes. Their sounds helped him have the courage to stay in the chair by the door.

More leaves, dry brown mummies, fell from the tall oak outside to tumble and dart toward the Pipers' big weird house. It was already getting dark out, and he nervously wondered how he was going to get out of trick-or-treating this year. Carmen had told him not to play sick again because everyone would be suspicious. He glanced at the bowl of treats, slowly reached for a packet of candy. It wouldn't take long to eat enough sweet candy corn to really get sick. He'd get in trouble, but it would be worth it . . .

. . . because the night was alive with burnt pumpkin and rainwater and wind.

Ricky . . . Sicky . . . Ricky . . .

"Ricky!"

He jumped as his brother's strident voice yanked him from the spell cast by the greenjacks' voices.

"Robin!" He forced himself to straighten up and make a fist. "I oughta smack you!" His brother was a ghost, his short body hidden beneath a floor-length sheet that had eye holes and a mouth hole that their mom had outlined with red paint. She'd brushed phosphorescent paint on his costume too.

Robin peered up at him and giggled. "Scared you!"

"Did not!"

"Did so. Scaredy-cat!" His gaze fell on the candy corn. "And you're stealing the trickertreats!" he whispered. "I want some too!"

Ricky tossed the packet to Robin, and he tore the cellophane and made a show of holding it to the costume's circular mouth hole and pouring it in.

"Robin Piper!" Their mother's Deep Voice, the one that meant you were in trouble, stopped him cold. "What did I tell you about taking candy?" She approached Robin and lifted the sheet from his head.

Ricky couldn't help giggling. Robin's mouth was so full that he couldn't quite close it, and you could see the orange and yellow candy corn tips poking from between his lips. His chipmunk cheeks poked out like Louie Armstrong on TV playing his trumpet. Ricky giggled harder, even though Mom threw him an angry look too.

She crossed her arms and stood glaring down at them as Robin tried in vain to start chewing. "Go in the bathroom and spit those in the trash, then brush your teeth."

Still trying to chew, Robin pivoted on his hands and went through the wood-paneled family room behind the living room, heading for the downstairs bath. A moment later, Ricky heard the toilet flush, then the water being turned on.

"Ricky?"

"What, Mom?"

"Did you give him that candy?"

He didn't answer.

"Did you?"

"He trickertreated me. I had to."

She tried to look stern, then gave up, leaning over to run her hands through his hair and kiss the top of his head. She was pretty and she had the same color hair as he and Robin. His dad called it yummy chestnut. He was always saying silly things and touching Mom's hair or kissing her neck, and she seemed to like it a lot. She had green eyes—Dad called them cat's eyes. She called Dad's eyes "mystery man blue." His parents acted weird sometimes, and even though he and Robin would roll their eyes and make disgusted noises, Ricky secretly liked it.

"Boo!" Something grabbed Ricky's ankle, and he yelped, flying out of his chair. "Robin!"

His brother laughed. "Gotcha!"

"That wasn't nice, Robin," Mom admonished.

"Sorry." He smiled sunnily at Ricky, then at Mom.

" 'Sokay," Ricky said, his heart still pounding. Robin could pad around like a cat—you never heard him come in a room unless he wanted you to. Sometimes Dad jokingly threatened to buy him tap shoes for his hands.

Mom looked from boy to boy. "What am I going to do with you two?" She bent down and slipped Robin's ghost costume back over him, then plucked a stray thread from Ricky's costume. "That's better. Where's your mask?"

"Over there." Unenthusiastically, he pointed at the plastic skeleton face he'd left on the couch.

"So are you two ready to go trick-or-treating?" she asked.

"Yeah!" Robin cried.

"Dad's not home yet," Ricky said.

"I know, sweetie. Daddy's going to be a while because he has to finish some reports for work."

The doorbell rang, the young voices behind it giggling and screeching for treats. Before Mom could answer it, Carmen bustled into the room, took care of them, and returned to the kitchen.

"Shouldn't we wait for Dad?" Ricky persisted.

She laughed. "No. Carmen will hand out the treats, and the three of us will go by ourselves."

Usually Dad handed out treats—he loved jumping out from behind the door and yelling "boo!" at the kids—and normally Mom and Carmen both went out with the twins, Mom pulling the red Radio Flyer wagon Robin rode in, and Carmen holding Ricky's hand. This sudden change of plans was too much for Ricky, and he decided it was high time to get out of trickertreating.

"I think it's gonna rain some more."

"I don't think so, Rick." She stared hard at him. "Are you still afraid, sweetie?"

Oh, yes, he was afraid. "No," he said stoutly. "I gotta go to the bathroom!"

He shot out of the chair and ran through the family room, past the bathroom, laundry room, and into the kitchen, where Carmen was drying her hands on a dish towel that had dancing spoons embroidered all over it.

"Carmen!" he whispered.

She turned, a solidly built yet beautiful woman of twenty-five, who kept her thick black hair pulled into a bun at the back of her head. "What?" she whispered back.

"You *gotta* go trickertreating with me!" he said desperately. "Please! Or tell Mom I'm sick! Tell her I have a bellyache! You gotta do something!"

"Ricky, come here." She sat down on a kitchen chair, and as he moved into her outstretched arms, she watched him with her chocolate brown eyes. "I'm not gonna tell your mama that you're sick this year. We already talked about that, remember?"

He nodded impatiently. "Please, you have to go with me. You *have* to!"

She took his shoulders and pulled him close and spoke softly into his ear. "I tried to talk your mama into staying to hand out the candy so I could go with you, but she wouldn't listen."

"You gotta make her!"

"Listen, Ricky. She wants to go because she loves you so much. And she loves Halloween—why do you think she goes to so much trouble to make those costumes for you and Robin? She can't wait to take her boys out. She told me so."

He stepped back slightly, trying to look really, really piti-ful. "Please?"

Carmen took his hands. "Remember your favorite story, Ricky? About Thomas Piper?"

He nodded. "Thomas McEnery Piper. He was my great-great-great-grandfather."

"You told me Thomas was a really brave boy and that you wished you could be like him, didn't you?"

He looked down, on the verge of tears. "I guess so."

"Well, *I* know you're just as brave as Thomas. You just don't know it yet, so you need to prove it to yourself. Going out tonight will help you do that."

He shook his head. "No."

"Yes, Ricky. Have I ever lied to you?"

He shrugged. "Guess not."

"I know you sat in your papa's chair by the front door for a long time tonight. I'm proud of you. It took a lot of courage for you to do it."

"I stayed twenty minutes," he said finally. "I didn't think I could do it."

"You're a brave boy, Ricky, just like Thomas Piper. You just don't give yourself enough credit. But after tonight, you will. Just stick close to your mama and your brother, and the whole time, make believe that *you're* Thomas Piper."

Icky Ricky; come and play, Picky Ricky, hey.

"But *they're* out there." He could hear them even as he spoke.

"They can't hurt you. And they can only scare you if you let them. Ricky, you can decide not to be scared, just like Thomas." She smiled conspiratorially. "You know what'll help?"

"What?" he asked, nearly convinced.

"Be nasty. When no one's looking, stick out your tongue at them!"

He almost smiled.

"They have no right to scare you, so just tell them, real quietly, to go stick their heads in dog doodie."

He giggled. "They'd probably like to do that."

She ruffled his hair. "You."

"Carmen?"

"What?"

"What about Big Jack? He can hurt me."

She studied him a long moment. "Well, what do you do in the daytime if you see a strange man coming toward you?"

"Stay with friends or cross the street."

"Okay. Remember, you said that anyone can see him, so that means he's not gonna come after you when people are around. Just treat him like any other stranger."

"Are you sure you can't go with us?"

"Yes. And I'm also sure you'll be fine. While you're gone, I'll make sure your window's shut tight and I'll double-check the lock on the cellar door, just so you feel extra safe when you get back."

He tried not to tremble. If Carmen really believed he was as brave as Thomas Piper, then he didn't want to disappoint her. "Okay."

She gave him one more big, cushiony hug. "You're a brave young man, and I know you'll be fine. You have to tell me all about how you whispered bad names at the jacks when you saw them."

"Pottyface?" he suggested coyly.

She laughed heartily. "That's a good one. Try it, but make sure your mama doesn't hear. And Ricky?"

"Uh-huh?"

"If you get a Snickers bar, will you give me a bite?"

"Sure."

"Now, go. Your mama and brother are waiting for you."

He hesitated, trying to summon up a brave smile. At first he couldn't do it, then Carmen mouthed "pottyface" at him, and he cracked up.

"Little boys," Carmen said, smiling. "You all like the same disgusting things."

Still giggling, he returned to the living room. "Didja fall in?" Robin asked. Mom was closing the front door after handing out more candy.

"Bite me," he told his brother, as he glanced fondly at Grandfather's portrait.

"Richard, *what* did you say?" his mother asked sharply.

"I said I'm ready," he said quickly, and pulled on his mask.

She stared, not quite fooled.

"He said—" began Robin.

Oh no, he thought.

"—I'm ready," his brother finished.

"Oh," said Mom.

He looked at Robin, surprised that he'd covered for him. A second later, Robin pulled on his hand, and he squatted down.

"You owe me all your Tootsie Rolls for that!"

"One."

"Three."

"Two."

"Boys?" their mother said, raising her eyebrows.

"Two and a half," Ricky hissed.

"Deal," Robin said. "Okay, Mom, we're ready."

3

"Thank you, Ricky," Carmen said, biting into the Snickers bar he'd fished out of his bag. He'd insisted on giving her the whole thing even though it was the only one he had. "You're the nicest boy in the world."

"You're welcome," he mumbled around a sticky Yabba Dabba.

Everyone else had gone to bed, and as they sat at the kitchen table, just the two of them, Carmen watched the little boy carefully. He was so small and so afraid, and she'd felt terrible when she'd had to stay at the house instead of going with him tonight, even though she knew his mama wouldn't let him out of her sight.

"Is it good?" he asked.

"Mmmm. Very good." She resisted the urge to grab him and hug him.

Truthfully, she knew he had to go out and face his fears, to learn to be less dependent on her, but it hurt her to let him go, because he was so small and she was so afraid for him.

Ricky had been her favorite ever since she'd come to work here the week after the boys were born. Of the two, Ricky was the most fragile. He was so serious and so easily frightened that he reminded her of a wounded deer. Robin, despite his handicap, was all sunshine and smiles, and very capable of taking care of himself. The brothers were an odd pair.

She felt bad for Ricky because no one believed him when he said he saw the greenjacks, and now that he wasn't a baby anymore, she was afraid that his parents would think there was something wrong with him. His mama had been asking her recently if he'd said anything about the greenjacks, and reluctantly Carmen had lied. When she decided to talk to Ricky about it, she was surprised to find out that he already knew his parents were worried. So, even though she wasn't entirely sure it was the right thing to do, she helped him, coaching him, reminding him, trying to build his confidence.

He didn't need to be afraid of the dark, for instance—not in the house—but he was so sensitive. She thought that perhaps he really did see greenjacks since her uncle's talk of *elementales* sounded very similar. But whether he could or he couldn't wasn't the problem. His fear was, so she told him over and over that nothing could hurt him if he wasn't afraid, and tried to play on his love of the stories about Thomas Piper. She watched him now: so serious, so sad. He tried so hard. The fact that he had gone out tonight could only be a hopeful sign.

She finished the candy bar. "Thank you, Ricky. Now, tell me, how was it tonight?"

He smiled, his lip trembling almost imperceptibly. "It was okay.

"What did you see? Anything?"

He hesitated. "Greenjacks. Mostly they were all over our yard, but there were some hanging around other people's yards, too, especially on our street." He smiled, more bravely. "I did what you said. I pretended I was Thomas." The smile suddenly broadened. "Know what I did?"

"What?"

"I flipped the bird at one." He giggled.

"I told you to stick out your tongue, Ricky," she said reprovingly. Carmen missed crotchety old Grandfather Piper, but he'd sure taught those boys some bad things.

"I did that, too, but the bird was more fun. You do it like this." He made a fist and extended his third finger proudly.

She cupped the offending hand in hers. "I guess your mama didn't see you do that?"

"Uh-uh."

"Your grandfather shouldn't have taught you that."

"Is it as bad as 'bite me'?"

"Worse. It's real, real dirty. Don't do it again, okay?"

"Okay." He dug a packet of Sweetarts from his bag and ripped them open. "Want some, Carmen?"

"No thanks, Ricky."

"I miss Grandfather," he said around a mouthful of candy. "He told me about the greenjacks."

"I know." His brown hair was still pasted damply against his forehead from wearing the skeleton mask all evening, and she reached out and pushed it from his face. She wondered if Ricky would have all his problems if his grandfather had kept his creepy old stories to himself. Who could know? And whether he saw greenjacks or only thought he did, it didn't matter, because she loved him blindly and she'd do anything for him. For good or bad, nothing could ever change that. It made her heart ache just to look at him.

"Ricky?"

"Huh?" He had a Mallomar half-crammed in his mouth.

"Did you see him? Big Jack?"

"No," he said, swallowing. "I guess not."

"You guess?"

"I thought I did for a second, in a tree on Penerosa Street." He picked up a box of Good & Plenty. "But it was windy out there, so I was probably wrong."

"You're gonna be sick if you eat any more candy tonight. Have those tomorrow, okay?"

He nodded.

"Ricky?"

"Huh?"

She hesitated, then decided to say what she had to say. "Ricky, you know you don't ever have to pretend to me. If you see something, you tell me. No one else will know."

"Okay." He pushed candy off the table into his bag and stood. "Are you gonna go to bed now?"

That was his way of making sure he didn't have to go up the dark stairway by himself. "Sure," she told him, glancing at the clock. "You know what? It's past eleven. I guess Big Jack has less than an hour left to play his tricks, huh?"

He gave her a genuine smile in return. "Yeah." He fell into her arms for a hug.

They walked up the stairs together, taking care to be very quiet. She told him to make sure and brush his teeth for a whole minute, kissed him good night, then made a show of switching on the night-light in the hall between the bathroom and the twins' bedroom. She walked to her room, around the corner from the others, but stood waiting by the open door until she heard Ricky safely enter his bedroom.

4

"Robin?" Ricky whispered as he pulled the bedroom door closed behind him. The night-light was out again, and swallowing his fear, he made himself bend down and feel for the wall socket next to the door where it was plugged in. *Nothing to be afraid of in here.*

His fingers found the socket but no night-light. "Robin!" he hissed.

No reply.

Robin, who loved to tease him by taking the little light and hiding it, seemed to be fast asleep. Ricky could see him buried under the blankets on the twin bed catercornered from his, and he was too angry at his brother to be afraid. "I'm turning on the big light, you turkey fart."

He waited a second, heard no giggling from the bed across the room. If Robin were awake, he would have cracked up. Grandfather had talked about turkey farts last year at Easter after dinner and several beers with Daddy. The brothers had practically wet their pants with hysterical glee before Mom came in and let Grandfather have it for saying "fart" and Dad for letting him. Mom was really ticked.

"Turkey fart," he said again, hopefully.

Nothing.

He flipped on the light switch, but Robin didn't stir because he was completely hidden in his blankets. At least his rotten brother hadn't figured out how to get up high enough to unscrew the overhead bulb, Ricky thought as he took off his costume and pulled on his pajamas. At least he hadn't *yet*.

Holding his breath, Ricky tiptoed across the room to the window that overlooked the three-acre front yard and the oak tree. Carmen had promised to lock it, but he had to check, had to put his hand under the curtain and feel the latch, make sure it was turned. He didn't even consider looking. Last year when he looked, he'd seen Big Jack looking back at him, scratching at the glass, tap tap tapping. *Ricky come out and play* . . . He shivered as he reached behind the curtain.

His fingers found the cold metal lock. Either Carmen had forgotten or Robin was messing with him again, because it wasn't latched. Stomach churning, he frantically twisted the lock closed.

The job done, he suddenly felt proud of himself, and almost as brave as Thomas McEnery Piper, not only because he'd flipped the bird at the little jacks, and hadn't panicked when the night-light disappeared, but because he'd calmly—well, pretty calmly—locked the window.

Smiling to himself, Ricky turned right and faced the foot of his brother's bed. Robin was so balled up in covers that he couldn't even see his hair. For a moment Ricky considered yelling boo and tearing the blankets from him. Maybe he'd get a glass of water from the bathroom so he could throw it on him.

No, he decided, he'd probably just end up getting in trouble. He'd cook up a safer trick tomorrow. Briefly he glanced at the wall of closets, saw with satisfaction that they were safely closed, then returned to his own bed, which was set against the inside wall as far as possible from the window and within reach of the overhead light switch. Last January Mom and Dad had redecorated the room. They put up wallpaper covered with drawings of sheriff stars, boots, six-shooters, lariats, and cowboy hats. Then they hung pictures showing cowboys, Indians, and lots and lots of horses. Ricky loved everything about the room except for the tree outside the window and the niggling fear that there might be a secret passage hidden in the closet somewhere.

There were all kinds of stories about the house and its hidden passages. His great-great-grandfather Conlin Piper—*Thomas's son,* he realized with a little thrill—had come here from Scotland and built the first house in Santo Verde: this house. Grandfather had always laughed and said that old Conlin was too creative for his own good and that he'd built a hodgepodge of a house with a maze hidden inside it. Conlin Piper had been in the Royal Navy, and Grandfather claimed he'd found a pirate's treasure, and had built the tunnels to hide his loot safely. Dad said the story about the loot was poppycock, but that the tunnels were real, and he'd even shown them the ones behind the built-in book-shelves on either side of the fireplace downstairs. One side was fake. The bookshelf turned around to reveal a little square room in which Conlin supposedly hid a deserter dur-ing the Civil War. Behind the other, though, was a dusty staircase, so low and narrow that a grown-up would have a hard time using it. It led straight up into utter darkness.

Yawning, Ricky pulled his yellow chenille bedspread down and climbed aboard, then crawled to the end of the bed, flicked off the light, and crawled back up, pushing his bare feet quickly, safely, between the clean white sheets.

Tonight he felt so brave that he didn't pull the covers all the way over his head. He knew Big Jack was outside some-where, but the window was locked, and before long, the clock would strike twelve and the creature would be gone for another year.

Lying there in the dark, he realized that he felt better than he ever had in his life, and it was all because he'd walked right past the greenjacks, refusing to listen when they called his name. Instead, he'd pretended to be Thomas and lifted his mask and stuck out his tongue. Later, he'd really, truly flipped the bird at one. He thought his ancestor would be proud of him tonight.

Outside, the wind picked up and oak twigs scratched at

the window. Ricky shivered with sudden alarm: What if he'd made the greenjacks angry? *They can't do anything to you!* Only Big Jack could hurt him, and he was locked out. Calm again, Ricky stretched and wiggled his toes, knowing for the first time in his life that things were going to be better now. Maybe the fear would never go away entirely, he thought sleepily, but he'd be like Thomas McEnery Piper and not be af—

"Ricky!"

His eyes jerked open.

"Ricky!" It was Robin's voice, muffled and distant.

He's still under the covers. Ricky realized that his twin was going to try to play a trick on him. Tonight it wouldn't work, he thought smugly. Not tonight.

Outside, the wind howled and distant thunder rumbled.

"Ricky!"

"What?" he whispered.

"Ricky!"

"What?" he called, a little louder.

Something tapped on the window. Suddenly he felt cold.

"Ricky!" The tapping grew insistent. "Open up!"

He slid from the bed, hesitating at the light switch, deciding to brave the dark because Robin was making so much noise that their parents might wake up. If they saw the light on under the door, he'd get in trouble for sure.

He padded to Robin's bed, paused, then poked his finger into the covers just as a brief flash of lightning lit the room. "Whatcha want, you pottyface?" He poked again, harder, and realized he felt nothing under the bedspread but a wadded-up blanket. Thunder boomed just outside. Ricky nearly jumped out of his skin. He glanced around nervously.

Tap tap tap. "Ricky!"

Just as the rain began to fall, he understood. His stinkpot brother got himself locked outside while trying to play a trick on him.

"Ricky!"

The storm noises would probably keep his parents from hearing anything, and the sudden delight he felt at having

Robin's trick backfire helped him fight down his nervousness about having to open the window again. Probably Robin was planning to scare him—he'd done it once before—by climbing out the window and pretending to be Big Jack.

The first time he'd done it, last March, Ricky'd been so terrified that he'd screamed. Mom and Dad had come running, and boy, did Robin get in trouble when they saw him sitting out there in that tree. Ricky had hidden under his covers and cried half the night, even though Robin kept trying to apologize. By the next morning, he wanted revenge, but he didn't get any because he didn't know how.

But oh boy, he sure knew how now. He'd let his twin sit out there all night. Or maybe an hour, anyway. Let him sit out there and get all wet, and then Robin would think twice before he tried to play another joke on him.

He fluffed up the lump of blankets Robin had left and returned to his bed, thinking that if his parents did come in, he'd just pretend to be asleep. Could he help it if he'd locked the window without knowing his brother was out there playing a trick on him? No, he couldn't.

He sat on the edge of his bed.

Tap tap tap. "Ricky! Ricky! Wake up, dummy!"

He swung his feet up, slipped them between the cool sheets.

"Ricky! Let me in!"

"No way," he whispered.

Then, abruptly, two words popped into his brain: *Big Jack*

"Cripes." He slipped off the bed and walked quickly across the dark, shadowy room. He'd gotten so full of himself for being brave that he didn't even think about the fact that it was Halloween night when he'd locked his brother outside. "Cripes," he whispered again. Even rat-fink Robin didn't deserve to get snatched by Big Jack. "Cripes." He pushed the curtains open.

A skeletal face leered in through the glass, a green glowing face that grinned from ear to ear. With a small yelp, he jumped back. Then he heard Robin call his name again and saw his brother's hand rap on the glass, and realized his turkey brother had tried to scare him with his own Halloween mask.

Drawing a deep breath, he undid the lock. Robin backed up a little way to a thicker part of the wobbly branch he sat on and waited while Ricky pushed open the window. Wind yanked leaves from the tree and splattered sharp raindrops against his face.

"You took my mask, you fart," Ricky whispered. "I oughta leave you out here all night."

Robin pushed the mask up on top of his head. "I thought you'd want Big Jack to trickertreat you, Ricky!"

"Shut up!" Ricky ordered, not at all amused. "Get in here."

"Why? You scared old Jack's gonna get in?" Robin grinned, full of the devil. "I'm gonna tell Mom you told me 'shut up.' "

"You just said it, too."

"Then I'm gonna tell her I saw you flip old man Clegg the bird."

"Did not."

"Did so."

"Did not."

"I saw you."

"I didn't flip off Clegg, I flipped off—"

"Who? Huh? Who?"

Ricky shrugged, not wanting to say. When Robin was in the mood to tease, anything made him worse. "Come inside. Mom 'n' Dad are gonna wake up."

"Good thing for you old man Clegg's blind as a bat or you'd be nailed already. If you give me all your Tootsie Rolls, I won't tell. You already owe me two and a half for earlier. Now I want 'em all."

Carmen always said Robin was a Tootsie Rollaholic, and Ricky guessed she was right. "I'll give you one more."

"Three."

"Two and that's fi—"

Behind Robin, near the heart of the oak, a thin branch

moved against the wind, bending itself around the trunk. Ricky felt his jaw drop open, and knew his brother said something, but didn't understand the words.

Time slowed to a crawl as he watched the branch encircling the trunk. At the end of it were five long twigs, jointed and flexing like human fingers. A second branch, identical to the first, snaked around the trunk from the other side.

A creaking sound. Wind sighed. Rain in his face. Ricky's ears filled with roaring blackness, and the same blackness appeared in spots before his eyes and filled his stomach with nausea. But he couldn't look away.

"Hey, butthead!" Robin called. "Wake up!"

Time began to flow again. "Get inside," Ricky ordered. "Now!"

"No way, José, not until you give. Three more Tootsie Rolls or I tell."

"Come in *now!*"

Alien laughter exploded inside Ricky's head, a gale of it, similar to the greenjacks' windy cackling, but deeper, more powerful, a hurricane rather than a breeze. Oblivious, Robin continued his teasing, but Ricky couldn't even hear him over the roar of Big Jack's voice.

He leaned out the window as far as he dared and extended his arms to his brother. "Come on!"

Don't be afraid of me, Ricky, I'm your friend.

Slowly, so slowly, the skeletal arms crept up around the oak, the stick fingers crunching as they gripped the bark. The thought of the creature hidden behind the trunk terrified Ricky, and he had to force himself not to turn and run.

I love you, Icky Ricky.

Then he saw it peering at him from behind the trunk. It was a skull, like a twisted burl of wood, human-sized, leering, grinning with wood-chip teeth, the eye holes so black, they seemed to suck light into them.

Icky Ricky, I want you, yes I do do do.

The laughter deafened him as the creature pulled its body higher, and higher. Ricky blinked, and in the instant his eyes were closed, Big Jack must have leapt, its sounds masked by the storm, for now it stood arrogantly on a thick limb a few feet behind Robin.

Lightning flashed. Thunder rolled.

Big Jack looked like it did last year, only clearer and closer, so close, too close. The monstrosity resembled a human skeleton, but with bones made of tortured bark and buckled wood. Naked white roots, like nerves, twisted through its limbs, and leaves and vines filled its chest, throbbing green tendrils that twined along its extremities like blood veins. One thick vine coursed up its neck, pulsing—*jugular vine*, Ricky thought, fighting the urge to laugh or scream or throw up, he didn't know which. Big Jack opened its mouth, and wet waxy leaves crept from the corners of its smile, growing perceptibly, reaching toward him.

Toward Robin.

Horrified, Ricky jerked backward. His head thunked against the sash, but he barely felt it.

Robin pointed at him and began giggling.

He forced himself to lean forward again. "Robin, you jerk, get inside!"

"Why?" Robin grabbed the limb he balanced on with both hands and pushed his body up. "Wanna see me do a handstand?"

"No!"

"What's the matter, little brother? Is bad old Big Jack out here?" His eyes twinkled. "It's not midnight yet. I guess he's around somewhere, huh?" He giggled.

"He's behind you."

Robin made a face. "Yeah, and so's the tooth fairy." He pushed up and down on his arms, doing the spider imitation.

It took all of Ricky's courage to climb onto the window-sill.

Ricky, Ricky, be my friend, you won't be afraid anymore.

Big Jack stepped closer.

Ricky balanced himself on the ledge, his outstretched fingers only inches from his brother. "Give me your hand," he said, vaguely aware that tears were running down his cheeks and into his mouth.

"Cripes, Ricky, don't cry, I was just fooling around," Robin said. "I'll come in. Jeez, I didn't mean to—"

He froze as skeletal hands clamped down on his shoulders. He turned his head and saw the woody fingers, then slowly turned back to Ricky, no fun in his eyes now, only raw, incredulous horror. A soft moan escaped his lips.

Now or never, Ricky. Will you save your big brother? Now or never, Icky Ricky!

Ricky felt the thing trying to suck his will away with its charcoal eyes.

"No!" Carefully, his gaze never leaving Big Jack, Ricky climbed back through the open window, then wriggled back out, this time on his stomach. To keep from falling, he hooked his feet on either side of the window, then, inch by inch, pulled his upper body onto the nearest branch, not stopping until his body would stretch no farther.

His brother was within reach, but he was like a statue, his hands cemented to the branch, his body still raised above it as Big Jack's viney claws dug into his shoulders.

Ricky slapped at his twin. "Robin! Give me your hand! Hurry!"

Dully, his twin looked at him, focusing only when Ricky grasped both his wrists and began yanking him forward. "Ricky—"

"Come on!"

Suddenly Robin let go. Ricky caught him and, with all his strength, began to pull him inside, realizing that his brother was paralyzed with fear. He grunted with effort, determined to win this battle with Big Jack. Robin cried out as the creature renewed its painful hold on his flesh.

Ricky struggled, gaining an inch, losing one. "I got you, I got you, I got you!" He repeated the litany as he worked, aware of Big Jack's laughter in his head and of Robin's shock-white face and fathomless eyes. "I got you!" Panting, Ricky held on. "Robin, I got you!"

Suddenly the monster released its hold. Ricky almost lost his balance as Robin fell from the limb, but he hung on to his brother's wrists, his hands slippery in the rain, gulping air, struggling to keep his feet wedged safely inside the window. After an eternity, Ricky began to pull him up, his back and arms screaming with the effort.

Robin was a foot from the window, Ricky half-inside, when Big Jack struck, sweeping across Robin, its storm of laughter echoing madly in Ricky's head. The sharp wooden hands grabbed Ricky at the elbows, pinching and holding until his fingers turned numb and started to open against his will.

Hey. Ricky, time to play!

Robin began to slip from his grasp. "No!" he cried, but his voice was lost in the howl of the storm. He watched in horror as Robin began to slip.

The wind screamed and then he saw Robin grab a branch two feet below. He hung on, then began pulling himself back up the tree.

And then Ricky couldn't see anything because Big Jack was all over him, grabbing, touching, plucking at him. Wind swirled around them, wet and rotting and green like cold swamp water. It whistled among the bony branches with a life of its own, mingling with the laughter of the thing itself.

Big Jack dragged him out of the window and into the tree. It hugged him against itself, smothering him in its green darkness, bruising him on its bark and bones. It paused for an instant, staring into Ricky's eyes until he thought he would faint. Its gaze drained him of his will while its arms crushed the life from him.

"No! Let him go!" Robin yelled from behind them.

Ricky only saw him for an instant, hanging on to the tree limb with one hand, pounding and pulling on Big Jack with the other. "Let him go!"

The thing paused, its grasp loosening slightly. Ricky drew a breath, coughing, and watched as Robin tore at Big Jack, ripping out the root nerves, yanking the blood vines. It seemed amused until the boy snapped off two of its gnarled toes. Then the swamp wind rose again, Big Jack's howl of anger within it, a part of it.

"Punch him!"

Robin's words startled him into action. Ricky fought, pulling and twisting the foliage guts, trying to break off ribs. The monster howled furiously as Robin attached himself to one of its legs and started ripping it apart.

Steeling himself, Ricky reached for Big Jack's neck and wrapped his hand around the thick, pulsing jugular vine. He pulled.

Howling, Big Jack let go for a bare instant, but that was enough. Ricky sprang back, grabbing the tree trunk and re-gaining his balance. Something cold splashed across his face and mouth. It tasted of plants: Big Jack's blood.

Ricky edged around the trunk as the thing reached for him, backed farther as he watched his twin do a monkey-climb right up the monster, ripping and tearing and shredding the vines as he moved. The thing put its arms around Robin as he reached its chest.

Two blocks away, the bells of Our Lady of Guadalupe began chiming the measure of prelude that would ring in the hour.

Midnight. The first bell rang.

Big Jack's almost out of time! Ricky edged forward to help his brother, who still tore at the monster's chest. "Get him, Robin!" he cried. "Hang on!"

Two chimes. With one hand, the thing shoved Robin's head into its torso, smothering the flailing boy. Its laughter blended with the rain as it extended its other hand and beckoned Ricky closer. *Come with me and I'll let your big brother live.*

Three. *I'm supposed to die! Not Robin!* Ricky stepped nearer.

"*No!*" Robin yelled, his voice muffled against the creature. He punched into the thing with all his might, over and over.

Four.

Green fluid still pulsed from the broken vine in Big Jack's neck, and green slime dripped from its mutilated torso, but still it held Robin. The vines growing from its mouth began to twine around his face.

Five chimes. Big Jack extended its hand again. *Come with me or he dies dies dies.*

Six. He couldn't let Robin die for him. Swallowing, Ricky reached for Big Jack's hand.

"NO!" Robin screamed as the creature's hand closed painfully on Ricky's wrist.

Seven. Big Jack paused, glanced at Robin, then stretched out its other arm, holding the boy far away from its body. Suddenly it let go, but Robin was already clinging to the arm, hanging on as Jack tried to shake him off. Face smeared with green, eyes fierce, he screamed, "No!" and refused to fall.

Ricky twisted in Big Jack's grasp, and suddenly the grip became so tight that he felt as if his bones were being crushed. He cried out, nearly fainting with the pain.

Eight. Robin swung across Big Jack's body and grabbed the arm it held Ricky with. With all his might, he began to tear at Jack's forearm, using every muscle in his hands and arms, using his teeth to bite, doing everything to make the monster let go of his brother. The monster tore at him, but he didn't seem to notice.

Nine. The wooden wrist began to crack. Robin twisted the wood fiercely, and it broke. He ripped a vine with his teeth and the hand came off, still attached to Ricky's arm.

Ricky staggered back against the tree trunk, breathing heavily, holding his wrist.

"You can't have him!" Robin screamed.

Ten.

Big Jack pulled its mangled arm back and again shoved Robin's head into the mass of oozing mashed foliage behind the ribs.

Eleven.

"Robin!" Ricky cried.

Robin's mine, little Ricky, icky little Ricky. He can't see like you can, but he's mine now. Better watch out!

Twelve. Midnight, November 1.

The leaves on the vines growing from Big Jack's mouth withered in an instant, turning brown and flying away on the breeze before the final bell finished echoing. Big Jack laughed again and let go of the oak, Robin trapped in its arms.

"No!" Ricky cried as they fell.

In the first minute of November first, Ricky stood in the branches of the old oak tree, barely aware of the rain beating monotonously against his face. He clung to the trunk and stared in shock at Big Jack's body on the ground twenty feet below. He craned his neck, trying to see Robin, but the boy was lost in the rain, buried in the dark visceral vines of Big Jack's remains.

The scene was lit by moonlight and the rainbow of Malibu lights that lined the paths crisscrossing the immense forest of a front yard, and as Ricky watched, a dozen little green-jacks gathered around the ruins of Big Jack. An instant later, a dozen more glimmering forms poured from the lifeless body of their king. A strong wind suddenly rose and the body began to break apart, the arms and hands and legs becoming nothing more than harmless twigs and branches. The roots and leafy vines crackled brown as they dried up and rode away on the wind.

Big Jack was gone for another year, and only the unmoving form of Ricky's twin lay within the circle of little jacks.

"Robin." Ricky moaned the name, and the greenjacks looked up at him briefly, then turned their attention back to Robin. They started to move around him. Ricky realized that they were fighting over his brother's body.

He realized that Robin was unconscious, not dead, just like Thomas in Grandfather's stories. That meant a greenjack could force Robin out and take his body—just as Big Jack had promised. Quickly Ricky started to climb down the tree. He had to get his twin into the house before they took him.

But the handholds ran out after a few feet, and it was too far to jump. "Robin," he whispered. The jacks barely glanced at him as he crawled back up the tree and into his window.

Once inside, he glanced briefly down and saw that the circle of jacks was moving wildly, violently, melding, com-

ing apart, melding again. Quickly he took the back stairs
past Carmen's room and down and around through the
kitchen and dining room, not caring about the darkness, caring only about his brother.

Don't let them get you, Robin, don't let them get you!

He crept across the living room, avoiding the spots where
the floorboards would creak. The drapes were drawn, and
for once, he wished they weren't. *Don't let them get you,
don't let them, don't let them.*

Quietly he reached up and pulled the wrought-iron bolt
on the arched front door, then grabbed the handle and
pressed the thumb latch. It clicked softly open. He waited a
moment, then, slowly, silently, he pulled the heavy planked
door open. His heart thumped as he got ready to run out
and down the steps to the oak, to rescue Robin and carry
him inside to safety.

"Hi, baby brother."

"Robin!"

Bathed in the yellow glow of the porch light, Robin
waited on the welcome mat, resting on his hands, peering
up at him. He was soaking wet, and a small trickle of blood
oozed from a cut hidden in his hair. Otherwise he looked
fine. Below, at the bottom of the wide steps, the amorphous
shifting shapes of the greenjacks cavorted and tumbled in
the grass. *I'm not afraid of them anymore.* The realization
astounded him even more than Robin's amazing recovery.
I'm not afraid. Suddenly he knew what it must feel like to
be a grown-up. Smiling, he turned his attention back to his
twin.

"Robin, you're okay! I was afraid you were—"

"Dead?"

"Knocked out. I thought you were knocked out!"

"I was."

His twin's crooked smile made the hairs on the back of
Ricky's neck stand on end. Grandfather's familiar words flit-
ted through his mind.

*. . . his father held a sword in his hand, ready to run the
body through if his son had become a changeling.*

"Whatcha thinkin'?"

"Nothing. Are you okay?"

"Okeydokey, icky Ricky."

Stunned, he stared at his brother. Ricky *knew,* beyond all doubt, that he had never, *ever* told anyone about the name the jacks called him: It was too humiliating. His bladder let go. It didn't matter. "What?" he whispered.

"I'm okay."

"Did you hit your head?" he asked timidly, wanting to believe that he'd imagined his brother's rhyming reply.

"Just a little. Just enough." He crossed the threshold, his movements lacking their usual grace, and stared around the room as if it were something new. "Shut the door, Picky Ricky. Let's go to bed."

In shock, Ricky loitered a moment in the open doorway watching the greenjacks as they capered in the rain. One, dimmer than the others, did not jump or dance, but stood motionless under the tree, near the place where Robin had fallen. A chill raced up Ricky's spine.

Robin? he thought hard at the figure.

And he thought he heard his name, called softly, but it was lost in the leaves that chattered in the breeze.

"What's going on here?"

Ricky whirled at his father's voice and saw his parents in their robes and slippers, standing at the bottom of the living room stairs. His dad's arms were crossed, but his mother stepped forward quickly.

"You're wet. You're both wet!"

Immediately Robin began to cry. "I fell," he sobbed.

"Fell?" Mom scooped him up, mindless of his wet clothes and the leaves and dirt sticking to him. "From where? Are you all right, honey?"

He threw his arms around her neck and clung, his face buried against her shoulder, sobbing and heaving as he never had before. It was a show. Ricky cringed, wondering what would come next.

"I fell out of the tree," he wailed. "I'm sorry! I didn't mean to—"

"Rick?" His father loomed over him. "What were you boys doing?" He looked him up and down, mouth set in a grim line.

"I—I—Robin went out the window and—" He silenced, knowing he shouldn't tell the truth because they wouldn't believe him.

"It's all my fault," Robin bawled.

Amazed, Ricky stared at him.

"I was playing a trickertreat on Ricky." His voice hitched dramatically over a series of whimpers. "I . . . I wanted to scare him. I lost my balance, and Ricky tried to save me."

"There, there . . ." His mother turned slightly, and Ricky could see Robin's face over her shoulder.

His eyes were black as night, and his expression was gleeful and scary at the same time. The little-boy voice that issued from his mouth didn't match the way he looked. "Oh, Ricky, I'll always remember how you tried to save me." His hand crept into his mother's hair, bringing a lock of it to his face. He smelled it, smiling. Then, to Ricky's horror, he stuck his tongue out and licked it. The smile broadened into a jack-o'-lantern grin, and all the while, Mom kept patting his back, unaware. Dad, not noticing, crossed to the open door and closed it.

"Ricky?" His mother said. "That was very brave of you to try to help your brother, especially when he played a bad trick on you."

"I'll pay you back, I promise," Robin said. Slowly he extended his tongue and licked the satiny robe his mother wore.

"It's okay," Ricky said softly. "He bumped his head," he added. "It's bleeding."

Oh!" Mom pulled Robin away from her, as Ricky hoped she would, and examined his head. "Frank, do you think we should take him to the hospital?" She glanced at Ricky. "Go on up and get dry and go to bed, honey. Everything will be all right."

He left his parents discussing Robin's bumped head as he trudged upstairs. At the top, he found Carmen staring down

at the scene below. Silently she walked with him to his bedroom, then waited outside the door until he came out in
fresh pajamas.

"Are you all right?"

He nodded.

"Do you want to tell me what happened?"

"Uh-huh."

"Come on, then." She led him to her room around the
corner, and they sat together on the little sofa bed she kept
for when one of her sisters came to visit. "Okay, Ricky,"
she told him. "Tell me. It will be our secret."

He did as she asked, leaving nothing out because he knew
she wouldn't just tell him he was crazy.

She asked, "So you think your brother's changed,
Ricky?"

Confronted so bluntly, he had to stop and think. That was
exactly what he thought. And he had proof because of the
name: *Icky Ricky.*

He swallowed his pride and told her about the name.

"Maybe you said it in your sleep, Ricky." She regarded
him solemnly. "Do you think you might have?"

More than anything in the world, he wanted to believe
that what Carmen suggested was true. "Maybe," he said,
knowing he hadn't. Suddenly he realized he'd have to go
back to his room soon and see his brother. That frightened
him so much that his stomach hurt.

Carmen leaned over and kissed his cheek soundly. "It's
late. Let's talk about it more tomorrow. You want to sleep
here tonight, Ricky?" she asked, as if she knew what he was
thinking.

He nodded gratefully.

5

Legs legs legs legs legs. Balanced on his hands, he padded carefully down the staircase, his abbreviated body held up high so that it didn't thump much against the steps. *Legs legs legs legs legs.* Icky Ricky was cowering in Carmen's room, maybe sleeping, maybe not, and the parents were back in their room with the door closed.

Legs legs legs legs legs. Despite the blood in his hair, he'd convinced them he was fine, so the mother had dried him and tucked him into bed. He liked that a lot, the feel of the rough towel on his skin, the feel of her hands, the smell of her hair, her skin, the minty scent of her breath.

He snickered, remembering how upset Ricky had been when he saw him lick Mom's hair. Poor Ricky, icky Ricky, crazy, crazy, sicky Ricky.

The parents talked and talked before falling asleep, and impatiently he'd waited until they'd been silent for a long time before leaving the bedroom. It wasn't much fun being alone, but he amused himself by looking through icky Ricky's dresser and toy chest until he knew it was safe to leave.

It was just as well he'd been left alone for a while, he decided. Because of the head bump, the memories buried in his brain had been a little fuzzy at first—the memories of the house, the parents, Carmen, and especially icky Ricky, but now they were flowing into place and he knew he'd be fine, no matter who he ran into.

Legs legs legs legs legs. He hated Ricky for having the legs, but this body had some advantages. Though Robin's balance and grace were still a little messed up, they were improving rapidly and six steps from the ground floor, he let loose a whispery little laugh and flipped his body up above his head and finished his descent in handstand position. Delighted with his progress, he turned and quickly raced back up the stairs, then, still in a handstand, dashed down the hall, past his room and around the corner.

Legs legs legs legs legs. He paused a moment, waiting until he discerned the soft sawing snore coming from Carmen's room, then, arms pumping, he dashed along the long hallway that led to the back stairs. His descent was perfect this time, and he made no sounds but for the soft pad-padding of his hands against the lovely grass-colored carpet and the rhythmic murmur of his breath and his muted giggles. At last he entered the kitchen and caught the perfume of ripening pears, the tang of orange peel, and the warm smell of the bread baked earlier that day.

He crossed to the refrigerator and, balanced on one hand, used the other to open the door. He pushed it wide so that the dim light from the interior could illuminate as much of the room as possible, then he began investigating the Kelvinator's contents.

"Mmmm-mmmm-mmmm-mmmm-mmmm, what's this, what's that?" Gleefully he opened a yellow Tupperwear container, and sniffed at the gelatinous brown lumps within. "Beef, beef, beefy beef," he whispered, sticking his finger in the cold gravy. Delicately he sucked the finger clean. "Mmmm." Lifting the bowl to his face, he dipped his tongue into the gravy and lapped up a morsel of beef. He chewed slowly, savoring the meaty flavor, memorizing the rich odor of flesh laced with onions, garlic, and bay, and the feel of its greasy, grainy texture. Before replacing the lid, he used his tongue to smooth the surface of the coagulated sauce.

Licking his lips, he replaced the container precisely where he'd found it before eagerly studying other items on the lowest shelf.

"Butter, butter, mmmm-mmmm butter!" He removed the cover, then ran the flat of his tongue over the yellow surface, careful not to leave any marks. He loved butter, the slick way it felt in his mouth, so rich, so . . . There was something more, but he didn't know what to call it.

So many tastes and smells and textures to examine and sample—*Said Simple Simon to the pieman, let me taste your wares, hairs, cares, dares.* The rhyme came to him, making him feel warm and tingly inside. He had a dab of catsup, a lick of sour cream, then an egg, consumed whole, crunchy shell and all. A drink of milk threatened to overflow his mouth and belly, so he spat the rest back into the carton.

Legs legs legs legs legs. Logy and full, Robin ascended the kitchen staircase, tired, moving slowly, the bump on his head making him feel achy and irritated, not caring much if his body thumped the steps now and then. Even so, he paused in the bathroom to open the hamper and examine the dirty laundry. He withdrew a shirt and sniffed it carefully, memorizing the scent of the father's sweat, then exchanged it for a pair of feminine underwear. He studied item after item, with nose, mouth, and eyes, never tiring until he had examined every last piece of clothing. Finally he replaced everything in the hamper and returned to his bedroom. He climbed onto Ricky's empty bed, removed his pajama top and underpants, then rolled around on the sheets.

When he tired of the activity, he dressed and moved to Robin's bed by the window. With effort, he unlocked it and opened it as wide as it would go and perched on the ledge.

The rain had stopped and there was no wind. The silence choked his ears until he began grinding his teeth just to hear something. Soon he began humming to himself, wishing icky Ricky were here so he could listen to him breathe, wishing he were here so that he could have a little fun.

In the darkness he longed for a whole body, to have legs to run with and senses that could see the greenjacks and hear their songs. Most of all, he longed for revenge against Ricky, who had everything he so desired. For the new Robin Piper, the loneliness was overwhelming.

6

July 22, 1974

Tonight the refrigerator held clusters of purple Concord grapes to stuff into his mouth, and he did, cramming it so full that he could barely close his jaws over them. Next, oh joy, a covered dish of olives, black finger food, salty and iron-tasting, reminding him of blood. The olives made him crave meat, and he had to reach as high as he could to grab the white butcher paper containing a mountain of hamburger. He opened it and nibbled the raw meat delicately, savoring each taste. Then, before rewrapping it up so carefully that no one would suspect it had been touched, he ran his smoothing tongue over the rest of the mound, leaving his saliva on what his family would eat.

He never grew tired of touching other people's things, of leaving something of himself upon them, so they would unknowingly consume his bodily secretions, or wear them against their bodies. It was one of many pleasures that helped him deal with his anger at Ricky for the legs and eyes denied him.

Eating was another, but now his stomach was full, so he shut the refrigerator and padded to the kitchen door, swung onto the stool next to it, and silently undid the lock and chain, ready for another sort of indulgence.

A moment later, he was in the backyard, hidden in the

darkness of a new moon. He breathed in the night air, feeling the summer darkness surround him, the cool wind like water on his face. A hint of eucalyptus lay under the soft sweetness of the citrus trees, the gardenias and jasmine, and beneath that, a cold-water smell and the bubbling of a waterfall. He glanced at the half acre of orange and lemon trees, at the path leading toward the cottage where Grandfather Piper had lived. It had been locked and dark for nearly two years, but now that Carmen and Hector were getting married, it was being cleaned out and fixed up so that they could live in it. The parents had hired Hector full time to act as gardener and handyman.

Robin was pleased about the marriage, because that meant the bitch wouldn't be hovering around icky Ricky at night like she did now.

The cold-water smell grew stronger, and he turned toward it, smiling in the dark. "Hi, hi, hi, hi, hi," he called wishfully. The new moon held little power, and he neither expected any answers nor received them, but ever since he'd discovered that very occasionally he could hear the greenjacks' song, he was compelled to try. He treasured the times he had sensed the presence of the jacks. It was a salve for his loneliness.

Legs legs legs legs legs. Hatred for icky Ricky, with his long legs and special senses, washed over him. He'd get the cowardly little shit eventually, get him good. He could get him anytime with a pillow over the face or a conk on the head, especially after Carmen moved out, but what he really wanted was to get him on Halloween, to give him a trick-ertreat he'd never forget.

Robin waited until later, when they were in their beds, to tell old Icky he was going to make sure he never lived through another Halloween. Ricky didn't say anything, just jumped up and hightailed it for his precious Carmen's room.

But Robin meant what he said. This Halloween he'd do the big trickertreat, or if something went wrong, the next. He could wait a long, long time.

Sniggering, he started down the path that led from the

backyard, down through the long, narrow side yard, with its thick border of oleanders and liquid amber trees, and finally to the front corner of the house. The front was even bigger than the back, covering three acres, and so surrounded with willows, elms, pines, and filled with fruit trees, flowers, ferns, and exotic broad-leafed tropicals, that you couldn't even see the street, Via Matanza, beyond them.

The yard that icky Ricky so hated was a park crisscrossed with brick and stone paths that were constantly overgrown by the grass and bushes, no matter how often Hector pruned or mowed. To Robin the place was a paradise, the plant life an announcement that the greenjacks were present. Again he took in the scents, the blend of aromas from the plants and the trees and the koi pond, the wonderful koi pond, a hundred feet distant.

Ignoring the light-lined brick path that led to the pool, Robin moved across the yard, enjoying the thick dampness of the lawn beneath his hands. He paused, reveling in the spongy coolness, and noted how his nails dug into the moist earth, snickering when he detected the cold wriggling sliminess of a night crawler as it passed between his fingers.

Reaching the flagstones that surrounded the koi pond, he crossed them—hard, cold, interesting. The pond itself had originally been a kidney-shaped built-in swimming pool, so it was huge and deep. But many years ago, Grandfather Piper, who hated to swim, had painted it dark blue, put the rocky rustic edge on it, and built the tall stony waterfall right over the tall diving platform. And then he had filled it with fish and water lilies.

At the water's edge, Robin halted, lowering himself onto his stomach to lie between the colored lights on the cold stone so that he could stare at the water, smell it, and dangle his fingers in it to attract the fish.

"Boy kois, toy kois, fishies, fishies, fishies!" He wiggled his fingers and they came, the fishies, gold and red and bronze and black, kissing his fingers, looking for food. Finally his favorite arrived, the huge white one that everyone called the Professor. It had black circles around its eyes that

looked like spectacles. He waited for it to mouth his fingers,
then deftly he snatched the fish up in both hands and lifted
it from the water.

"Hi, fishie, fishie!"

The koi barely wriggled in his powerful grip, and he fan-
cied that it studied him as intently as he did it. Gently he
kissed the creature, and found it cold and wet but full of
life. Its odor was of algae and dark, cool water. It gasped,
needing to breathe, suffocating on air, and quickly Robin
ran his tongue over the creature's scaly side, tasting salt and
stagnant water. " 'Bye, fish, go, fish," he whispered, and
thrust it into the water, watching until the sleek white shape
disappeared into the bubbles of the waterfall on the far side
of the pond.

He loved the fishes. On warm nights he'd slip into the
water and swim with them. The thought made him remember
Ricky, locked away up in their room, and he turned and
gazed up at the bedroom window. The light was out, but he
thought he saw the curtain move behind the glass. Hoping
he was watching, Robin waved, then pulled his T-shirt over
his head and tossed it behind him. A moment later, his
shorts—the mother made them for him with a little fly and
no leg holes—and underpants lay beside it. He waved again,
loving the way the air felt against his skin.

Ribbet. At the sound of the frog, he flipped himself silently upright. *Ribbet.* Near, he thought. *Ribbet.* Near and
nearer. Another frog answered, in a deeper voice, from somewhere near the waterfall. Still another joined in and another,
and soon the air was full of *ribbets* and *robbets,* croaking
music high and low and in between. Pleased, he listened to
the symphony, and when it was at its peak, he rose on his
hands and lifted all the way to his fingers, his version of
tippy-toes. Fingers aching with effort, he moved silently
around the pond to the rocky waterfall, watching for a frog.
Despite the Malibu lights, it was difficult to spot even one,
for they sought out the shadows.

The invisible singers continued their melody as Robin
settled his body next to the waterfall. He waited, listening,

and while he did, he glanced up at the house and saw the bedroom light come on. Icky Ricky was up for sure. Grinning, he thought his scaredy-cat brother probably had to go pee, because he always had to turn on the light before he could even get out of bed.

Ribbet ribbet. Something moved in the darkness, and suddenly, right in front of him, he saw the dark shape of a large amphibian. It hopped even closer, and Robin grabbed it, squeezing hard to keep it from slipping out of his grasp.

The other singers fell silent.

He touched the frog, smelled it and tasted it, then spat at the bitterness. Then he worked its legs, pumping them up and down, up and down, fascinated. *Legs legs legs legs legs.* He petted it, stuck his fingers in its mouth, and looked up and smiled when he saw Ricky's silhouette in the bedroom window. Probably Ricky couldn't see him right now, but he could certainly remedy that.

Sticking the frog's legs in his mouth, ignoring the bitter, moldy flavor, he clamped his teeth down on them so that, no matter how hard it kicked, it couldn't get away. He rose on his hands, moved around to the back of the waterfall, and nimbly climbed to the top.

Settling his body on the smooth stone just above the water spout, he waved at his brother. Icky Ricky saw him, but didn't wave back. That was fine by Robin.

Legs legs legs legs legs. He took the frog from his mouth, wiping his lips and spitting, then held it up for Ricky to see, one little foot in each hand.

"Legs legs legs legs legs," he whispered, holding the frog up above his head. Slowly he began to pull the legs apart. The frog made a sound, a funny little froggy-scream. Then, after a long moment, its skin made a ripping sound and the creature came apart. Blood spattered like raindrops across Robin's face and into his open mouth. "Legs legs legs legs legs," he said, tossing the dismembered halves into the pond.

He lifted himself up on his hands. "Icky Ricky, icky Ricky, come out and play," he called, his voice melding with the waterfall and the night breeze. "Come out and swim with me." Laughing, he propelled himself over the waterfall, into the pond, surprising the fishies, and washing frog's blood from his skin. *Legs legs legs legs legs.*

7

Locusts. The air hissed with their high, dry sounds, rasping, phoneline electric, screaming outside the car. Rick Piper cringed as he closed the window. He hated the locusts. He hated the desert.

Until he turned right on Vegas Boulevard and saw that the thermometer on the First Interstate Bank read 104 degrees, he wasn't even aware that his shirt was plastered to his body. *You're losing it, Piper.* Sighing, he loosened his tie, switched on the air conditioner, and let the chill air turn his sweat to ice.

Sinatra dobedobedoed at him when he turned on the radio. Wincing—a reflex born in childhood—he switched to the news. The stations rarely played any music he liked, and carrying cassettes in the car in this heat was a bad idea; they melted.

The desert, thought Rick, sucks. Clear, sunny, and hot, the weatherman was saying, yesterday, today, and tomorrow. It never changed. When he was a kid, he'd thought Southern California had no weather. Lord, had he been wrong about that.

If you don't like it, you can move. He glanced at the envelope on the seat beside him. The letter from George McCall, his attorney, had arrived two weeks ago, and he still hadn't answered it. He didn't know how. It was about Aunt Jade and her deteriorating mental state, about the house and its own state of deterioration, about sewer lines, property taxes, and a host of other aggravations related to home ownership.

The house in Santo Verde provided all the frustrations and none of the benefits, but that was his own fault. Sell it, he thought. Put crazy old Jade in a rest home with part of the proceeds. He should have done it years ago, but he just kept putting it off. He'd had title to the place since his twenty-first birthday, but he hadn't been back since he'd left for college. *Time flies.* He realized he hadn't seen it in nearly twenty years.

LOOSE SLOTS! a computerized sign blazed as he passed. Shaking his head, he thought, *You hate this place,* for maybe the hundredth time since the letter had arrived and maybe the millionth since he'd moved here in '82. *You hate the heat. Christ it's only June first and it's over one hundred.* He squinted into the sun, a headache coming on. *You hate having your kids grow up here with gambling and drinking and sex advertised on every other billboard.* Shelly's attitudes had already been affected by her surroundings, and he knew it was only a matter of time before it rubbed off on Cody, too. He could take them back to Santo Verde, enroll them in good schools, fix up the house, and live a normal life again. That was something they hadn't done since Laura was killed by a drunk driver, when Cody was barely a year old. The poor kid didn't even remember his mother.

He'd been considering a move for sometime, and now the time had come to make the decision. His contract with the local station would be up for renewal at the end of the month, and though he liked doing the show, he didn't need the work. Too, in the last few weeks, pressure from station management—a group of disturbingly sharp, closely related men who referred to themselves as "the boys"—to sign a contract that would tie him up for three years had increased to the point that he was coming home with headaches and acid stomach nearly every evening. Lately he'd been wondering if he might wake up some morning and find himself nose to nose with a horse's head.

Moving to California to take care of family matters was something "the boys" would probably understand.

Since he'd started hosting the program, a show that was similar in style to "Consumer Crusader," his syndicated newspaper column, he'd been away from home more often than not, leaving Shelly to her own questionable devices and Cody to sitters he never quite trusted. No, he didn't need the show. Besides, if he really needed the money—or the ego gratification—he'd already been approached by a Los Angeles station about doing a five-minute spot several times a week on a local morning news show. It paid almost as well as his weekly half hour, required far less work, but unfortunately would require him to get up at three in the morning Monday, Wednesday, and Friday. Still, it was his if he wanted.

All you need, Piper, is your column. Ten more newspapers had just contracted for "Crusader," and that meant he'd soon be appearing in virtually every major metropolitan area in the nation every Sunday. What more *could* he need? And if he just did the column, he'd be home a lot more, which meant he wouldn't feel so guilty all the time.

He knew the kids needed a more wholesome environment; a world-class gambling town wasn't a fit place for a teenage girl or a little boy ready for kindergarten. It wasn't a fit place for a single father, either. He shook his head. *Better be careful, Piper, or you'll talk yourself into this move.*

Joe Piscopo, bulging with obscene, oily muscles, smiled smugly down at him from a billboard by the MGM. Yeah, Rick thought, he hated it here. Except for one thing, the one reason he had moved here in the first place: It never got dark on the Strip.

He turned left on Flamingo Road, wondering if he was ever going to stop carrying around a childhood fear of the dark—the *greenjacks will get you if you don't watch out.* A simple fear of the dark ruled his life, deciding where he could or couldn't live, letting it control his every move. *Ridiculous.*

Don't think about it! Abruptly his memory tried to shut down, just as it always did when he thought too much about his past.

Not this time, he ordered himself. *Not this time, no.* He had to think about it because it was time—past time—for him to take control of his life. At. seventeen, when he first came here, his fear was ridiculous, but to continue to carry it around all these years was borderline psychotic, or something equally abnormal. "Hell," he said, and hung another left.

A moment later, Rick pulled into the garage beneath the Paradise Towers, found a space, and parked. *Home, sweet home.* He stepped out of the air-conditioned Celica and into the shadowed, cloying heat. The air smelled like stale cigarettes—not just in the garage, but everywhere in the vicinity of the Strip. That was another good reason to return to California—not that the air was more healthful, it just smelled like it was, especially in Santo Verde in the spring when the citrus orchards were in full blossom. Despite himself, he smiled as he grabbed his briefcase, locked the car, and crossed to the elevator.

The refrigerated air in the hall on the fourteenth floor outside his apartment smelled like stale cigarettes, too, and spilled booze. "Shelly?" he called as he unlocked the door. "Shelly? You here?" Sometimes the ventilation screwed up and he'd wake up in the night smelling old smoke from Dakota and Lil's apartment next door, or worse, dog-shit cigars from his other neighbor, a fat, froggy guy named Mancuso who worked weird hours and wore dark suits, even in August. "Shelly? Cody?" He tossed his briefcase on the couch.

Except for Quint, his huge orange cat, who was fast asleep in the center of the dining room table, the place was deserted. "Scat, cat!" he ordered by rote, and as usual, Quint blinked at him with utter boredom and went back to sleep. "Cheeky bastard," Rick said, completing the ritual.

He glanced at his watch. Six-ten. Shelly had promised to pick up her brother by five and bring him straight home. Irritated, he dialed the sitter's number and found out, as he expected, that Cody was still there.

The current sitter lived on the fifth floor, and precisely three minutes and forty-five seconds elapsed between the time Rick hung up the phone and when he rang the bell. Tapping his foot, checking his watch, waiting for the door to open, he realized that his darling daughter had been late coming home four nights out of five this week.

"Mr. Piper! Come in, come in!"

The door opened and Marlene Poom beamed at him through a blue tobacco haze,

"Mrs. Poom, I'm sorry about this."

She took his arm and leaned familiarly against him. "I'm just going to have to take you over my knee and give you a good spanking if you don't remember to call me Marlene," she told him, batting her eyelashes.

Now, there was a horrifying thought. "Marlene," he said quickly, "I don't know what kept Shelly. She should have been here over an hour ago."

Mrs. Poom, her big-boned face mummy brown from the desert and tautly stretched from the plastic surgeon, beamed at him and blew a smoke ring in his face. Rick was only five nine, and that gave old Marlene a good half inch on him. That was another good reason to move: Most of the women in the building were performers and stood about six foot four. Mrs. Poom claimed to be a former show girl her-self—probably from around the time of the last gold rush. He tried to avoid another face full of smoke.

"Shelly's a pretty young girl, and she probably has lots and lots of boyfriends," Marlene Poom was telling him.

"That's what I'm afraid of."

"Daddy!"

"Hey, Cody!" Rick squatted, and the little boy careened into his arms. The brim of his red cowboy hat smacked into Rick's nose, bringing tears to his eyes. He stifled the urge to swear. Cody probably heard enough of that from Marlene.

Cody took his hug and pulled back, filled with dimples and glee. Except for the Piper dimples and dark blue eyes, the boy looked so much like his mother with his straight gold hair, full lower lip, and turned-up nose. Sometimes it hurt to look at him. He still missed her so much that sometimes in the middle of the night he'd wake up in a panic because he'd reach for her and she wasn't there.

Mr. Piper. I'm afraid we have some bad news . . . Your wife's been in an accident . . . A drunk driver on the wrong side of the divider . . . Sir, we think it would be best if you didn't look at the body . . . He'd never seen her again, he knew Shelly still missed her and wished Cody could have known her . . . sweet Laura. *Keep it up, Piper, and you're going to lose it in front of the dragon lady!* He cleared his throat. "I had a hard day, kid," Rick grunted. "I need another hug."

Cody obliged.

What if you take him to Santo Verde and he sees them too?

"Dad-dy!"

"Huh?" Rick plastered a smile on his face and focused on his son. *Get a grip! There's nothing to see!*

"Lookit what Marlene gave me." Cody dangled a pair of fuzzy pink dice in front of his eyes. "We went to Carnival Town today and played the racehorse game and Marlene won and she gave them to me. Wanna bet, Daddy? Double or nothing?"

Rick cringed. "Not today, buddy." Carnival Town had a kiddieland above the casino with live circus acts, which were fine, and carnival games that somehow seemed harmless at a county fair but like a gamblers' training center inside the casino. He glanced at Marlene Poom, who smiled at him as she lit a fresh cigarette off the old one. "Uh, Marlene, I'd really prefer that you don't take Cody into the casinos."

"Oh, don't be such an old poop," she scolded. "You've been there, I'm sure. It's not like we're playing poker or anything. It's very wholesome."

He snorted. "Wholesome isn't the word I would have used."

Marlene just shook her head and gave him a pitying smile. He had been to Carnival Town plenty of times during his college days, and the place was sleazy, all the more so because of the cotton-candy atmosphere it traded on. Not long ago, he'd run across a photo of himself and Craig Costello, the strangest friend he'd ever had, fondling one of the breast cream cones that adorned the walls. The gigantic plastic cones were filled with fleshy pink plastic ice cream, each scoop swirled into a half dozen voluptuously feminine mounds, every one tipped with a red nipplelike gumdrop.

"Well, Mr. Piper," Marlene commented between drags, "you look pleased with yourself. Just what are you thinking about?"

"Nothing. Just a little indigestion." He scooped Cody into his arms and crossed to the door, holding his breath against another exhalation of smoke. "We'll see you Monday, Mrs. Poom."

"Marlene, honey. Marlene." She held the door. "My goodness, when you call me 'Missus' it makes me feel like I'm fifty years old!"

Since she was at least sixty, Rick thought as they headed for the elevator, she ought to be happy.

"Daddy, what are we gonna do now?"

"We're going to find your sister, and she's going to help you take a bath while I make dinner," Rick said, stepping into the elevator.

"Why do I always have to take a bath when you get home?" Cody squirmed out of his arms. "I never used to have to."

"You never used to spend all day with Mrs. Poom. Her cigarettes make you smell bad."

"And they're bad for me, too. They eat my lungs. A man on TV said so."

"I know, buddy. I know." They exited at their floor, and Rick almost asked Cody what he'd think of living in California in a real town, a real house, with real flowers and trees.

What if he sees them? He stopped the thought. Stupid childhood fantasies. *Grow up, Piper! You were a psycho child!* "Where do you think your big sister is?" he asked.

"Lemme down." The boy squirmed to the floor and ran down the hall, coming to a stop in front of their neighbors' apartment. *"Shelly!"* he screeched, and began pounding furiously on the door.

Two apartments down, Don Mancuso opened his door and glared suspiciously out at them. Rick smiled and shrugged as he hissed at Cody to be quiet. Mancuso's frog face disappeared an instant before Lil Magill opened her door.

"Cody! Cody Piper! What're y'all doin' here?" She grabbed the boy and hugged him, muffling his delighted laugh between her breasts. "And there's yore cute li'l ol' daddy! Come on in, Ricky. Bet y'all are lookin' for Shelly. Well, she's on back there." She flicked her shiny red nails vaguely toward the bedroom. Garth Brooks wailed faintly through the closed door.

"Thank God," Rick said. At least she wasn't out roaming around with that pack of overripe future beauticians she called her friends.

"Y'all want me to call her or you wanna be sociable and come in for a few?" Lil asked.

As long as they weren't fighting, Dakota and Lil's antics almost always took care of his headaches. "I'll be sociable," he told her with a grin.

"Good." Lil Magill, all six feet two inches of her, stepped back to let him enter the apartment. A Moonbeam Nights dancer, she had an Amazonian body and copper hair—its color as fake as her Georgia peach accent—piled up to add another three inches to her height. Rick enjoyed her as long as she wasn't trying to seduce him. Lil could have virtually any man she wanted, but when the mood struck—generally after a couple drinks and the Sunday afternoon airing of "Consumer Crusader"—she wanted him.

It wasn't Sunday, but she reeked of alcohol, and Rick carefully kept his gaze above her breasts as he passed her. Whenever she wanted to embarrass him, she'd point out that they were just "kissing level" to his mouth.

"Hiya, Piper!" Dakota O'Keefe, Lil's roommate and Rick's best friend, strutted out of the kitchen, dressed in an apron, bra, and Jockey shorts. He held a potato peeler in one hand, and a drink in the other. Dakota, formerly Duane, worked for the Chambre du les Femmes show, and when he had his makeup on—he specialized in Marilyn and Madonna—he was as stunning as Lil, which shot the hell out of Rick's theory that show girls were all cloned on a ranch out in the desert somewhere, probably near a nuclear testing site.

"Here's your scotch, Lil. Last call. Remember, you have to go to work." He looked Rick up and down appraisingly. "Nice suit. It's a Blass, isn't it?"

"Uh, I don't know. Could be."

"Piper, dear, you're a TV star and you look—mmmmm." Dakota smacked his lips, doing the sweet transvestite from *The Rocky Horror Picture Show.* "You look good enough to . . . You look so good in your clothes, dear, you really ought to know who you're wearing," he finished, tousling Cody's hair.

"Thanks." Rick suppressed a smile. "So is my daughter making a pest of herself?"

"Nah. She's tryin' on clothes." Lil scooped Cody into her arms. "What else you think a teenage gal's gonna do?" Cody laughed gleefully as she rubbed noses with him. "You gotta let me help her pick out some new stuff, Ricky. She's got a real nice figure, an' she oughta be showin' it off."

"Magill! For Christ's sake, a father doesn't want his daughter showing off her figure!" Dakota frowned. "Honestly, Piper, all Lil thinks about is her body!"

"And *you* don't, Dakota?" Lil laughed. " 'I do think mah breasts are bigger than yours! I got more feminine hormones than you do, Magill. And ain't mah skin so soft and purty? Bet you all wish you had skin's nice as mine.' Jumpin' Jesus,

Dakota! Except for that big old dick of yours, you ain't nothin' but the vainest—"

"Magill, don't say 'dick' in front of Cody," Dakota admonished. "It's not nice!"

Clutching the squirming boy to her bosom, Lil shook her head. "Ah won't say 'dick' if you'll quit callin' everyone by their last names. God, I hate that, don't you hate that, Ricky?" She didn't wait for a reply. "Lord, ah'm gonna be late for work." She placed Cody in Rick's arms, then turned and planted a big kiss on Dakota's lips. "See you later, sweetie. You keep your hands off Ricky, ya hear?" She snatched her bag and keys from a hook by the door and exited in a flurry of perfume and hairspray.

"I'm sorry, Rick," Dakota said, locking the door. "Lil wouldn't watch her language in front of the pope." He crossed his arms, staring at the door. "I think it's about time for her annual vacation at Betty Ford," he added, embarrassed.

"Don't worry about it." Rick felt sorry for Dakota, who spent much of his time apologizing for his roommate's frequent scenes. He glanced toward the bedroom. Country music always gave him an inexplicable urge to throw his head back and howl like a coyote. "I'd better get Shelly."

"I'm hungry," Cody said.

"Look, why don't you stay for dinner? There's plenty." He glanced toward the door. "Lil wasn't supposed to work tonight, but one of the other gals called in sick."

"I wanna stay," Cody said, wiggling from Rick's grasp. "Can we, Daddy?"

"Please," Dakota said. "You'd be doing me a favor."

"Well . . ."

Dakota smiled. "You know you can't say no to me, Piper."

Certain the invitation was sincere, Rick grinned. "Sure. What's cookin', good-lookin'?"

"Coq au vin." Dakota, queen of the double entendre, cracked no smile.

"Sounds great."

Dakota nodded. "I hope so. Piper, we need to have a chat. Cody, you want to watch TV while your daddy and I get dinner ready?"

"Yeah!"

"Okay. You can go turn it on. You know how, right?"

"Yeah!" Cody ran across the room, grabbed the remote control, and plunked himself down on the floor in front of the set. An instant later, Roadrunner and Wile E. Coyote were vying with Garth Brooks for aural dominance. Somehow, Rick thought, that seemed appropriate.

The bedroom door opened and the singer drowned the cartoons.

"Turn that down, Shelly!" Dakota immediately yelled.

The sound went down, fractionally, then Shelly strutted out of the bedroom wearing one of Lil's gowns, a strappy, spangled, peach-colored piece of spandex that revealed enough skin to keep Cher happy. She'd piled her long golden hair high on her head and sprayed it with blue glitter that matched the eye shadow coating her lids. In one hand she held a mirror so she could admire herself, and she used the other to hike up the skirt. Except for the length, the gown appeared to fit perfectly. It made her look twenty-five or maybe even thirty-five years old. Obviously, Rick thought as his stomach turned to lead, she'd stuffed the bodice. Overstuffed it.

"Lil! What do you think?" Shelly asked, undulating closer, her eyes on the mirror.

Oh, God, maybe she hadn't stuffed the bodice, Rick thought as she neared. *My daughter looks like a stripper.* The lead sank deeper.

Dakota glanced at Rick, then cleared his throat. "Lil's not here, hon."

"Doesn't this look great, Dakota?" she chirped, never looking up from the mirror. "This dress makes my boobs look absolutely like double Ds! I'm going to go to Victoria's Secret tomorrow and buy a push-up bra. Man, it'll drive Starman nuts, and I bet I could get a really *good* job in a casino."

"Oh, my God." *Did I say that?* Rick thought he might have.

"Daddy!" Shelly screamed. "How *could* you!" Crossing her arms over her breasts, she turned and ran back into the bedroom, slamming the door behind her.

"How could I what?" Rick asked slowly. He felt like he'd been punched in the gut.

"Come on in the kitchen, Dad," Dakota said, pushing him ahead. "Time to talk."

"Who's Starman?"

"The rim job she's got a crush on. Sit." Dakota pointed at the dinette set in the corner of the small, neat room. Numb, Rick did as he was told.

"I've got to get these potatoes going before my coq gets too soft," Dakota informed him in his best breathy contralto.

O'Keefe smiled, and Rick realized he was trying to lighten things up, but it wasn't going to work, because his shock was transmogrifying into anger. "Did you *see* her?" he asked, trying hard to keep his voice steady.

"I saw her. Don't get too upset about the clothes, Rick. She's just doing what comes naturally."

Not trusting himself to speak, Rick stared dully at Dakota, at the apron declaring him to be a "Hot Dish."

"She's playing dress-up, Piper. All little girls like to play dress-up." He smirked. "So do some little boys."

"She's not little. She was falling out of that dress."

"Filling up, not falling out Look, Piper, big or little, we all like to try on clothes, so quit worrying about that. You've got bigger fish to fry."

"Starman?"

"Don't let the name fool you. He's just a bellboy at Bally's. I took a look. Not a brain in his head, just a penis on legs. Wants to be a rock 'n' roll star."

"That's supposed to make me feel better?" Rick closed his eyes. "Are they having sex?"

"I don't know."

"She's only sixteen."

"Oh, grow up. And open your eyes, Piper; you're giving

me the creeps. How old were you when you had sex for the first time?"

"That's different."

"Bullshit. How old were you?"

Rick resisted the urge to close his eyes again. "Fourteen . . . But I was a boy."

"So who'd you have it with, another fourteen-year-old boy? Or the family sheep, maybe?"

"Dakota—"

"You had it with a fourteen-year-old girl, right, Piper?" He chuckled obscenely. "Or maybe a thirteen-year-old girl, you cradle robber, you."

"If you want the truth, it was a seventeen-year-old girl."

"Whoa, Ricky!" Dakota poked him in the arm. "You seduced an older woman! I'm impressed."

"Well, no . . . She, ah, seduced me."

"I'm even more impressed." Dakota put two fingers under Rick's chin and forced him to look him in the eye. "The only thing you're worried about here is that your sixteen-year-old daughter might be having sex. Why? Because you did and because you know how guys think. But there's more to your problem with Shelly, and now that you've told me about your experience with the older girl, I think you know exactly what it is."

"I don't know what the hell you're talking about, O'Keefe."

Dakota snatched his fingers back and crossed his arms, studying Rick. "Yes, you do." He tapped his foot impatiently. "Your real problem is that Shelly is a lot like that seventeen-year-old who seduced you. She knows what she wants and she takes it."

He thought about that a moment, then nodded slowly. "You're right." He felt like giving up as he spoke the words. "You're absolutely right. Dakota, I can't control her anymore. She's too young, she's going to get into trouble. I wish I understood her as well as you do."

"You have all the answers, Piper, but you're too close. You can't see them for looking."

The kitchen door flew open and Shelly, dressed in jeans and a tight yellow tank top, glared at them. "I'm going out. I have a date."

Rick started to rise. "It's a school night. You can't—"

"A study date, Dad," she said in disgust. "At the library. I'll be home around eleven."

"Shelly—"

But she was gone before he could say more.

"Rick . . ."

Rick stared at the backs of his hands, his emotions furious and futile. "There must be some way to control her."

"Don't try to control her; you'll just make it worse. Try to guide her, without her knowing it. If you try to do the old laying-down-the-law routine, she'll go dead opposite. She's strong-willed as hell. Smart, too. She's feeling her oats right now." Dakota shook his head. "That's what I wanted to talk to you about. It's not boys or clothes you have to worry about. It's Shelly herself. She's too impatient for her own good. She wants it all—money, glamour, power. And you're right. She *is* going to get into trouble. I'm afraid Lil isn't helping much, either."

"What do you mean?"

"Oh, she's been introducing her to people, trying to help her get a job."

"In a casino," Rick said darkly.

"Not exactly. Shelly can't work in a casino. She can't be on the floor where drinks are served; you know that. The FBI checks for age of majority. Lil's trying to help her get a job in a show. She believes she's doing her a big favor. I've tried to stop her, but . . ." Dakota shrugged. "Lil's pretty strong-willed herself. She means well."

"Oh, shit. The stage. This is supposed to make me feel better?"

"Hell no, Piper. I just thought you should know what's going on."

"Oh, shit," Rick repeated. "This all ties in with something I wanted to talk to you about."

"What's that?"

"I'm considering getting out of Vegas," Rick began.

Dakota raised his eyebrows. "Really? What about your show?"

"KBUK wants me to renew—an extended contract—but I've been thinking that it would be good for the kids to live in a real house in a real world. I knew Shelly had an attitude, but I didn't realize how bad it's become. Her performance tonight pretty much made my decision for me."

"You're thinking of buying a house in the 'burbs?" Dakota sounded pleased. "Make sure you get one with a pool."

"Actually, I'm thinking of moving back to Southern California. Back to Santo Verde."

"Santo who?"

"Santo Verde. It's the town where I grew up."

The greenjacks'll getcha if you don't watch out!

"Get over here and help me with the potatoes." Dakota crooked his finger at Rick, then turned and walked to the sink. "I'll peel, you slice." He handed him the knife, then tossed a peeled potato his way. "Santo Verde, huh? As a recovering Cathaholic, I find the name fascinating. I wonder which saint it refers to. The Green Saint. Saint Patrick?"

"No, it refers to . . ." Rick paused, his stomach twisting into an old, familiar knot.

"Spit it out, Piper."

Greenjacks, Big Jack, they're gonna get you!

"Something more . . . primitive."

Dakota raised his eyebrows and waited.

"My great-great-grandfather founded the town, and the name has to do with an old family legend. Santo Verde is named for a nature god that some of the Piper clan can supposedly see."

"I love it," Dakota said, starting another potato. "Are you talking about Pan?"

Rick considered. "Something similar to Pan and his satyrs, yes. The Pipers called them greenjacks."

"That's *so* romantic, Piper." Dakota paused. "Your family's from Scotland, correct?"

"Yeah."

"So why Santo Verde? Why not McPan or McJack or something?"

Rick chuckled, despite himself. "Conlin Piper used the Spanish words because he had moved to the Southwest and because he loved Mexico. He thought it was more appropriate." Rick laughed again. "Actually, 'Santo' is Italian, but he wasn't too far off."

Dakota nodded. "So what exactly is a greenjack? Does it have hooves and horns?"

This is your chance to talk about this stuff like an adult, Piper. Don't blow it! "Nothing like that," Rick said lightly. "They're more like trolls or fairies, They aren't material, except on Halloween night, when they get together and build *the* Big Jack. They build it out of twigs and branches and leaves, and Big Jack can grab you and take you away until midnight, November first." He smiled nonchalantly, hoping Dakota wouldn't notice that his hands were trembling. "At least that's how Grandfather always told the tale."

"I guess it's true what they say about you Scotsmen being mystical," Dakota told him. "That's a marvelous story. I guess Big Jack's a lot like the Green Man in England."

Rick rooked at him in surprise. "Yeah."

"I remember him, then."

"You do?" he asked, the skin on the back of his neck prickling up.

"When I was little we went to the Met in Central Park all the time, and I'd spend hours looking at those English hunt tapestries, you know? I loved them because they were puzzles. If you looked hard enough, you'd see the Green Man somewhere in the art. He was hard to spot because he always had leaves growing out of his mouth and he'd be peeking out from between the trees." Dakota laughed. "I guess it was the medieval version of *Where's Waldo?*"

Icky Ricky, come out and play, hey, play.

Rick shivered as the familiar voice played through his mind.

"Piper, what's wrong?"

"We're digging up old memories, O'Keefe. Ones I'd just as soon leave buried."

"For Christ's sake, Rick, don't tell me you were afraid of the Green Man?" Dakota looked incredulous. "He was into sex and orgies and all the finer things in life."

"I was terrified," he confessed. "I grew up on a steady diet of those stories, and the ones my grandfather told weren't about sex, they were about stealing the bodies of little boys. I took them very seriously." He tried to laugh but it was a sick sound. "I was an overly sensitive child."

Your body, Ricky, give us your body . . .

"Body theft," Dakota mused. "Every time my aunt Irene visited us—she was from Ireland—she told stories about the fairies and leprechauns. They'd take a human child and leave one of their own in its place. There was a name for it—"

"A changeling," Rick supplied, glad that Dakota knew so much. It was just too juvenile and ridiculous to explain in detail.

"Yeah, that's it," Dakota agreed. "Maybe you can answer a question for me, Piper."

"I'll try."

"What I always wondered when Irene told those stories was *why. Why* would these incredibly nifty beings want anything to do with humans when they were so free the way they were? That just never made any sense to me."

Rick smiled wanly. "Without physical bodies, they can't feel or taste or smell—"

"Or have orgasms?" Dakota smirked.

"Or have orgasms," Rick agreed. "They want sensation, like we have. The grass is always greener, you know?"

"Okay. Go on."

"I don't know about all the other tales, but in the Piper clan stories, anyone's body would do in a pinch, but what the greenjacks really wanted was the body of a person who had the sight. The ability to see and hear them."

"Why?"

"Grandfather claimed it was because they got very lonely if they couldn't communicate with their own kind."

"That makes sense," Dakota said. "So, Piper, did you ever see any of the little devils?"

Rick's cheeks grew hot. "I—I thought I did," he stammered. "But I had an overactive imagination when I was a kid."

"You don't sound like you're very eager to move back to the old hometown. Why not go somewhere else? Or do you have family there or something?"

"A senile aunt, but she's not the reason for going back. I own the family estate."

"Estate? You're rich? Piper, you devil, you never told me—"

"I'm not rich. The family money that my parents left for maintaining the place is about gone. It's more a matter of cutting expenses, if you want the truth. The place is an estate more because of the size of the property than because of the house. It's big, but . . ."

"So sell it."

"I've thought about it, but with the market so soft, if it sold at all, it wouldn't draw anywhere near what it's worth."

"So where's Santo Verde?" O'Keefe asked, evidently oblivious to the tremble Rick heard in his own voice.

"It's in San Bernardino County, maybe fifty or sixty miles east of Los Angeles."

"Nightlife?"

"Not that I know of."

"Sounds boring."

"It's a little bourgeois, but it's nice." He paused. "Well, the Piper house isn't bourgeois. It's decidedly weird. Conlin built what he liked, so it's sort of part Carpenter Gothic and part Spanish hacienda. It has Victorian cabinetry and Spanish wrought iron. Some of the doors are arched, some are square. There're even a couple stained-glass windows." He chuckled. "Calling it 'eclectic' wouldn't begin to describe it. Oh, yeah, it's full of secret passages."

"I *have* to see this place."

"If I pack up and go, you're more than welcome," Rick told him. "Its only about four hours from here, but it's very different. It's citrus country, nestled in right up against the mountains. In the thirties and forties a lot of the movie stars used to live out there. It's scenic. *Very* scenic." His stomach twisted as he heard himself add, "It's the greenest place you'll ever see."

"Dakota?" The door opened and Cody peered in. "Is dinner almost ready?"

"Another half hour. Why don't you take a banana and watch another cartoon show?"

"Okay." The boy reached up and took a piece of fruit, then disappeared back into the living room.

Dakota turned back to Rick. "So this house you own is the same one that you grew up in?"

"The very same."

"So how come you've never mentioned it before?"

"There are some bad memories . . ."

The greenjacks'll getcha if you don't watch out.

"How do you mean, 'bad'?"

"Oh, you know, goofy stuff mostly. Kid stuff." *Boy, does that sound stupid!* His hand trembled as he sliced a potato.

"Goofy? Kid stuff'?" Dakota stopped peeling to stare at him. "Come on, Rick. You think I can't see that this 'goofy kid stuff' is eating you up? It's why you've never gone back, isn't it?"

Rick said nothing.

"No more bullshit, Piper, dear. What's the real story?"

"There's nothing else, Dakota, really. The place is a little run-down," he added quickly. "At least that's what my lawyer says, but it's solid. It's in the best part of town, and the schools are excellent, but . . ."

Ricky, icky Ricky, Ricky, icky Ricky.

"If it's so great, then what the hell are you raising kids in this hellhole for? Gambling, drinking, drugs, hookers . . . *Mormons,* for Christ's sake . . ."

Icky Ricky, I'm gonna getcha, Icky Ricky.

"Rick! Watch out!"

Startled, Rick jumped, dropping the knife. It clattered into the sink.

"Jesus Christ, Piper! Let me see that."

Rick recoiled as Dakota's water-cold hand grabbed his left wrist.

The potatoes he'd sliced into the colander were turning red. He watched bright blood splash into the white sink as Dakota pulled Rick's arm toward him.

"You're bleeding like a sieve." O'Keefe pulled a wad of paper towels from the holder and wrapped them around Rick's fingers. "Jesus, I can't even see which finger you cut. Piper, you're as white as a baby's butt. Are you okay?"

"Not one of my smoother moves," Rick said as he took charge of his hand, pressing on the towels to stop the bleeding. It was starting to hurt.

"Are you okay?" Dakota repeated.

"Fine. Got any Band-Aids?"

"Just a sec. Let me rinse the blood off these potatoes before it soaks in or something. What Cody doesn't know won't hurt him. Keep hanging on to those towels."

Rick almost smiled. Dakota was nothing if not practical. He loosened the pressure, but the artery was still pumping. He tightened up again, feeling a little dizzy.

"You're shocky. Sit down," Dakota ordered as he left the room. A moment later, he was back with a box of adhesive bandages and a bottle of iodine.

Carefully Rick unwrapped the hand, and everything south of his abdomen tried to climb to visceral safety as the pad of his middle finger, nearly severed, started to come away with the towels. Gingerly he loosened it and let it fall back over the wound.

"You need stitches," Dakota said.

"No, I don't," Rick answered.

"If that finger was your throat, you'd be dead."

Rick snorted. "Don't be so dramatic, O'Keefe. It's not my throat."

"Well, it's gaping. What are you planning to do? Staple it shut?"

"That's a thought," he said, trying to ignore the throbbing. "But let's try a Band-Aid first."

"You need stitches. The fucking thing is positively grinning at me."

"It's cut on the bias," Rick said, keeping his voice light. "All I need to do is tape it down. It'll glue naturally." It was everything he could do to control his trembling. "The Band-Aid, please?"

"Suit yourself." Dakota shrugged and unwrapped several bandages. Wearing a disgusted expression, he handed over one, then another, his lip curling as he watched Rick tape his flesh back together.

"I can't believe you did that yourself," he said as Rick finished. "I'd pass out. Shit. You forgot the iodine. We'd better—"

"No. I don't need it. I bled out all the impurities."

"What? Have you got a death wish? If it gets infected—"

"I don't get infections," Rick said lightly. "I have the constitution of an entire bottle of antibiotics."

"Piper, you are acting extremely weird. What are you, afraid of doctors?"

Quit 'cher fuckin' cryin' boy, and take your whippin' like a man! a new voice screamed in his ear. Dear God, how could he have forgotten about Uncle Howard? His head spun as he wondered what else he'd forgotten.

"Piper, you need stitches, so quit your macho man act!" Dakota stood up. "Come on. I'll get Cody and we'll run down to the emergency room—"

"Lay off, already!" Rick barked. "I cut my fucking finger, big fucking deal. I'll live."

His harsh words made Dakota flinch as if he'd been slapped. Instantly Rick felt terrible.

"Sorry," Rick muttered. "I didn't mean—"

"Mellow out, Rick," Dakota interrupted. "I've never even heard you say 'fuck' before, and now you say it twice in one breath. Just a wild guess, hon, but I'd say something's wrong."

Get out of my face! he wanted to scream. Instead, he spoke casually. "Nothing's wrong. It was just a stupid accident." God, it hurt so bad, he could hardly stop clenching his teeth to talk. The only thing worse than the pain was the humiliation.

"If I cut myself like that, I'd be squalling so bad, my face would be puffy for a week, and I'd be getting stitches and pain pills. Look at you, pretending it doesn't even hurt."

Rick said nothing. It took every ounce of control not to scream at Dakota to shut the hell up or to humiliate himself by admitting it hurt.

Crybaby, titty mouse, Ricky got a whipping! I'm gonna tell Uncle Howard, and then you'll get another! Crybaby, titty mouse.

"Rick!"

"What?"

"Here! Take these!"

Dakota stood in front of him holding aspirin tablets and a glass of water. Rick hadn't even realized he'd moved.

"Thanks."

"You're welcome." Dakota went back across the room and took a bottle of wine and two glasses from a shelf. "Merlot, Cypress. A ninety-nine. I hid it from Lil. She wouldn't appreciate it." He uncorked the bottle and poured, handed a glass to Rick.

"Thanks again."

"Welcome again. So what's eating you? When you cut yourself we were talking about Santo Verde. You said you have bad memories. They must be doozies."

If you tell, they'll take you away, away, the little men in their white coats will come and take you away, away, away.

Old memories, presumed dead, old voices, *his* voice, came alive in his head. "No, not especially, but I hadn't thought about all those stories my grandfather used to tell in years." Rick sipped the wine, then downed half the glass at once. "Going back to Santo Verde is sort of like going to the dentist to get a bad tooth pulled. You don't want to do it, so you put it off, hoping it'll get better. Maybe it seems like it does, sometimes, but it only gets worse and worse until you take care of it, once and for all. Refill, please?"

"You're intriguing the hell out of me, you mysterious

man." Dakota refilled Rick's glass, then topped off his own. He sniffed the wine. "It has a good kick, not to mention the nice bouquet. And the afterbirth is purely delightful." Suddenly he nailed Rick with a look. "So what was your grandfather, a sadist?"

Rick laughed, his stomach already warm. "No, he was great. He was sort of stuffy like the professor in 'The Paper Chase,' but he was full of the devil, too. My problem was that I was overly impressionable and ridiculously sensitive. My brother wasn't and, oh, I don't know . . ." Rick swallowed hard. *My brother.* He'd said it aloud.

"I didn't know you had a brother."

"His name was Robin." Rick had never told anyone even this much about his past, but suddenly, almost against his will, it came bubbling out. "I was an easy target for Robin. He was . . . precocious and spent a lot of time feeding my fears, telling me that the jacks would steal my body while I was asleep, things like that. He liked to tease."

"He sounds cruel."

"Little kids are always crueL" He drained another half glass in one fell swoop; then laughed uneasily. He paused while Dakota crossed the room, stirred the potatoes, then withdrew a fresh bottle of wine from the back of the cupboard and opened it. "Want to smell my cork?" he asked as he returned to the table.

Rick smiled and waited for his refill. He already felt a little smashed, a little better.

"Tell me more." Dakota's gaze was frank. "Did you hate your brother?"

"Christ, O'Keefe. What kind of question is that? How could I hate my own brother?" The wine went down like water. "I sure got pissed at him. One Halloween Robin pulled this joke on me. He made me think the greenjacks had taken him."

"How do you mean, 'taken him'?"

"He pretended to have a new personality—like a jack had possessed his body. And I, idiot that I was, believed it and thought I was next. Isn't that stupid?"

"It's not stupid," Dakota said. "Could your brother see these things?"

"No." He finished another glass and swallowed hard. "But I thought I could," he confessed. "I was the only psycho."

"Don't get maudlin on me, Piper. It's a waste of good wine. So are you still afraid? Is that why you haven't gone back?"

If you tell, they'll lock you up and throw away the key.

"Oh, maybe a little." Rick smiled to imply that he was joking. His whole body was warm now, and the finger had stopped hurting. "It's a lot more than that. My parents died, and the Wicked Witch of the West and her alcoholic husband came to take care of us. I guess I mixed the greenjack stuff into everything else that happened, and it's all left a bad taste in my mouth."

"Both your parents died?"

Rick nodded.

"An accident?"

"Shit, you're nosy, you know that?"

O'Keefe smiled smugly. "Sorry. If you don't want—"

"They were murdered."

"God, I'm sorry. I didn't realize—"

"It's okay. You couldn't know."

"What about your brother? Do you two get along now?"

"He died, too. An accident." Rick realized he'd hit another hole in his memory. "Anyway, not too long after that, I moved here and enrolled in UNLV. I've never gone back."

"I'll bet you felt guilty as hell for hating your brother, then having him die and all."

"I told you, I didn't hate him."

"Of course you did. Maybe you loved him, too, or maybe you didn't, but you *had* to hate him for scaring you. I would've hated him. It's perfectly natural."

If he hadn't been drunk, Rick would have been furious over Dakota's words, but the wine allowed him to see their truth. "Dakota, you're either horrible or wonderful, I can't decide which. How can you be so fucking blunt about things like that?"

"I almost succeeded in killing myself once. After that, it was either finish the job or face my problems head-on. I couldn't live with the lies anymore. It hurt too much." Dakota patted Rick's uninjured hand affectionately. "You're developing quite a gutter mouth, Piper. I'm proud of you. Now, tell me about your brother. I take it he was older than you?"

"No." He paused. "Well, strictly speaking, yes. By five minutes. Robin was my identical twin. Well, almost identical."

"Different personalities, obviously."

Rick nodded. "Also, Robin was handicapped. He was born without legs."

"My God, you must have been terrified before your kids were born!"

"No, it wasn't inherited. It was a fluke, a condition called Streeter's dysplasia, where part of the fetus gets cut off from—"

"That's enough," Dakota interrupted, "If you say more, I'm going to toss my cookies."

"Sorry. The point is, I think that my having legs may have made him a little antagonistic toward me." He was mortified to hear himself let loose with a stupid drunken giggle.

"Piper, dear, you have a gift for understatement. He probably *hated* your guts because you had the utter audacity to have legs." He paused. *"I* would have."

Infinitesimally, the weight in his chest lifted. "You *really* think so?"

"Shit, Piper, you think you're the only person capable of petty thoughts? Hell no. Wanting something someone else has is how wars are started. Of course he hated you. I hated my big sister because she had breasts." He ran his hand over his torso and grinned. "I'm over it now, of course, because mine are bigger than hers."

"You hated your sister because she had breasts?" Now, *this* was interesting. "Honest to God?"

"Yeah, I really did. I was horribly jealous because she had what I wanted—a female body. I didn't really understand it at the time. It took a couple years with a good therapist before I got what was going on. Piper, that's what you ought to do. See a therapist. I know a great one in California. He moved there a couple years ago. I can give you his number"

They'll lock you up and throw away the key key key.

"Thanks. I'll get the name if I think I need it."

Dakota nodded. "Do you know where Sylvan Heights is?"

Rick looked up, surprised. "Yeah. It's not far from Santo Verde, but I don't care how close this guy is, I'm not interested in—"

"No, no, no. I didn't know exactly where it was. My sister just moved there."

"The one with the breasts?"

"Watch it, Piper. She might be able to help you."

Rick made a face. "I don't need any help."

"She's an optometrist." Dakota wiped his lips and cocked his head. "I was just thinking—maybe you did see something weird when you were a kid. You ever get your eyes examined?"

"Two months ago. Healthy, normal, twenty-twenty."

"Still, if you told her about it, she might be able to tell you something."

"Dakota, if you tell her—or anybody—one word of this, I'll—"

"Your secret's safe with me. You won't have any trouble, anyway," he added. "You've found an outlet for your imagination with those crazy columns of yours. You'll be fine—I guess I was just looking for an excuse to have you and Audrey meet."

"I don't—"

"She's just your type, Piper. Divorced, barely fills an A cup, five foot three, HIV negative, and disgustingly well read." Dakota grinned. "Want her number?"

"I haven't even decided to move for sure. Don't try to fix me up yet!"

Dakota topped their glasses. "You'd like her."

Rick snorted into his wine. "Jesus, O'Keefe, brothers are supposed to beat up guys who try to screw their sisters."

"Shit, Piper, I didn't say you could screw her. You know, you're becoming positively vulgar? I said you should meet her." Dakota set his glass down and examined his lacquered red nails, a Mona Lisa of a smirk plastered on his face. "I've done that."

"Done what?"

"Punched out a guy who messed with my sister. I pack quite a powerful left hook, you know."

Rick grinned in amazement. "An obnoxious boyfriend?"

"Her husband."

"Why?"

"He beat her up, the son of a bitch." He took a deep breath, then exhaled, relaxing until the pinched look left his features. "Look, enough about that cretinous puddle of scum. I've got to whip these potatoes before they turn to mush. I'm positively starving."

"You want any help?"

"Thanks, no." Pans clattered as Dakota fussed around the stove. "You know," he called, over his shoulder, "you'll probably have trouble with Shelly about this, but it'll work out eventually."

"O'Keefe?"

"Hmmm?" he asked, stirring gravy.

"That guy, Starman, that bellboy Shelly likes? You checked him out?" he asked guiltily. He hadn't even known the guy existed.

"Took a look, asked some questions. I was afraid he might have, you know, connections . . . to certain unsavory organizations. He doesn't." Dakota glanced over his shoulder. "You're feeling like you're the world's worst father, aren't you, Piper? Well, don't. Shelly's an adolescent, which automatically means she's not going to tell you squat. Sometimes she confides in me a little."

"Why you and not me?"

"Because you're her father. Piper, plug in your brain. You were a kid once What teenager tells their parents *anything?*"

Dakota smiled and put a hand on his hip. "She talks to me because I'm sort of a big brother to her . . . and big sister."

"You're right again." Rick stared at Dakota. He wore no makeup, but his face—its features strong in a woman, delicate in a man—were disturbingly beautiful, genderless in the way of the faces of angels in some Renaissance paintings. Rick thought: *Boy, am I drunk.*

"What're you smiling about, Piper?"

"Thanks for looking out for my daughter, Dakota. You're an angel."

"Thanks. You know, Cody's going to absolutely be in heaven if you do this."

"I hope so," Rick replied, thinking about his son's Piper blue eyes.

8

Rick's stomach held an ocean of aspirin, and he was feeling a little seasick. Between his efforts to ease the dull headache, relax his tense neck muscles, and kill the throbbing pain in his hand, he'd taken too many pills. Now, lying on his back at four in the morning, watching the lights from the Strip splash their gaudy reflections against the bedroom window, aware of the warm weight of the cat, who had plastered his furry orange body against his side, Rick reached for the antacids and tumbled out the last two. The bottle had been half-full when he'd gone to bed.

Quint's tail beat angrily against his leg as he crunched the Tums—the feline considered such noises beneath contempt but the thrashing gave way to basso profundo purring as soon as he began scratching behind its ears. The cat, he reflected, had trained him well.

A car alarm began wailing somewhere below. He listened briefly to make sure it wasn't his, then turned his thoughts to the evening and wondered again if it had been worth the physical discomfort he now felt. He decided that maybe it had, in a sort of roundabout, somewhat humiliating, way.

At some point during the long, blurred postdinner conversation, Dakota had called him a control freak. Rick had laughed to hide his annoyance, but now he admitted to himself that O'Keefe was right. He'd never opened up, even as much as he did tonight—but then he'd never gotten so drunk either, not even in college. He never let himself, for fear of . . . for fear of what? Losing control, of course. Tonight's reaction to the liquor had been decidedly weird. He wasn't a teetotaler; he'd split a couple bottles of wine with friends any number of times, and usually it just relaxed him a little and made him sleepy. But tonight . . . tonight, probably because of the stress and moronic finger slicing, he'd slobbered sentimental gratitude on Dakota and, as a result, wasn't sure he'd ever be able to look him in the eye again, despite the fact that Dakota insisted he'd done nothing to be ashamed of.

Voices, a man and a woman arguing, passed by, and a moment later, a door slammed farther down the hall. It was never quiet here. Rick wondered if he could sleep in a place without voices and horns and sirens. And lights. *Grow up, Piper.*

He smiled to himself, remembering that he'd told Dakota stories about Aunt Jade's poodles. He hadn't thought of them in years—in fact, he'd forgotten about them until the moment he'd brought them up.

Remembering the dogs had been an eye-opener for him. He'd never seen the humor in them before. If most of the things he'd blocked were as stupid and innocuous as that, then the move home would be a very good thing for him as well as for his kids.

Then again, maybe Dakota was full of shit. Still, it was the first time he'd ever told anyone about his brother. Too, he was glad he'd talked about the dogs. Later, he'd even made a few jokes about Jade's bizarre sexual proclivities, and he was perversely pleased with himself for making fun of a territory so long self-forbidden. The words had tumbled out, nasty little nuances seduced by a nice red wine. And he'd loved it, absolutely loved it, and only wished he'd done it sooner. The wicked delight he had felt—and was still feeling—was as exciting as an altar boy's first forbidden peek in a *Playboy.*

All in all, he couldn't remember when he'd had a better time, throbbing hand and all.

"What a miserable little kid I was," he told the cat as he scratched behind its ears. "I never laughed." God, he'd been a serious, oversensitive little—

Gonna cut your legs off icky Ricky.

"Be quiet!" he whispered. Acid, hot and burning, seeped into his throat. The unbidden words, as always, delivered in his brother's voice, were nothing but symptoms of his own oversensitivity. He knew that most kids would have laughed off the nasty things his brother said. Most kids—like his brother, for instance—would have delighted in his grandfather's greenjack stories, but not Rick. Sometimes he hated himself for being who he'd been: a cowardly, overly imaginative child who grew up afraid of everything and haunted by untrustworthy memories. Perhaps now, things would begin to change.

For all he knew now, Robin might have been a wonderful kid. Rick's memories of his childhood were deformed, his imagination twisted. If he could imagine seeing and hearing greenjacks, for Christ's sake, certainly he could imagine things about his brother that weren't true. But why? Maybe Dakota was right. Maybe he should talk to someone.

If you tell, they'll take you away, they'll think you're crazy, crazy, crazy.

The headache beat against his skull. What did he have to tell, anyway?

Secrets.

Telling O'Keefe about Jade was a joke when compared to the *real* secrets. There were things about Robin and about Carmen—perhaps even about himself—that were too terrible to ever recall. He hoped that seeing Carmen and Hector wouldn't bring any of them back—he doubted that it would. They were purposely buried far in the past.

Secrets.

About death. About murder.

Silent tears blazed trails from the outer corners of his eyes to the pillow beneath his head. How much was real? Any of it? All of it? How much was imagination born of guilt? Maybe Dakota was right, maybe he did hate his brother, even though he had no right to. *After all,* he reminded himself, *I was born with legs.*

If you tell, if you tell, if you tell . . .

His brother's voice, always his brother's voice. He wondered if he would ever be free of it.

No, he thought, as his eyelids grew heavy. *Because it's your voice too.*

9

"Ricky? Ricky, is that really you?" said the voice on the telephone.

"Yes, it's really me." Rick stood at his bedroom window or his office window, depending on the time of day—and squinted into the afternoon glare. After a moment, he turned the wand controlling the heavy vertical blinds and watched the slats of sunlight grow narrower and narrower. "It's been a long time, Carmen." This morning he'd told the boys at KBUK he was leaving the show, and now there was no backing out. He had a stomach full of butterflies as he sat down in his chair, leaned back, and put his feet on the desktop.

"Say something so I know it's you," Carmen ordered.

"What? Why?" Her request made him nervous. When Robin was alive, there had been good reason, but now . . .

"Please."

"Is something wrong?"

"No. No. Just tell me something only you could know."

"Okay." He smiled to himself as a memory came. "You and I shaved Jade's poodle after it crapped on the couch. You told her the vet did it because it had lice."

"Ricky, it's so good to hear your voice."

"Carmen, why did we have to do that?"

She hesitated before she answered. "I'm getting to be a

superstitious old woman, Ricky. I'm scared of ghosts, that's all. Mr. McCall told me you'd be phoning. How are you?"

"I'm fine." *She's afraid I'm Robin, back from the dead,* he realized. Had she always been so superstitious? Yes, maybe she had. Perhaps this woman, the only person he trusted after his parents were killed, had unwittingly helped him become the nervous wreck he was today. "I have kids," he added.

"Kids? More than one?"

She knew about Shelly. He'd sent her a Christmas card the year his daughter was born, but he was pretty sure that was the last time he'd been in contact with her. "I have a son, too. Cody. He's five."

"How is your wife, Laura?"

"She died four years ago."

"Oh, Ricky, I'm sorry."

"Me too," he said simply. "Carmen? Did George tell you why I'm calling?"

"Yes, Ricky. You're coming home. Hector and I are so happy!"

"I'm glad," he said uncomfortably. "Uh, Carmen, what's the situation with Jade? Is she as eccentric as ever?"

"Madre de Dios, that woman. She's still crazy, and she's still got those stinking little dogs."

As her poodles had died—they seemed to meet with more accidents than anything else on earth—she had had each one stuffed. By the time Rick had left for Las Vegas, there must have been more than a dozen of them holding their various eternal positions around the house. "Does she have a living one now?" Rick asked.

"Two," Carmen said sourly.

"That's too bad," he said, thinking that Quint would have a great time terrorizing the creatures.

"You're telling me." Carmen paused. "Miz Jade's getting a little senile, too. She's supposed to keep those damn stuffed dogs in her apartment, but I keep finding them all over the house. She claims she isn't responsible." She snorted. "She's never been responsible, that one. Butter wouldn't melt in her mouth, and she's crazy as a loon."

"Apartment?" Rick asked hopefully. "Do you mean she's living in the cottage now?"

"No. We still live there. Miz Jade doesn't climb the stairs so well anymore. Remember how the downstairs is built in a circle, you know, the kitchen, dining room, living room, and then you go through the wide archway into the family room, past the bathroom and laundry room, and back into the kitchen, right by the back stairs?"

"I remember."

"Hector put folding doors on the arch between the living room and family room, and another door between the bathroom and laundry room so that your aunt has her own apartment. Remember that little room at the back of the family room?"

"Mom's sewing room?"

"Yeah. That's her bedroom."

The idea of having that woman and her dogs so close was revolting. "Carmen, how would you and Hector like to live in the main house? We can put Jade in the cottage."

"No, Ricky. She'd have a fit, and I don't think I can live in that big house. I'm sorry."

"I understand," he told her, deciding not to pursue it any further until he saw what conditions were like for himself. Chances were, he'd have the horrid old woman put in a rest home. "Carmen? Can you do me a favor?"

"You name it, Ricky."

"If I can tell you exactly when we're arriving, could you make sure Aunt Jade isn't home? Keep her away for a few hours?"

Carmen's laugh was hearty. "Sure. Are you afraid she'll scare your children?"

He smiled. Carmen always knew him so well. "Cody can probably handle her," he said, thinking of his unflinching acceptance of Mrs. Poom, "but my daughter . . . well, I want her to see the place first. She's very unhappy about leaving her friends."

"I understand. I think that's a good idea."

They talked awhile longer, making plans and arrangements. Finally Carmen announced that she would take Jade to the Melrose District in L.A., let her get her hair done, then turn her loose in the Poodle Peddler, an overpriced purveyor of useless doggie products. All he had to do was give her the high sign.

Hanging up, Rick realized his butterflies were gone and that he honestly felt good about the plans he was making. He'd thought about it for a week after the binge with Dakota, then called George McCall and told Cody and Shelly. Shelly had a temper tantrum and threatened to run away, but fortunately she ran in Dakota's direction, and he extolled the virtues of California boys, or something along those lines. At least that had turned her from teenage histrionics to accusatory glares and calm, sullen acceptance.

He'd leave the childhood fears behind and concentrate on learning to be a homeowner. His only problems would be those of the real world. He'd get a couple years worth of columns out of it, on everything from putty knives to paint to lawn sprinklers. And if Jade was too weird, he could afford to put her in a retirement home, or even rent her a small house and caretaker. He leaned back in the desk chair and put his feet up. Twining his fingers into a pillow for his head, he felt that he'd done the right thing.

He just wished the goose bumps would go away.

10

"No! I won't have it!" A queen on her throne, Jade Ewebean stomped her foot so hard that the two white poodles at her feet yelped and shook in doggy terror. "If he thinks he can just move in here like he owns the place, then he's very mistaken. This is *my* house. *I* live here!" She looked down, saw the poodles watching her, and instantly her expression metamorphosed from beetle-browed fury to sappy adoration.

She patted her lap. "Come here, my widdle wuvems. Come here, Mister Poo; you, too, Stinkums." The poodles danced on their hind legs, each pawing at one knee. "Oh, what sweet wittle poodley-pies." The dogs went nuts with joy as she scooped them into her bony lap. "Is you my babies? Is you? Oh yes, you is! Kiss mama now! Kiss mama!"

Eagerly they licked their mistress's withered, rouge-stained cheeks while Jade giggled and cooed like the nasty old lady that she was. Carmen Zapata felt the urge to puke as she watched the disgusting display.

She disliked the dogs almost as much as she despised Jade Ewebean herself. It had been bad enough back when Jade had kept only one dog, but for the last two decades, it had been double the puddles, double the crap, and double the whining and yapping. In a way, Carmen didn't blame

her: The animals died so regularly that the old *puta* almost
needed a spare.

Dios Mio, but she hated coming into Jade's quarters. It
smelled of moldy poodle fur and old-lady sweat, and it made
Carmen sick to see all those horrible dead dogs. All of them
were some shade of white, ranging from ancient yellow to
moth-eaten gray. One, its fur slowly tearing away in hideous
clumps, reclined on top of the old Zenith TV, its glass eyes
catching and reflecting the light cast by the lamp on the
table by Jade's padded rocking chair. Carmen didn't remember its name any more than she remembered the names of
two dozen other dead dogs that filled the apartment, but
Jade knew all of them. Carmen suspected she identified
them by the "lifelike" poses the taxidermist had tortured
them into for all eternity. It was a sin against God.

The woman went through more poodles than ever should
have been allowed into the world to begin with. They all
died in strange accidents, and Carmen held the secret belief
that crazy old Jade did them in when the mood struck, then
forgot all about it. The last death, a little less than six months
ago, nearly proved it. The dog had peed all over Jade's bedspread only hours before Carmen had opened the dryer and
found its stiff, dead body, along with half a roll of fabric
softener sheets.

Horrified, she'd put the carcass in a garbage bag outside
the back door, intending to have Hector dispose of it, but
before long she saw Jade handing it over to the kid from
Seymour Taxidermy. A month later, the creature reappeared,
its leg in an eternal lift. When Jade was mad at her, Carmen
would find it poised over the pair of slippers she kept by
the back kitchen door. Normally, though, the old woman
liked to have it stand over a bowl of dusty silk philodendrons
she had in her bathroom.

Tired of listening to Jade's incessant baby talk, Carmen
cleared her throat. "We have to talk about Ricky and his
family," she said sternly.

"It's my house." She sniffed. "Richard wasn't nice to his
aunt Jade, so he can't visit. You can tell him that for me."

"Listen, Mrs. Ewebean, this isn't your house. It belongs to Ricky. He's just been kind enough to let you live here, so if you want to stay, you better treat him nice. Otherwise *he'll* send *you* away." Saying those last words felt so good that Carmen had to bite her tongue to keep from listing off all the reasons Ricky might kick her out. "Do you understand what I'm saying?"

"Ooh, Mister Poo is kissing his mommy, yes he is!" She kissed the dog back, square on the muzzle, then put her nose against the other one's face. "Stinkums, Stinkums, Stinkums, that's your name, uh-huh, yes it is. And do you know why, Stinkum-winkum, do you know why? Because you used to poot so bad when you was just a wittle bitty boy. Cute wittle puppy poots, that was you."

Carmen crossed her arms, thoroughly sick of the senile old crone. *Why don't you die? Put me out of your misery!* "Jade Ewebean!"

That got the *puta*'s attention. Her nostrils flared and her watery green eyes flashed as she glared at Carmen, her hands stiff in the poodles' fur. "How dare you talk to me in that tone of voice!"

Carmen stepped forward until she was looming over Jade, her stare so fierce that the old bitch didn't say a word. "Now, you listen good, because I'm only gonna tell you this once more. This house is Ricky's. If you're not nice to him, he'll send you away, and I'll say good riddance."

"Well, I nev—"

"Be quiet." Madre de Dios, *help me. before I strangle her with my bare hands!* "Listen. He's gonna have his two kids with him. His teenage daughter is going to be sad about leaving her friends, and his little boy is gonna feel lost in this big old house. So you're gonna be just as nice to them as you are to Ricky." She paused, savoring the bomb she was about to drop. "And you're gonna be nice to his cat, too."

Jade's nose curled as if she were smelling something bad. "Cat?" She stood, sending squealing poodles tumbling to the floor. "Cat?" Her voice rose an octave.

Carmen smiled like the Madonna herself. "A nice cat," she said serenely. "Maybe it will catch some of the mice we got running around in the walls."

"He can't bring a cat in here. Who does he think he is?" Jade sputtered with anger, little flecks of foam at the sides of her mouth.

"He's your landlord, that's who he is, and if those nasty little dogs of yours chase that cat even once, you'll be very, *very* sorry." Placing her hands on her hips, she added, "I always protected Ricky from you, and now I'm gonna protect his whole family from you. And that includes his cat."

"He can't—"

"Yes he can. He can do whatever he wants, and you better give him some respect. You remember how you treated him? Always teasing him, always making fun of him? Punishing him for being afraid? You remember that, *Tia Puta?*" Carmen felt like she might be foaming a little herself. She'd held this back for years, and now it poured out like water. "You remember how mean you were to him? Well, you better hope he's nicer to you than you were to him."

"Get out," Jade said without much fire. "Get out."

Carmen turned on her heel and walked through the archway into the living room, then pulled the triple-fold birch doors closed behind her.

She moved quickly through the dining room, pausing to flick a speck of dust from a blue vase in the center of the table. Tomorrow, before Ricky's arrival, she'd fill it with giant marigolds from the garden, his favorite flower ever since she'd explained to him that in Mexico, people believed that the flower could keep them safe on *El Día de los Muertos,* when spirits roamed the world. "Ricky." She whispered the name with fondness and dread, and wondered how he'd changed over the years.

In the kitchen, Carmen poured herself a cup of coffee and sat heavily at the kitchen table, her thoughts turning back to Jade Ewebean. It had been a month since she'd told Jade about Ricky coming home, but the old woman acted like she didn't remember. Carmen suspected that the forget-

fulness was an act, an excuse to fly into a rage every time
her nephew was mentioned. Jade feigned senility and help-
lessness whenever the mood struck, but in truth, the woman
forgot nothing. That wasn't to say Jade wasn't crazy as a
loon, because she was, and had been for years. Living in
this house with nothing but poodles and ghosts to talk to
had taken its toll.

It all served to make the woman impossible, and Carmen
hoped Ricky would remove her immediately. Her and her
dogs, living and dead. She hoped Jade wouldn't upset Ricky
too much.

He'd always been such a timid boy, and she hoped he had
found his courage in the years away from the house. On the
phone he sounded like a fine, strong man, though she
thought she detected a telltale trace of hesitation when he
spoke of the house.

To be honest, Carmen was surprised he was coming back
at all.

Something skittered in the wall, a chipmunk or perhaps
a rat. The sounds always chilled her and made her think of
the way Robin would race through the secret passages on
his hands.

The door separating Jade's apartment from the laundry
room and kitchen was ajar, and Carmen could hear her talking to herself. She did that frequently. Carmen crossed herself and whispered a spell her uncle had taught her—one
that, like marigolds, protected you from the spirit world.

It wasn't regular old-lady talk, not senile ramblings, but
insane babbling that was always the same. She talked to
Ricky's dead twin, saying obscene things, dirty things,
sometimes moaning and giggling like a schoolgirl. Sounding
as if she were having sex. Hearing that over and over was
what made Carmen nervous. Robin was dead, but she
thought that perhaps his spirit continued to walk the halls
and roam the passages within the house. *"Madre de Dios."*
She crossed herself again.

11

The drive across the desert from Las Vegas, Nevada, to Santo Verde, California, had taken five stressful hours. Between Shelly's sullen silence, the cat's yowling, Cody's manic good cheer, and Rick's own doubts about the intelligence of moving back, it had, in fact, been hell on wheels. But now, as he pulled past the open iron gates and up the long, long driveway into the veritable jungle surrounding the Piper family elephant, Rick had to smile as Cody oohed and ahhed as if he'd never seen a tree before. Of course, he hadn't seen that many.

Rick noticed that the front grounds were more overgrown than ever. After parking the car next to the stone path that led to the house, he thought that he might enjoy doing some of the work himself.

"Look, Daddy!" Cody cried in his ear. "Lemon trees! Can we make lemonade?"

"Sure, we can do that." Farther up the driveway, past the garage and outbuildings, Rick saw a slice of the modest citrus grove behind the house. The trees were lushly green, some laden with lemons, most with still-greenish oranges. Rick knew the Zapata cottage was nestled within the trees, but he had little memory of the back otherwise. He'd rarely entered the grove, because the crush of trees, even in broad daylight, had frightened him.

"Can I pick some lemons?"

Rick turned to look at his son. "Later, okay?"

Cody nodded, his attention focused on unbuckling his seat belt. "Okay!" In a flash, the boy, eyes bright with excitement, was out of the car.

"What a dump," Shelly observed as she opened her door. "This place is a wreck."

"We're going to fix it up," he told her as he stood and stretched. The cat yowled from his carrier on the backseat. "All right, already." Ignoring the cat's accusing glare, Rick pulled the cage out and set it on the ground at his feet.

"This is cool!" Cody cried, and took off at a tear up the long driveway. A moment later, he was back. "I like it, Daddy! I'm gonna look at the front yard now."

"Don't go near the pond," Rick called after him. "It's dangerous."

"I won't." The boy disappeared down a shady pathway.

"It sucks," Shelly countered. "It's filthy and I want to go home. Now." She put on her little-girl face. "Please, Dad? I could go live with Dakota and Lil. I want to go home."

"We *are* home," Rick said firmly. "You'll love it. It just needs a little paint."

"Like a million gallons," she said, already reverting to her I'm-a-teenager-and-I-hate-you voice.

"Hush," Rick said softly. Shelly was wrong—it wouldn't take a million gallons; twenty or thirty would do the trick. The stucco, once a pale peach, had faded to the color of unwashed flesh, and the formerly white trim was dirty gray and peeling. He wondered if the interior was as bad. Over the years George McCall had repeatedly told him the place needed fixing up, but Rick hadn't wanted to hear it because there wasn't enough money in the estate account for renovation of the house or yard. Frankly, he'd gone out of his way to ignore this place, hiding his head in the Las Vegas sand every time the subject of the house came up.

Now he'd have to do something, and he thought it might

be fun to do some of the work himself. *My poor wallet.* Fixing up the place should raise the property value enough to make it salable if he decided he just couldn't stand living here.

The neighbors would be pleased. They probably hated the Pipers at this point. Fortunately, the house couldn't be seen from the street, but the overgrown foliage that hid it probably horrified the owners of the huge Victorians, Tudors, and haciendas that lined Via Matanza. Those houses had perfect paint and perfect yards, not a blade of grass out of place, while he had an award-winning collection of shaggy bushes and award-winning weeds.

He picked up the carrier and started toward the house, his heart thumping unreasonably hard. "Come on, Shel," he said, and reluctantly the girl dragged her feet behind him.

Wildflowers exploded in the beds lining the walkway, and the grass was very long, making Rick recall that while the neighbors had their lawns mown once a week, Piper grass demanded cutting two or three times a week. Grandfather always said it was because the greenjacks lived here.

Rick forced the thought away, his gaze falling on the koi pond a hundred feet in front of the house. It was full of dark green water, and lilies floated on its scummy surface. A memory, so vague that it consisted only of the smell of cold, swampy water and an overwhelming feeling of dread, made him stop walking. *What? What happened there?* He shivered, despite the heat, relieved that memory wouldn't come.

"Dad?" Shelly asked sullenly. "You got a problem?"

"No," he said as he realized he was standing in the shade of the old oak. The gnarled wood rose out of the ground, twisting and knotted, a trunk so thick, it would take three people to ring it with their arms. Rick had hoped that the tree wouldn't seem so huge now that he was grown, but it was even bigger than he remembered. Staring at the trunk, he recalled his old fear of the tree, recollecting the cold terror he felt whenever its upper limbs scratched against his bedroom window on the second floor. The window was dark behind the leafy branches, and he found that he felt no fear now. Pleased, he wondered if he'd feel the same way after sunset. *Yes,* he told himself forcefully, *I will.*

"Let's go inside," he said as Cody ran up. He took the key from his pocket.

"Where's that housekeeper you said we get?" Shelly asked. "Where's your aunt?"

"Carmen took Aunt Jade shopping. They won't be back for hours." *I hope.*

The black iron handrail flanking the steps leading up the wide front porch jiggled when Rick grabbed it. The art of reattaching metal to stucco, or whatever was beneath it, was a mystery to him, but he felt sure he could figure out how to do it. In all honesty, it sounded like fun. *Maybe this is what the nesting instinct feels like,* he realized with amusement.

The top step was loose, too, he noted as he stepped onto the wide wooden veranda. A moment later he noticed a frayed wire on the porch light and that the doorbell was broken. The house was definitely going to be a challenge. At least the heavy, dark door, arched and adorned with black iron fixtures that made him think of the Spanish Inquisition, appeared to have nothing wrong with it. He inserted the key and pushed the door open.

The house exhaled a pleasant, nostalgic breath of lemon wax and cinnamon potpourri, though the underlying odor— poodle—was nowhere near as pleasant.

"It's big!" Cody said, running into the middle of the room and turning in circles. "It's got stairs!"

Smiling, Rick found that the living room looked eerily as he had remembered, only older, tireder. The dark green wool carpeting had been cleaned within a thread of its life, and many of the same pictures decorated the walls, including his parents' Robert Woods prints and Jade's horrid big-eyed children and dog prints—poodles, of course—from the sixties. The portrait of Grandfather Piper that used to have the place of honor above the reclining chair had been removed, and he wondered where it was. It had been the only decent piece of art in the house. In its place was one of the hydrocephalic children with hyperthyroid eyes holding an equally deformed poodle in a beret.

From his carrier, Quint let out a bloodcurdling yowl. "You said it, cat. These pictures have got to go." In fact, it was all going to go, he decided, and if Jade didn't want to hang the big-eyed children in her room, he'd toss them in the trash. The little U-Haul trailer he'd towed behind the car contained a half dozen exquisitely framed Edward Hopper prints as well as a few carefully chosen original pieces by relative unknowns who also captured the dark Americana feel Rick had first discovered in Hopper's work. He liked the darkness at the edges, the bright, sunshiny houses with inhabitants staring uneasily off into the shadows and woods, as if they were waiting for

something

to emerge.

Piper, he told himself with a little chill, *you're twisted* But he felt so good that he didn't mind. Here he was, standing in the place he feared most in the world, and he was thinking about painting and redecorating. It made him feel like he'd broken free of a set of chains he'd worn all his life.

The van would arrive with his furniture next week—not a lot, but nice, and it would fit in here—and he could buy whatever else he needed. Happily he envisioned polished wood floors with Navaho area rugs. With paint and plaster patch, a level and a sander, he'd scour away the bad memories. He'd rip away the bad things, like the forest green carpet that reminded him of grass in shadowed woods and the heavy, dark draperies that matched. He'd get white vertical blinds, put them under light nubby drapes, lined to keep the darkness out at night. And the sun out in summer, too. *I'm not afraid!* He was very nearly giddy.

The thick swirled plaster on the living room walls was dirty and yellowed, as was every other wall in the house, he assumed. No one had painted since his parents died—and it was obvious that even Carmen's deadly bucket of TSP couldn't get rid of the years of tobacco yellow from Uncle Howard's nasty little Tiparillos.

God, I'd forgotten that. He had a sudden clear image of Uncle Howard tilted back in a white metal chair, feet up on the front porch railing, a fifth of Jack Daniel's sticking out of his crotch. *Little brown turd, don't I love you,* that's what he sang to his Tiparillo, as he sat out there getting meaner and meaner. When it got too cold, he'd come in and do the same thing in front of the TV, tilted back in the recliner. Howard would croon to himself and watch the fights, grabbing whoever walked by and demanding this, cussing that, taking an occasional punch.

He used to pretend to be asleep when Uncle Howard was drinking.

Surprisingly, he was glad to have this memory. It seemed so . . . so normal. An abusive drunken uncle made more sense than little green men flitting around in the trees.

"Dad?" Shelly asked impatiently. "Dad?"

He looked at her. "Yeah?"

"Jesus, you're always telling me that *I* space out. You—"

"Don't be rude."

She glared at him, and he had to remind himself how unhappy she must be. He said no more, but it didn't lessen his desire to lock her in the closet until she was ready to leave for college.

"What's back there?" She pointed at the wooden folding doors sealing the living room arch.

"That's where your aunt Jade lives. The rest of the house is ours." He walked over to the monstrous brick fireplace, thinking that it, like the oak tree, was as big as he remembered. "So, Shelly," he said, seeing that his daughter was peering up the stairwell, "how do you like the house?"

Shelly replied with a sullen glare, but Cody came running out of the dining room, calling, "It's great!" He crossed to the fireplace, tried to look up the chimney, then moved to one of the built-in bookcases beside it and counted the shelves, patting all the ones he could reach. Rick hoped he didn't accidentally find the secret latch that would open it, and resolved to fill both cases with books as soon as possible.

Shelly snapped her gum. "This place is boring," she said, popping her gum. "It's totally dead."

Silently Rick counted to ten. "Give it a chance, Shel."

"I hate it here." *Snap. Snap.*

I will not blow up I will not blow up I will not blow up. "Please, Shelly," he said, trying to sound patient and understanding. "Give it a chance." *She's just left all her friends behind in Vegas,* he told himself again. Friends like Starman the Bellboy and Lil and that girl gang she ran with. Okay, not a gang exactly, but he didn't like the way they all wore at least two pierced earrings in each ear. Several had nose piercings, too. It wasn't natural. At least he'd removed his daughter before she'd put extra holes in her lobes. Probably. Casually he tried to catch a glimpse of her ears.

"What?" she whined, catching his gaze.

"Nothing." Her ears were hidden in her hair. Probably just as well, he decided. What he didn't know wouldn't hurt him.

"Where's my bedroom?" Cody asked.

"Shall we go upstairs and pick one out?"

"Yeah!"

"I'm choosing mine first," Shelly announced. "I'm older."

"Shelly," he said evenly. "I thought you might like the big bedroom in front."

The room he and Robin had shared was the second largest in the house, and in deference to his old fears, he decided that, for his own piece of mind, it would be best not to put a male Piper in that room. For Shelly, however, it would be perfect. "It's nice and airy," he told her. "You'll like it."

"Is it the biggest bedroom?"

"Except for the master suite, and I'm taking that," he said firmly.

"I don't want it if it's got stupid paint."

"You can choose your own paint, dear heart," he said, knowing he'd live to regret his words. No doubt she'd choose black.

She nodded. "Show me."

Rick walked up the stairs, Cody dancing ahead, Shelly dragging behind. With every step he saw new projects, from replacing the worn carpeting to replacing a missing bracket on the dark mahogany handrail. At the top of the stairs, he set the carrier down and opened its door. Tentatively Quint peered out, took a step, two, sniffing, then all at once, took off down the hall.

"Dad?"

"What, Shelly?"

"Which way is the room?"

"It's right there," he said, leading her to the first door on the right.

She pushed it open and walked in. Then he heard her moan. "Gawd, this is *gross.*"

"Of course it's gross," he said, irritated.

"What?" she whined.

"Nothing." He entered the room, not remembering the cowboy wallpaper until he saw it. He'd loved it, but it explained Shelly's reaction to the room.

"It's just the same as it was when I was little," he said softly. "But we'll take care of that, pronto, Shelly. First project, I promise."

She didn't answer, and he just stood there, staring, and feeling far less fear than he'd expected. He remembered being terrified here, between Robin's tricks and the greenjack stories, but now it was just a room that he'd shared with his brother until Carmen and Hector moved into the cottage and he inherited her room. He'd rarely entered this room after he was nine or ten years old.

"Daddy!"

He turned to see Cody behind him, grinning like he'd won the lottery. "What, Cody?"

"Please, I want the cowboy room! I love it! Please!"

Damn. "Cody, we'll put new wallpaper—with cowboys or spacemen or dinosaurs, anything you want—in any other room. I think your sister needs this great big room. She has so many clothes that she'll want that whole wall of closets."

"He can have it," Shelly mumbled as she turned and left the room.

Thanks a lot. "Cody? Wouldn't you rather have new wallpaper? This is kind of dirty and old. Look, there's a rip in it."

The rip—a gouge, really—was right over his old bed. Sudden images assaulted his brain, visions of Robin sitting on his chest in the dark, grinning and giggling and stabbing a butcher knife at the wall above his head.

Are you scared, icky Ricky? Gonna wet your pants, little brother?

No, Rick told himself, *this is just another example of your oversensitivity.* Robin had been teasing him with a toy knife, a rubber dagger, and he'd twisted the memory into something that had never happened.

Then how did it gouge the wallpaper?

"I don't care about an old rip. I want this room. I like it. I really, really, *really* like it." Cody showed his dimples.

"But . . . why? I'll get you new wallpaper."

"I like it because you had it when you were little. Please, Daddy?"

He was about to arbitrarily say no, but common sense made him hesitate. What could it hurt? Even if the knife had been real—and of course it wasn't—what did it matter now? Robin was gone and the past was . . . the past. Cody knew nothing of Rick's twin or of the greenjack stories. "Sure," he said, finally. "I guess you can have this room if you really want it."

His newfound nonchalance deserted him as he spoke the words, and the hairs on the back of his neck stood on end. *Grow up, Piper!*

"The rooms all suck."

"Shelly, you're back."

"I guess I'll take the one at the end of the hall. The one with the bathroom."

"Sorry, kid. That's the master suite. It's mine."

"You said I had first choice."

"I also said the master is mine."

"I'm the girl, I should get the bathroom."

He grinned at her. "But I'm the grown-up."

If looks could kill. "That's not fair."

"Fairness has nothing to do with it, darling. This is a family, not a democracy."

"But I should get the bathroom. I'm the girl—"

"And when you're the girl—woman—paying the bills, you'll get to claim the room with the bath."

She set her lips in a thin line. "Maybe I'll run away."

One. Two. He wouldn't lose his temper. *Three. Four.* Maybe he would. *Five. Six.* Running away was a new threat. *Seven. Eight.* Maybe he should just give her the suite. *Nine.* Maybe he should send her to a nunnery. Or a military school. *Ten.*

"You may choose from any of the other bedrooms on this floor," he said, surprised and pleased at the firm finality in his voice.

She tried to make him spontaneously combust with her eyes. "Then I'll take the yellow one. The one as far away from you as possible."

"That's fine, Shelly. As I said, you can choose your paint." He smiled pleasantly. "Anything but black."

She moaned and rolled her eyes, then flounced out after he complimented her, quite sincerely, on her uncanny imitation of Lurch on *The Addams Family.*

A moment later, Rick realized that she'd chosen Carmen's old room, the one that would allow her the most freedom. Its door was around the corner from the main hallway, and the kitchen staircase was immediately accessible. He almost went after her, suspecting that her prime motivation in making the choice was the ease with which she could sneak out of the house. *Don't accuse her unjustly,* he told himself, knowing that, not only would he feel terrible for misjudging her, but that he didn't want to plant the idea in her head if she hadn't thought of it herself.

"I'm starved!" Cody yanked Rick's hand insistently. "I wanna eat."

"Well, then, we'd better feed you." Rick checked his

watch. It was almost two in the afternoon, and he wondered how the kid had held out so long. Excitement, maybe.

Although Shelly had her license, he had never let her drive the Celica in Vegas. He made a few brownie points with her now by asking her to drive into town and pick up lunch. It was miraculous how her sullenness let up as he dangled the keys over her hand.

12

McDonald's had never smelled so good. When Shelly returned a half hour later bearing burgers, fries, and chocolate shakes, Rick was pleased to see that his daughter was actually working at maintaining her sour attitude. He detected a trace of enthusiasm lurking behind her studiously indifferent stare and Walkmanned ears.

They ate in the kitchen, which still had the yellow spoon-and-fork wallpaper Rick had helped his mom put up at age five or six. The 1950s round-shouldered refrigerator, gingerbread trim above the window over the sink, and yellow and white counter tile gave the room a kitschy look, as if it had been done over by a nostalgia nut. Rick liked it very much, but he always had: It reminded him of his mother.

The cat, lured downstairs by the perfume of Big Macs, made its grand entrance shortly after they opened the sacks. After taking his due, a quarter of a patty and a piece of bun, the cat stalked back into the dining room.

" 'Scuse me a minute." Rick shoved the last of his sandwich in his mouth and followed Quint, somewhat concerned about hidden poodles and open windows. There didn't seem to be any, but when the animal came to the closed doors to Jade's quarters, it sniffed, put its ears back, and growled, then assumed the imbecilic openmouthed, cross-eyed position of felines who didn't like the smell of something. Obviously Quint didn't like poodles.

Rick chuckled, until the cat suddenly turned around and sprayed the entry doors with everything he had, not once, but twice.

"Quint!" Rick scolded. The cat's acknowledgment was a scathing glance, then it flicked its tail, cat for *fuck you,* and marched back upstairs.

Rick looked around for something he could use to wipe up the urine, secretly pleased with the cat's editorial comment. Locating a box of Kleenex on a lamp table, he took a handful and wiped up the mess. Rising, he looked around to make sure the kids weren't watching, then tried the center latch on Jade's doors. It was locked from the inside, which was just as well: A herd of dead poodles lurked within, and he didn't want his son discovering them by himself.

"Dad?"

At Shelly's voice, he whirled guiltily.

"Yes, sweetheart?" He hid the wadded Kleenex in his hand, feeling like he'd been caught doing something wrong.

"Can I take the car again? I'd like to drive by the high school." She gave him a killer smile.

"Well," Rick began as Cody bounded by on the way back up to his new room, "I don't know . . ."

"I won't be too long, I promise, and I'll be really, really careful."

"I guess it would be okay," he said finally. He knew her charm tactics were purely false, a manipulation she knew would work, but as he handed her the keys, he told himself that the sooner she got to know her new home, the sooner her pleasantness wouldn't be an act.

"Thanks, Daddy!"

He watched her drive off, then headed back up the stairs, deciding it was time to investigate the so-in-demand master suite. He paused to check on Cody, who was happily counting sheriff's badges on the wallpaper, then continued on to the suite.

They died in there . . .

He swallowed hard, staring at the closed double doors. Why did he want this room, with its horrible memories,

memories he'd never been able to block, no matter how hard he tried?

Perhaps it was a knee-jerk thing: This was the grown-ups' room, after all. Or maybe it was the fact that there were good memories associated with it too. That was it. He smiled with the realization that Cody wanted his old bedroom, dingy cowboy wallpaper and all, for the same reason he wanted this one: because it was his parents' room.

He felt like he was six years old again as he opened the doors. The room was nearly as large as he remembered, with shining hardwood floors beneath scattered braid rugs, and aging white curtains over the windows. The double bed was the same one his parents had slept in.

The murder bed.

He shut off the thought. It was the same 1940s waterfall headboard, but a different mattress, not his parents' mattress. This mattress had a history he didn't want to think about for various tawdry reasons, the primary one being that it had been Jade and Howard Ewebean's conjugal bed for many a year, and the secondary being the occasional, unthinkable visitors Jade had invited into it.

Robin's riding the range tonight, Ricky, boy, hi ho, Silver! You don't know what you're missing!

He wouldn't have believed it if he hadn't seen it.

Disgusted, he studied the yellow hobnailed bedspread. It belonged to the Ewebeans. *The stories it could tell.* His parents had a handmade quilt, with a white background emblazoned with a blue and green wedding ring pattern, It had been stained and sodden with blood the night he found them.

At least you don't believe in ghosts, Piper. Purposefully he crossed the room, flopped down on the bed, and found the mattress to be an unendurable landscape of hills and valleys. Too small, too. He was used to his king-sized water bed, warm in winter, cool in summer, and only fifty percent waveless because he'd decided a little sloshing would keep him young. He stared at the ceiling and decided that the minute the furniture arrived, he'd get rid of the dark forties stuff and install his smooth bleached oak furnishings, his spread and curtains. It had all been dearly acquired on Gallery Road in Santa Fe, southwestern as all get-out and perfect for this house, primarily because it would help exorcise the memories of his parents' murder.

"Merowlll." Quint thunked his feline bulk onto the bed and nonchalantly padded onto Rick's stomach, centering himself. The cat hooked Rick into his stern orange-eyed gaze, and began kneading some serious bread in the breastbone region.

He scratched Quint behind the ears. He had the right idea, and Rick decided to take a lesson from the animal and make this house his own. He'd put his mark on it just as surely as Quint had on Jade's doors, though, he amended, with perhaps a tad more savoir faire.

He smiled, comfortable for the first time since they'd arrived. Gently Rick pulled the fuzzy paws forward, and the cat settled down, eyes dosing, purr rumbling. A nightly ritual done in daylight, he thought as his eyelids drooped, a good omen or not?

13

"Oow! Jesus! Get off me!" Rick's eyes flew open to see the cat, ears back, tail huge, clinging like Velcro to his chest. Its claws sank deeper into his chest as Rick tried to pull it free.

"Damn it, Quint! Get off me!" He shoved the cat, and this time the claws ripped free, taking skin and cloth with them. "Damn! Jesus Christ!" Quint hissed and sprang away. A moment later, low growling commenced beneath the bed.

Rubbing his chest, Rick sat up and looked around the shadowed room, disoriented, his brain muddled with sleep. "Be quiet!" he whispered, but Quint ignored him, and continued to growl steadily. Rick's mind started clicking things into place, and suddenly registered alarm. The last time Quint had acted like that was when a burglar had broken into the apartment. Swinging his feet off the bed, he thought *Robin!*

Rationality took over an instant later, and disgusted with his first reaction, he crossed the room and switched on the light. His watch read five o'clock—he'd been asleep for more than two hours. Where was Cody? Shelly? His car? He hadn't meant to leave them alone.

The cat's growl suddenly swelled, almost covering the sound of a door opening downstairs, and volleys of high-pitched yipping heralding the arrival of Aunt Jade and her poodles. "Lord, give me strength," he whispered as Quint swatted the heel of his shoe from beneath the bed. The cat was going completely out of its mind now, making high-pitched growling-yowling-chewing noises full of evil intent. "Come on, kitty," he coaxed. "Calm down. They're just dogs. They're no match for you."

Quint, always a smart cat, *huffed* a couple times, then quieted.

"Cody!" Carmen's contralto overrode the yapping. "Hi, Cody!" As Rick straightened his clothes and combed his hair, he heard his son say something, though Rick couldn't make out the words. An instant later, hands clapped, once, twice, and Carmen snapped a command in Spanish that Rick recognized from his childhood. She'd told Jade it meant "Hush, love pups," but the true translation was something like "Shut up, you stinking little turds!"

Next he recognized Jade's gratingly nasal voice complaining about something. Knowing Jade, it concerned the presence of a child in her house.

My house, Rick corrected. *And the old bitch is razzing my son.* That, he decided, as he closed his bedroom door and headed for the stairs, wouldn't happen more than once. Jade had been the evil stepmother incarnate and had made his childhood miserable. Not Robin's, just his. Robin had entertained her. "You bitch," he muttered, reaching the stairs. The fear she had instilled in him as a child had turned to hatred about the time puberty hit. And that was good because if he'd had anything more to be afraid of, he would have lost his mind.

"Ricky?" Carmen called as the poodles renewed their yapping. Steeling himself, he reached the bottom of the stairs. *Here we go,* he thought, stepping into the living room. *Show time.*

"Daddy!" Cody, safe in Carmen's arms, giggled happily "Lookit! Those are the doggy rats you told me about in the car, huh, Daddy?"

Carmen grinned as she approached him. Transferring Cody to her ample hip, she hugged Rick with her free arm, then soundly kissed his cheek. "You're so handsome, Ricky. So handsome."

He felt himself blush. For a moment he couldn't hug her back because there was something, some little thing on the edge of his memory, something about Carmen Zapata that worried him, though what it was, he didn't know. More subconscious hooey, he decided, and forced himself to return the hug.

"You haven't changed a bit," he told her as he began to relax. He'd forgotten that being hugged by Carmen was one of the better things in life. He'd forgotten how comfortable she was, how warm and safe she felt. Even now that he was taller than she, he still felt engulfed by her. Suddenly he felt good about being here because she was exactly what Cody needed.

"You're a good boy, Ricky, to say I haven't changed. But I'm an old lady, fifty-five."

"That's not so old."

"You can see the gray hairs and the crow's-feet and you still say that." She beamed at him. "Thank you."

Carmen in a blue flannel nightgown, the rotting green odor of the koi pond clinging to her. It's our secret, Ricky.

He pulled away.

"What's wrong?"

"Daddy's funny," Cody said.

A throat was cleared. Dogs whined, and a grown man winced at the noise, which sounded like sandpaper on dry snot.

"Aunt Jade," he said smoothly, "I hope you're well."

"Doggy rats," she intoned. "Explain doggy rats."

She stood by the sofa, her dogs' red leashes wrapped around her. All he could see of them were their snarling, cowardly muzzles poking out from behind her legs. Jade herself had changed little, except that the tall, heavy-boned woman was thinner and slightly stooped now.

As always, she wore too much makeup. Her foundation had sweated into the loose wrinkles on her face, emphasizing the clownish circles of rouge ornamenting her prominent cheekbones. Worse, mold blue eyeshadow covered her eye-lids from the clumps of mascara on her eyelashes all the way up to her plucked-out and painted-on eyebrows. A single wart with two wiry black hairs grew on the side of her nose.

The woman, Rick thought, was a witch, and her expensive but out-of-date—and season—clothing only emphasized the effect. She wore a long black batwing jacket and matching straight skirt that ended, regrettably, above her bony knees, and her red scoop-necked blouse showed off her crepey cleavage to great disadvantage.

The only change was her hair. Formerly mouse brown, it was now jet black and swept up in some sort of beehive throwback. More than anything, Jade Ewebean looked like Cruella DeVille with a hangover.

"I'm waiting for an answer, Richard," Jade said.

Do you have any idea how much I despise you? The woman had made his life hell, though he had to admit that she'd had one positive influence on his childhood. If she hadn't made him quite so miserable, he might not have graduated high school early and had an extra year away from her.

If you hadn't been such a wimp, Piper, you might have gotten away even sooner. His feelings ranged from disgust to amusement when he thought of how he'd removed himself from his impossible home life. He got straight A's, then ran away to college. It never occurred to him to do what kids did in books and movies. He could have run away and joined the army or even gone hog-wild and run off with the circus.

The circus. The carnival.

Delia.

The name brought a physical jolt. *Delia.* Oh, God. Delia. She'd been with the traveling carnival that arrived in Santo Verde each July. He'd met her on the Fourth of July only a few days before his parents died. How could he forget about Delia? She was the first girl he'd ever kissed, the first he had loved.

"Ricky? Ricky?" Carmen shook his elbow. "Is something wrong?"

"No. It's just strange to be back here."

"Yeah," Carmen said, pointedly glaring at Jade. "Some things never change."

Jade stared down her nose at Rick. "I'm waiting for your explanation."

I don't have to answer her, Rick thought. *I can tell her to go to hell.* He opened his mouth, then closed it again. *I'm an adult. I should be civil.*

Luckily, Carmen spoke for him. "You leave him alone. This is his house and he's the boss now."

Jade harrumphed, but something in her posture changed. Obviously she was aware of the truth in Carmen's words.

"Richard," Jade sniffed, doing a turnaround reminiscent of Shelly's teenage manipulations, "this woman doesn't know her place. I worked my fingers to the bone taking care of you, and what do I get in return? A rude maid that I can't fire."

Thank God. "If you'll recall," Rick replied calmly, "my parents stipulated in their will that the Zapatas would stay on as caretakers as long as they wanted." If it hadn't been for Carmen, he never would have survived long enough to leave Santo Verde. The Zapatas were free to leave, of course, but the Ewebeans had been forbidden to fire them.

Jade strode toward Rick, bringing the poodles and an almost visible cloud of perfume with her, Rick tried not to recoil as she laid a spotted hand on his wrist. As tall as he, she looked him straight in the eye. *"You* can fire her, Richard. I did everything for you; I think you should do this one thing for me. Fire her. Get me a nice maid, one who shows me some respect." Her grip tightened.

"No." He'd never directly crossed Jade and her horrible temper before, and he found it felt very good.

Her nails dug painfully into his flesh. "You *must."*

"I won't fire her, Aunt Jade."

"I insist."

"No," he repeated. "But maybe . . ."

"What?" The claws loosened slightly.

"Maybe you would prefer to live in a nice retirement home?"

The hand flew from his wrist and slapped his face, hard. "How dare you, you—" She drew her hand back to strike again. Rick caught it and held on, which wasn't easy. The woman was surprisingly strong. Somewhere in the background he heard Carmen first call on the Mother of God, then cut loose with a stream of Spanish invective centered around the word *puta*.

"Don't do that again, Jade," he said with deadly calm.

"Boy, is Daddy p.o.'d," Cody told Carmen. "He only talks real quiet like that when he's p.o.'d."

One of the poodles yipped, then attacked his leg, not biting, he realized, but wrapping its paws around him and rubbing. *Just like his mama,* he thought as he kicked it away without taking his eyes off Jade. "Listen carefully, Aunt Jade. If you ever do that again, I will send you and your dogs away. Behave yourself, and you may stay in your apartment. Do you understand?"

Immediately she switched back to simper mode. "Oh, Richard, I'm just an old lady. Sometimes I just blither on, you know. You'll forgive me, won't you, dear? My, my, you're so handsome. You look so like your brother, but you have a kinder face. A younger face, more boyish."

Carmen had warned him that Jade was losing her mind. God, she gave him the creeps talking as if Robin were still alive. He let go of her hand. She didn't move away, but stood her ground, keeping that brown-nosed smile painted on her face. The old bat, he believed, was possessed more of cunning than senility. He cleared his throat. "Abide by my rules, you can stay. Upset my family and you go. Another thing. Keep your dogs in your apartment. I don't want my cat upset either."

"A cat?" Her lip curled. "You have a cat?"

"Yes."

"She knows that already, Ricky," Carmen hissed.

"I hate cats."

"I hate poodles."

"Cats live outside."

"This one's a house cat. He never goes outside."

"Where are you going to keep him, then? In your boy's room?"

"The cat gets the run of the house, except for your apartment."

"But I was here first," she said in a victimized voice.

"No, *I* was," Rick said firmly. "I just left for a while. *I* own the house, not you."

"My poor little puppies are used to their freedom."

"Don't let her fool you, Ricky," Carmen said. "I never let those dogs loose in the house. They pee everywhere."

Rick took sudden perverse pleasure in knowing the poodles would be blamed for Quint's misbehavior.

Cody squirmed out of Carmen's arms and squatted to peer at the animals. "What're their names?"

Jade said nothing, so Carmen leaned down and whispered something in the boy's ear. He giggled with delight.

"She told him something dirty," Jade sniffed. "Do you want a dirty woman like that around your boy?"

"Yes." Rick found Carmen's occasional earthy language delightfully creative, and she saved any true obscenities she deemed necessary for her native tongue. The Spanish epithets for the Ewebeans had helped get him through his childhood. They thought the words and phrases were respectful; they were anything but. *Tia Puta,* as far as Jade knew, meant "Aunt Beautiful."

"Carmen says the dogs' names are Mister Poo and Stinkums," Cody announced. His giggling reached hysterical proportions.

"You can't touch my babies," Jade said haughtily.

"We wouldn't dream of touching them, Aunt Jade." Rick said demurely. Outside, he saw Shelly pulling into the driveway.

"See that you don't." Jade turned, almost tripping on her dogs, inserted a key in the lock on the folding doors, and slipped through, revealing none of the interior. Rick heard the lock click on the inside.

"Good riddance," Carmen muttered. She opened the front door just before Shelly knocked, and smiled at the girl. "You must be Shelly. I'm Carmen."

"Hi," Shelly said as she walked in. At least she'd used a pleasant tone of voice.

"You just missed the doggy rats," Cody told her. "They smell yucky." He giggled, then added, "So does Aunt Jade."

Shelly sniffed the air, her nose curling. "Opium," she said. "A whole case of it."

Cody considered this a long moment. "She should just say no."

"Dad?" Shelly asked, her tone perceptively sweeter. "There's a mall here. Why didn't you tell me?"

"It's news to me, sweetheart."

"Can I have some money? I could get some clothes for school."

"I suppose," Rick said, digging out his wallet. He found two twenties and handed them to her. "Receipts, change. I want to see what you bought."

"Be back by seven," Carmen added. "For dinner."

Shelly nodded at Carmen, then turned back to Rick and batted her eyelashes at him. "That's not much money. Could I have your MasterCard, Daddy?"

Borrowing his car, being promised a car of her own—something he'd agreed to consider during the endless drive across the desert—and borrowing his plastic, all in one day? *She's going to milk me for all the guilt and presents she can because of this move.* He knew he had to stop it now. This wasn't going to be much fun.

"Can I, Daddy?"

"No, Shelly."

Her face clouded. "That's not fair!"

He plucked the twenties from her hand.

"Daddy!" she cried, shocked.

"What's not fair? That you can't use my money, my car, and my credit rating anytime you want?" He paused. "Lis-

ten, Shel, if you want money from me, then you're going to
have to work for it."

"Doing what?" Sarcasm edged her voice.

The snotty tone made him want to slap her, but he knew
bemusement was the best revenge. "How about gardening?
You could help Hector," he suggested with a smile. He
glanced at Carmen, not wanting her to think he was insulting
her husband. "This place is too much for just one man during the summer."

"It's usually not so bad," Carmen said quickly. "Hector's
been in bed with a virus all week."

"Gardening." Shelly looked like he'd told her to scrub
the house down with a toothbrush. "You're kidding, right?"

"No, I'm not. Look, hon, I know you don't want to garden, but I have to pay an extra gardener. Hector needs the
help. I'm going to have to hire other people to fix things up
around here, and it's going to take a lot of money. So why
don't you look for a job so that you'll have all the spending
money you need? Maybe check McDonald's or the A & W
or—" he paused, trying to get her interest up "—maybe at
one of the clothing stores you like. Then you could afford
all the clothes you want, and you wouldn't have to fight with
me about it."

"In Vegas one of my friends worked at The Gap," she
said thoughtfully. "She had an employee discount." She gave
him one more daddy-dearest look. "Okay, I'll look for a job
at the mall. Can I have the money back, please, Daddy? I
need to dress nice to get a job."

He handed the twenties back. "It may take a little while
before you find work," he cautioned, but she just kissed his
cheek and raced out and climbed in his car—without asking.
Shaking his head, he watched her drive off.

Carmen was smiling at him "Kids."

"You said it."

"Daddy?"

"What, Cody?"

"Can we go exploring?"

Ah, an easy one. "Sure we can."

Carmen pulled a ring of keys out of her pocket. "I got these made for you. They've all got ID tags, so you go look around while I see how Hector's doing."

"Thanks, Carmen. I'd like to say hi."

"In a day or two, okay? I'm afraid he still might be contagious."

"Sure. Give him my best."

14

His father's workshop looked the same as it had the last time Rick had seen it, so many years before.

"Wow!" Cody stared at the huge room, then trotted around, heedless of the fine layer of dirt that coated everything in the room. In the boy's wake, dust motes danced up into the light.

Rick sneezed.

"Is this a barn?" Cody asked, turning a circle in the center of the room.

"No. It's a workshop. A *big* workshop."

The huge, high-ceilinged room was light and airy, because of its white paint and the high windows and skylights built into it. "Conlin Piper had this built so he'd have a place to build his sloop," Rick explained.

"What's a sloop?"

"A big sailing boat. After he built it, he used this to store the boat in the wintertime."

"Where'd the boat go?"

"It and Conlin were lost in an accident on Lake Arrowhead many years ago."

"Oh. What's that?" Cody pointed at a covered vehicle in the far corner of the room.

"I don't know. Let's look." He crossed to the shrouded form and lifted the edge of the tarp. Something scuttled beneath the canvas.

"Christ!" he cried, dropping the cloth and leaping back.

Cody giggled. "You're funny, Daddy."

Immediately he felt foolish. "I think we have rats," he told his son. "Move back a little. We'd better set some traps before we do any more exploring."

"But what's under there? I want to see."

"You can see it later. It's your aunt Jade's old car."

Cody nodded, satisfied. "What's that?" He pointed at the ceiling this time.

Rick looked at the equipment hanging from the huge center beam. "It's a winch." He remembered sitting on the workbench and watching his dad hoist an engine out of an aging Ford. "My dad used it to pull engines out of cars."

"Why'd he do that?"

"He liked to build new cars out of old ones. I hoped the Monster was under the tarp, but your aunt must have sold it."

When I get through with this car, Ricky, his father would tell him, *I'll keep it for you until you're old enough to drive.* Rick smiled sadly. Dad was killed before the car could be completed.

"What's the Monster?"

"He named the car for Frankenstein's monster because they were both built out of old parts."

Cody laughed, delighted.

His dad had worked on the hotrod through most of Rick's life. Remembering all the hours he'd spent out there with his dad, talking, laughing, working, planning, made him realize that he'd forgotten many of the good things from his childhood, not just the bad.

Tears sprang in his eyes, and he roughly wiped them away. Relieved that Cody hadn't noticed, he crossed to the workbench. A small hand-lettered sign hanging above the counter read, IF IT WORKS, TAKE IT APART AND SEE WHY. Rick smiled, blinking back more tears. His father always joked that it was the Piper family motto.

God, he missed his father.

"Daddy?"

His own son took his hand and tugged. "What's wrong, Daddy? Are you crying?"

"No, no. Just got some dust in my eyes. What do you say we see what's in these drawers?"

They opened drawer after drawer, and Rick was glad to find that evidently only the hotrod had been removed. The metalworking tools were all there: the acetylene torches, the cutting tools and hammers. Two welding masks filled one drawer. They'd called them Martian masks, he and his dad. None of it had been touched since the last time he'd used them, a few months before leaving home.

Three tall cabinets stood at the end of the long workbench. Rick opened the first one and let the good memories stored within flow over him, He'd spent a lot of time out here helping his dad—the workshop had been a place where he didn't have to contend with his brother, and that made it all the better. As time passed, he'd even found a hobby of his own, one that pleased his father, who wasn't at all concerned that Rick wasn't especially interested in building cars. Instead, he built metal models, which were a lot better than the plastic Revels of the Mummy and Dracula, because he built them from scratch, with only his dad, and later, Carmen, lending an occasional hand.

Gently he lifted a foot-tall brass and copper piece out of the cabinet. He'd built it several years after his parents died.

It was a skeleton, begun as an *El Día de los Muertos* figure meant to be a Halloween gift for Carmen. Originally it held a guitar he'd snipped and torched from distressed metal and wore a sombrero, but those accessories were stored in the back of the cabinet because he'd transformed it into a sculpture of Big Jack, giving it a spray of little copper leaves to hold and filling its rib cage, with more. As proud as he was of it, he couldn't bear to look at the piece, and hence, he'd never given it to Carmen.

"Wow! What's that?"

"It's sort of a Halloween ornament," Rick said, handing the figure to Cody. "In Mexico they make all sorts of skeleton decorations for the Day of the Dead." Involuntarily he shivered, but forced himself to go on. "Usually they're made out of papier-mâché, but I made this one out of metal."

Cody turned it in his small hands. *"You* made this?"

He couldn't help being pleased as hell. "Yes. When I was twelve or thirteen. Do you like it?"

"It's cool!"

"Would you like to have it?"

"Yeah!" He turned it in his hands. "What's he holding?"

"Leaves. They aren't too good, are they?"

Cody shrugged. "Why's he got leaves?"

No jack stories, Rick thought. "The Mexican figures usually hold something representing a person's profession or hobby. A doctor might have a stethoscope or hypodermic, a singer might carry a guitar—"

"This one's a gardener, right?"

"Right."

Cody continued to turn the figure in his hands, and his happy expression filled Rick with more pleasure than he'd felt in a long time. Smiling to himself, he looked back in the cabinets, saw his other, lesser efforts, and remembered how much he'd enjoyed working with his hands. *Maybe I'll take this up again,* he thought. *Maybe Cody would like to learn how.*

A sculpture hidden behind some copper squares caught his eye, and he lifted it gingerly from the shelf. It was a small, angular horse, the last thing he'd worked on before he'd left home. He turned it in his hands, thinking the workmanship wasn't too shabby. The horse and its saddle were complete, but he'd never even started the horse's rider, Don Quixote. *Knight of La Mancha,* he thought fondly. *Slayer of windmills.* His hero.

Pretty weird hero, Piper. But there was something grand about the character, something he had always admired and identified with. *You identified with the quixotism, Piper, because you were as nuts as the don was.*

Fondly he turned the figure in his hands, thinking that

he'd like to do this again someday. He envisioned a life-size Don Quixote mounted near the koi pond, his tribute to Cervantes and Daumier, and craziness. *What the hell. I think I'll do it.* It would be a talisman to keep his own imaginary demons at bay.

"Daddy!"

Rick whirled to see Cody backing slowly away from the shrouded car. He took three quick steps forward and snagged his son up, scratching his wrist on the skeleton the boy clutched to his chest.

"What's wrong, Cody?"

"There's somebody in there."

Rick could feel Cody's heartbeat hammering against his hand. He tried to sound calm. "Why do you think someone's in there?"

"I looked. I looked under the sheet, and somebody looked back."

"From where? The car?"

"Uh-huh." Cody buried his head against Rick's shoulder.

"Cody, listen to me. You didn't see anyone. You just imagined you did."

Ricky, you didn't see anything. You imagined it. How many times had he heard that himself? And now he was saying it to his own son.

"I saw it."

"I'm going to set you down and we'll both look, okay?"

"No."

Relieved, Rick patted his son's back, keeping his eye on the car. "Listen, Cody, I'm sure there's something under there, but it's just a rat. A big old rat. That's probably what you saw, that or your own reflection in the glass."

"Uh-uh. No way."

"If you're sure, then I *have* to look, Cody."

The boy backed into the workshop's doorway. "Okay. Look."

Heart pounding, Rick flung the tarp back. But there was nothing in the car but mounds of antique trash and stuffing from the seats. He took a deep breath. "It's rats, Cody.

They're nesting in the upholstery. He dropped the tarp back over the Rambler. "Let's go in now, son. Tomorrow we'll buy some traps."

15

Shelly returned from the mall with a poet shirt, a pair of Guess jeans, and eighty-five cents in change, knowing her dad was going to be pissed. He was totally hung up on value-shopping, as he called it, which meant he thought she should buy last season's clothes for next season, or worse—for the following year. Christ, he could be a pain in the ass.

She locked the car and knocked on the front door, and Carmen, who seemed okay but kind of nosy, let her in. As she carried her bags up to her room, she thought that at least Dad probably wouldn't make her take the clothes back—he'd say she should, but he was a softie, and she'd get off with the same old lecture, which was an annoying but small price to pay. She removed the tags from the clothes before putting them away, just in case.

Dad wasn't that bad overall, she guessed. He was just really, *really* ignorant. He'd always tell her he'd get smarter when she was twenty-five or so, and she knew that was supposed to be a joke, but it really pissed her off. The man could be so self-righteous.

Closing the closet, she crossed to the north window and opened it, breathing in the cool, citrus-scented breeze. Below, she could see the shingled roof of Carmen's little house rising up in the middle of the citrus orchard. It'd be great having all that fresh-squeezed available anytime she wanted it. Except for squeezing it, of course—but maybe Carmen would do that.

In a way, she realized, she was glad they moved here, because her father probably wouldn't be on TV anymore. Almost all her friends—her *girl*friends—went nuts over him, always wanting to come over and stuff. They'd act stupid and flirt when he was around, and when he wasn't, they'd tell her how lucky she was, how cute he was, blah, blah, blah. That bimbo Sally Dugan, who was a grade behind her, for Christ's sake, even had the audacity to ask if she thought her dad would go out with her. Shelly wanted to freak, but instead she told Jill to go ahead and ask, because if there was one good thing about her father, it was his frigging code of honor. That's what he called it.

The good part was that she knew he'd never screw around with her girlfriends, even if he found a whole pile of them in his bed. The bad part was that he quizzed her dates to hell and back and he didn't approve of half of them. He'd let her go out, but he didn't approve. To his credit, he'd only forbidden her to date two guys. The first was Sterno Stevens, who rode a hawg—and she was sort of glad Dad had interfered since Sterno was trying to talk her into getting his name tattooed on her butt. The other was Starman Henessey. That happened only a few weeks ago, and she'd almost run away over it. Dad would shit a brick if he knew that Starman himself had talked her out of it.

She turned to the west window and pushed it open. There wasn't much to see, just a flagstone path leading toward the front yard and the little roof over the kitchen door below. And a lot of green. Grass, pine trees, honeysuckle, junk like that. Sighing, she flopped on the queen-sized bed. Dad sure made life hell when he didn't like her dates. That's why she'd tried to keep Starman from him—he was twenty-two and definitely off limits, if Daddy had his way.

She sat up and looked around the room. Something was missing. A television set.

There was one downstairs in the living room, and she decided it was time to get acquainted with it. She rose and left the room, going around the corner to the main staircase since she didn't want to go through the kitchen and have to bullshit with Carmen.

Entering the living room, she quietly approached the TV.

"Girl, what's your name?"

Shelly jumped about out of her skin, then whirled to see a gross old lady sitting in the easy chair, a pair of whining poodles in her lap. Jade.

"I gotta go," Shelly said.

"No, girl. Sit down. What's your name?"

"Shelly."

And hell began. She sat there and listened to the old battle-ax yammer on and on and wished she hadn't come back to the house so soon. She even started to wish she'd taken the Celica back over the Cajon Pass, and had just kept driving until she was back in Las Vegas.

Jade was telling her all about her poodles, but Shelly was thinking about the day. She'd checked out the town, and decided it wasn't as nerdy as she'd feared. The mall was small, but it contained all the right stores: The Gap, The Express, and Nordstrom's. And on the outskirts of town there was a real prize, the A & W root beer stand her dad had mentioned. The parking lot had been filled with mini trucks, four-by-fours, Trans Ams, and restored classics, the kind of cars acquired by rich teenagers—the kind she wanted to be friends with. Her spirit had soared as she pulled Dad's flashy little Celica into the lot. Inside, she found extremely cute guys behind the counter, who, it turned out, would also be seniors at Santo Verde High. One of them introduced her to some of the other kids in the restaurant, and by the time she finally left, she felt like she'd already made some friends.

Now here she was, back home, ready to forgive her father, at least as long as he didn't bitch too much about the new clothes. But he was nowhere to be seen. Instead, she was trapped by Jade, who was every bit as horrible as her dad had said. And more.

"What kind of name is 'Shelly'?" The old Ewebean fixed her beady little eyes on her. "What's it short for?"

Shelly resisted the urge to shrink back in the ratty gold easy chair. She glanced out the living room window, but no one was coming to save her. "It's not short for anything. It's my name."

Jade sniffed, and the smelly poodles at her feet both looked at her. "Poor excuse for a name. It's not surprising, I suppose, considering your father."

"What do you mean by that?"

"Richard was always a . . . a weak child. He had no backbone. He was afraid of his own shadow. A weak man chooses a weak name." The old bat shook her head.

She'd never thought about her name much, but now she felt like defending it—and her father—but she couldn't make herself meet that steely-eyed gaze. She looked at her knees instead. "My father," she said softly, "isn't afraid of anything."

"Shelly, you're back early."

She looked up to see her dad standing in the dining room doorway, along with Cody. His dark hair was windblown, and his normally pale skin was flushed with color. He looked like he'd been running. Her brother's eyes were bright as he trotted across the room and thrust something copper-colored at her.

"Look, Shel, look what Daddy gave me. He made it when he was a kid."

Normally she would have said something obnoxious, but she was so glad to see them, she took the thing and turned it in her hands. "Cool," she told Cody. "What is it?"

"It's a Mexican Halloween skeleton."

"For *El Día de los Muertos,* "Dad explained, as if that was supposed to mean something to her.

Jade snorted. "Useless junk."

"I like it," Shelly said, looking up at her father. "I didn't know you were an artist, Dad." She threw Jade a fuck-you glance.

He looked amazed, then smiled and shrugged. "It could be better. Did you have a nice afternoon?"

She nodded. "I put in job apps at The Limited and Miller's Outpost. I met some kids at the A & W, too."

He smiled. "That's where I used to hang out. Everybody showed off their cars there."

"They still do, Daddy. All the kids had cars, nice cars. Do you think . . . I mean, the high school is so far away . . ."

"We'll find you a car, hon."

Shelly hardly believed her ears. She'd wormed a promise to think about it out of him while they were driving here, but this was a voluntary statement: It meant a whole lot more. She handed the metal skeleton back to Cody, then grabbed her father and hugged him. "Thank you, Daddy."

He beamed at her. "A girl's gotta have wheels, right?"

"Right," she said, vaguely aware of Jade's disgruntled snort. "Can I have a VW Bug?"

"Maybe. If we can find a good used one."

"What kinda car did you have, Daddy?" Cody asked.

"I didn't have a car," he said, staring in Jade's direction.

"Why not?" Shelly asked in amazement. "Your family was loaded."

"He didn't need a car," Jade intoned. "And, Richard, *she* doesn't need one either." She pronounced the last word "eyether," which further irritated Shelly.

"I'll be the judge of that, Jade."

The old lady stood, her poodles tumbling forgotten to the carpet. "Why don't you be a man for once, Richard? Don't buy the girl's affections. Be a man. Your brother, he's a man."

Shelly saw her father's face go dead white, his lips thin to a grim line. "Robin died before he became a man, Jade," he said.

"You're wrong, Richard."

"Shelly," her dad said, in his scary calm voice, "have you seen Carmen?"

"No."

"She's in her house," Jade said, settling back in her chair. "Feeding her husband. Come on, Mister Poo," she said, her voice turning to a sugared coo as she patted her lap. "Come kiss Mama, Stinkums."

The poodles jumped onto her lap and began licking her ugly red cheeks.

"Cody," Rick said, "go on up to your room and get ready for bed." Shelly thought he sounded really weird.

"But I didn't have dinner yet."

"Then go up to your room and get ready for dinner," he said in the quiet voice that meant trouble. "Now."

Shelly nudged her brother, and he took off; he recognized the voice, too. The poodles yapped madly as he tore up the stairs.

"Shelly," he said, ignoring Jade, "would you go out back and ask Carmen if she's cooking tonight? Tell her it's fine if she doesn't want to. We'll go out."

"She already said she's cook—" She paused, realizing he was trying to get rid of her. "But I'll go make sure," she finished quickly.

"Thanks, hon."

She entered the hall, then moved into the shadows to listen.

"Jade," her father said a moment later. "As I told you before, if you want to remain here, you will not question how I handle my children, nor will you insult any of us. But there's one more condition I forgot to mention earlier. You won't mention my brother again, in front of me or my children."

"Too bad you're not more like your brother, Richard."

"He's dead, Jade, so don't talk about him like he isn't. He's been dead for a long time.

"Only to you. But you wanted him dead, Richard. You were so jealous of him, so jealous of your poor little brother."

Confused, Shelly listened closely. She knew her father had a brother—a twin, not a "little" brother—and that he'd died a long time ago, but that was all she knew. Dad didn't like to talk about him.

"The subject is closed," her dad said.

Jade just giggled like an over-aged schoolgirl. "How I love him, his attentiveness, his charm. He's afraid of nothing.

He's not like you at all, Richard. And you, you had the legs. What a waste. He should have had legs, and you should have been the freak."

It was everything Shelly could do to not burst back in and ask what they were talking about.

"Be quiet, Jade."

"You had legs, but you were so jealous of him," Jade continued. "He tells me, you know. Him with his poor little body." Her voice became dreamy. "Such nice, strong arms. And so much fun. His eyes glint with fun. He's not a poop, like you. He knows how to live. How to love a woman. He's a *real* man."

"You whore," he said in that same deadly quiet voice. "You slept with your own nephew, you filthy, fucking whore."

Shelly, shocked, stepped backward and bumped into a dining chair. It crashed.

"Shelly!" Her father's voice was serious and stern.

"Yes, Daddy?" she peeped, scared to death. He never, never used words like that.

"Come here, please."

She did, wondering what he was going to do. He sounded crazy-calm, like he did when he'd told her Mom had died.

She almost flinched when he put his hand on her shoulder. Behind her, she could feel Jade's eyes boring into her back. "Shelly, did you eavesdrop just now?"

"Yes."

"I'm glad."

"You're glad?"

"Because I have to tell you some things, and I've been putting it off. Now I have to tell you. Please go check with Carmen, then meet me upstairs, in the study."

"Study?"

"The room with all the bookshelves."

"Oh, yeah, right."

This time she didn't wait to hear more.

16

"So, Shel, to sum it up, I had a crummy childhood. I was a chicken, and my brother was a bully. We were a charming pair. There were a lot of hard feelings. Things we didn't work out before he died." Rick hesitated, then added, "Things we probably wouldn't have worked out anyway— and that's why I've never told you much about my brother. There's nothing very good to tell."

Shelly nodded thoughtfully, and Rick had a glimpse of what she'd look like as an adult.

"Dad? Can I ask a question?"

"Sure."

She hesitated. "It's really gross."

He could guess what was coming, and controlled the urge to say no. "Ask away."

"Did your brother *really* sleep with Aunt Jade?"

Yep, that was the question. Although he was glad he'd told her the basics, he would have just as soon skipped this part. "You shouldn't eavesdrop."

"I'm sorry."

"Don't do it again."

"I promise. So is it true?" she persisted, too eagerly.

Well, he told himself as he looked into his daughter's sharp green eyes, *the truth will out.* "Yes," he said simply. "It's true."

"How do you know?"

"I saw them."

"That *is* disgusting." She made a face. "How *could* he? I mean, besides it being incest and all, how could he lay— sleep with that old bat?"

Gonna make more little Piper boys. You can fuck her, too, icky Ricky.

"Dad? Are you okay?"

Rick rubbed his temples, a futile effort to exorcise his brother's voice.

My voice?

"Da-ad!"

"I'm sorry." He smiled. "It's hell getting old. What were you saying?"

"Why would your brother go to bed with that shriveled-up old bat? Was he crazy?"

"I think maybe he was so angry about his deformity that it made him a little crazy. It made him hate me, too. Here I was exactly like him but complete—I had legs. No wonder he spent most of his time torturing me. It was very important to him to prove himself worthy physically. He always wanted to race down the stairs—he could go faster on his hands than I could on foot. And he thought of himself as a—" Rick floundered for a word other than *cocksman*— "a lady's man," he finished lamely.

"It sounds like your brother was a certified jockstrap."

Rick laughed. "I think you're right."

"Dad? Did your parents know he was mean to you?"

"I think they might have suspected," he replied as old pain welled up.

"You didn't tell on him?"

Shifting uncomfortably, he glanced at his watch. "Shelly, it's getting late, and I really need to catch a shower before dinner."

She studied him a moment, then rose. "Okay. Thanks for telling me that stuff, Dad. It sure is weird."

"Yeah, I know. I'll see you downstairs."

She left, and a few moments later, he stood in his dressing room and pulled a change of clothes from his knapsack. His gaze fell on the corner where he'd hidden the night he and Robin overheard their parents discussing them. He shivered as he turned to look at the low cabinet that contained the passage door they had entered through. Though he hadn't blocked this memory, he had filed it very deeply.

A moment later, he stood under the hot water, letting it beat down on him, washing away the grime, but not the memory of the night he spent in his parents' dressing room. Brought to the surface by an innocent question from his daughter, it refused to sink again.

June 7, 1975

"Come on, baby brother. We're going to have some fun." Before he opened his eyes, Ricky felt Robin's eyes boring into his flesh and smelled his Tootsie Roll–scented breath. There was no reason to pretend to be asleep: Robin would only get rougher and rougher until he could force him to reply.

"What time is it?" Ricky murmured, trying to sound unafraid.

"It's almost ten, icky Ricky, almost ten, and we're going for a run."

Ricky opened his eyes as Robin yanked him upright. "I'm sleepy."

"Come on, come on! Get in the closet, sleepy Ricky."

"Okay." Rubbing his eyes, adrenaline waking him up, Ricky crossed the room, Robin cavorting around him, herding him. He climbed into the closet, and Robin hand-flipped in after him, then pushed the hidden lever to open the passage.

There was no point in refusing to go with him any more than there was a reason to ask him where they were going, so Ricky crawled into the darkness after his brother. As they passed the staircase that led down into the bookcase opening in the living room, Ricky heard the television set: His parents were still up.

That meant they wouldn't be going down to the kitchen. That was one of Robin's favorite things to do, ever since Halloween almost three years ago. Ricky had seen him leave on his midnight excursions any number of times. Usually he disappeared into their closet and took the passage down to the bookcase door, sometimes he took the stairs, front or back, and other times he went right out the window and down the tree.

Several times Rick had been forced to go with him. To make him go, Robin threatened to do all sorts of horrible things to him, including throwing him out the window and being smothered in Saran Wrap.

Robin often spent half the night roaming the house. He liked to start in the kitchen, first going through the refrigerator and tasting almost everything in it. Ricky had seen him spit in the milk, and once, he peed a little in a fresh pitcher of lemonade. The next day, watching Mom and Dad drink it, Ricky was almost sick, but Robin had reminded him that they were already pretty sure Ricky was crazy and would think it was his idea.

But the worst was the night that Robin had held him down and forced gobs of raw hamburger into his mouth. He'd thrown up bloody red meat into the toilet, and it looked and smelled like guts. He could barely think about it, even now.

"Come on," Robin whispered. He led him away from the comforting sounds below and into a dark, claustrophobic crawl space. Ricky was entirely lost, but Robin moved quickly and easily through the dark, almost as if he possessed a sixth sense that let him see in the dark. *He's a greenjack* Ricky reminded himself. *He probably* can *see in the dark.*

They descended no stairs tonight, just crawled through the passages hidden on the second floor. "Here we are, sleepy Ricky," Robin said at last. "You go first."

Knowing that argument was useless, he slipped past his brother and found himself in a small cabinet, empty except for a couple pairs of Mom's shoes.

Robin made him climb out. They were in their parents'

bedroom—their dressing room, to be exact. "Hide there," Robin ordered, pointing at a dark corner behind a rack of coats. He did as he was told, then Robin cozied in next to him. "Now we wait," he said. "And if you make a noise, I'll tell them *you* made *me* do this."

Soon their parents arrived. Ricky cringed into the darkness upon seeing their feet, seeing them slip their shoes off. He looked away when Mom's hand appeared, rolling down a stocking, but Robin craned his head, wanting to see more.

A minute later, the feet disappeared into the bathroom, and as soon as the shower came on, Robin said, "They're gonna do it tonight."

"Do what?"

"It, stupid. They always do it Friday night."

"Do what?" Ricky's insides were crawling.

"Sex, asshole, sex. They'll turn on the radio and then they'll do it."

Ricky and Billy Galani had been walking home from school last spring when they saw a little dog and a big dog stuck together on old man Clegg's lawn. When Billy finally stopping laughing, he told Ricky they were having sex. That was pretty much all he knew about sex except for the kissing and hugging stuff, which he thought might almost be sex.

As soon as Mom and Dad were in bed, Robin moved to the very edge of the dressing room so that he could see them. Ricky stayed where he was, a horrible sick feeling in the pit of his stomach.

"Shall I turn on the music, Grace?"

Their father's voice was easy to hear and understand.

"In a minute. I don't think I'll be able to relax until we make a decision about sending Robin away to school."

Ricky saw his brother's back stiffen.

"I know, Gracie. We have to make a decision."

"There's something I haven't brought up that might be important to our decision." She hesitated. "It's about Ricky."

They're going to send me to the funny farm instead! His heart in his throat, legs cramping, Ricky almost lost his balance.

"What about Rick?"

"I think he's afraid of his brother. I know that sounds silly, but . . ."

Robin's head swiveled, and his hateful gaze fell on him. Ricky shrank farther into the corner.

"I don't think it's silly," Dad said. "I've noticed it too. It's just that the boy's afraid of so many things."

"I know. Frank, do you think that Robin's scaring him on purpose?"

"Well . . . I never mentioned this before, you know, boys will be boys, but Robin does have a mean streak in him."

"What do you mean?" Mom asked.

"I caught him with a nest of baby birds. They didn't even have feathers yet. He was—" Dad's voice cracked. "He was doing things to them."

"What things?"

"You don't want to know."

"Tell me."

"He was tearing them apart with his bare hands. Tearing the wings off."

Mom made a shivery noise. "All the more reason to send him to the special school. He needs counseling for his handicap."

"Yes, I agree." Dad was quiet a moment. "About Rick. You know, he's always been terrified by those greenjack stories Pop used to tell. I wonder if Robin repeats them."

"To scare him?" Mom asked.

"Yes."

"But why would he want to scare his own brother?" she asked.

"For the same reason he maimed the birds," Dad explained. "He has no legs—so he cripples the birds. With his brother, it's jealousy. Poor Robin. He looks at Rick and sees a perfect mirror image—except that it's more perfect than he is."

I want your legs legs legs, Icky Ricky, and your eyes, too, boo hoo! His brother's voice in his head was so real that

Ricky jumped before he realized Robin wasn't really speaking.

In fact, his twin was paying no attention to him now. Robin splayed his hands on the carpet and began pushing himself up and down in the slow, controlled way that always meant he was angry. Ricky didn't dare move, even when a charley horse knotted one of his calf muscles.

"Robin's always so concerned about Ricky," Mom said. "You know that Ricky's been asking to move into Carmen's room after the wedding?"

"Yes."

"Well, Robin came to me and cried, saying he didn't want to sleep alone."

"Now, *that's* interesting." Dad's voice got a little louder. "He came to me, too, but he didn't cry. He said that he didn't think Ricky should move because he shouldn't be alone when he has nightmares. Grace, I think Robin told us each what we wanted to hear. Robin's the one who doesn't want him to move. Robin also told me that Ricky sleepwalks. Is that true?"

"I've never seen him sleepwalk," Mom replied. "I think that's an out-and-out lie."

"Let's tell Rick tomorrow that we're going to let him move. It won't hurt anything, and it might help."

"What about the boarding school?"

Dad cleared his throat. "It's a good school, expensive, but within our means. I'll call them tomorrow and get Robin's registration going."

Robin settled down onto his body and made fists with his hands. Sparks seemed to fly from his eyes when he turned a slow, deliberate stare on Ricky.

"Good," Mom said. "You know, Frank, I hate to admit it, but sometimes I'm even a little afraid of Robin. He's always so sunny and happy, but sometimes there's something so cold in his eyes."

"I guess we should have had this talk a couple years ago," Frank said. "I should have seen it sooner. When Rick's with me out in the workshop, Robin's never around, and Rick is so . . . so *normal*. When he's not afraid, I think he's far more normal than his brother."

Robin silently slapped a fist into his open palm.

"Then separating them is the right thing. It's settled." Dad's voice dropped a little. "A little night music, my dear?"

"I'm ready."

Ricky heard a click, then the radio came on, filling the air with classical music.

Even after the soft moans and whispers began, Ricky didn't dare move. He couldn't even feel his legs anymore. Robin remained by the doorway, never glancing at Ricky, his attention utterly on their parents' activities. His face was hard-set in an ugly, frightening scowl.

Time passed. Soon Ricky's mind' felt as numb as his legs. Despite his fear of his brother, he was nodding off when a hand touched his shoulder.

"Shhh!" Robin hissed in his face.

The music was off and Dad's soft, steady snore filled the room. Dazed, Ricky looked around, his eyes coming to rest on his brother's, a foot from his face. The look in them brought him to full terrified alertness.

"Into the cabinet, icky Ricky," Robin whispered.

Carefully he tried to move, but his legs were rubbery. An instant later, the pins and needles started, and Ricky groaned.

"What's wrong?"

"My legs are asleep."

Robin started to laugh. He covered his mouth with his hands and shook with glee, little raspy sounds escaping. Finally he stopped and grabbed Ricky by his pajama collar. "They think they're gonna send me away, icky Ricky, and it's all your fault! You know what that means?" he whispered hoarsely.

Ricky stared dumbly at him.

"You know what that means?"

He shook his head no.

Robin pulled him forward until they were nose to nose. His breath stank. "It means you're dead. I'm gonna getcha, icky Ricky, and I'm gonna getcha soon. Way before school starts. Not even gonna wait for Halloween. Crazy hazy Ricky, numb and dumb. I'm gonna kill you. Nighty-night."

He let go of Ricky, then slipped silently into the cabinet and was gone.

Rick turned off the shower and stepped out, pulling the towel roughly over his body. He'd spent the rest of the night hiding in the dressing room. His fear of Robin, and what revenge he might take, overrode the joy he had felt over his parents' words.

He pulled on his fresh clothes and drew the comb through his hair. It was a wonder, he knew, that he had survived.

"Dad!" Cody called from the hall. "Carmen says come and eat!"

He smiled at the sound of his own son's voice. "Coming, kiddo!"

17

It was nearly midnight, and Rick lay on his bed, exhausted, yet unable to sleep in this roomful of memories. He was also concerned about the cat, who was acting decidedly strange. Not only had Quint refused to leave the room again after the one foray downstairs, but he hadn't even left his hiding place under the bed when Rick had come back upstairs. Silently he cursed Jade's poodles.

On his way down to dinner, he worried a little about dealing with open drapes and windows because he just didn't have enough energy to deal with his neurosis or psychosis or whatever the hell 'osis he had. But he needn't have worried: All the drapes were closed. Silently he had blessed Carmen, who had remembered. He blessed her again at dinner as her cooking rekindled his appetite: He'd forgotten that Carmen was a killer cook.

The only negative thing at the dinner table had been Jade. Evidently she'd used up her day's supply of nastiness, as well as any brain cells that were still functioning properly, and this combination put her in a bizarrely jovial mood that was harder for Rick to tolerate than her previous nastiness and hostility.

He was almost certain she'd forgotten his warnings about mentioning Robin, because she brought him up about every five minutes, usually to remark obscenely on his prowess as a lover. Shelly seemed to find it disgusting yet funny, and

Cody was too busy building things out of his mashed potatoes to pay the least attention.

Rick, however, hated every last minute and was grateful that Carmen hustled her back to her quarters as soon as they were done eating.

Then, after she showed Shelly and Cody how to operate the TV set in the living room, the housekeeper had turned her attention on him.

"Come on, Ricky, you help me clean up and I'll give you a treat." She nodded her head toward the kitchen, and he followed her, happily remembering all the other times she'd said that, then shared a private stash of cookies or cupcakes with him.

They did the dishes by hand, she washing, he drying, and when they were done, she brought out the treat: a fifth of Sauza Gold and two shot glasses. She brought them to the kitchen table and poured two shots.

"This isn't what I expected." He grinned and tossed back a shot.

She matched him. "Yeah, you thought I was gonna give you a Snickers bar, right?"

"That's right," he said with total honesty. "So how do you stand doing dishes by hand?"

"There aren't that many dishes, Ricky. Besides, I've always done them this way. I don't know what I'm missing." She patted his hand.

"Dishwashers are a necessity of life. Mine broke down once and I couldn't get it fixed for a week. After three days, we were out of dishes. We had to buy paper plates and cups and plastic forks."

She laughed. "You're supposed to wash the dishes every day, buster."

"Well, I tried. I put them in the sink with hot water and soap, then I went to write my column. By the time I was done, the water was too disgusting to put my hands in."

Carmen snorted. "So what'd you do? Hire somebody to do it?"

"Well, yeah. Shelly said she'd do it for twenty dollars, so—"

"Twenty dollars? Ricky, you must have money growing out your butt!"

"No, but it seemed reasonable. It was such a disgusting job and all."

"Boy, that girl sure knows how to work her daddy!"

"Yeah, I know. Anyway, tomorrow we'll order a dishwasher."

"I'm not gonna argue with you!" She poured another round. "One more to help us sleep. I read your column every week, Ricky. It's good. You're pretty funny, you know that?"

"Thanks. I enjoy it."

They talked for a few more minutes, she bringing him up-to-date on the repair of the house, Hector, and the neighbors, he telling her about his life in Las Vegas.

"Carmen? Does Jade always talk about Robin so much?"

She studied her hands. "Tonight was worse, but she's never stopped talking about him. The dirty old woman."

"Do you think she's dangerous? To the kids?"

Carmen considered. "Only her mouth."

"Good." Rick twined his fingers behind his head and stretched against them. "I'm bushed. Shall we call it a night?"

"In a minute. Ricky, I want to ask you something."

The tone of her voice gave him a chill. He said nothing.

"Did you see them?"

"Them?" he asked, knowing very well what she meant.

"Them. Don't play with me."

"That was a long time ago. I was a scary little kid. My imagination—"

"Have you looked?"

"No. There's no need."

"Madre de Dios, you're telling me you don't believe in them anymore, but you won't look out the window? I think you're lying to yourself."

"Would I come back if I believed in them?" He held the shot glass with both hands to hide their trembling.

She stared holes through him. "No, I guess you wouldn't. I'll tell you what I think, Ricky. I think you better take a look, just to make sure."

"And what if I see them, then what do I do? Check myself into an asylum?"

"Quit feeling sorry for yourself. You just go look out the window and you'll be free of them, once and for all."

"Maybe."

"Does Cody know the stories?"

"No."

"Good. You make sure and have him look out the window tomorrow night, and make sure you're with him, whether you saw them or not. He's young enough, he'll tell you if he sees something. If he does, I think you better go back to the desert."

"You really believe—"

"I just believe anything is possible." She stood up. "Come on. You gotta look."

"Carmen—"

"We're gonna get it over with. Come on."

She took his trembling hand in her firm, dry one, making him feel seven years old again. Meekly he let her lead him into the living room. Cody and Shelly were sprawled in front of the TV, Cody fast asleep. Carmen let go of his hand, stepped forward, and scooped Cody into her arms. "Okay, Shelly, time for bed."

"What? It's too early!"

"I know. But your dad and I want to talk."

"Dad, can't you talk in the kitchen?"

"There's a little TV on the dresser in my room," Rick told her. "You can take it in your room for now."

"Little?" she asked doubtfully.

"Shel, Carmen and I want to watch something on PBS."

"What?" she whined.

"An opera," he said.

"Yeah," Carmen lied. "When your dad was little, we always watched the opera."

Shelly rolled her eyes. "You're kidding."

Rick put his arm over Carmen's shoulders. *"Rigoletto.* Hey, I have an idea, Shelly. Why don't you watch it with us? You're old enough to enjoy—"

"No, thanks." Shelly stood. "I'll take him," she said, lifting Cody from Carmen's arms. She started up the stairs.

"Night, Shel."

"Night."

Carmen crossed to the set and turned it off, then flicked off the light switch. "You can see better if it's dark. You ready?"

"Sure," he said dully. Outside, a summer breeze had come up, and he told himself he didn't hear his name within it.

He controlled the old panic quite well as he waited for her to return to him. Suddenly his hand was in hers again and she was leading him forward, toward the window. "Don't trip," she said as he raked his shin on the end table by the easy chair. She led him to the center of the picture window. "Stay there."

He closed his eyes and waited, listening to the drapes open, listening just as he had so many times so many years ago. He swallowed, feeling as if he were in front of a firing squad.

Her hand returned, and he could feel her standing next to him. "Ricky, look now."

He couldn't open his eyes. The wind called.

"Ricky?" She waited.

"I can't."

Both her hands enveloped his. "Yes, you can. You have to."

"No." His voice broke.

"Ricky, they can't get you in here."

You jerk, he thought fiercely. *You asshole, you moron. You're making a fool of yourself. Again.* He was afraid he was going to cry.

Carmen's voice was soft and gentle. "Remember Thomas, Ricky? Remember him?"

Thomas McEnery Piper. He remembered his first hero, the one preceding Don Quixote. Slowly, he opened his eyes.

They were out there in the night, dancing beneath the oak, their voices riding the wind. In the night. In the wind. *Ricky . . . Ricky . . . Ricky . . .*

"No," he whispered.

"You see them?" Carmen asked.

He pulled away from her. "No. Good night, Carmen."

Barely controlling his panic, he took the stairs as sedately as he could, then, out of sight, he trotted to his room. The door had no lock, so he shoved a chair under it, then threw himself down on the bed and stared at the ceiling, his eyes wet.

Since then, he'd gotten up to check on Cody, and found him peacefully asleep in the bed nearest the door. The curtains weren't closed, but that was fine because he could see that the window was locked tight. Shelly, too, was fine, asleep on the bed, the TV still playing. He'd turned it off and returned to bed.

That was an hour ago. He stared at the ceiling a moment longer, then rose and walked into the dressing room.

After that night, when they'd heard their parents talking about sending Robin away, Ricky's spirits had briefly soared, but Robin took his revenge so quickly and gleefully that his life grew instantly worse.

Before June 7, the night of the eavesdropping incident, sleeping in the same room with Robin had been a trial that he could stand because he knew he could go to Carmen's room if it got too bad. But on the night of June 8, he nearly didn't make it.

June 8, 1975

Ricky had almost asked to sleep in Carmen's room, but he didn't want to do it in front of his parents—he worried that they might ask him why—and he couldn't get her alone. Finally he'd gone to bed, and was so tired that when he saw that Robin appeared to be asleep already, he didn't even wonder if he was playing possum or not. He didn't have the energy to wonder. Sometime later, he awoke.

Eyes in the dark.

Ricky felt them staring at him, watching him, and he pulled the covers around his body, over his head, and waited, almost suffocating in the close crush of blankets, feeling the eyes boring into him, feeling his own hot breath push the sheet in, out, in, out, like a doctor's mask on TV. His fear receded slightly as he made believe he was Hawkeye Pierce performing open-heart surgery and everyone was cheering and applauding, especially his parents and even his brother. Then, finally, the inevitable song began.

"Ricky, icky Ricky, I see you-ooo."

"Stop it," Ricky whispered into the sheet.

"Stop it, drop it, says icky Ricky." There was a thump as Robin dropped to the floor. "Whatcha scared of, sicky icky?"

"Nothing!" Ricky pulled the covers from his face and gulped the fresh, cold air. "I'm not scared of nothing!" But it took every ounce of courage not to hide his head again.

"Nothin'?" came his brother's voice, closer now. "Not afraid of nothin'? Liar, liar, pants on fire. Icky Ricky, you're afraid of me! Me! Me!"

Panicked, Ricky reached for the bedside lamp and turned the switch. Nothing happened. He tried again.

"Maybe it got unplugged, picky Ricky. Why don'tcha come down here and look?"

Ricky bit his lip to keep from crying. "Stop it!" he pleaded.

Robin didn't answer. Instead, Ricky heard his brother's hand-slaps as he crossed back to his own bed, the creak of the handgrip attached to the headboard, the protest of bedsprings as he swung energetically back onto his bed.

Burrowing into his covers, Ricky relaxed slightly. Usually Robin's teasing only lasted a few minutes, and though he still imagined he could feel his brother's eyes on him, he closed his own, hoping the worst was over, letting drowsiness overtake him slowly, peacefully . . .

"It's kinda hot in here."

Startled, heart pounding, Ricky awoke, knowing time had passed, but not how much. The bed frame creaked, and he saw Robin's silhouette across the room. He was perched on the end of his bed, next to the window.

"Don'tcha think it's kinda hot in here?" As he repeated the words, he turned the latch. Thin moonlight slashed the room as the white curtains fluttered with the incoming breath of night air.

Ricky . . . Ricky . . . Ricky came the voices on the wind.

"Ricky, Ricky, Ricky," sang Robin.

Ricky pulled the covers back over his head.

"Icky Ricky, Icky Ricky, come out and play." Robin bounced up and down on the bed, babbling softly.

"Close the window," Ricky begged.

"It's only open a little," Robin said innocently.

"Please." Ricky choked on the sudden flood of tears. For a short time, he'd lost his fear of the greenjacks, but under Robin's constant threats to throw him out the window, the fear had returned.

"Crybaby, titty mouse."

Suddenly Robin swung off his bed, and almost instantly was on top of Ricky. He yanked the covers once, twice, and Ricky lost his grip.

"Hi, hi, hi, icky Ricky!" Robin's strong hands clamped on Ricky's throat and started to press.

"It was kinda fun fuckin' with you, baby brother." He seemed oblivious to Ricky's thrashing. "But we're not gonna play anymore." He laughed through his teeth, hissing like a snake. "I'm not gonna kill you, icky Ricky, don't worry, I'd never kill you. I'm just gonna take you outside."

Ricky coughed, his vision blurring. He stopped fighting, unable to think.

A second later, Robin's hands loosened, and Ricky gulped air as his twin grabbed him around the waist and yanked him off the bed. They rolled in twisted somersaults across the floor, Robin propelling, Ricky unable to fight, barely able to breathe. By the other bed, Robin let go and climbed up on his bed. Before Ricky could drag himself away, Robin reached down and grabbed him under the armpit and hauled him onto the bed as if he weighed nothing.

Ricky . . . Ricky . . . Ricky . . .

"No!" Ricky choked on the word. "No!" He kicked, but Robin only laughed and pulled him up against the open window. He pinned his arms with one hand and clamped the other over his mouth.

"Shhhhhh! You're so stupid, icky Ricky. You're such a scaredy-cat. You don't know anything!" As he spoke, Ricky cringed, hearing adult fury hiding behind his brother's falsely cheerful tones. "Be quiet and listen, Ricky Piper, Ricky Diaper. You don't know what you're missing. If you go outside with me tonight, you get to live forever. You don't have to go to bed or eat your vegetables. You can do anything you want and never get punished. You get to play all the time!" He grinned. "Would you like that, little brother?" The hand was lifted from his mouth. "Would you?"

"No!" Ricky whispered.

A string of drool dripped onto his cheek. "Aw, come on, icky Ricky. If you don't go with me, I'll tell the folks all about how you don't think I'm your brother, and then they'll know you're the crazy one and they'll have the men in the white coats come and take you away, away." Robin's teeth glinted in the streak of moonlight. "Hee hee, ha ha, ho ho!" He paused. "They already decided you're crazy anyway. They changed their minds again. I heard them talking again this morning. They're going to send *you* away, not me."

"You lie." Ricky hissed.

"I heard them. They don't like you anymore, Icky Ricky; they've decided to send you away and keep me here. So why don't you go with me outside instead? It'll be a lot more fun, it really will. And you get to see your real brother. He misses you, Ricky. He misses you a lot."

"No!" Ricky whispered. "You killed him. You took his

body away, and nobody knows he's alive. He can't talk to anybody."

"No, no! That's not true!" Robin sounded happy and sincere now. "He has lots of new friends. Friends you can have too. Friends you can share. All we did was trade bodies for a while, just like trading marbles or baseball cards. I'm letting him use my body while I use his. He has legs now, Ricky. He's happy because I gave him my legs."

"You want *my* legs!"

"Shhhhh! You don't want Mommy and Daddy to hear you, do you? If they hear you saying crazy things again, you'll be sorry!"

"You just want my legs!" Ricky repeated, but more softly.

"Not true, baby brother. I want your eyes, too." Robin pushed him up against the windowsill. "I only want you to share, Ricky. Is that a bad thing? To share with friends? Robin's sharing and he's happy. He has legs. But he misses you. He wants you to come out and play."

"You lie," Ricky whispered again.

Robin's expression changed, hardened into a scowling mask, the eyes glittering like black onyx. Strange eyes, animal eyes, not his brother's eyes. Ricky moaned as Robin twisted one hand into his hair and pulled.

"If you won't go with me willingly, then I guess it's time to play, little brother," he whispered. He grabbed Ricky under his arms and lifted him up into the window. "We're gonna go down there, and I'm gonna choke you just a little more, and then you get to see your brother again."

Ricky . . . Ricky . . . Ricky . . .

Gathering all his will, Ricky kicked Robin as hard as he could. His brother fell back on the bed, clutching his stomach.

"You little shit!" he hissed. "You little shit!"

Ricky started screaming, his voice loud and raspy, not stopping as he hopped down from the window and ran across the room.

"You stupid little shit!"

As he was about to open the door, he heard his parents'

door open and close, his mother's hurried footsteps, his father's slower, heavier ones just after. He sighed, and sat on the edge of his bed. He might as well let them think he had a nightmare, because even though they might be on his side now—he wasn't entirely sure—they'd never believe that Robin tried to kill him.

As the doorknob began to turn, Robin grinned and propelled himself across the room and onto Ricky's bed. Then his twin's arms were around him again, so tight he could hardly breathe. "You little shit," he whispered again, and began rocking him back and forth in his arms, a pretend soothing for the grown-ups to see.

Light bloomed overhead and then his mother was at his bedside, his father standing behind. He could see Carmen waiting behind them in the doorway.

"Another bad dream, Ricky?" his mother asked, her gentle embrace removing him from Robin's rough one.

She smelled good, like Breck shampoo and Ivory soap, and Ricky nodded, burrowing into her shoulder, putting his arms around her neck, letting himself cry just a little.

"Do you remember the dream, Rick?" his father asked softly.

"I forget," he muttered, clinging to his mother.

"He just screamed," Robin said. "He screamed and I woke up."

"It was good that you tried to make your brother feel better," Dad said hesitantly.

"Yes," agreed Mom, though she glanced oddly at Dad as she said it. She stroked Ricky's hair and rocked him.

"Is there anything you need to tell us, Rick?" Dad asked.

He was tempted to tell until he saw Robin's threatening glare. "No."

Dad stared at him a moment, then nodded,

"Frank, would you mind shutting that window?" Mom asked as she continued to hold Ricky.

He saw a look pass between his parents, then Dad said, "Robin, I thought you learned your lesson about that window when you were seven." He closed the window and turned the latch.

"I was hot," Robin said softly. "I'm sorry, but I wasn't playing. I think maybe I have a fever."

Mom let go of Ricky and felt his twin's forehead. "Well, you're a little warm, I guess."

Dad picked Robin up and carried him back to his bed. "No more open windows, son," he said, tucking him in while Robin smiled angelically. "You get some sleep now."

"Thank you, Daddy."

Dad returned to Ricky. "What about you, Rick? Do you think you can go back to sleep now?"

"Can I sleep in Carmen's room?" he asked.

Mom and Dad exchanged glances. "Sure, honey," Mom said. She kissed his forehead, then stood. Ricky ran past her, out of the room, and took Carmen's hand.

"See you later, Ricky," Robin called.

In the hall, Mom kissed him again, then a concerned look crossed her face. "Look at those dark circles. A little guy like you shouldn't have such big circles under his eyes."

"I'm okay," Ricky said.

"He just needs sleep, Miz Piper, and I'll make sure he gets it." Carmen smiled. "I don't allow bad dreams in my room, so you don't have to worry about him anymore."

He stayed with Carmen that night, and all the nights thereafter, until, on June 25, she and Hector were married, and he inherited her room with the nailed-shut passage in the closet and the lock on the door.

Suddenly the cat jumped on the bed, startling him from his reverie. "Well, it's about time," he said as Quint planted himself on Rick's chest and began to knead with his claws, eyes half-closed, purr rumbling, looking completely happy and moronic. Absently Rick petted the animal. He'd acquired Quint four years ago, a few days after Laura was killed. He'd had to be strong for Shelly and Cody, but he had no one to

lean on himself, and the lonely nights were especially bad.
Over and over again, he'd wake up sobbing and reaching for
his wife, and he didn't know how he could go on without
losing his mind. Then Dakota O'Keefe, a new neighbor he
barely knew at that time, knocked on the door and showed
him a tiny orange kitten, no more than a month old. Dakota
had found it abandoned in the alley behind the theater where
he was working. It needed to be fed with an eyedropper
every hour, he'd explained, and he couldn't do it because he
had to work, and his roommate was allergic to cats. He
begged Rick, who worked at home, to watch it for a day or
two while he tried to find it a good home.

Reluctantly, still in a depressive haze, Rick took the kitten. Within an hour it had burrowed into his shirt and fallen
asleep against his heart, remaining there while Rick worked
on his column. That night he put it to bed on a finger towel
in a shoe box lid that he placed on the nightstand. When the
dream about Laura's death came, he woke up sobbing, and
found the kitten snuggled up between his shoulder and neck,
watching him, purring as hard as it could, and gently batting
at the tears as they ran down his cheek. They'd been together
ever since. The cat knew his moods and had proven itself to
be a great listener. Rick could tell it anything.

He scratched behind Quint's ears. "I thought I saw the
greenjacks," he told it. "You know what that means?"

Quint purred louder and settled down, watching Rick
through slitted eyes.

"It means I'm nuts," he told the animal. "Completely,
utterly bonkers."

The cat purred.

"Ready for the rubber room," he added, almost asleep.

Ricky . . . Ricky . . . Ricky . . .

Fear exploded within his gut, and the cat exploded on top
of it, digging in its claws and hissing, before racing for its
spot under the bed, where it started growling with a vengeance.

"Shit!" Had he dreamed the voices or not? he wondered.
Either way, he'd scared the piss out of the cat.

"Shit!" he repeated. He got out of bed and knelt on the floor, pulling the bottom of the bedspread up. "Hey, cat, come on out. It's okay."

Quint stared at him, unblinking. The growling ceased.

Icky Ricky, icky Ricky, come out and play.

The cat hissed, the sound turning into a high-pitched yowl. Ears flat back, Quint swatted at Rick's face.

"Christ!" He pulled back just in time. "What the hell's the matter with you?" The feline moved farther under the bed, growling.

Hey, icky Ricky, come and play, hey . . .

The cat growled again.

The voices, Rick thought. *He hears them, too.*

Hey, Ricky, come and play . . .

Softer now, fading into the night. They never called for long, he remembered. Never for long.

18

"Daddy!"

Cody's call brought Rick instantly to consciousness, his stomach lurching behind somewhere, his brain dizzy, disoriented, and alarmed. The cat sprang off the bed, growling.

"Daddy!"

"I'm coming!" He staggered to the bedroom door and fumbled with the lock. "What's up?" Seeing that his son was fully dressed, he glanced at his wristwatch, was appalled to see it was past ten A.M.

His son stood a few feet back from the door, staring at something on the floor. "Lookit."

He followed Cody's gaze down to the stuffed poodle standing just outside his door. It was bluish white and wore a purple rhinestone collar, its hind leg was held lifted, ready to urinate. Rick pulled his bare foot back without thinking.

"You're funny, Daddy!" Cody giggled, squatting to study the animal.

"Did you put this here?" This was the dog that Carmen had talked about, the one she found dead in the dryer only six months ago.

"Nah. It smells yucky." Gingerly Cody patted its head. "But it wasn't here when I went downstairs before."

"When was that?"

"I dunno. It was light out, though. Carmen said I was an early bird and wanted to know if I eat worms." He giggled. "I said no, so she made me breakfast. She *cooked,* Daddy. Pancakes, just like at McDonald's, only better."

"Well, Cody was Aunt Jade up?"

He made a face. "I didn't see her."

"Where's your sister?"

Cody shrugged. "Can I go now?"

"Where are you going?"

"Carmen's gonna let me pull weeds!"

Rick had to smile. "How fun."

"Yeah!" Cody's voice betrayed complete sincerity.

"Don't go near the pond."

"I know. Carmen said." He turned and skipped back toward the stairs.

With a last withering glance at the petrified peeing poodle, Rick shut his bedroom door.

Fifteen minutes later, feeling considerably more human, he reopened it, snagged the poodle by its raised leg, and walked toward the back stairs. Pausing, he knocked on Shelly's door, but there was no reply, so he headed on downstairs, the poodle held distastefully out and away from his body like a lethally loaded diaper.

Carmen's arms were in dish suds up to the elbows. "Sleep okay?" she asked without turning around.

"Like the dead."

"Sometimes the dead don't sleep so good."

He'd never known how to react to Carmen's dire pronouncements, so he did what he'd always done and ignored it. The cheerful morning light that streamed in through the windows made her superstitions seem especially silly. "Jade paid me a visit sometime this morning," he said.

"Oh?" Drying her hands, she turned to face him, her eyebrows rising as she saw the dead dog. *"Madre Dios."*

"I found it outside my door." While he was dressing, it had occurred to him that maybe Jade had picked up the odor of cat piss and was getting even, but he decided not to mention this possibility to Carmen.

"That filthy old *puta.*" Carmen took the dog from Rick. "Excuse me a minute." She stomped through the laundry room and pounded on the locked hall door, the back entrance to Jade's apartment.

Rick couldn't quite make out what they were saying, but Jade sounded haughty, and Carmen, heated. A moment later she returned without the dog. "She says she didn't do it. You want some breakfast?"

"No, thanks. Well, who did it, if she didn't?"

Carmen crossed herself. "She did it. *Mentirosa.* She does it all the time."

"Menti . . . ?"

"She's a liar, Rick. She lies."

"Has this happened before?"

"Sure. Every time I find that dog standing over my slipper, she says she didn't do it. You should have a good breakfast."

"I can't eat in the morning. Who does she say takes them?"

"She takes them, Ricky. I told you."

"Are you sure?"

"Ricky, I don't even want to say it." Carmen crossed her arms and nodded. "Crazy old *puta.* She's lost her marbles. Like I told you last night, she talks about him all the time. He makes love to her, he sneaks food from the fridge, he steals her dogs. She does whatever she wants, then blames him. Can you believe it, the stories she tells? She's loco, that one."

"Are you sure she's not dangerous, Carmen? Really sure?"

"I wish I could say no so you'd have an excuse to send her away, but she's harmless, except for the sex talk. And she'll get into your refrigerator and get her germs in your food—you should get a lock for it or she'll get her germs in everything. You should lock your bedroom, too. Sometimes she goes upstairs, you know." Carmen paused. "It's not good for you to skip breakfast, Ricky."

"I always skip breakfast, so you don't need to remind me anymore," he said with a smile.

"Okay, okay," she said quickly. "Tell me about last night, when we looked out the window. Did you see th—"

"Excuse me," he interrupted, having no intention of talking about last night either. "Do we have a Sears catalog around here somewhere? We should pick out a dishwasher."

"They don't have the catalog anymore. But there's a store in Montclair and another one in San Bernardino. Take your pick." She blew air noisily out her nostrils. "But first we need to talk about the greenjacks."

"I'd better go now," Rick said quickly. "I have to get back and get to work. I'm way behind on my columns."

She shook her head, "poor, little Ricky" written all over her face. "Whatever you say."

"Are there any features you especially want on the washer?"

"I really don't need it, Ricky." Her tone betrayed her continuing irritation with him.

"Well, I do," he said lightly. "What am I supposed to do on your day off? The three of us will use up every dish in the house in twelve hours, we always do. And if you're gone for more than a day, well . . . I have to have a dishwasher."

She started to protest.

He held his finger to his lips. "Shhh. It's for me, okay? I'm buying. But you can use it if you want."

"You want some lunch?" she asked, glancing at the kitchen clock. "It's almost lunchtime."

"No, thanks." The clock was a circa *1965* plastic plate, olive with copper hands and numerals, uglier than sin. As soon as his stuff arrived, he'd replace it with his own kitchen timepiece, a reproduction of a vintage yellow and white rhinestoned Felix the Cat clock with the ticking tail and shifting eyes.

Rick smiled, suddenly understanding her. She'd spent her whole life watching out for him, and now he was back and her instincts were up and saluting. "Carmen, I ate so much last night that I won't eat again for a week. Stop worrying about me. I'm going to go out for a while. Is it okay if I leave Cody with you?"

"Of course it is! You know Shelly took your car, right?" She saw the look on his face. "She said you knew."

"She lied," he said, suddenly tired. "Do you know where she went?"

"She said she was going to the mall to put in job applications at some more stores."

"Well, don't let her take my car again without double-checking."

"I'm sorry, Ricky. I didn't realize—"

"It's not your fault, Carmen. I should be apologizing to you. I can't believe how badly she's behaving."

"No, she's just being her age." Carmen smiled wryly. "Of course, she's doing it in spades."

"She's very difficult for me to control."

"We'll turn her around. Kids that age, you give 'em a little bite of cake, they'll take the whole thing." She shook her head. "A lot of little kids are cruel. A lot of big kids are selfish."

"Cody's not cruel."

"Neither were you, and he's a lot like you, just happier. More outgoing. But he hasn't started school yet either. He'll have to learn to be a little mean so he can take care of himself." She paused, considering. "You never liked school very much, did you?"

"No," he admitted. "But it wasn't that bad. I knew how to stay away from the bullies." *And everybody else,* he thought.

"Cody will have it easier because he doesn't have the pain you had."

Rick's throat tightened up. "Carmen—"

"We have to talk, Ricky. We both have things we need to say to each other." Her voice was fierce with emotIon. "You know? You remember?"

Carmen kneeling by the koi pond, pushing her hands into the cold corrupt water, so green, so alive . . . Our secret, Ricky, our secret . . .

Roughly he shook his head. "No. I don't remember."

She studied him a moment, then drew a key from her pocket. "Here, you can use Hector's truck. He's better today, but he's not going anywhere."

"Thanks." He accepted the keys and opened the back door, then turned and looked at Carmen once more. "I'm sorry," he told her quietly. "Sometime we'll talk."

"Okay."

19

Having picked out a dishwasher and arranged for delivery, Rick left Sears, stopped at the market for Pepsi and rattraps, and returned to the house shortly after one. Pulling into the driveway, he was annoyed to see that Shelly was still gone, but he hid his irritation as Cody raced to greet him.

"Daddy!"

Rick swept the mud-caked child into the air, eliciting a volley of delighted giggles. "You making mud pies, Cody?" He set the boy down.

"Hector and I are pulling weeds!"

"How you doing, Rick?" Hector asked as he approached.

"Fine." Shaking hands, Rick thought that the small, lean man hadn't changed except for the salt and pepper at his temples and in his mustache. "Should you be working today? Carmen said you were pretty sick."

"I'm fine. I just had a little flu bug, but you know Carmen. She'll try to make you stay in bed if you've got a hangnail."

Rick agreed, then asked Hector if he thought the koi pond could be turned back into a swimming pool. They discussed the possibilities for a few minutes until Cody insisted he and Hector had to get back to work.

Indoors, Rick let Carmen feed him lunch, and was relieved when she didn't try to bring up the past. In fact, except for Shelly's stunt, everything was going very, very well. Before going upstairs to work, Rick and Carmen divided up the rattraps, and he didn't protest when she said she'd do the house and the root cellar. He took his out and placed them in the garage and toolshed, then finally entered the workshop.

He didn't lift the tarp off the car this time, but toed a couple bait boxes in underneath it, and placed the rest in the base cabinets.

Time to get to work, Piper. He had a column due in two days, and he couldn't be late with it. Normally he kept the syndicate supplied with at least six weeks worth of columns, but he'd gotten lax lately. They had nothing in reserve, so he not only needed to get this one done, he needed to write several more, pronto.

I'll go up in a minute. He'd been thinking about building a big Don Quixote off and on ever since he'd found the unfinished sculpture yesterday, and he was dying to see what he'd need in the way of supplies. He would allow himself that, he decided, before he went in and got to work.

He began pulling equipment and metal from drawers and cabinets, setting it out on the counters, taking stock, and making plans in his head. At one point he nearly went inside to find a notebook so that he could write down the particulars of his project, but remembering that before he'd worked with no plans, only sight and intuition, he squelched the urge. He would design the don by the seat of his pants.

Minutes turned into hours, but Rick, feeling at peace and happier than he'd been in years, had no notion of time until the workshop door opened. "Dad?" Shelly asked. "Carmen told me you needed to talk to me?"

Reality came crashing rudely back.

"Shelly, you took my car without permission," he said as he set down a box of flaring tools.

She looked at the ground. "I thought you wouldn't mind."

"Why would you think such a thing?" His stomach started twisting up. Shelly could frustrate him like no other.

"Well . . . you let me take it yesterday."

"You asked permission yesterday."

"I didn't want to wake you up, and it was for a good reason: I put in job applications all over town and—"

"Damn it, Shelly! You know perfectly well that you have no excuse for what you did. It was wrong. Why can't you admit it?" Crossing his arms, he took two long strides toward her.

"I thought—"

"You didn't think, Shelly, you just assumed you'd pull another one over on dear old Dad. You've taken advantage of me for the last time."

"Daddy, I didn't mean to—"

"I knew it would be hard on you leaving your friends back in Vegas, and I've tried to be extra nice to you. But instead of appreciating that I let you use my car yesterday, you decide that gives you carte blanche to take it whenever you please."

"If you'd buy me a car, it wouldn't be a problem anymore."

One. Two. She's your daughter, you can't kill her. *Three. Four. Five.* Maybe you could ship her off to a nunnery. *Six. Seven.* The pressure in his ears and the black spots in front of his eyes started to diminish. *Eight. Nine.* Carmen would help him with her from now on. *Ten.*

"Shelly," he began calmly. "Let's talk about what you've asked for in just the last two or three days."

She rolled her eyes and started to back out the doorway.

"Don't move," he ordered.

"Da-ad . . ."

"And don't whine. Now, if I remember correctly the day before we left Vegas, you said you needed a NordicTrack—"

"Well, I do."

"Shhh. The same day you said your ears stick out too far, and you'd like to have cosmetic surgery to pin them back."

"They do! They're horrible."

"You have very nice ears, as I recall. Of course, I haven't seen them in years because they're hidden under your hair." He smiled sweetly. "But if you keep interrupting me, I'll be glad to pin them back for you."

She glared, but said nothing.

"In the car coming here, you asked for blue contact lenses. But your eyes are twenty-twenty."

"My eyes are drab."

He shook his head, almost amused. "Your eyes are the same green as your mother's were, and hers were beautiful."

Shelly didn't respond, just stared at something on the floor.

"You also asked for a car, cable television, your own phone line, and a television for your room. First, how do you propose I pay for all these things?"

"You should take that spot on the morning news like you were talking about?" she asked meekly.

Lord, why did I tell her about that? "If I did take it—and frankly, getting up at three in the morning three days a week doesn't appeal to me—I would use that money to fix up the house.

"Listen, Shelly, I'm not saying you can't have those things you want. I'm saying you're going to have to pay for them yourself."

"You said you'd buy me a car!"

"Unless things change around here, that won't be happening."

"Can I use yours?"

"Nope. You blew that today."

"Then how am I supposed to get a job if I don't have a car?"

"Ride your bike." As he spoke the words, he realized the movers hadn't arrived yet. He glanced at his watch, saw that it was nearly six, and figured they'd pull in tomorrow.

"I hate you!" Shelly cried. "You're mean and I hate you and you're horrible and disgusting!" Her shot taken, she turned and flounced out of the workshop, slamming the door behind her.

Rick shook his head, knowing she'd calm down soon enough, then put his tools away and went in to clean up for dinner.

20

Dinner was a Carmen Zapata specialty: pork loin, slow-roasted until it fell apart under a fork, black beans, sliced radishes and tomatoes, guacamole, sour cream, fresh salsa, and warm flour tortillas to wrap it all up in as one saw fit. Food of the gods. Rick now sat in the lumpy old recliner and stared at the television without digesting what he saw because all the blood in his brain had gone south to help digest the obscene amount of food he had consumed. He felt logy and content.

He'd insisted that Carmen and Hector join them tonight, and they'd had a wonderful time, especially since Shelly and Jade, the current malcontents, had refused to join them for dinner. Jade wanted to watch television in her room, so Carmen had taken her a tray, and Shelly pretended to be too infuriated to eat. That didn't bother Rick at all, because when he'd checked his car to make sure it was locked—it wasn't—he'd cleaned out a pizza box, McDonald's wrappers, and three large soda cups.

Carmen and Hector had gone home nearly an hour ago, and now he and Cody had the place to themselves.

His son was sprawled on the floor in front of the television, his head propped up in his hands. They'd flipped a coin for the early evening reruns: heads, *Murphy Brown*, tails, *Married with Children*. Cody, with tails, had won. As he watched, Kelly Bundy miscalculated and walked into a wall.

Rick stifled his laugh, because, while he didn't believe in censorship, he wasn't sure he should let his son know he was amused by dumb-blond antics.

His gaze drifted to the draped picture window, and almost instantly, he heard their voices.

Ricky . . . Ricky . . . Ricky . . .

Shivering, suddenly wide-awake, he wondered if he'd always heard the voices only when he thought of them. It certainly seemed so now. Back when he was a kid, he'd thought about them all the time, so he had no way of knowing, did he?

He'd been a regular little obsessive back then.

Carmen's admonition to find out if Cody could see them had haunted him since last night. *Now,* he decided, *it's time to find out.* Steeling himself, he tilted the lumpy old chair upright and rose, stretching, fighting down the anxiety that was already threatening to turn his knees to rubber. *Thomas Piper,* he reminded himself, *wouldn't be afraid.* His hands trembled. He felt like a child.

Remember the Halloween when you stuck out your tongue and flipped the bird to the jacks? Remember how brave you were . . . for a few hours, until Robin climbed out in the tree and you saw—

"Bull," he said aloud.

"What, Daddy?"

An ad was on, and Cody was staring at him.

"Nothing."

"You wanna have some ice cream? Carmen said we can make sundaes. There's Redi-Whip and cherries and chocolate sauce."

"Not now, sport. Maybe later."

"But—"

"We just had dinner. I'll pop if I eat anything else."

"I'm starved," Cody whined, but the ads were over and his interest was back on the set.

"Later." As he spoke, Rick crossed to the window and, without pausing to reconsider, pulled the drapery cord.

The greenjacks were out there, faint in the summer dusk,

a dozen of them, maybe twice that, it was always hard to tell. The evening wind was up, and they moved through the blowing grass and tumbling leaves, dancing and cavorting among them, human yet not human, possessing faces yet featureless. As he watched, they became aware of him, turning, coming closer. Watching him.

The panic started low in his abdomen, spread heavily into his legs and arms, making his brain dull and frantic at the same time. *Pretend you're Thomas.* Carmen's words echoed in his head, and he did what she'd said, though he felt like a fool.

Several came closer, melding together to form long-limbed wraithlike figures tall enough to peer in the window. He barely retained control of his bladder, but then he thought: *I'm Thomas. I'm not afraid.*

The old trick helped. For the first time in his life, he remained calm enough to examine them, to really see how they resembled liquid mercury, unable to retain form when they melded together, but were merely long-limbed and ghostly. *I'm not afraid,* he thought again. And he began to believe it. He tried to think of them as fog shifting in the wind.

Ricky, icky Ricky, sicky Ricky, Ricky, Ricky, Ricky.

The voices stirred his fear, and he tried not to hear them. Most of the greenjacks remained back beneath the oak so that they could see and be seen, though the formless wraiths stayed at the window, sometimes showing a suggestion of hollow eyes or a mouth, though never for long.

On his seventh Halloween, he'd gone out among these creatures and found that he was able to live through the fear. To transcend it. Then the few hours of freedom were cut short later that night when Robin climbed out the window and . . .

What? Rick wasn't sure. Robin had changed, he knew that, but was it because he'd grown sour over his handicap, or had Rick, always so guilty over his normalcy, merely read more into his brother's teasing than he should have? The notion that Robin had switched bodies with a greenjack seemed ludicrous to Rick now.

It had to be nonsense. But here he was, a grown, hopefully rational adult, and he was looking at greenjacks and listening to their rhyming catcalls. He smiled sadly. *I'm nuts,* he thought, *that's it. But at least I'm not afraid, thanks to my patron saint, Thomas.*

Slowly he raised his right hand to the window, made a fist, and extended his middle finger. It felt as good as it had when he was seven. He lifted his other hand, fisted, extended that finger, too, mouthing the words "screw you."

There was a reaction of sorts: The voices dimmed slightly—probably in amazement, he thought wryly—and their movements slowed down. The wraiths at the window seemed less stable than before. Experimentally he wiggled the fingers, pistoned his hands up and down half an inch.

"Daddy!" Cody's arrival at his side was so loud and un-expected that Rick froze where he was.

"Daddy! You're making a flip-off!"

"No I'm not." His hands slowly obeyed his order to un-clench.

Cody giggled. "Who you flipping off, Daddy?"

"No one, Cody. I was doing, ah, isometrics."

"What's that?"

"Exercises."

"Well, it looked like flip-off, Daddy. Do you know flip-off?"

"Yes, I do. But who taught you, young man?"

"Lil." He giggled and slapped his hands over his mouth, then spoke between his fingers. "She showed me how, but she said I couldn't tell you. You won't tell on me, will you, Daddy?"

"No. As long as you don't do it anymore." *That bitch.* Of course, he himself had learned it from his grandfather, but the knowledge had come vicariously. That was . . . nor-mal, but for Magill to purposefully teach a child . . . *that bitch.*

He stared at the jacks. As darkness grew, their activity, if it had indeed slowed, now increased again. They reminded him of ants, so ceaseless were their movements.

Rick's heart lurched as he saw one, especially dim, just becoming visible as the night grew darker, standing by itself under the oak. Its very stillness made it noticeable.

It reminded him of the one he'd seen the night Robin changed.

Bullshit, he told himself. *Don't even think it.* But he couldn't help himself, and his next thought was strong and hard and directed: *Robin.*

The greenjack looked and raised one arm—Cody yanked on his shirt cuff. "Whatcha looking at, Daddy?"

Jesus, he'd forgotten about his own kid. Glancing down, he saw Cody staring up at him, a quizzical look on his face. Rick swallowed. "What do you think I'm looking at?"

Cody pressed up against the glass. "Cool!"

Oh, no. "What's cool?"

"The wind. It's blowing good!"

Thank you, God.

"Daddy, let's go outside and smell the wind!"

"No, Cody, I don't—"

"Please, Daddy, please!"

"It's dark out."

"Not very. Come on, just for a minute. Please?"

He tried to spot the dim greenjack, but it was nowhere to be seen. "I don't know."

"Please?"

What could it hurt? He'd been among them before, hadn't he? Suddenly it seemed like a good idea, a final step to cure him of his fear. "Okay, but just for a minute."

"Yay!" Cody took his hand and dragged him to the front door, waiting impatiently while he undid the bolt. Slowly the door creaked open, and they stepped out on the wide front porch.

The jacks saw them.

"This is fun!"

Rick swallowed his fear as the greenjacks gathered at the base of the steps. Suddenly Cody let go of his hand and raced down the stairs. Rick cringed as the creatures, giggling and singing, surrounded his son.

"Come on, Daddy!"

"Coming." *Dear God, what am I doing?* He took one step, two, finally all six of them. Then he was standing on the stone walk at the base of the stairs, and the little jacks lined the border.

Cody, on his knees in the grass, windmilled his arms and giggled.

Rick could feel the jacks, like cool breezes, touching his legs. *I'm Thomas,* he told himself again, feeling foolish as hell. *I'm Thomas and I'm not afraid.* Heartened, he stepped off the path and sat down on a wrought-iron bench in the grass near the oak.

They gathered around him and they felt very cold, chilling his legs. Gingerly he reached out. A jack flickered through his hand, a cold, slimy feel. It returned, impaling, itself upon him. Repulsed, Rick drew back.

"Cody, let's go in now."

"Just a second, Daddy."

Rick stood, his legs swathed in repulsive greenjacks. A deep chill enveloped him. "Let's go, sport," he managed as he looked around, hoping to see the solitary jack again. He saw nothing, and the voices were growing louder. Too loud.

"Now, Cody."

"Just another minute."

"Well, I'm going to go make myself a sundae. If you want one too—"

Cody was past him, up the steps in a flash. Rick followed quickly. Before he closed the door, he took one last look, and for a moment he thought he spotted the solitary figure, but in an instant it was caught in the midst of the others, lost to his eye, but not to his mind.

21

The phone woke him at eleven-thirty.

"So how's it going out there in the butt end of California?"

Rick chuckled. "I miss having you around, O'Keefe."

"You just miss my gutter mouth." He paused. "You're lonely. Want my sister's phone number?"

"Stop trying to fix me up, Dakota. Listen, I'm building Don Quixote for the garden. Wait'll you see it. When do you think you'll have a chance to visit? You've got a standing invitation, you know."

"Wait a minute. You've lost it, right? You're on drugs? The old twat with the poodles raped you? What the hell does 'I'm building Don Quixote in my garden' mean?"

"For my garden. It's metal sculpture. I used to do it when I was a kid."

"Piper, I'm impressed. You're a Renaissance man, and here I thought you only excelled at writing cleverly snide comments about trucks, and bras, and cake mix. Guess I'll have to get a look at this. Does he have a big, hard lance?"

Rick laughed. "He will. The biggest one you ever laid your eyes on, O'Keefe."

"I'll visit soon." Dakota spoke in his sultriest voice. "Can't pass up the world's biggest lance, right?" He chuckled. "But what will your neighbors say?"

" 'How'd that guy get such a big, buxom blonde to pay attention to him?' is what they'll say."

"And I'll just smile and tell 'em that you can lick your own forehead. You'll never be lonely again."

"Bite me," Rick said, and instantly regretted the words because Dakota said he'd be glad to.

"So, Piper," he said after a few more minutes of banter and innuendo, "Have you see any of those jack-off things you were telling me about?"

"Greenjacks, not jack-offs." Rick paused. "But I like your term better. Wait a minute, Christ, I told you about those, didn't I?"

"That and more, Piper, dear. You're such an easy drunk, you *had* to tell me. You were *compelled.* But you didn't answer my question. Have you seen any jack-offs?"

He almost lied, then thought: What the hell? "Yeah, Dakota, I saw some. Isn't that a kick?"

Dakota didn't tease. "Does Cody see them?"

"No, it's just me. Nobody else is crazy. Same old story." He tried not to sound bitter.

"You're not crazy, you're just feeling sorry for yourself. Knock it off." Dakota didn't say anything else for a moment. Then: "What about that fat-bottomed cat of yours? Has he seen anything?"

"No, he just hates the poodles. And I don't blame him."

"Have you held Quint up to the window and shown the things to him?"

"No." Rick hesitated. "He did act odd last night at the same time as I imagined I heard the jacks. But I think it was coincidence."

"Maybe, maybe not. Look, cats are always staring at things normal people . . . Sorry Rick, you know what I mean—"

"Yeah, yeah, go on."

"Well, cats see things people don't. They stare at things in corners, and sometimes their fur stands on end."

"That's called a pylo-erection, O'Keefe," Rick said lightly. "Just thought you'd like to know."

"I know that. We always had cats. I know all about them." Dakota gave a small, throaty laugh. "I knew what I was doing when I went to the pound and chose Quint."

"You said you found him—"

"Well, I saved him from the gas chamber. He needed you, Piper, but I think you needed him more."

"I don't know what to say."

"Say thanks."

"Thanks," Rick repeated. "Really, thanks."

"You're welcome. Now, seriously, first chance you get, have the cat check out the jack-offs. See what he does."

"I hate to say it, but that's a good idea, O'Keefe."

"Of course it is, sweet thing. Call me back soon and tell me what happens."

22

After hanging up on Dakota, Rick went to check on his son one last time and was surprised to hear him giggling. He paused outside Cody's bedroom and waited a moment.

"Cody Thomas Piper," his son said softly. More giggling. "I wanna be a cowboy." Muffled giggles laddered the scale and down again. "Five."

"Cody?" Alarmed, Rick rapped on the door twice before opening it. In the shadows, he could just see his son's form in the bed nearest the window.

"Hi, Daddy!"

Rick flipped the overhead light on, making Cody squint and rub his eyes. "That's too bright!"

"So what's going on, sport?" Trying to appear casual and easygoing, he crossed to the bed and sat down next to his son. The frame creaked, a familiar sound.

"Nothin'."

"Who were you talking to?"

"My friend."

"Where is he?"

"You can't see him."

"Can *you* see him?" Rick asked, alarm returning.

Cody just giggled. "Of course not! You're silly, Daddy. He's invisible."

Rick felt better. Shelly had invented an invisible playmate

that lasted her entire seventh summer. This sort of thing, he could deal with. "What's your friend's name?"

"Bob," Cody told him solemnly. "His name's Bob."

Shelly's friend had been named Joyce. *What normal names children give the invisible,* he thought with amusement.

"Well, Cody, I heard you laughing in here. What were you guys talking about?"

"Bob wanted to know my biology."

"Your biology?"

"About me."

"Biography."

"Uh-huh. I told him about me and about you, too. That you're a big TV star."

"Was a little star," Rick corrected. "But thanks. It's kind of neat to have your own kid brag about you."

"Are you gonna be on TV again?" he asked hopefully.

"Maybe after a while." He might have to take the job if he was going to do all the renovations on the house that he planned. "It's getting late, sport."

"But Bob wants to talk some more."

"Not tonight." Rick raised his voice slightly. "Cody's going to sleep now, Bob. You can talk to him again tomorrow, okay?" He waited a moment, his ear cocked. "Bob said good night."

"No he didn't," Cody replied.

"He didn't? Well, what was that he said then?"

"Nothin'. He didn't say nothing."

"Anything," Rick automatically corrected. "Well, maybe he can't hear grown-ups. You tell him."

The boy was a born giggler, but once he got it out of his system, he looked around the room and announced, "Daddy says I gotta go to sleep now, but we can talk tomorrow. Okay? Bob? Okay?" Cody looked at Rick. "He won't answer me."

"Well, he probably went to sleep." He leaned down and kissed his son's forehead. "You too." He rose and walked to the door. "Good night, Cody."

"Night."

Rick flipped off the switch, adding, "Good night Bob," as he pulled the door closed. He smiled to himself.

Cody's giggle broke the silence.

"Cody?" he called sternly.

"Bob says good night," Cody called.

"Go to sleep, kiddo," he admonished. Shaking his head, he returned to his own bed. His son hadn't seen the green-jacks, but he turned right around and invented an invisible friend. He wondered if Cody would imagine greenjacks if he knew the stories.

As Rick lay down and switched off his lamp, he wondered if he himself would think he saw them if he hadn't been told the stories. He honestly didn't know.

23

Despite, or perhaps because of, all the memories he'd allowed himself yesterday, Rick slept like a baby until he awoke at eight Wednesday morning. Relaxing, staring at the ceiling, enjoying the morning sun, petting his cat, and feeling serene and calm, he was at peace for about three minutes.

"Shit." The serenity was swallowed by a rush of stomach acid that came with the sudden realization that he had a column due day after tomorrow and he hadn't even given it a moment's thought. "Shit." He didn't know what the hell he'd write about since he'd misplaced his notes on athletic shoes during the move.

He dragged his unwilling body out of bed and rubbed the small of his back. Among other things, he expected the furniture movers to show up today, and Lord, would that be a blessing for his abused spine.

In the shower, he stood under the water and let it play over his face and shoulders. "Massage," he said, not minding the water spraying into his mouth, only wishing he could adjust it to pound the tension out of his shoulders and neck. "I need a shower massager." He smiled: He'd buy several and write about those. He could test them this afternoon after working up a sweat moving a little furniture with the van guys, or after horsing around with his sculpture, and write his column tonight. It would be easy and fun, as columns allowing vague sexual innuendo and double entendre always were, the paper would spring for the shower gadgets, and he'd have an afternoon of—he groaned, but thought it anyway—good clean fun.

When he exited the shower with its puny little sprayer, he heard Shelly outside his door, calling his name in a dull, whiny voice.

"What, dear?" She hated to be called "dear," and he hated to be whined at. Synchronicity, he decided, pulling his jeans on.

"Can I take the car today?"

"No."

"Why not?" Hormonal teenage whining, four-star quality this time.

"Number one, it's my car. Number two, I told you yesterday that it's off limits."

"That's not a good reason."

"I can't think of a better one," he called smugly.

"Daa-ad, I need it. I *have* to go back to the mall."

"You've spent two days there already."

"I was doing job interviews."

"All day?"

"Daa-ad!"

He pulled on loafers, smirking because she was getting ticked, taking untold pleasure in applying karmic torture. "Have you actually applied anywhere, Shel?" he called. "Give me the truth, I can take it."

"Yes! Everywhere! And I'm supposed to be back at Nigel's Beauty Supply at eleven for an interview with the manager. I think she might hire me."

"That's great. You can walk."

"Daa-ad! My hair'll get all screwed up."

"Messed up. I'll drop you off, and you can walk home when you're done."

She mumbled something unintelligible but unmistakably rude, so he cheerfully informed her that if the movers showed up soon, she could take her bike. She mumbled something else, then begged him for a ride at ten-thirty. He made her wait a moment, then told her he'd do it. She left after that, doing sort of a combination drag-stomp to show him he wasn't being a good, cooperative father.

The jeans were okay for another day, but the socks were the last pair, and the dressing room was practically bare. He needed to do laundry. The meager supply of shirts he had brought in the car had dwindled to one slightly used blue-stripe button-down and a gaudy blue and black rayon shirt with distant Hawaiian bloodlines. He chose the Hawaiian, and as he slipped it on, his gaze dropped to the three twenty-four-inch base cabinets built into the wall.

Tense with memories, he hooked a finger around the door handles of the one he thought hid the secret passage. He pulled it open and peered inside, jumping when Quint, afflicted with terminal curiosity, rubbed up alongside him.

The empty cabinet had two wooden shelf supports attached halfway up. The shelf itself lay in the bottom of the cabinet, making him suspect that no one had used it in many years. Then he realized that the Ewebeans probably just threw their belongings inside without ever worrying about refinements.

He reached up on the inside back and felt for the lever, found it easily, and pushed it. Silently, surprisingly, the hidden panel in the back of the cabinet slid open, revealing the utter blackness beyond.

Involuntarily he shivered as cool air wafted over his face. Something scuttled somewhere in the passage, something small and blessedly distant. *More rats,* Rick thought, *more D-Con.* Quint hissed, then stepped tentatively toward the darkness.

"Uh-uh, no way, cat. You're not going in there." He pushed the animal away and released the lever to close the panel, then rose and crossed to the bedroom dresser, where he'd left the Pavilions bag containing the D-Con. After grabbing a few traps, he retrieved his little high-beam flashlight from his duffel bag and returned to the cabinet.

The cat watched balefully as Rick kneeled down and

opened the cabinet. After he readied the bait traps, he pushed
the lever again and watched the panel reopen. He flicked on
the flashlight.

*If Robin hadn't eavesdropped that night, would they still
be alive?*

Rarely had he let himself consider that possibility, but the
police had never caught the murderer. Robin did have his
reasons: School was going to start in a week, and he'd be
sent away. After his attempt to get Rick out the window
failed, he might have been desperate enough . . .

*Nonsense. You saw him that night in a clean yellow-
striped nightshirt.* Besides, as strong as he was, Robin hadn't
even been able to force him out the window.

*Quit driving yourself crazy, Piper! Set the damn traps and
close this thing before the damn cat climbs in!*

He shined the light into the opening and gasped when he
saw the knife.

It lay just inside the passage, and seeing its long, thin
blade filled his guts with ice. Carefully he picked it up by
the end of the handle and brought it out where he could
examine it more carefully. It was a filleting knife, its twelve-
inch blade coated with dust, its cork-covered handle speck-
led with blackish stains. *Blood.*

The murder weapon.

Suddenly nauseous, Rick threw the knife back in the passage. He let the panel close, barely recognizing the strangled
whimper he heard as his own. He slammed the cabinet door
shut, then rose, frantically searching the bedroom, then the
bathroom, for something he could use to secure the cabinet
doors. Frustrated, he ended up standing in middle of the
dressing room, telling himself he didn't need to secure anything. That's when he noticed the wire hangers hanging right
in front of him. He snagged one and unkinked it, then
quickly ran the wire through the cabinet handles and twisted
it tight, so that nothing could get in.

Or out.

He sat back, breathing hard, still queasy, and feeling very

childish and ashamed. Quint, who cared only about his stomach, circled around him, yowling.

"I put that wire there to keep you out of the cabinet," he told the cat. Instantly he felt better, because he could tell anyone who wondered, including himself, that the cat was the reason. The wire would do until he could disable the panel. He grinned. The cat would be his excuse to nail up every panel in the house.

He busied himself, trying to forget about the knife in the passage. After feeding the cat, he called to verify that the movers would arrive, then gathered his laundry and carried it downstairs, only to find Carmen tossing Cody's clothes in the washing machine. Silently she took his clothes from him, looked them over, then threw them in with Cody's things.

"I can do our laundry, Carmen."

"Hey, don't worry about it. I get paid for this, remember?" She eyed him. "What's on your mind?"

"I need a hammer and some nails."

She raised her eyebrows but didn't ask questions, just directed him to the toolbox on one of the laundry room shelves. He took a handful of tenpenny nails and a claw hammer. "I'll bring this back later."

"Hold on, Ricky. You're gonna let me feed you breakfast today."

"Well, coffee, maybe."

She made him eat toast, too, then they lingered over second cups while he told her about the movers and jotted down what he wanted them to put where, and whether to leave, store, or get rid of various pieces of furniture already in the house. When he told her, with great delight, to take down all the hyperthyroid paintings and return them to Jade, Carmen nodded approvingly.

"But the most important thing is to make sure all the furniture in my room is taken out and the new stuff put in. If I have to spend another night without my water bed, my back's going to be ruined for good."

"A water bed." Carmen made a funny face, "I didn't know you were such a playboy, Ricky."

"I got it for my back, not for . . . that."

"I'm teasing you, Ricky." She laughed. "You're so serious. How do you write those funny columns?"

Embarrassed, he shrugged.

"You ready, Dad?" Shelly swept into the room on the heels of her words. "We have to go! I can't be late."

He glanced at his watch. She was right. "Okay." He glanced at the hammer and nails on the table. "I'll get those later, Carmen. Is Cody around? I can take him with me—"

"He went to Home Depot a while ago with Hector. They're buying weed killer and things. That boy of yours just loves working in the yard."

Rick found that mildly amusing. "I hope he's not driving Hector nuts."

"No, he loves the company."

"Let's *go,* Dad!"

24

Armed with half a dozen decadent handheld shower massagers, Rick returned a couple hours later to find a moving van blocking the driveway, several roomfuls of ratty furniture stacked by the garage for the Salvation Army to take, and four burly guys with terminal butt-crack dragging his own furniture into the house, none too carefully. Carmen, hands on her hips, seemed to be in her element as she ordered them around.

"Need help?" he asked her.

"No, I'm fine," She lowered her voice. "Morons, they're morons. They bang up everything."

"That's what they're paid to do," he said lightly. He didn't want to think about it.

Rolling her eyes, she looked heavenward. "They did the three bedrooms first. Cody's in his room putting away his things."

"So my bed's up there?"

"Yeah, but I think they broke it. It's in a bunch of pieces."

"It's supposed to be," he said, then realized she was teasing him again. "If you don't need me, I'm going to go put it together."

"You should make them do it."

He shook his head. "Like you said, morons. It only takes a few minutes if you know what you're doing." He paused. "Oh, Christ, the cat. I left the cat up there."

"I know, don't worry. I put him in my house."

"You're an angel."

"I know," she said, and blessed him with a smile.

"Call me if you need me."

"Sure, Ricky."

Upstairs, he found Cody having a great time unpacking and generally making a mess. Watching him, Rick thought that it would be a good idea to nail the closet panel shut right away, not only to keep Quint out, but because if Cody discovered it and went inside, he could be bitten by a rat. Since he didn't know about the passages, he was unlikely to find it, but Rick decided he'd get to it, along with all the other panels in the house, within the next few days. The old beds and dressers were gone, replaced by his son's roomful of high-impact white furniture, and topped off by his race-car bed. The room looked a million times better.

He left the boy shoving Legos in one of the drawers beneath the closet and walked down the hall to his room.

"What a relief," he said, looking in. Despite the stacks of packing boxes, the master suite looked bigger than ever with his smooth bleached-oak furniture in place of the heavy, dark stuff. He set to work on the bed and, an hour later, had the mattress filling with the help of a garden hose he'd borrowed from the toolshed. Meanwhile, Rick attached a shower head, assured Carmen he was almost done using up all the hot water, and put away some of his clothes.

Twenty minutes later, the bed was filled. He coiled the hoses and headed downstairs, thinking that since he couldn't test the shower massage until the water heater refilled, he'd kill an hour by starting work on the frame for his metal sculpture. That was, if Carmen didn't need him.

A moment later, as Carmen shooed him out the front door, Shelly returned to announce she'd gotten a job at Nigel's Beauty Supply and that she could get makeup really cheap. Her sullenness had evaporated completely, and when she whirled and kissed him on the cheek, he was filled with desire to buy her a car, cable, a phone, and whatever else she wanted. He refrained from saying so, and as he walked to the workshop, he contented himself by hoping that having a job would teach her some respect—if not for him, then for his wallet.

25

Two hours later, he pushed the welder's mask back and surveyed his work. It didn't look like much, but it was big. He grinned. The base and half the horse's frame were complete. It was merely a stick figure, a simple skeleton upon which he'd build. Tomorrow, after the column was safely sent off, he'd finish the knight's form, and after that, he'd start the real work: the painstaking heating, bending, and cutting of the metal he would weld together to eventually create his horse and rider.

Now, however, the dinner hour was closing in, and he needed to take a shower or three very badly. Grabbing his shirt from the stool where he'd left it, he thought about putting it on, then used it to wipe his brow instead. He paused, looking at the frame. "What the hell," he said, and pulled the mask back over his face, deciding to allow himself just a minute more to complete a couple little finishing touches before cleaning up for the night.

"Hi!"

Startled, he turned, taking the acetylene torch with him, accidentally pointing it toward the friendly feminine voice.

She stood about ten feet away and was in the process of stepping farther back, her eyes on the flame.

Flustered, he shut off the torch's valve. "Sorry," he said, putting the tool down. "I didn't mean to— You startled me."

"I didn't mean to startle you," she said, retracing her steps. "Your housekeeper said I'd find you here."

Three feet from him, she halted. Rick stared dumbly, aware that she was the least Vegas-like female he'd seen for some time. She was no more than five three, with slender bones and small breasts. She wore a scoop-necked white tank top, tucked in to her jeans, and her mane of gold-red hair floated around her shoulders. *This woman is my type,* he thought, remembering Dakota's efforts to fix him up. He'd have to explain that to O'Keefe sometime.

"I'm Audrey," she said, extending her hand and smiling.

"Rick—" He snatched his hand back before it reached her, shoved the mask up, reextended his arm. "I'm Rick Piper. I'm afraid you have the advantage . . ."

"Oh." She looked flustered this time. "You didn't know I was coming?"

"No," he said sheepishly. "I don't even know who you are." *But I'd like to find out.*

"My brother was supposed to phone you to let you know I'd be bringing this by." She pulled an Express Mail envelope from her shoulder bag and handed it to him.

"Your brother?"

"Duane."

"Duane?" he asked, puzzled.

"Oh." Her smile lit up the room. "You probably call him Dakota."

Before he could react, she was talking again, words spilling out in a nervous rush. "He said it came for you Monday and that it was vital you got it, but he didn't have your address, so he sent it overnight to me and asked me to bring it over and make sure I gave it to you yourself." She smiled. "I just live over the hill in the Heights."

"You're Dakota's sister?" he asked in amazement. He owed Dakota an apology. O'Keefe did know his type.

Audrey smiled. "He described you to me, but you don't look quite like I expected."

In response, Rick set the letter down and pulled the welder's mask from his head and placed it on the workbench.

He looked down, saw the dirt and dust caked on his chest, hands, and arms, the stains on the jeans, and wondered what his face looked like. He grabbed his shirt and wiped his forehead. "I'm a mess, aren't I?"

She laughed, just a throaty little chuckle, and he liked it very much. He thanked God for California girls. The Beach Boys were right.

"Duane talks about you sometimes," she said. "He always says he wishes your, ah, sexual persuasion was, well, different." She blushed.

"I'm glad it's not," he heard himself say. In Las Vegas, sex was a buy-and-sell commodity, and Rick hadn't responded mentally or physically to a woman in a long, long time. Now his brain was alert, and there was an embarrassing twitch in his shorts. "Dakota's a very good friend."

She nodded. "He's a good guy." She continued to study him. "You're not small at all."

Before it dawned on him that she was talking about his height, he'd grabbed his shirt and draped it over his arm so it would conceal any embarrassing bulges in his jeans. "Small?" he asked, his voice cracking. He felt as if he were fourteen again, very embarrassed and very friendly.

"He said you were short. I thought you'd be five two or something."

"Five nine without shoes."

She grinned. "That's tall. Men taller than that give me a stiff neck." Suddenly she blushed. "I—I'm sorry, I don't know what gets into me sometimes. I didn't mean that the way it sounded . . . I mean . . ." She regained her composure with visible effort. "Aren't you going to open that?"

"Huh? Oh, yeah. I guess I should." He snagged the envelope, fumbled, finally ripped it open. Inside was a folded piece of paper. A single sentence, in Dakota's flamboyant hand, occupied the entire page: "I told you you'd like my sister." He stared at it. Stared some more.

"Is something wrong?"

"No. I, uh, hell. Here." He thrust the note at her.

Audrey stared at the note, then blushed to the roots of

her hair. "That rotten brother of mine," she began. "I was so nervous coming here because he kept calling me and telling me that . . . that . . . Christ. This is ridiculous." She took a deep breath. "I think Duane's playing matchmaker."

Rick nodded. "Dakota told me you were my type. I didn't believe him."

"He told me the same thing about you. I didn't believe him either."

"Want to have dinner with me?" he asked solemnly.

"Yes," she replied, her voice controlled and dignified.

"Want me to shower first?" he inquired even more gravely.

"That would be *very* nice." A giggle got loose, and she clapped her hand over her mouth. "I'm sorry," she said a second later. "This is all so weird."

"It is," he agreed, putting away his tools.

"So what is that?"

"It's a metal sculpture for my garden. With any luck, it'll look a little like Don Quixote." He closed the last cabinet. "Did your brother happen to mention I have children?"

"Yes. Why?"

"Just checking. You can see the house while I clean up. I have to take a shower," he added unnecessarily. Then he blurted, "I have to take several."

She laughed. "What?"

On the way into the house, he explained, then left her with Carmen and Cody while he went upstairs.

Half an hour later, Audrey drove them to Briarwood, an English pub with sawdust on the floor and a piano player who wore a garter on his sleeve and played Joplin at the correct tempo, something that constituted heaven as far as Rick was concerned. Sitting there drinking pints of Ballards while they waited for their food, he felt as if he were renewing an old friendship, not on a first, blind date that had been engineered with absolutely no subtlety whatsoever.

"I've never been here before," Rick said.

"Do you like it?"

"Love it." The piano player launched into "The Pineapple Rag." "This is my favorite kind of music."

"Really?" Audrey studied him. "You're not just saying that, are you? Duane didn't tell you?"

"Tell me what?"

"That I'm nuts for this stuff."

"Rags?"

She nodded. "Rags, jazz, pretty much anything written between *1895* and *1925.*"

Dream woman. "No, he didn't tell me anything except that you were just my type."

She smiled. "Sometimes my little brother's pretty smart."

"So," Rick said, studying her clear green eyes, "I hear you're an optometrist."

"And you're a journalist. I've been reading 'Consumer Crusader' for years. Duane said you did a TV show in Vegas." She waited as the matronly waitress set platters of fish and chips in front of them.

"You folks care for malt vinegar or lemon?"

"Lemon," Rick and Audrey said in unison. *This is too good to be true,* he thought. *Way too good.* Something had to go wrong soon.

"Lots of lemon, tons," Audrey called after the server. "So are you going to do a new show?"

"Not unless I need the money."

"Are you a writer first and consumer advocate second, or the other way around?" She paused, a piece of fish raised to her lips. "I'm sorry. I'm asking too many questions."

"No, it's fine. I like both, but I guess I lean toward the consumer side. My first year in college, I discovered all those books on subliminal advertising, and it kind of bloomed from there." He smiled.

They talked through dinner about things he couldn't recall later. The time flew by, the ale loosened them up. "So what has your brother told you about me?" he asked over coffee.

"Not a lot. He told me who you were, which was a kick

since I always read your column, and I think I already told you that. He described you as 'regrettably straight,' that you had two kids and wanted to get your daughter away from Vegas."

"Did he tell you why?"

"Oh, boy, did he." She sipped her coffee. "That came out the other night after he had another fight with Lil. He said she's encouraging your daughter—"

"Shelly."

"Thanks, encouraging Shelly to become a show girl." She shook her head. "I wish Duane would kick Lil out, once and for all. She treats him like dirt, but the poor guy never could resist a stray."

Hearing that gave Rick pause.

"Is something wrong?"

"I might be one of his strays."

She reached across the table and squeezed his hand. "No. Lil was a prostitute. Couldn't get a job. He helped her clean up her act." She smiled. "As far as you're concerned, Duane's a wee bit star-struck."

Rick squeezed her hand back, and neither let go. "You're not," he said coyly.

She laughed, a delightfully musical sound. Her hand was on top of his, and she slowly moved her finger over his palm. It drove him nuts. "I guess not," she agreed.

"Are you sure Dakota didn't say anything about me?" he asked.

"Like what?"

"Well, did he say anything about my eyes, for instance?"

She cocked her head. "Your eyes? No, I don't think so. Why?"

"Oh, I don't know," he said casually. "I just wondered if he'd said anything else. I used eyes as an example . . . a paean to your profession."

"He didn't say a word, Rick, but he should have. You've got the most incredible dark blue irises. Are they contacts?"

"Nope. They're characteristic of the Piper clan."

"Well, they're gorgeous." She finished off her coffee. "What'dya say we blow this Popsicle stand?"

"What do you have in mind?"

"How about a yogurt stand? There's one just down the street. We can walk."

A few minutes later, they were strolling along the Via Pecado, downtown Santo Verde's picturesque main street. White firefly lights twinkled in the limbs of the small trees lining the sidewalks, and warm yellow glowed from the storefronts of the restaurants and businesses still open. They bought chocolate cones at the yogurt stand and continued to stroll. Rick had never willingly walked in town after dark before, but wasn't too surprised to find that on these civilized streets, there were no greenjacks to torment him.

She'll drop you like a hot coal once you tell her you see little green men, so you'd better not talk about eyes anymore, Piper, not if you want to see her again.

"Is your last name O'Keefe? Dakota mentioned that you used to be married."

"See? He *did* tell you something about me. Yes, it's O'Keefe. I was young and stupid when I got married. It didn't last long, and I threw the name out with the husband." Sidelong, she looked at him. "Did Duane tell you why we broke up?"

He almost said no, then decided bluntness had worked fine so far. "Yes, he did. Dakota was bragging about his left hook, and I asked him who he hooked. He told me." He waited, but she said nothing. "He said the man abused you."

"That's a nice way of putting it. He broke my jaw once. My wrist, too. He was a drunk. Lil's a drunk, too. I wish Duane would learn from my mistakes. He sure lectured me about Ron, so you'd think he'd learn."

"How long did you stay with him?"

"Too long. Five years. Let's sit." She indicated a white bench outside Much Ado About Books, a venerable bookstore where Rick had bought all his Batman comics way back when. "I don't know how much longer I would have stayed if Duane hadn't grown up and caught him shoving me around."

"He abused you the whole time?"

She nodded, gave him a half smile. "Hard to believe I'd stick around?"

"Actually, it is. You seem very sure of yourself."

"After I left, I lived with Duane for a while. He was pretty screwed up himself; he hadn't discovered his true calling yet. I also went to a shrink, who told me I had to stop feeling like I deserved to be treated like dirt. Ron always told me I deserved what he dished out, and I took it for truth. My therapist said it was because I had one of those deadly cold daddies who was into bare-butt spanking. She also thought he'd abused me, but I don't recall. Those are such in things right now, blaming everything on your parents and being sexually abused. I'd prefer to think I got screwed up all on my own."

"Adults do screw up their kids, though," Rick ventured.

"Sure, of course. But I learned that instead of blaming your problems on other people, you look at them as your responsibility. To overcome them is your challenge. It's the only way to grow. At least the only way I could. Your yogurt's melting."

Rick looked down and saw that his hand was shrouded in melting chocolate. Absently he wiped it off, then tossed the remains of the cone and the napkin in the trash can across the sidewalk.

"Good shot."

"Go on" he said. "Please."

"I'm not boring you?"

"No! The opposite." The things she'd said made him want to tell her about Robin; he was bursting to spill his guts. But he didn't dare. "You were saying?"

She smiled uncertainly. "Oh, well, I just decided to take responsibility for my own self-destructive tendencies, and I overcame them." She smiled. "For the most part, anyway. In the process, I went back and got my O.D., took some assertiveness training, and tried to get it together."

"From the looks of things, you've more than succeeded."

She blushed. "Thanks. It's taken ten years and lots of hard work to get where I am now. I opened my own office last year." Her nose crinkled as she grinned. "I'm pretty proud of that."

"You should be."

"My mother used to call me 'Little Audrey,' like in the comics?" She made a face. "And my dad called me his calico kitten."

"That's nice," Rick said, confused.

"Yes, but I took it to mean I was powerless."

"I had a cute little marmalade kitten," Rick said. "He grew into a big bruiser who takes crap from no one." He smiled. "Especially me." He took her hand, and she immediately twined her fingers among his.

"I like your attitude, Rick." She turned on the bench to face him. "So what about you? Any brothers or sisters?"

"A brother," he said, "Deceased."

He used discretion as he talked, describing his twin's handicap, touching on the greenjacks, mentioning that he was a gullible kid who believed the stories and, hence, was teased by his embittered brother. When he got to the part about his parents' murder, he only said that it happened. "I was afflicted with Ewebeans after that," he finished.

She chuckled. "That sounds like a horrible disease."

"It was. Is. You didn't see her, but Aunt Jade still lives in the house. She keeps poodles, and when they die, she gets them stuffed."

"So how'd you turn out so normal?" she asked.

He laughed, long and genuinely. "Boy, have I got you fooled."

"Well, then, I guess I'll just have to work on figuring you out. You look tired, Rick."

He glanced at his watch. It was already past ten. "I don't want to go home yet," he said conspiratorially. "Do you?"

"No. There's a jazz club a couple miles from here down on the boulevard. They serve gourmet coffee. I'm not up to any more drinking," she said apologetically.

"Me either. But jazz sounds fine."

On the way to the car he stopped to call home. Carmen answered, said everything was fine, did he have his key, and have fun. He'd had one phone call, a person, sex unknown, named after a state, who wanted Rick to call back.

They stayed out till midnight, talking like old friends. Then Audrey declared morning would come too soon and she drove him back to his house, pulling all the way up the long driveway and turning the car around in the wide parking area in front of the garage.

The lawn was crawling with greenjacks, and Rick's stomach twisted so hard, he thought he was going to vomit, even though he still sat in the passenger seat. *You have to walk through them. Do you want this woman to think you're nuts? Remember, they can't hurt you.*

"Rick, what's wrong?"

"Nothing," he told her. "I, ah, just realized I have work tonight. I need to take five more showers and write my column before noon tomorrow."

"Poor guy," she said from the driver's seat. "It's a dirty job you have to do."

They laughed, then slowly, slowly, leaned together, eyes locked, lips trembling. Anticipation wove through his body, made it tingle deep in his abdomen and long into his limbs. Hour-long seconds passed, deliciously, then their lips met and it was a first kiss, chaste, gentle, and warm. Exciting.

After, they pulled back enough to gaze at each other. Audrey's nostrils were flared and her pupils were so big, they looked perfectly black.

Rick took this as a good omen. "Can I see you again?"

"I was afraid you'd never ask," Audrey murmured.

They agreed on dinner and a movie for Friday night, then Rick reluctantly got out of the car. She waved and drove away.

Icky Ricky, dicky Ricky, Ricky, Ricky, play today!

Thomas, Thomas, Thomas, he thought back. *Thomas, Thomas, Audrey, Thomas.* By the time one more Audrey slipped between the Thomases, he was at the door without breaking into a run.

Shelly was in the living room watching an ancient God-zilla movie. "Hot date, Dad?"

She was still in a good mood. "Dakota's sister, Audrey. Dakota sent her to see how we're doing. She's pretty nice."

"Yeah, I bet!" Shelly teased him for another minute, then brought him up-to-date on her new job, which she'd begin tomorrow, the brands of makeup they carried, and all sorts of other things he didn't actually care about, but loved be-cause it meant he was back in communication with his daughter. He listened attentively, noting that not once did she demand any material gifts. Tomorrow, he decided, he'd call the cable company. One could only do without *South-park* for so long.

Within a half hour she wound down, and together they closed up the house and went upstairs. Still energized from his time with Audrey, Rick managed to install two of the shower heads, one in each upstairs bath, and test them. Stretching luxuriously in his bed, enjoying the warmth and the way it felt against his neck and back, he thought that in the morning he'd switch them for the others, and test those before doing the column. "Life is good," he told the ceiling.

Beside him, Quint flattened himself out to soak up every square inch of warmth his body would allow. The cat always seemed to know exactly where the warm spots were, and it occurred to Rick that he'd read somewhere that they could see infrared-heat waves. *Cats can see things we can't.* That's what Dakota had said when he urged Rick to see if Quint could see the jacks. He couldn't get to sleep because he had Audrey O'Keefe on the brain. Part of it was delightful, part of it wasn't. If they continued to hit it off, what would she say if he told her about the jacks? That would be the end of it: Nobody wanted to date a psycho.

"Okay, cat, let's take a walk." He rose, slipped a robe on over his shorts and T-shirt, then scooped up the cat, holding it against his chest so it was looking over his shoulder.

The house waited silently as he walked quietly down the

front stairs, then tiptoed across the living room, praying that
Jade's poodles wouldn't hear him. Without pausing to think
twice, he slipped between the draperies and the picture window.

They were out there in the grass beneath the oak, doing
their endless dances. Slowly they became aware of him and
turned to watch him as he watched them, a few moving
closer to the window.

Behind him, muffled noises from Jade's room startled
him. He listened a moment, and realized that the old lady
was talking in her sleep, giggling and moaning, sounding
like she was—*how disgusting*—making love. The cat
growled low in its throat, prompting Rick to scratch its ears
to calm it. He waited, but Jade continued to make her obscene sounds. *To hell with her.*

Icky Ricky, come play, hey, Ricky.

The cat didn't react this time, but its ears were aggres-
sively forward, its attention focused on Jade's folding doors.

Several greenjacks melted together and oozed up, wraith
like, just outside the window. "Okay, kitty," Rick whispered
as he turned the cat toward the window. "Look at this."

Two seconds passed before the cat reacted, then Quint's
muscles tensed, its claws sinking into Rick's arm. Ears
back, the cat growled, not low and menacing this time, but
the high-pitched panicked sound of a frightened animal.
The wraith shifted toward the left, and the cat's head moved
with it.

Suddenly the cat hissed and tore Rick's flesh, frantic to
get away. "Jesus," he whispered as he clamped one hand on
the front paws, and trapped the back under his arm. He was
barely able to keep from yelling as the feline's hind legs
kicked his side through the thick robe.

"Shhh!" He slipped out of the drapes and moved to the
stairs and up, the sounds of Jade's now loud moaning mixing
with the cat's whining snarl.

Finally he entered his room, shutting and locking the door
before letting the cat free. Quint hissed again, then disappeared beneath the headboard of the bed.

26

Rick finished his column with an hour to spare, which was fortunate since he hadn't had time to hook up his fax, so at eleven-fifteen he drove downtown and had it sent from a stationery store.

After that, not quite ready to return to the house, he cruised through Santo Verde. The older business and residential areas had changed very little, retaining their old-fashioned, moderately well-to-do charm, but the outskirts of town had grown tremendously between the new housing tracts, condos, and businesses. As he passed the mall, he stifled the urge to stop in and see how Shelly was doing— she'd hate that. When she'd come to the study this morning to tell him good-bye—she'd conned Hector into giving her a lift—she'd still been in her newfound good mood, and he hoped it was going to last. If it did, he decided to buy her an inexpensive new car for her birthday next month.

As he drove away from the new area and back toward the house, he turned off on Cuerpo Podre and took the long, winding avenue until he arrived at the tall wrought-iron arches of Santo Verde Cemetery. He paused, then turned in, deciding to pay a visit to his parents' graves.

The cemetery, which occupied a series of small rolling hills, looked much as he remembered it, filled with oaks and pines and oleander hedges, very green, very peaceful. At least in the daylight hours. *I'll bet this place is infested with greenjacks at night.* He smiled grimly. Since the cat's reaction last night, he couldn't help thinking that maybe he really was seeing something, and had decided that after he got to know Audrey better, maybe he would ask her about variations in people's vision. Very subtly, of course.

He pulled over and parked the car, then plodded up a steep pathway. Soon he reached the oldest section of the grounds, The Garden of Souls, a place rife with looming crosses and pensive angels. Here and there stood ornate family mausoleums dating back to the early nineteenth century. They constituted California's version of ancient history.

Rick wandered among the monuments, reading the names and dates, noting signs of earthquake damage, perversely wondering how far down the ground squirrels burrowed.

Strolling down the other side of the hill, he entered The Eternal Playland, one of the children's burial areas. Some of the graves here were new, and one even had a Lucite covering that protected a color portrait of the dead child's smiling face. Chilled, he averted his eyes and continued quickly along the narrow path until he reached The Forest Eternal, an older area containing the Piper plots.

Despite his other fears, Rick had always enjoyed coming here, even as a child. He'd favored it over the regular park because everyone here was . . . quiet. He smiled to himself. And though he himself had no intention of ending up here— cleansing flames and a brisk ocean breeze were his preferences—he especially liked this area because of the decidedly nonreligious monument central to the family domain. Like the angels and cherubs and obelisks elsewhere in the park, it was a marble sculpture, but this, chiseled by an Italian artist friend of Conlin's, was a Scottish piper, complete with bagpipes and kilt. As a child, Rick came here often to sit at its feet. Sometimes he talked to it, pretending it was his ancestor Thomas. Who knew? Maybe it was. He found he'd still like to think so.

He stood before the piper and studied the strong taciturn

features shadowed under its tam. It stared back, bearing little resemblance to any of his relatives, living or dead. He stuck his hands in his pockets. "How's it hangin', Thomas?" Belatedly he looked around to make sure no one heard him, and was relieved to see that only the ghosts, if any were around, might have heard. Secure in his isolation, he approached his brother's grave. "Robin Emeric Piper," he read aloud. "Born 1965. Died 1981. Beloved nephew."

Aunt Jade, of course, had chosen the epitaph. "Beloved nephew" was putting things mildly.

Looking at the grave had little effect on Rick. He didn't miss his brother, hadn't shed a tear when he'd died. He was numb, unfeeling, where Robin was concerned. Beneath the numbness there was something else, something he didn't like to think about.

Dakota's voice intruded: *Of course you hated him.*

Maybe . . . *Was he really as cruel as I remember?* he wondered. Certainly he liked to tease, but Rick had been so . . . so touchy. So oversensitive.

Slowly he moved to the Celtic cross ten feet behind Robin's marker. PIPER was chiseled into the cross arm, and at its base were the words TOGETHER IN LIFE AND IN HEAVEN. Below the cross, to either side, were two flat bronze markers, one for Franklin Richard Piper, 1940–1975, the other for Grace Dorian Piper, 1946–1975.

As Rick knelt in the grass between the markers, hot tears sprang to his eyes. Flowers, he thought, he should have brought flowers.

September 1, 1975

They died during the dog days, on a night so hot and humid that the water coolers did nothing but release warm steam through the ceiling vents. They were off now, and the night was quiet except for the soft whirring of the ceiling fan.

Since moving into Carmen's old room in July, Ricky, no

longer having to contend with his brother's tricks, or oak limbs tapping on the window glass, slept better than he ever had before.

But tonight sleep would not come, and unaccountably nervous, he'd gotten out of bed to check the twist-lock on the doorknob half a dozen times. Now, at five past midnight, he lay on top of the damp sheets and listened to the heavy silence, while sweat trickled off his forehead. His head felt thick with the heat, and able to stand it no longer, he rose and went to the window overlooking the backyard, his fear of the night and the greenjacks now secondary to the stifling misery of the room. Turning the latch, he pushed the window open wide.

The cooling breeze fluttered the curtains around his face, evaporating perspiration from his forehead, from the lids of his closed eyes.

At that moment he realized that he hadn't heard the greenjacks calling him tonight. Even with the window open they remained silent.

He opened his eyes and peered out, but saw only the dim yellow glow of Carmen's porch light within the dark orchard.

No greenjacks.

No crickets.

Wind ruffled through his hair like familiar fingers, and despite the heat, goose bumps prickled across his neck.

The wind died.

Time ended.

Something was going to happen.

The night waited, the wind, the boy.

He crossed to his desk and sat in the chair. He folded his hands on the blotter. And waited.

Somewhere, a board creaked, once, twice. It might be his brother wandering through the secret passages, spying on others while they slept. Or perhaps it was only the house settling in the heat of the night, its timbers like heavy, swollen limbs.

He sat, listening, unmoving, staring at the Felix the Cat clock above his desk, glancing at the Batman calendar hanging beside it, considering minutes, days, and hours, thinking about how slow time passed when something was about to happen.

At 1:15 he heard new noises downstairs, faint sounds muted by the thick walls of the house and his own closed door. He sat up straighter and listened carefully. *Robin's in the kitchen.* He imagined his twin basking in the cool breath of the open refrigerator, balancing on one hand so that he could reach up and take the milk carton from the top shelf, then settling down on his legless body to take a drink, swirl it around in his mouth, and spit it back in. He would carefully close the carton and replace it before committing his other mischiefs, which might be running his tongue over the butter, or chewing small wads of raw hamburger before working the fouled pieces back into the main lump of meat.

At 1:35 there was silence once again.

An instant passed and it was 1:51. Ricky wondered what Robin was doing now, whether he had returned to his room or was still roaming the house . . . If Robin didn't want you to hear him, you didn't hear him.

The clock over the desk said 2:15, and it was just as hot and sticky as it had been at midnight, and Ricky, still wide-awake, continued his vigil. To pass the time, he thought about his brother, and how he would be sent away to a special boarding school in a week's time. Ricky could hardly wait, and each time Robin teased him now, he reveled in the knowledge that soon he would have far less to fear. That knowledge had carried him through the endless hot days and nights of July and August.

Three o'clock in the morning. Even though his brother was still here, Ricky knew, he had already begun to relax, to feel safer within these walls. But not tonight. Instead, the tension, the anticipation he felt, had wound tighter and tighter, and before long, he knew he would snap.

At 3:15 he heard something that sounded like a human whimper, followed by a thump.

He waited, unthinking, unfeeling. Numb.

At 3:20 the house sighed and settled as the night exhaled its first cool breeze into the room.

Ricky remained at his desk, back straight, hands neatly folded, a schoolboy ready for his lessons.

At 4:30 in the morning, the first glimmering of dawn shone in the east window next to the desk.

And broke the spell.

Woodenly he rose and walked slowly to the door. His stomach had tied itself in knots because it knew the waiting was over. He put his ear to the door, listened, heard nothing, then lay down on the floor and peered through the narrow space between door and carpet. The hallway was deserted.

Standing, he unlocked the door and slowly opened it.

The house lay still in the predawn shadows as he ventured into the hall.

Turning the corner, he cautiously approached Robin's room, and was relieved to see that no light shone from beneath his door. Ricky tiptoed past, then continued down the corridor until he arrived at his parents' room.

His brain, dazed and paralyzed by something unidentifiable for these last few hours, suddenly came to life. Why was he here? Why was he about to disturb his parents so early in the morning? He found he didn't know, but to do so was an imperative he could not ignore.

Raising his hand to knock on the door, he realized that Robin might also hear, so instead, he clutched the doorknob and slowly turned it. As the door swung silently inward, he heard the steady whirring of the ceiling fans within the room.

"Mom?" he whispered. "Dad?"

They didn't wake up, so he stepped inside, then, still fearing that Robin would hear, closed the door behind him.

"Mom?" he called. Then again, a little louder. "Mom?"

In the bathroom, a faucet dripped.

He approached the bed, his heart thundering against his rib cage. Although the windows were open and the cool northerly breeze had picked up, his parents' bedroom, hot and close, was foul with a heavy, hot smell that made the hairs on the back of his neck prickle up.

He stepped closer to the bed, thinking that it was strange that Mom and Dad were under their quilt on such a hot night. Shrugging to himself—grown-ups did all sorts of weird things he didn't understand—he reached out and tapped the quilt, about where his mother's shoulder should be.

She didn't wake up.

"Mom?" he asked, poking at the quilt a little harder.

The material felt funny, sticky-damp. "Mom!" He practically yelled it, fear curling through his bowels.

"Dad!" Leaning across her, he shook his father. "Dad!"

Suddenly he lost his tiptoed balance and fell on them, landing facedown, mouth open, on the quilt. Abruptly he became aware that the sticky dampness was everywhere, and as he breathed in its rusty metal smell, he realized it was in his mouth and he recognized the flavor of blood from a hundred cuts he'd licked, from a bloody nose last year, from . . .

"Dad! Mom!" Falling backward, he screamed their names. "Wake up!" he cried as he backed toward the wall. He gulped for air. "Please wake up!" Frantically he felt for the light switch, smearing his hands over the wall. "Wake up," he pleaded once more as his hand hit the switch.

Light bloomed overhead.

For a moment he couldn't comprehend what he was seeing. The white homemade quilt with its blue and green wedding ring patterns had turned red. His mother's eyes were open, her mouth, too, and briefly he thought she was about to speak to him. Then he realized that her head was tilted back at an unnatural angle.

He moaned. Her head was almost off her body, there was red meat in her neck, and white bones, gleaming. Beside her, his father . . . His father was the same. Ears ringing, Ricky sank to the floor, blackness invading his vision.

Ricky's stomach moved, roiling, and as he vomited, he saw their blood all over his clothes, his hands, and knew he had their blood in his mouth. He vomited again.

He tried to stand up, couldn't. *Have to get out of here! Have to! Now!* Grabbing the doorknob, he pulled himself up, refusing to look at the bed, refusing to think. As he tried to open the door with his slippery, sticky fingers, he heard himself crying but thought it was someone else. Finally he got the door open and slammed his body out into the hall.

"Ricky!" Robin was watching him from the threshold of his room. "Hi, icky Ricky! Wanna play?"

Ricky stared at him without comprehension.

Robin grinned.

I'm gonna getcha, icky Ricky, I'm gonna getcha good!

Ricky ran, racing down the stairs, tripping and rolling down the last ten, not even aware that he'd broken his arm as he regained his feet, only aware that Robin might be following him as he started running for the kitchen.

The glass in the back door was shattered, the screen torn, and the door stood wide open. As he raced into the backyard, into the orchard, he heard Robin call his name, heard his hand-slaps, but he kept running, running, running, until he reached Carmen's doorstep.

As he pounded on the door, he glanced back. No one was there.

Between the grave markers, Rick Piper wept silently. He wept for himself and for his parents.

He wept for what might have been.

The days after the murder had been a blur. He spent the first two in the hospital, and there had been so many questions, so many policemen, so many nightmares. Eventually the police announced that the house had been broken into, nothing stolen, except for a stainless filleting knife from the kitchen that never reappeared. It was presumed to be the murder weapon. Though a few suspects were questioned, no arrests were ever made.

And Robin didn't go away after all.

That was a long time ago. Wiping his eyes, he stood and

brushed grass from his pants. *A very long time.* He moved
away, only to stop once more at Robin's grave. "You couldn't
get me, so you killed them instead, didn't you?" He kicked
a small stone, and it hit Robin's marker with a thunk. "I
hated you. I still hate you."

Admitting it made him feel better. The only thing he still
couldn't reconcile was the childish notion that his brother
had exchanged bodies with a greenjack, when logic dictated
that the handicapped boy had gone mad.

He stared at the grave and tried to understand his brother.
It must have been hard to be handicapped, he told himself.
*It must have been awful to look at me every day and wonder
why you were the one without legs. No wonder you hated me.*

And no wonder I hated you. "You told me I was crazy,"
he whispered bitterly. "You told me they were going to send
me away. You threatened me and called me names. You told
me you were going to kill me. And you *tried.* Goddamn you,
you *tried.*" Unthinking, he kicked the headstone. It hurt like
hell and increased his fury. "Goddamn you, you even said
it was my fault they died! Fuck you!" He raised his voice,
not caring if anyone heard. "Fuck you! Fuck you!"

The tears came back, hot and furious, tears of anger and
hate and frustration. He dropped to the ground, exorcising
twenty-six years of anger and hurt.

Finally the tears dried, and then, guiltily, he realized why
he had never declared his hate and anger toward Robin before. *He saved my life that Halloween night when we were
seven. He let Big Jack take him instead of me.*

"Oh, God," he moaned, falling to his knees, knowing he
himself was mad. "Oh, God."

Finally, slowly, he regained control of himself. *Can't think
about this.* Rising, he knew he still couldn't handle the
memories, the confusion that went with them. He washed
his face at a water fountain and went back to the old Garden
of Souls section to lose himself in other people's history.

27

"This house is riddled with secret passages," Rick told Audrey as they sat at the kitchen table after their date Friday night. "The blueprints disappeared way before my time, so I don't even know how many tunnels there are." He sipped his coffee. "This morning we had that installed—" he pointed at the new dishwasher "—and the workmen broke into a passage we didn't even know existed."

"Really? In the kitchen?" Audrey said over her coffee cup. "Maybe your great-grandfather liked to sneak midnight snacks without his wife catching him."

Eat it up! Robin whispers, shoving raw hamburger down his throat. Eat it up!

"You look like you've seen a ghost, Rick. Are you all right?"

"Fine." He didn't think the raw-meat story would be appropriate. "My brother traveled the tunnels all the time," he added lamely.

"You didn't?"

"No. I've been in them, but not willingly. When I was very young, my grandfather took me through a few of the main ones, which was okay, but later, Robin knew how to force me to go with him."

"Most little boys would love secret tunnels in the walls."

She paused, studying him. "I take it your brother made that miserable, too?"

"Yes, that and the fact that I was ridiculously afraid of the dark." He set his cup down. "I still don't like it. Grandpa Piper's stories about the greenjacks had more effect on me than they should have."

"Greenjacks," she repeated. "You mentioned them before. What are they, anyway?"

Over fresh cups of coffee, he told her Grandfather's stories, surprised and rather pleased to find he still knew them word for word. "Pretty silly stuff to be afraid of, huh?"

"No, it's not silly at all. Fairy tales are the worst! I was scared silly by Hansel and Gretel." She pushed red hair away from her face and lowered her voice conspiratorially. "When I was about five, my favorite uncle, Craig, told me the story. I was okay at first, just really impressed, you know? But then, every time he'd come over, he'd say, 'Let's see if your fingernails are clean.'

"The first time, I didn't know what was going on. I held out my hands, and he examined my fingers very closely, very seriously. Uncle Craig was a big, tall man with lots of black hair, one long eyebrow, and a very deep voice, so when he looked at me from underneath his brow and intoned, 'Well, those nails are pretty dirty. I guess we won't have you for dinner . . . this week!' I was sure he meant it." She looked at Rick. "So can you guess what I did after that?"

Rick shook his head. "What?"

"Every Sunday, before Uncle Craig came over, I'd go out in the backyard and frantically scrape my nails in the dirt until they were caked! I was scared to death of the man, scared to death. And he never even knew it."

"How old were you when you lost your fear?"

"I didn't. Uncle Craig got killed when I was seven." She smiled thinly. "It was tragic, really. He worked for CalTrans. They were paving part of I-10, and he had a freak accident with a steam roller."

Rick decided not to smile.

"The last time I dug in the yard was right before we went to the funeral." She stifled a giggle. "You know, just in case. At the service, I was sitting next to my mother, and I remember hearing her make this little 'tsk tsk' sound, you know? I tried to keep my hands hidden for the rest of the day." She sipped her coffee. "About a month later I overheard her telling my dad how much my hygiene had improved lately."

"Thank you," Rick said.

"For what?"

"That story."

"Oh?" She raised her eyebrows quizzically.

"I've never thought about other people's reactions to fairy tales before." He shook his head, amazed. "Never. I can't believe how shortsighted I've been. I mean, I knew I overreacted because I judged my reaction against my brother's opposite one. It's never occurred to me that anyone else would take a story as seriously as I did."

"Well, I sure did. Lots of people do. That's a pretty insulated view you had there, Piper."

"I never talked to anybody about it. Robin constantly told me I was crazy and if I told about any of it—fear of the greenjacks, fear of my brother—the grown-ups would find out I was nuts and send me to an asylum."

"What a cruel little monster he was! You must have hated him."

"When Dakota said that, I denied it. Now I know it's true." He shook his head. "It just never occurred to me that anyone else might be frightened."

"Well, plenty are. We all talked about it when we were kids." She paused. "By 'we,' I mean girls. I think there's a difference between the sexes. It was okay for us to be afraid and to talk about it, even to enjoy it." She smiled. "Every time we had a sleep-over, we had a seance and ended up screaming ourselves silly. But little boys have to pretend to be brave. And males don't seem to talk to each other about serious stuff. It's 'Hey, Bud, pass me a cold one,' or 'Yo, Jo, lookit da tail on that chick.' "

Rick laughed. "There's a lot of that. But look at Cody. He's not into impressing anyone with his testosterone yet, but he seems to have no fear of the dark, or anything else in particular. Driving here from Vegas, he wanted to stop up at Madland, you know that old West movie place up on I-15 by Madelyn?"

"Out of Barstow?"

"Yeah." He paused. "There were ads along the road for the Haunted Mine Ride for a hundred miles before we passed the place, and I was starting to wish I could chloroform the kid." He pitched his voice up an octave. " 'Daddy, I wanna go in the haunted mine! I wanna see ghosts! Are there zombie miners there?' " He laughed.

"Are you still afraid of things like that?" she asked softly.

"Yes." He'd never admitted it before, but it seemed fine to tell. "I did not want to go in there. Fortunately, we were on a schedule. But it made me feel funny knowing that if there had been time, I would have found a way out of it."

"Do things that jump out at you really bother you, like the ghouls in the Haunted Mansion at Disneyland?"

"God, I've never been in there. I'm afraid of making an ass out of myself, squealing or something. I'm a roller coaster man myself," he added in the deep, stupid voice he equated with rednecks.

She smiled briefly. "You didn't answer my question. Is it the dark or things jumping out at you that you can't handle?"

"Let's put it this way: My brother thought the height of amusement was jumping out of dark corners and yelling boo. He didn't do it too often," he added, studying his hands. "He always waited until some time had passed and my guard went down, then 'boo!' and he'd laugh and laugh. It made me jumpy. I ended up with nerves of cellophane."

"You learned to always be on your guard. It must have done wonders for your self-confidence, too," she added dryly.

"Oh yes, wonders." He drained his cup. "More?"

"Sure."

He took their cups to the counter and poured more from

the Mr. Coffee. "The last thing I meant to do is whine about my past," he said, sitting back down.

"Lord, you're hard on yourself, Rick!" She paused. "Can I ask you a question?"

"Sure."

"It's a weird one."

He laughed. "Go ahead."

"Those greenjacks. Did you think you could see them, like the boy in the stories?"

Rick slopped his coffee. "What?"

"You did, didn't you?" she pressed. "It's no big deal. Lots of people think they see things. Not just kids. Every other person in Ireland would probably say they've seen a leprechaun or fairy at one time or another." She smiled. "Nowadays people see little gray aliens, but it's all the same thing. I think."

"Yeah, I used to think I saw them. I thought—still think—I probably just wasn't too well adjusted."

"Well, you had a sadistic brother, and a lot of these things are tied up with abuse. A person can't stand thinking that someone who supposedly loves them is hurting them, so they invent something else to take the blame. From what I've read, it happens a lot."

"That makes a lot of sense." He paused. "And it probably applies to me. No wonder your brother was always telling me to see a shrink," he added casually. "Listen, Audrey. Can I ask you a weird question too?"

"Fair's fair."

"Well, in your practice, have you ever run in to anyone who can see things other people can't? Like infrared rays, for instance?"

"That used to happen to cataract patients, but that's not what you mean, is it?"

"No, I mean naturally. Like cats see infrared."

She considered. "It's possible, but it would probably be impossible to detect during an eye exam unless it was a person with an ocular deformity. James Thurber had that problem. The brain fills in what the eye doesn't pick up."

She smiled. "But he put it to good use—he put the things he saw into his cartoons."

"What about someone with twenty-twenty vision? Could they see something?"

"Rick? Do you still see them?"

"No, no, no, of course not," he replied hastily, then started to skate. "I have a cousin back in Scotland who says he's seen them all his life. He's intelligent, has a good job, and seems perfectly sane. But he sees them. I've just always wondered if maybe he really does."

"What does he say they look like? Are they solid?"

"No, not at all." He described them briefly, leaving out all mention of Big Jack.

"Something like that sounds like it's in the realm of light waves, so it's possible." Audrey studied him a long time. "Let me do a little research."

"If it's any trouble . . ."

"None at all. It's fascinating. I saw a UFO once, but when I made the mistake of reporting it, the authorities told me I was seeing things." She gave him a wry smile. "But I know what I saw—I just learned not to tell anyone about it."

"I believe you," Rick said sincerely.

"I thought you might," she replied, giving him a look that made him certain she knew there was no cousin in Scotland.

"Let's talk about something else," he suggested quickly.

"Okay. The other night you promised to tell me about your old girlfriends."

"I did?"

"Uh-huh. So who was your first?"

He hesitated only briefly. "Her name was Delia."

"And how old were you?"

"Ten."

She smiled. "Tell me all about it"

"It's pretty weird."

"All the better."

He smiled and sat back in his chair. "Her full name was Delia Minuet, and I met her at the carnival on Independence Day Weekend in 1975."

July 4, 1975

The Masello Brothers Carnival and Sideshow arrived in Santo Verde just in time for the July Fourth weekend of Ricky's tenth year. According to his dad, the carnival had come to town at this time every year for as far back as he—and even Grandfather Piper—could remember, but this was Ricky's first visit.

Last year they'd been on vacation at the Grand Canyon, and before that, other vacations, chicken pox, and the mumps had made them miss it.

Now Ricky, standing next to Mom on the warm, clear morning, could hardly wait as they stood in line for tickets. The red and gold banner, the colorful pendants waving across the whole front, the smells of popcorn and cotton candy on the warm breeze, and most of all, the rides. Behind the buildings and tents, he could see the top of the Ferris wheel and the dinosaur back of the Wild Mouse, not to mention whirling umbrella chairs and the occasional lift of an octopus arm.

"Lift me higher, Dad! I wanna see!" Robin, already riding high in their father's arms, almost managed to pull himself onto his head before their dad boosted him onto his shoulder.

Inside, it was even better. Ricky played ring toss and won a rubber snake, rode the roller coaster with Dad, then consumed a cone of sticky pink cotton candy and two snow cones.

Only two things marred the first couple of hours. One was when he and Daddy and Robin rode the Ferris wheel together, and Robin, seated between them, whispered to Ricky that he was going to push him off the swinging bench when they reached the top.

That wasn't too bad because he knew his brother wouldn't do it, not with Dad around. It was the horror ride that was the really bad thing.

From the moment he laid eyes on Train to Terror, Robin

wanted to ride the little cars into the horrors hidden in the darkness beyond. And he wanted his brother to ride with him. Just the two of them, he kept insisting, It would be fun.

Ricky equally did *not* want to ride, not at all, but especially not with Robin. His lower lip kept trembling and he was afraid he was going to start crying any second now. Just looking at the ride scared him so badly that he could hardly think. He didn't want anyone to know how afraid he was, because at every opportunity Robin reminded him that if they knew, their parents would think he was crazy and send him away. And even though he'd actually heard Mom and Dad say they thought Robin was scaring him and that they were going to send him away to school soon, Ricky realized he wouldn't quite believe it until it happened.

"Come on," Robin goaded. "Ride with me, Ricky."

Ricky shook his head no, and his father squatted down and looked him in the eye. "It's just a ride. You love roller coasters, right?"

"Well, yeah."

"This is just a different kind of ride. It's fun. And it's safer than a roller coaster any day." Daddy patted his shoulder. "You know your brother can't go on all the rides you can go on, and he'd really like you to go on this one. I think that's nice, and I think it would be nice if you did, don't you?"

It wasn't nice. He wanted to get him on the ride, then scare him or push him out of the car or Ricky didn't know what. Something awful.

"Why don't we all go on the ride?" His mother stepped forward and put her hand on Ricky's shoulder. "This ride scares me, so maybe Ricky can ride with me and you can ride with Robin?"

Robin looked mad, but Daddy nodded. "That sounds like a good plan, don't you think, Rob?"

"Okay." He smiled so wide that it looked like his face would split in half. "But maybe you should ride with Mommy if she's scared. Then I can still ride with Ricky. That'd be *really* fun. Huh, Ricky?"

But his mother was already leading Ricky toward the ride. "Maybe next time, dear," she told his twin. She and Dad exchanged glances.

"Rick's riding with your mother, Robin," Dad said firmly.

Trembling, Ricky allowed Mom to lead him into the next car. It looked like an insect, shiny black with blood-red trim. Just before the screaming darkness swallowed the car, he glanced back. Daddy and Robin were right behind them. Robin grinned at him and slowly drew his finger across his throat.

Quickly Ricky faced forward, and Mom put her arm around him and pulled him close. He muffled his eyes and ears against her body, stuffing his fingers in his ears and squeezing his eyes shut for good measure.

And he endured. After an eternity, she gently pulled his fingers from one ear and told him it was almost over. As they emerged into light, she assured him he didn't look like he'd been afraid at all and told him she was glad he let her hang on to him.

Ricky knew that wasn't how it worked and he knew she knew, but in that moment he loved her so much, it hurt, because she let him keep his dignity.

A little later, they had lunch (corn dogs dipped in French's mustard, and Cokes with tons of crushed ice—the best junk food on earth), then went to a magic show where a man with a curly mustache sawed a lady in half. Ricky hated it, but didn't know why. After that, they saw a show in the big top with clowns in a car and a trapeze act that looked like fun.

When they exited the big top, Ricky spotted a long tent painted with a series of wonderfully weird pictures. A man at the ticket booth was talking about the pictures on a loud-speaker, and Ricky halted, mesmerized by the voice and the pictures. There was one of a cow with part of a second little cow growing out of its side standing by a goat with four eyes, two on each side of its face. Other pictures showed two babies joined at the chest, Siamese twins, he realized; a cocker spaniel with a horn growing out of its forehead; and a man with pins stuck in his skin. The last painting was of a family that didn't look quite right, and the banner over it said THE SMALL FAMILY! LIVE! DIRECT FROM THE CAVERNS OF CONNEMARA.

"Can we go in there?" he asked his parents.

His father looked at Robin, then Mom. "I don't think that's such a good idea, Rick."

"I want to go in too," Robin said.

Their parents looked at each other for a long time, and finally Dad nodded. "Okay, just for a few minutes, though." As he bought the tickets, he said, "It's all fake."

There were all sorts of things in jars, some so goopy you couldn't tell what they were. Maybe some were fake, like the cow—you could see the stitches—and the four-eyed dog didn't look real either. But the Siamese twins, Ricky was sure, had been alive at one time. They floated in formaldehyde in a huge jar, and you could even see the fine hair coating their bodies. They were face-to-face, eyes closed, arms around each other in an eternal embrace. Awestruck, saddened and fascinated, Ricky stood there until a tap on his shoulder made him look up. Robin had craned over to whisper, "Someday I'm gonna put you in a jar, just like that."

Ricky ignored him, his attention already caught by a sign directing them toward the Small Family—SEE THEM IN A REPLICA OF THEIR OWN HOME! LIVE! the sign said. He walked down the short corridor and came into a little room with a stage that looked like a cave—a funny, brightly painted maw with shamrocks and curly-looking kids' furniture. Folding chairs were set up on the floor below the stage.

"Audience," he heard a man's voice call from behind the stage. "Somebody get out there."

Embarrassed, Ricky turned to leave—his family hadn't followed him in yet—then a kid's voice said, "Hi."

He turned back and saw a little girl who was very short and had kind of a large head and long arms. Her long brown hair was tied back with a blue ribbon, and she had big blue eyes. When she smiled, she had dimples.

"We'll have a show in ten minutes," she said.

"What's your name?" he asked, walking closer.

"Delia Small." She giggled. "Mr. Masello, the owner, he said we have to be the Small family. Get it? Small?"

"Uh-uh."

"We're dwarves, you know." And she whistled a few bars of "Hi ho, Hi ho." "Dwarves. Freaks."

Ricky was shocked. "That's a bad word."

"What is?"

"Freaks. My parents said so. Doesn't it make you mad when you get called that?"

"No."

"What's your real last name?"

"Minuet. Like a song. I think that's a much better last name than Small, but Papa says Mr. Masello knows what's best."

"I like your name," Ricky said.

"What's *your* name?"

"Ricky Piper."

"Hi, Ricky."

"Hi, Delia."

They looked at each other and giggled. Then he whispered, "My brother's a freak, but no one's supposed to call him that."

"Is he a midget?" she asked.

"No. He's got no legs."

"He's a half boy?" she asked excitedly.

"Huh?"

"A living torso, but with arms. He has arms?"

"Sure. He walks on his hands."

"Mr. Masello would kill to get a half boy."

"I don't think he's for sale," Ricky said, then paused. Then he grinned. "But I wish he was!"

They giggled. "Is he rotten?" Delia asked conspiratorially.

"He tries to kill me." He said it like a joke.

"That's pretty rotten," she said, and Ricky Piper decided he was in love.

"There you are!" Ricky's mom walked up. "Don't wander off like that. I was worried about you." She turned and called, "He's in here, Frank."

"This is Delia," Ricky said.

"Hello, Delia," Mom said.

"Hi, I gotta go get ready for our show. You'll stay, won't you?"

"Can we, Mom?"

"Sure."

Delia disappeared behind the set just as Rick's dad came in, Robin in his arms. Other people soon followed, and in a few minutes the chairs were filled. Delia, her parents, and little brother came out and did a skit about mining gold in Ireland. It was silly. At the end, when they took their bows, Delia grinned at him and waved. Next to him Robin leaned over and said, "Your girlfriend's funny-looking," and without a second thought, Ricky punched him in the stomach.

"Richard Piper!" his mother said. "What on earth?"

Robin was staring at him with a funny look on his face, sort of a cross between amusement and fury.

"He said something bad about Delia."

"Well," said his father, "we expect you not to solve your problems with your fists, Rick. Apologize to your brother."

"I'm sorry," he said, and it was easy because he felt suddenly brave and knew he wasn't sorry at all.

"That's okay, Ricky," Robin said like some Goody Two-shoes kid off a TV show. "I had it coming."

How could he compete with that?

They stood to leave, and as they filed out, he heard his dad tell his mom that it was nice to see he had backbone. He smiled to himself, still shocked that he'd pounded Robin.

Outside the tent, a tall, dark-haired man stopped them, saying to his father, "Hello, sir, did you enjoy the show?"

Frank Piper nodded.

"I'm John Masello. My brother Vince and I own the carnival." He looked at Robin. "And what's your name, young man?"

"Robin," he said brightly.

"I bet you can do some pretty neat tricks, huh?"

"Sure."

"What is it that you want, Mr. Masello?" Dad asked. He sounded angry.

"I noticed that this young man is special and I was wondering if, since you were at the freak show, you might be interested in giving him a better life."

"What are you talking about?" That came from his mother, and she didn't sound happy either. Delia chose that moment to come out of the tent. She stood next to Ricky and listened intently.

"People with deformities often like to be with their own kind," Masello said. "This boy could make huge sums of money and have many, many friends who would never judge him by his looks." The circus man pulled two cigars from his pocket and offered one to Rick's dad, who shook his head. "Forgive me for being forward," Masello continued, "but would you be interested in letting Robin here travel with our show?"

"I told you he'd do anything for a half boy," Delia whispered to Ricky. "Those cigars are imported from Cuba!"

Ricky stifled a giggle.

"His contract would be very lucrative," Masello went on. "He'd make enough for his handsome brother here to go to college, and he could keep the whole family in—"

Say yes, say yes, say yes. Ricky prayed.

"No," Dad said with stern finality. "We're not interested."

"Let me give you my card—"

"No, that won't be necessary." He turned to his family. "We're going home."

"Ricky," Delia said. "Can you come back? Tonight, maybe?"

Go outside at night? For an instant he almost said yes, but common sense set in.

"No, but I live just two blocks from here. Could you sneak over to my house?"

"Ricky, come on," called Mom.

"Just a second."

"What's your address?"

"It's 667 Via Matanza. That's—"

"I'll find it. Can you meet me outside?"

"You don't have to sneak. My mom won't mind. How early can you come?"

"Six-thirty?"

"Come to the door at six-thirty. She'll invite you to dinner."

"Really?"

"She invites everybody to dinner."

"That sounds great." She paused. "Will your brother be there?"

"Yeah. Why?"

"What's wrong with him?"

"He was born that way."

"No, not that. He's . . . I don't know, creepy. No offense," she added quickly.

"No offense. I think he's creepy too. You're the first person besides me to ever say that, though," he told her with delight. Maybe Delia would be able to see the greenjacks, too. But even if she couldn't, he could hardly wait to talk to her some more.

"See you tonight," she said.

"See you."

"How about some fresh coffee?" Rick asked, bringing the pot to the table.

"Thanks." Audrey pushed her cup toward him. "What a romantic story."

Rick shrugged.

"But I won't let you leave me in suspense. Did your mother invite Delia to dinner?"

"Yes. We had a great time, too. It was the first time I ever felt like I had a real friend my age—you know, the kind who understands things about you that would make other people think you're crazy."

"I know," she said softly.

"Anyway, my parents got a kick out of her—Delia was very mature for her age, very feisty—and I wished with all my heart that I could have her for a sister instead of Robin for a brother."

Audrey smiled. "I thought you said she was your first love."

"She was. We saw each other every day until the carnival left town, and my mother told her to come back the next year. But Mom and Dad died two months later."

"So you never got to see her again?"

He gave her a ghost of a smile. "I saw her. We just sneaked around after that first year."

"Why did you have to sneak?"

"My brother mostly. Plus Aunt Jade and Uncle Howard would have made fun of her."

She cocked her head. "A while ago you said Delia asked you what was wrong with your brother. What did she mean by that?"

He chose his next words carefully "He hated her from the moment they met. He even called her 'Troll' to her face. She stayed away from him, but it wasn't because of the name-calling—she could handle that. It was because she didn't trust him. I think she must have sensed his meanness." He gazed at Audrey, wanting to tell her the whole story, but afraid to.

"Delia had been raised in such a different way than most people," he ventured. "She really didn't notice physical things: They didn't mean much to her. So I think that because she didn't spend time feeling sorry for Robin or cutting him slack because he had no legs, she could sense his cruelty very easily. She hated his eyes," he allowed himself to tell Audrey.

"If you were identical twins, weren't they just like yours?"

"They were darker than mine, almost black," Rick explained. "Delia said that when she looked into his eyes, she could see he didn't have a human soul."

Audrey's green eyes had grown large. "That's a pretty strong statement for a little kid."

"Well, frankly, I didn't think he had a human soul either." The words were out of his mouth before he could stop himself.

"Rick, really?"

He nodded, his guts tying themselves in knots. How was he going to tell her more without sounding crazy?

"Why?"

"Because Robin told me so, and I believed him." He shook his head. "I always believed everything he said, and he claimed he was a little jack who'd possessed my brother's body, and that my real brother was outside with the jacks . . ."

"Don't stop now!" She gestured impatiently.

"Well, when we were seven, Robin pulled a Halloween joke on me that backfired. He took a skeleton mask and climbed out our window into the oak in the front yard to scare me. He wanted me to think he was Big Jack." Rick clutched the coffee cup to keep his hands from shaking. "To make a long story short, he fell out of the tree and hit his head. After that, he started claiming—but only to me—that he was a changeling or whatever you want to call it. He said what he really wanted was my body since I could see—" *Oh, shit,* he thought, *Oh shit, oh shit, oh shit.*

Icky Ricky, sicky Ricky, dicky Ricky.

For the first time tonight, he heard them. Had they been calling all along or had his guard just gone down? Or maybe he just thought he heard them. *I hear voices,* he thought. *Oh joy That probably means I'm certifiable. Just what Audrey wants.*

Audrey shook her head. "Children are incredibly cruel. You must have been terrified."

He took a deep breath, grateful that she'd said nothing about his slip. "I was incredibly gullible. I believed it all."

She reached across the table and took his hand. "Do you still?"

"No. Robin's personality changed when he fell on his head, so I assume he sustained some kind of brain damage."

She nodded. "Probably. But you still see the greenjacks, don't you." It was a statement, not a question, but her hand stayed firmly on his.

"N-No," he replied, flustered. "Like I said, I had a deadly imagination."

"The other night you told me you didn't want to judge yourself by your brother anymore. You're doing it."

"I don't understand," he said dully.

"You saw them, your brother didn't. I bet there are more kids who think they see things than ones who don't. I mean"—she grinned at him—"didn't you ever have an invisible friend?"

"Shelly did," he answered with relief. "And Cody's just acquired one." He smiled. "His name is Bob. Bob the invisible friend."

Their laughter broke the tension.

"My invisible friend's name was Miranda," Audrey said, "because that's what I wanted my name to be. The cutest girl in school was named Miranda."

"Cody doesn't know any Bobs," Rick said thoughtfully.

"Maybe he got it off TV. Bob Newhart, maybe?"

"I'll bet you're right." Rick stroked one of her fingers. "So you think lots of kids see things that aren't there?" he asked, trying to sound very casual.

"I *always* see prowlers if I let myself," Audrey confessed. "In shadows at night, my robe hanging on a hook by the door becomes a living, breathing intruder. It moves. My eyes see it. God, I hate sleeping alone."

He didn't say a word, just sat there and watched the color come up from under her collar, flushing her skin redder and redder until she looked sunburned.

"I wasn't coming on," she sputtered.

He squeezed her hand. "Too bad." Seeing the look on her face, he quickly added, "Since Laura died, I've been out half a dozen times, blind dates mostly, nothing serious. Not like . . . What I mean is, I haven't done this in a long time, Audrey."

"Me either." She squeezed back.

"Okay if I'm blunt?"

"You'd better be." She smiled softly.

"I'm in no hurry and I'm not going to rush you. In fact, I want to go slow." The truth was, *want* had nothing to do with it; he *needed* to go slow.

"An-ti-ci-pa-tion," Audrey sang softly.

"Yes, anticipation's good," he agreed.

They sat in silence a long moment. "Rick, you see green-jacks—saw greenjacks." She stared into her coffee cup. "I've seen a ghost. Have you?"

He thought about it. He'd been so hung up on his own brand of critter that he'd never thought about hauntings. "Um, no, I don't think so," he said finally. "You saw one, huh?"

Silently she got up and brought the coffeepot back to the table. Her hand shook as she poured. "Yes," she said at last. She overfilled his cup, slopping coffee onto the table. "Oh, sorry. She reached for a napkin, but he beat her to it.

"Relax." He blotted the spill. "Tell me about the ghost."

"I've never told anyone before."

"I won't tease you," he promised solemnly. "I'll believe you."

"I know. That's why I'm telling you, but, Rick . . ." She swallowed. "When I'd been married about a year, my mother died. She hated Ron and she'd begged me not to marry him, but I did anyway." She shook her head. "We fought and fought and ended up not speaking.

"The night she died, Ron had come home drunk." She looked down. "He beat me up. It was ten past midnight—I kept looking at the clock. Ron was snoring on the couch. I was in bed, and I hurt so much, I couldn't sleep. He'd punched me in the ribs several times," she added, her mor-tification obvious, "and I realize now I had some broken ribs. It even hurt to breathe.

"I hadn't spoken to Mother in nearly a year, and I was thinking about her, about how right she'd been about Ron. I was only nineteen, still so young and stubborn that I couldn't make myself call her and tell her so, but I sure thought about it. I wanted to go home, but my pride wouldn't let me.

"Suddenly I smelled her perfume—she always wore White Shoulders—and I opened my eyes. She was standing by the bed, plain as day. Just standing there looking down at me." Sudden tears welled and ran down her cheeks.

"God, I'm sorry," she said, picking up a napkin and dabbing at her eyes.

"It's okay."

She nodded. "She was dressed in a powder blue suit I'd never seen before, and she was a little plumper than I remembered. I remember what I said. I asked her a question. I asked, 'Are you going to take me home now?' She didn't say anything, she just smiled and held out her hands.

"I took them." Her own hands trembled as she spoke, and he took them in his, held them still. "Rick, her hands were as warm and solid as yours are now.

"I sat up in bed and put my arms out, and she sat next to me and pushed my hair out of my eyes like she always used to do. We stared at each other and I said, 'I love you, Mother,' and she said it back, but, Rick, I was looking right at her. I heard her, but her lips didn't move."

The hairs on the back of his neck rose.

"She held me," Audrey said softly, wonderingly, "and told me she loved me over and over.

"The next thing I knew, I woke up. The phone was ringing. It was my father, calling from the hospital. His voice was shaking. It was almost two in the morning. He said Mother had a stroke and she'd died at ten after twelve. There was nothing the doctors could do."

Silent tears ran down her cheeks, but now she smiled through them. "My mother came to tell me good-bye. I know it."

"That's beautiful," Rick said softly.

"Yes."

Close to tears, he wanted to confess, once and for all, that he still saw them. But he couldn't

28

"Dad!"

Jolted by the scream and the sudden pain Rick's fingers caused as they dug into her arms, Audrey pulled out of the good-night embrace.

"Rick?" He stood there, eyes glassy, chestnut hair mussed from her fingers, the color draining from his uncomprehending face. He didn't seem to see her. "Rick!"

"Dad!"

Slowly his head turned toward the staircase, and then the lost look left his features and everything clicked into place. "It's Shelly!" He turned and ran up the stairs, Audrey close behind.

"Dad!"

The cry was loud as they rounded the upstairs corner.

"Shelly!" Rick slammed against her door, then grabbed the knob and turned it, practically falling into the room as the door swung open. "Shelly!"

"My God!" Audrey whispered as she entered behind him. Shelly sat in the middle of her bed, clutching her covers protectively around her neck. Her nightstand light cast a yellow glow over the room and the things it held.

On the bed, on the dresser and chest and desk, were toy dogs. All of them were pointed at Shelly as if watching her, and they were all in different positions, everything from begging to lifting a leg to urinate. For a moment Audrey couldn't comprehend what she was seeing, then she remembered Aunt Jade and realized these were the deceased poodles Rick had mentioned. At the time, it was funny; they'd laughed over the story. Now it was horrifying.

"Daddy," Shelly whimpered. Her eyes were huge, her dark blond hair tangled around her face so that she looked like a little girl.

Rick swept a poodle off the bed with the back of his hand, then he had his arms around his daughter, rocking and consoling her, whispering, "It's all right, it's okay," over and over again. Shelly's shoulders shook with quiet sobs.

In a few minutes, the girl regained control. She looked up, directly into Audrey's eyes, and suddenly she felt like an intruder. "I'm sorry, I shouldn't be here. I'll go."

Shelly didn't react for a moment, then she mumbled, "No, it's okay." Then she made a face. "Man, what a feeb I am," she added shakily.

"No, you're not, Shel."

"You won't tell anybody that I screamed and stuff, will you, Daddy?"

"Of course not."

Audrey jumped as something grabbed her legs from behind.

"Cool!" Cody pushed around her and into the room. "Lookit the doggy rats! One, two, three," he counted, "four, five, six dead doggy rats. Cool!" He looked at his sister. "Did you steal 'em from Aunt Jade?" he asked, wonder and awe in his voice.

"Of course not, butthead," Shelly sneered. "And who told you, you can come in my room?"

"You screamed, huh?"

"Up yours!"

"Shelly's a screamer," Cody sang. "Shelly's a screamer!"

"Cody, be quiet," Rick ordered sternly. "Do you know anything about these?" He gestured around the room at the dogs.

Cody shook his head. "Uh-uh, no way. I bet Bob put 'em here."

Cody did it, Audrey thought.

"Cody," Rick said, "come clean." Obviously he, too, subscribed to the theory that a kid blaming an invisible friend was guilty without trial.

But the boy didn't giggle or look away from his father's eyes. "No, Daddy, I didn't do it."

"Shelly? What happened? Do you remember anything?"

"I woke up. I heard a noise and I woke up. I felt like somebody was watching me, and I wasn't sure if it was from a dream or not, so I turned on the light." She glared at Cody. "I'm gonna get you, you little turd."

"Shelly, no." Rick stood up. "I don't think your brother did it. I think your aunt did it." He glanced at Audrey as he added, "She's a few bricks short of a load."

Audrey nodded. Right before Shelly screamed, while they were in the front foyer indulging in a little lightweight necking, weird sounds had come from the old lady's room, moaning and whispering. Rick looked embarrassed and explained that she did that almost every night.

"Come on, Cody," Audrey said. "I'll see you to your room.'

Rick was gathering poodles and dropping them in an empty packing box still in the room, his face distorted by an expression of utter disgust. He looked up. "Thanks. I'll be there in a minute."

Cody took her hand and practically dragged her out of the room and around the corner to his room. "Come on! You gotta see my wallpaper! My dad had it too. It's the same paper, I'm keeping it."

He talked a mile a minute as he took her around his room, showing her his treasures, which seemed to involve Legos and plastic dinosaurs more than anything else. "And you know what? There's secret tunnels in the house."

"There are?" Rick had mentioned that he'd kept that information from his son. "Who told you?"

"Bob. He's my friend. He talks to me at night. Someday he's gonna show me the tunnels."

"Come on, you get in bed now."

"Okay." He dimpled up at her and jumped into his red race-car bed by the window.

A tree limb just outside scratched the screen lightly. *That's the tree Rick hated.*

"Kiss me g'night."

She smiled and did as he ordered. "Good night, Cody."

"Is your brother a boy or a girl?" he asked abruptly.

"A boy," she said immediately.

"How come he has boobies?"

Boobies? "Well, um, why don't you ask Duane about it when he visits? Or ask your father."

"Who's Duane?"

"Dakota. His real name's Duane. Dakota's his stage name."

Cody lay down. "Okay, g'night," he said.

As she left the room, Rick approached, carrying the box of dogs. He looked upset. "I told Shelly to make sure she locks her door from now on." He paused, grimacing. "I'm sorry. I'm really sorry about this."

"Don't be silly," she told him as they started down the stairs. "It's not your fault. By the way, Cody knows there are passages in the house."

Rick stopped in his tracks, "He does?"

"He says Bob told him."

Understanding dawned on his face. "Jade probably told him." He adjusted the box in his arms, his upper lip curling with distaste. "I'll just have to make sure everything's sealed up." He put the box of poodles on the floor at his feet. "I can't keep her in control. She must have gone up the front stairs while we were in the kitchen and put these things in there to scare Shelly." His face clouded.

"But Shelly said a noise woke her up, so it must have happened just before we got there."

He smiled grimly. "I have an answer for that, too. She went up the back stairs while we were out here."

"But we heard her making noises."

"Only for a few minutes when we first came out. We

were out here for"—he consulted his watch—"almost half an hour."

"Time flies when you're having fun," she said, smiling a little.

"Yes, it does." He reached for her, and she started to snake her arms around his waist. Then, from Jade's room came a moan, followed closely by Jade's clear, loud voice crying, "Fuck me!"

Shocked, Audrey looked at Rick. He looked back.

"Fuck me." Louder, more demanding. The words were followed by a series of obscene grunts and groans.

Rick turned beet red, and she was pretty sure she'd done the same.

"Fuck me!"

"Rick? Maybe she has, uh, marital aids? She's not all that old, is she?"

"Early sixties. Carmen told me she takes hormones."

"Fuck me!"

Audrey snickered. "Better tell the doctor to cut her dosage!"

Rick started laughing, pulling her close and burying his head on her shoulder to muffle the sound. She felt hilarity rising from a tickle in her abdomen, up, up, into her throat, and it exploded from her mouth, gales of it. She clung to Rick, trying to keep quiet, but he was shaking with stifled laughter also.

"What a night," Rick whispered, his words hiccuping over the laughter. "Fine Italian cuisine, slapstick movies, coffee and ghost stories, and"—he swept one arm grandly toward Jade's room—"and, the *pièce de résistance,* stuffed dogs and sex-crazed old ladies."

He laughed again, too abruptly to be able to muffle the noise. Audrey would have doubled up if she didn't have him to cling to.

The noises from Jade's room stopped abruptly.

"Oops," Audrey managed. "She heard us."

"Yeah."

"Or she shorted out her vibrator," she couldn't help adding.

Rick snickered again, and they silenced as they caught each other's gaze. Another good-night kiss was coming up quick.

Before their lips met, Audrey heard a key click in a nearby lock. She and Rick pulled apart, and as she watched the handle on the louvered door start to descend, her legs turned to jelly.

Rick simply picked up the box of dogs. Four stiff pink legs poked out of the top. She couldn't help herself; another hysterical giggle escaped.

The door opened and she beheld Jade Ewebean for the first time. She gasped, then clamped her hand over her mouth to trap the laughter that wanted to escape.

Jade's black hair floated in a tangled mess around a face coated with red lipstick, thick eyeliner, red circles of rouge, and sparkly white powder that had creased into her wrinkles so that they looked like scars. Mascara had smeared beneath her eyes. She looked like Bette Davis in *Whatever Happened to Baby Jane?* The face made Audrey want to scream. It belonged in a house of horrors.

But the tall, bony body made her want to laugh. The woman wore a peignoir set of red polyester and black lace. *Thank God she put on the robe,* Audrey thought, barely controlling herself. It was as sheer as the gown, but the double layer faded her body from what would have been horrific pornography to moderately disgusting translucence.

Rick had moved toward his aunt, and Audrey remained in the shadow of the staircase. The old bat didn't see her, but her reaction to Ricky was amazing.

"Richard," she crooned. "My sweet little Ricky. You've come to see your auntie, haven't you?"

"Jade—" he began. Immediately she cut him off.

"You're so like your brother, Richard, but you still look like a little boy." She unbuttoned her robe and let it fall open.

I'm in a Felini film. Audrey moved slightly so she could see around Rick. *Oh, my God!* she thought, shocked.

Jade's robe dropped to the floor, leaving her saggy body backlit by the lamplight from her room. The gown was short, and even in the dim light, Audrey could see the blue veins knotting her legs. Her gaze traveled upward and stopped. Jade had huge breasts, trussed into the gown's flimsy black lace bra. She squinted, not believing her eyes. A Fredrick's gown, she thought, seeing that the nipples thrust bare from the lace. They, too, were big and damp and lumpy, like two wads of red bubble gum. They looked rouged.

Jade kneaded one in her gnarled hand. "Come to your aunt Jade, Richard. Let's give you a kiss."

Rick's back had stiffened the moment she'd entered the room, and he hadn't moved since. Now he spoke, so low Audrey could barely hear.

"Don't do that."

"Why? Are you a bad boy? Got a stiffie for your dear old aunt?"

"You make me sick." The words dripped cold fury. "There are children in this house, Jade."

"I don't see any children now, Richard. Come here." She stepped nearer.

"What you do in the privacy of your room is your business, but don't bring it out here," he said icily. "If you do this again, I won't even send you to a rest home. I'll have you committed. Stay away."

She made an obscenely childish face. "You're no fun. You never were. You'd be so nice if you were like your brother."

"My brother is dead!" He nearly yelled the words, then was silent a moment, regaining control, Audrey realized. "Get out of my way, Jade."

"What?"

He stepped toward her. "Get out of my way. These belong to you. They belong in your room. I'm going to put them there, and they're going to stay there. If they don't, I don't care about the cost, you're out of here. You scared Shelly half to death." As he spoke he pushed past her, shoving her out of the way with the box. He disappeared into the room, and Audrey heard thumping as he dumped the dogs on the floor. "Don't upset Shelly or Cody again," he warned, re-appearing in the doorway.

At that moment she spotted Audrey. Jade's painted face was almost comic as it raced through a series of reactions. Then she laughed. It was a horrible sound, like fingernails raking a blackboard. "I see why you don't want your auntie, Richard. You fucked that flat-chested little whore instead." She sniffed. "You have shitty taste, nephew. Shitty." She spat in Audrey's direction. "Whore."

Rick's face had hardened into a stony scowl. He took a step toward Jade, his hands coming up. She couldn't see his face. If she could, Audrey thought she'd run. The open boy-ishness that so attracted Audrey to Rick had disappeared entirely, replaced by anger so potent that it seemed to come off him in waves. "Rick," she said tentatively. "Rick, it's okay."

He ignored her, hands level with Jade's neck, eyes glittering and furiously intent. Another step and he'd be on her.

"Rick!" Audrey cried. "Stop it!"

For an instant he focused on her. But then his hands closed on Jade's shoulders—not her neck, Audrey saw with relief. His fingers made white marks on the skin below her collarbone, and he forced her to turn around.

Audrey ran forward, reliving her own old fears. "Don't hit her!" she cried. "Rick! Don't—"

He turned the woman around and slowly forced her up against the wall. "I won't hit her," he said without taking his eyes from Jade's face. He kept her shoulders trapped against the wall. "She used to hit me all the time, Audrey. I didn't tell you about that. She used to take a belt to me. Once, she whipped me until my pants were shredded. I had to stay out of school for a week. She thought it was funny. Didn't you, Jade? You thought it was funny."

"Richard, don't be so mean." Jade's voice quavered. "You're hurting my shoulders."

"Rick," Audrey began, then stopped. There was nothing she could say.

"Richard, please!"

"Daddy?"

Audrey looked up, saw Cody rubbing his eyes at the top of the stairs.

"Go back to bed, Cody," Rick called, his voice only slightly strained. "Everything's okay."

"Okay."

Audrey was amazed that the boy obediently did as Rick asked.

Rick drew a deep breath and released it with a shudder, then let go of Jade. He bent and picked up the red robe and threw it at her. "Cover yourself up and never leave your room dressed like this again. My children and my friends do not need to see you like this. Neither do I."

"You'll never measure up to your brother, you little prick!" Jade spat at him as she flounced past, pulling the door closed behind her.

"My brother's dead," he said quietly as Jade's lock clicked home.

"Rick?"

He turned and looked at her, his face open again, boyish, but heartbreakingly sad. "Audrey? I'm sorry. I'm really sorry. I'll understand if you don't . . . I lost control."

She went to him and took his hand. "You didn't lose control."

"Yes, I did."

"No. I lived with a man who had no control, and because of that, I thought for a second that you were going to hit her. I'm sorry. If I hadn't been hit, I wouldn't have thought it."

"I wanted to hit her. I wanted to kill her."

Slowly she pulled him forward and put her arms around his waist. "I wanted to kill her, too, Rick." She smiled up at him. "Anyone in their right mind would want to kill her."

"Does this mean you'll see me again?" She felt his body

relax against her slightly. His voice trembled with caged emotions. She wished he would cry, but knew he wouldn't.

"Yes, I want to see you again. I mean, it can't get crazier than this, can it?"

He studied her a long time before answering. "Yes, it can."

Something in his voice, a finality, a surety, troubled her, but she looked into his eyes and said, "We'll just take it one day at a time, okay?"

"Okay."

They kissed chastely, and he saw her to the door. She thought it was odd that he didn't accompany her down the walk to her car, but then, he'd been through so much.

On the drive home, she wondered about him, thinking that there was more under the surface than she'd realized. At first she thought he was a sweet, sincere guy, sort of shy, very intelligent, and stamped with her brother's seal of approval, which was damn hard to come by. There was a darkness lying just below the surface, though, and she didn't know if it was something that could be exorcised or not. She also thought the cousin in Scotland didn't exist.

29

"Quint?" Rick called as he locked his bedroom door behind him. "Quint? Where are you, cat?" He waited a moment. "Here, kitty, kitty. Time to eat."

The cat wasn't answering. *Christ,* he thought, *on top of everything else, this is all I need.* "Quint?" He walked into the dressing room, automatically looking at the cabinet, relieved to see the hanger holding it shut. He scanned the floor and the shelves above the clothes racks. "Quint?"

The cat wasn't in the bathroom either. "Here, kitty, kitty."

Then he heard a hiss behind him and returned to the bedroom. "Quint?"

A low growl emanated from behind the headboard. Grabbing his flashlight from the nightstand, he got down on his hands and knees. "Quint?"

The cat was crouched at the halfway point in the eight-inch-wide space between the bed and the wall. Its ears were back and its eyes reflected green in the flashlight's beam. It growled menacingly.

"What's wrong, cat?"

Quint's only answer was another hiss.

"Okay, have it your way." Rick rose and went into the bathroom, poured fresh Iams in the dish and replaced the stale water. Usually Quint would come running when he heard the crunchies tumbling, but not tonight. *Why?*

A scrabbling sound in the wall gave him the answer. Rats.

Quint wouldn't know a rodent if it bit him on the ass. Maybe he'd seen one, smelled one, something. After all, Rick hadn't checked for entries into the room other than the passage. He squatted down in front of the bathroom vanity and opened the door, inspecting the openings the plumbing traveled through, and saw a small opening between the pipe and the cabinet. He reached up and retrieved his flashlight from the counter, shined it on the cabinet floor, behind the rolls of toilet tissue.

A mouse turd, just one, lay in the back of the cabinet. "Uh-huh, I see," Rick said, rising. "Ouch!" he cried, banging the back of his head on the counter. "Shit!" He rubbed the sore spot as he returned to the bedroom, got a bait trap, and placed it in the cabinet. "Here you go, you little son of a bitch!" He rose, successfully this time, and brushed his teeth, then stripped to his shorts. He'd had enough showers for one day.

After he climbed into bed, the cat joined him almost instantly, plastering his body against Rick's side, draping his head and arms over his shoulder. "You're a big baby, you know that? Big cat like you, afraid of a little bitty mouse."

The cat stared at him, unperturbed.

Usually Rick read himself to sleep, but tonight he snapped off the lamp and lay in the dark, absently stroking Quint's fur. "It wasn't a good day for me either, fur-ball."

The cat purred.

He didn't know what to do about Jade. She'd frightened Shelly, called Audrey names, and caused him to stop thinking and almost do violence. My god, he thought, if he hadn't been brought to his senses when he heard Audrey's anguished "Don't hit her!" he actually might have done it.

What if she parades around like that in front of Cody? The thought filled him with dread. Maybe he could rent her an apartment. She didn't really need a retirement home. She wasn't so old and feeble that she needed one. Or crazy enough to be locked away. And unless he buckled under and took the TV job, he couldn't afford it, so his threats were somewhat empty. *Rent her an apartment,* he advised himself, *and get her out of the house.* But even if he was only putting out another thousand or so a month for her upkeep, he'd still have to take the TV job, that or give up good restaurants, the theater, the symphony, and the occasional rock concert. There were other expenses to consider. Now that he had the room, he wanted to buy a real piano so that the kids—and he himself—could learn to play. His primary computer was getting old and crotchety, and he wanted a laptop so that he could work in bed, too. The kids needed things, the house, too, all items that he could eventually afford without going into debt if he just left Jade where she was.

Put her out on Sunset Boulevard and let her hook her room and board. He smiled devilishly. *You don't owe her a place to live.*

That was the ultimate truth. The Ewebeans had been their guardians, if you could use that word without laughing, after their parents died, but from the first, they did it only for themselves. The Ewebeans were just like the innkeeper and his wife in *Les Misérables.* He remembered clearly the day they showed up, a few weeks after their parents' death.

October 1, 1975

The arrival of Jade and Howard Ewebean from Larkin Hill, a little nest of inbreeding located in the northernmost reaches of California, did not fill Ricky with joy. These, his only living relatives, were people who rightfully belonged only in small, backward towns in the middle of nowhere. Here in Santo Verde, they qualified as the cream of the crap, as his father used to say. As they pulled up the drive, Ricky, watching with Carmen, had the sinking feeling that the Beverly Hillbillies were moving in.

He'd heard his parents talk about the Ewebeans, but he'd never seen them before. They were the only relatives left. His dad had sometimes joked that gypsies must have left his sister, Jade, on his parents' stoop one night, because she

didn't look or act like any of the other Pipers. Grandfather
had studiously pretended she didn't exist.

Seeing her for the first time, Ricky thought that, except
for the way her breasts were trying to pop the buttons of her
faded plaid dress, she looked a lot like the woman in the
painting called *American Gothic*. And Howard looked just
like the man, skinny and bald and sour. All he needed was
a pitchfork. Ricky stifled a giggle.

"Come on, Ricky," Carmen said, touching his elbow. "We
better be polite."

Heart sinking, he watched them climb out of a dirty,
smoke-belching pink and gray Rambler. Aunt Jade turned
briskly toward the open car door. "Come here, Buffems,"
she called in a cloying, nasal voice. "Come here, Buffem-
wuffems."

He heard yipping, and a second later, he saw a dog leap
from the car. It was a poodle, small and white, with a poofy,
goofy haircut and a green plaid collar studded with rhine-
stones. Its high-pitched frantic whining turned briefly into
a growl as it saw him, then Jade called it again, and it threw
itself into her arms. It was the most loathsome creature he'd
ever seen.

Then a girl slithered out of the car, and he forgot about
the dog. Ricky knew she had to be his cousin, Evangeline.
She was about three years older than him, and the look in
her pale muddy eyes, combined with the smile she bestowed
on him when she noticed him staring at her, said she'd instantly pegged him as kibble for the horrible poodle. His
blood ran cold.

"Oooh, wittle Buffems," Aunt Jade cooed into a fuzzy
pink ear. "Is you my wittle baby? Is you?"

Buffems licked her face, waggling its tail like a golfball
on a stick. Suddenly he saw its weenie stick out and rub
against Jade Ewebean. He slapped his hand over his mouth
a second too late to keep the giggle inside, and the sound
of it hung in the air like a big red arrow, pointing directly
at him.

Aunt Jade looked at him. Uncle Howard looked at him. Evangeline looked at him. Even the poodle looked at him.

"You," Howard Ewebean grunted. "Which one are you?"

Ricky stared dumbly at him.

"You deaf, boy?" Aunt Jade asked. "Answer your uncle."

The poodle growled, its gums obscenely pink.

"I, I—"

"This is Ricky," Carmen said, putting her hands protectively on his shoulders. He leaned gratefully against her.

"What's the matter with him?" Howard demanded. "He a mute?"

"No," Carmen said. Ricky could tell she was angry and trying to hide it. "He can talk, but he's just lost his parents, so he doesn't feel much like it, you know?"

Jade drew herself up to her full, considerable, height and threw her shoulders back. "You're the maid?"

"Housekeeper," Carmen replied with dignity.

"Well, you ain't going to be the maid long if you mouth off to me again."

"Miz Ewebean." Carmen spoke calmly. "Did you and Mr. Ewebean read all the legal papers?"

"Course we did," Howard grunted.

"Then you know you can't fire me. It's in the papers. My husband and I take good care of the boys and the house. We see nothing bad happens to any of them. The Pipers, they knew that and they put it in their papers. If you did read them, you know that too."

Howard grunted and blew his nose into a wrinkled handkerchief.

"We'll see," sniffed Jade. "We'll just see how much you'll care about those boys when you don't get your paycheck."

"The lawyer's office sends my money, and since you say you read the papers, you know that, too, so don't pretend to be stupid, Miz Ewebean. And don't pretend I am either. That way we'll get along a lot better."

"Look, Mama." Evangeline's voice was high and whiny, and she never took her eyes off him as she spoke. "Look at the boy. He's staring at Buffems like he never seen a dog before."

"You never seen a dog, boy?" Aunt Jade asked.

"Madre de Dios," Carmen said quietly to Ricky. One of her hands left his shoulder, and Ricky knew she was crossing herself.

"Speak up, boy," Howard grumbled.

"I—I've never seen such a fu—funny-looking one." A small hysterical giggle escaped, and he felt his face flush.

"It's a sin against God," Carmen hissed.

"I thought they had money," Jade said to Howard.

"They do," Howard said. " 'cause we got it too, long as we take care of their brats."

Jade nodded knowingly. "Pity. I guess having money don't mean having fashion sense. You're a stutterer, boy?" she asked.

Ricky shook his head no.

"Where's the freak?" Evangeline Ewebean asked loudly.

"You got him locked up somewhere?" Howard chimed in.

Carmen's hand tightened on Ricky's shoulder. "We don't call him words like that. His name is Robin."

"Yeehaw!"

As if in answer, Robin's joyful cry pierced the air. Ricky and the others turned toward the house, and Ricky watched the leaves in the oak tree move as Robin, invisible, climbed down from the bedroom window. Suddenly he dropped from the lowest branch to the ground. He landed on his hands, elbows flexing, and then he ran forward, hands hidden in the overgrown grass.

"Oooh, look at it!" squealed Evangeline.

The poodle let loose a hysterical volley of yaps and strained to get free of Jade's arms.

"Stop it, Buffems," she ordered. "Will you look at that thing move?" she asked.

"Hauls ass," Howard allowed.

Robin arrived at the walkway leading to the driveway, and the slap-slap of his hands hitting the bricks seemed very loud to Ricky. The Ewebeans just stood there and stared, Jade clutching Buffems against her breasts, until Robin arrived next to his brother. Ricky moved closer to Carmen.

"Hello, Aunt Jade. Hello, Uncle Howard." He paused, looking Evangeline up and down. "Hello, Evangeline."

She giggled.

"I'll be goddamned, if that ain't the goddamnedest thing I ever saw." Howard slowly shook his head. "Belongs in a circus. What'd you say his name was?" he said to Carmen.

"Robin," she said.

"Robin? Hell!" cried Howard. "He don't look like a robin. He looks like a lump to me. He oughta be called Lumpkin, 'cause robins got wings."

"He's gonna grow up and be third base," Evangeline supplied.

The poodle, still yipping, suddenly squirmed free of Jade's grasp. Instantly it turned to face Robin, its legs stiff, its lip curled. *Eat him,* Ricky wished, then closed off the thought.

"Lumpkin," said Robin merrily. "Lumpkin, Lumpkin, Lumpkin!" With that, he flipped into a handstand and ran, head down, across the yard, climbing the oak tree like a monkey.

"Don't that beat all?" Howard said, chuckling and sending his boozy breath in Ricky's direction. "That thing's gonna be a hoot."

"Give Ricky a nickname too," Robin yelled from the tree.

Howard snorted, but before he could open his mouth, Robin screamed, "He's icky Ricky! Icky Ricky! Call him Icky Ricky!"

The Ewebeans looked at Ricky and laughed.

Things deteriorated after that. Rick stared at the ceiling. Howard was a mean drunk, Jade was his match, and their daughter didn't fall far from the tree. Evangeline, at thirteen, was well into puberty and intent on torturing every male she came into contact with.

Rick yawned. The first few years were bad, but he still had his locking bedroom and Carmen. When he wasn't in school, he lived by spending countless hours at Carmen and Hector's or, if he couldn't, remaining locked alone in his room, reading, writing, thinking. The Ewebeans didn't miss him, the Ewebeans didn't care. At night, when he'd wake up screaming because he'd dreamed again about finding his dead parents, they ignored him or hollered at him to shut the fuck up.

Two years later, when he and Robin entered early adolescence, things became far, far worse.

A silent tear ran from his eye. Quint moved one paw up and touched it, just as he had when he was a kitten.

Rick stared at the ceiling. *I don't owe Jade Ewebean a thing,* Rick thought drowsily. *Not a damn thing. She owes me.*

30

After a month of work, Don Quixote still didn't look much like a knight errant, but his noble steed had taken on a distinctly horsey cast. Rick stood back and surveyed his work with satisfaction. The legs and tail were completed, and if not perfect, they at least had the long-limbed wraithiness that he so admired.

Scratching his chin thoughtfully, Rick studied the belly of the beast. He wasn't sure how to handle the penis, and as a result, he'd spent the morning perusing equine genitalia in his Metropolitan Museum of Art book. Eventually he decided that his horse must indeed have one, but wasn't sure of the logistics—macho or subtle was the problem now. After a final moment's thought, he chose subtle; nothing flashy, a simple Daumieresque pointy suggestion of stallionhood.

He used his discarded shirt to wipe the sweat from his forehead, then pulled the mask back down and went to work on the underside of the horse. After a few moments, he was snickering to himself, feeling juvenile, and wishing Dakota were here to crack a few of his off-color Mr. Ed jokes.

He'd heard from Dakota regularly. O'Keefe had made a point to phone him—as well as Audrey—every Sunday to get the lowdown on their latest date. Each week he also asked if he'd told Audrey that he could actually see the "jack-offs," as he called them. Rick would say no, he hadn't, and don't you tell her, either. Since the night he'd told her the tall one about the cousin in Scotland, he'd religiously sidestepped the topic every time it started to come up, and Audrey was kind enough to let him. He would have liked to know if she really had done any research, but it was easier to avoid the whole thing.

Still and all, things were going very well. Over the last few weeks he and his family had settled into a pleasant routine. Though Rick still avoided going out at night as much as he could, he found that his rather Pavlovian response to the phrase "I'm Thomas" helped him see the greenjacks as something more closely related to annoyance than crippling fear. It concerned him far more that he saw them at all, though the cat's reaction had made him suspect that he wasn't completely mad. That knowledge diminished his fears more than anything else, and perhaps that was why he'd originally told Audrey as much as he had.

As for Shelly, she spent most of her time at her job in the mall and the rest of it with new friends, other high school kids, none of whom, as far as Rick could tell, wanted to be exotic dancers or rock stars.

There'd been no serious trouble between father and daughter since she'd been working, and Rick had quickly rewarded her, and himself, with cable and paid half the fees to have her own phone line installed. So far, she'd asked for nothing else and had even talked about saving for a car. Impressed, Rick had started to secretly scan the used-car ads with the intention of giving her the surprise of her life for her seventeenth birthday at the end of the month.

Cody, meanwhile, had turned down Rick's offer of metal sculpting lessons in favor of studying under Hector Zapata's green thumb. Rick wanted to feel hurt, but gardening was so much safer than what he proposed that, in truth, he was more than a little relieved that Cody was occupied with vegetables, flowers, slugs, and snails, not to mention the coveted twice-weekly rides with Hector on the sit-down mower. Bob the Invisible One was still his best friend, but

Rick figured that once school started and Cody made some real flesh-and-blood friends, old Bob would be history.

Cody also adored Carmen, and she was as good with him as she had been with Rick. Her protective streak still ran deep, which made life much easier for him.

She and Rick got along fine now that she had ceased mentioning the need for the two of them to talk. As much as he loved her, he couldn't help being uneasy around her. He felt like she knew something he didn't, and suspected that it had to do with the fleeting visions of her in the blue nightgown, smelling of cold, still water, that had haunted him since his arrival. He couldn't shake it, but he couldn't place it either—not that he wanted to. He only wanted it to go away, and had come to suspect that the vision had something to do with whatever it was she'd wanted to talk to him about since his return. The past, he told himself frequently, was the past.

That old blast from the past, Aunt Jade, had behaved herself amazingly well since that one awful night. He'd barely seen her, and no more poodles had made unwanted appearances. He'd never gotten her to admit that she'd told Cody about the passages, but he was certain she had: She wouldn't look him in the eye when she denied it.

Rick had briefly feared that all was lost with Audrey after Jade's obscene demonstration and his angry reaction, but that wasn't the case, and their relationship continued, tentative and slow, but very enjoyable. Delicious, in fact.

He was falling in love, he knew that, and he didn't try to fight it. If they were to continue, he supposed he would eventually have to tell her the truth about the greenjacks. He couldn't lie to her forever. In the back of his mind, he had a partial plan that had something to do with waiting until Halloween and making sure she saw Big Jack—assuming, of course, the creature actually existed. So many of Rick's memories were elusive or nonsensical that he sometimes wondered if they were all false versions of what had really happened.

And that possibility was too upsetting to dwell on. He'd

decided the only healthy thing to do was to stop thinking about the past and concentrate on today: the challenges of home ownership, career, and family.

The only real problems he had were with the house and his own indulgences. He intended to begin renovations, but there was no time between his column and his sculpting. When he began the Quixote project, it was supposed to be something he did once or twice a week, a hobby, nothing more. But he'd become obsessed with it to the point that he'd apologized to Carmen for his laziness. Carmen, bless her soul, had responded that he actually *was* working on the house, because the sculpture would be a decoration for the garden. Thin as it was, he appreciated the excuse and used it whenever he felt guilty.

As he welded another seam together, he reminded himself that there were some things that needed to be done soon, excuse or no excuse. Although he'd driven two nails into the hidden passage in Cody's room, he hadn't sealed any of the others yet because he was still putting fresh bait inside them: It took a long time to do in twenty years' worth of rodents.

Even out here, there were still rodents. Frequently he heard their scrabbling around the ancient Rambler in the corner. He'd replenished the bait several times, but they kept coming.

"Ricky?" Carmen stuck her head in the open doorway. "You want some lunch?"

He turned off the torch and removed his heavy gloves and welding mask, which took the temperature in the work-room down about a million degrees. "Lunch?" His damp hair clung to his forehead, and he pushed it back with his fingers.

"I'm making chili dogs." She smiled. "Cody says they're your favorite."

"He does, huh? You never made hot dogs for me!"

"They had pork guts and hooves in them back then. I didn't want to poison you. I got chicken dogs."

"Beaks and claws!"

"Ricky!' She feigned anger.

"Sorry. Sure, I'd love one. Do I have time for a shower?"

"If you hurry!" With that, Carmen turned and walked quickly away.

A few moments later, Rick ascended the stairs, humming contentedly to himself until he saw that the door to his room was ajar. He knew he'd latched it—he always did.

Entering, he saw with relief that everything appeared normal and decided that Carmen must have come in to take his laundry basket and had forgotten to close the door.

"Quint?"

No answer. Shit.

By now he knew to check under the headboard for the cat. Sure enough, he was there, ears and whiskers flat back, unwilling to come out. The feline had uncharacteristically sulked virtually all the days they'd been here, acting frightened and nervous, and exhibiting none of his usual cocksure arrogance. Now he growled in a high-pitched tone that spoke of fear, not aggression.

"Quint?" he called, feeling on the nightstand for his flashlight. "Quint?" His hands closed on it and he brought it down, flicking it on and shining the beam on the cat.

The animal was soaking wet.

"What'd you do, cat?" he asked, chuckling.

The cat growled.

"I'll bet you saw a mouse and ran so fast, you tipped over your water bowl. Is that it, fur-ball?"

The cat was not amused.

Poor idiotic cat. Smiling to himself, he left Quint where he was, walked into the dressing room, and stripped, dropping his dirty clothes on the floor. He'd have to remember to put them in the hamper before Carmen saw them.

He entered the bathroom, surprised to see Quint's water bowl pristinely full, the floor around it dry. "Where the hell did the water come from, Quint?" he called as he opened the shower door.

"My God." He staggered backward, not comprehending what he saw hanging low in the shower. "My God." His bare buttocks hit the countertop and he stood there, blood pounding in his head, making him dizzy. He stared. "My God."

It was a poodle, soaking wet and limp, its white fur matted, its pinkish flesh showing between the clumps of fur. The shower massager's hose was knotted around its neck.

"Jade, you crazy bitch," he whispered as his heart slowed down. "Great, just great." She'd hung one of her damned stuffed dogs in his shower and probably ruined the hose to boot. *At least I have a couple spares under the sink.*

He put his hands around the animal.

The dog was soft and warm.

He snatched his hand back, moaning softly at the sight of the creature's black bulging eyes, thickened tongue, a little trickle of blood from one nostril.

Frantically he washed his hands, pushed the shower door closed with his toe, then pulled his dirty jeans back on.

The cat was her real target, he thought wildly. Jade had tried to kill his cat.

Slamming his door behind him, he flew down the front staircase to Jade's door. He yanked on the handle. Locked. "Jade! Open up!" he yelled. "Now! Unlock this goddamned door!" Inside, a dog yipped wildly.

Carmen raced into the room, Cody and Hector behind her. "Ricky! What's wrong?" she cried. "What is it?"

"She—she—"

Cody was clinging to Carmen's skirt, peering at him with wide eyes.

"Cody, it's okay, go to your room," he said as calmly as he could. The little boy stuck his thumb in his mouth and started toward the stairs. "No, wait!" God knew what else might be up there. "Don't go up there."

Out of the corner of his eye, he saw Carmen cross herself. "Cody," she said, "why don't you and Hector take your lunch over to our house. Your papa and I gotta, we gotta . . ." She faltered, looking at Rick.

"Plumbing problem," he said lamely.

"We gotta fix the plumbing, then we'll come over, too."

"Why you mad at Aunt Jade, Daddy?"

"Uh, I'm not mad." He could barely control his breathing. "We'll be over in a little while."

Jade's heavy footsteps could be heard approaching. "Hector," Carmen ordered, "Take him."

"Come on, Cody." Hector scooped the boy into his arms. "We've got Pepsi in our fridge," he said, leaving the room. "You want a Pepsi?"

"What happened?" Carmen whispered as Jade started to turn her lock.

"She hung one of her poodles in my shower," Rick whispered. "She knotted the sprayer cord around its neck. I think she tried to kill my cat."

Carmen stared at him, then hissed, "Shhhh!" as the door opened.

"What's going on here?" Jade's black hair was wild above a long green terry robe. She wore no makeup, and looked faded and dry and old. One poodle bared its teeth and growling from behind her calves.

"How dare y—" Ricky began.

Carmen grabbed the bare skin just above the back of his pants and pinched. He silenced.

"Well, what is it?" Jade asked huffily.

"Miz Jade." Carmen put her hands on her hips. "What were you doing just now?"

"Taking a nap," she huffed. "What the hell does it look like?"

"I thought maybe you were taking a shower."

She showed no real reaction to Carmen's words. "Why would I shower in the middle of the day? We were having our nap, weren't we, Mister Poo?"

"Where's Stinkums?" Rick asked calmly.

Jade looked flustered. "Stinkums? Come here, Stinkums."

She turned and disappeared into her rooms.

Rick started to follow, but Carmen grabbed him by the belt loop. "Don't tell her," she ordered.

"Why not? She knows. She did it."

"She wouldn't kill her own dog."

"Before you said—"

"Forget what I said!" Carmen snapped, her eyes fierce.

"Carmen, she's nuts. She tried to kill my cat."

"You told me that already, but I didn't see any scratches on her."

"She's probably wearing that robe to hide them."

"No. The cat would have scratched her hands."

He could hear Jade moving around in her room, calling Stinkums in a quavering voice. "Look, Carmen, she's the only one who could have done it."

"Don't say anything to her. Not yet."

"Stinkums?" Jade's voice was tinged with hysteria now. "Stinkums?"

"You do what I say, Ricky. Promise."

She smells of the pond, of cold water, rich with life and death . . . The front of her nightgown is sopping wet. "Our secret," she says. "It's our secret, Ricky. Forever."

"I promise."

Jade ran back into the living room. "Stinkums is gone! My little Stinkums!"

"We'll find your dog," Carmen said gently. "You go finish your nap. Ricky and I will find him."

Jade stared at them.

"Go on. He's around here somewhere. The bitches are in heat outside. I'll have Hector look out there."

Jade stared at them suspiciously, and Rick could barely contain himself. He trembled with an almost overwhelming urge to do violence to the woman until, staring at him in alarm, she slowly retreated into her room and shut the doors.

"Stinkums?" he heard the old bitch call as she turned her lock. "Stinkums?"

"Come on," Carmen ordered. He followed her into the kitchen, where she collected a garbage bag and a butcher knife. "Let's go," she commanded as she started up the back stairs. Silently he followed her, wondering what the knife was for.

At his room, she opened the door and went in. He followed, feeling impotently angry and afraid as she marched into the bathroom. He stopped to check behind the bed to make sure the cat was all right.

"Ricky, can you come in here?" she called.

Reluctantly he entered the bathroom and saw that she'd used the knife to cut the hose. The dog lay on the counter, and his stomach lurched as he watched her wiggle its head, then pry its mouth open and peer inside. *"Madre de Dios,* I don't know how she told those dogs apart," she said, still prodding the animal. "It hasn't been dead long."

"No."

"It's neck's broken. Must've snapped when it was hanged. Ricky, hold that bag open for me, please."

Jade's screams began as Carmen dropped the dog, shower head and all, into the bag. Startled, Rick dropped the bag, and it thumped sickeningly to the floor.

"Stinkums! What have you done with Stinkums?" She hobbled forward, and Rick could see that the stairs had taken their toll. As she passed the bed, Quint's horrifying yowl rent the air, followed by violent hissing.

Jade shoved past Rick, bending with surprising agility and grabbing the bag, muttering the animal's name over and over and over. She pulled the poodle from the black plastic and held it to her chest, kissing its dead muzzle, cuddling it, stroking it, talking to it.

Rick felt sick.

Jade rose on creaking legs, looked Ricky straight in the eye, and slapped him as hard as she could. "You're evil!" she cried. "You killed my dog! You killed my Stinkums!" She reached out to slap him again, but this time he caught her wrist. He wanted to twist it, to break it.

"I didn't kill your damn dog, Jade" He was shocked by the controlled icy coldness in his voice. He saw Carmen staring at him in surprise. "You tried to kill my cat," he continued, his voice growing chillier. "He got away, so you did this." He gestured sharply at the animal in her arms.

"No I didn't! You killed my Stinkums!"

"Maybe Robin did it," he heard himself say in a nasty,

sarcastic tone. "You blame everything else on him. Why not this too? Maybe Robin did it, Jade."

"Ricky," Carmen began.

"She's like a spoiled little kid," Rick continued. "She does whatever she wants, then blames my brother."

Carmen crossed herself.

Jade squeezed the poodle harder, and something disgusting leaked from its rear end. "I have to call Mr. Whalen," she announced, storming from the room.

"The taxidermist," Carmen said dully. She opened the vanity, removed a sponge and cleanser, and one of the extra shower massagers. "Here." She handed the head to Rick. "You fix this while I clean up."

Silently he did as she asked. Carmen handled problems with action; it didn't matter what the action was, but she believed you had to do something—vacuum, tie knots in string, scrub down the kitchen—it didn't matter what.

"Excuse me," he said, reaching past her for a wrench he'd left in the medicine cabinet.

Carmen watched him, amused. "You never did learn how to put away your toys, did you, Ricky?"

Her words eased the tension between them, and they quickly finished their work.

"Now," she announced, "I'm gonna call Hector." She went to Rick's bedside phone and dialed, spoke rapidly in Spanish, then turned to Rick. "Okay, let's get your cat's stuff. His box and his toys. Throw away the food—Hector's taking Cody to the store to buy more."

"What? Why?"

"Your cat's gonna live with us for a while. At night you can bring him back to sleep with you, but then you bring him right back."

"I don't see why—"

"He'll be alive, Ricky."

"Okay, but I'll feed him here—"

"No. You got too much rat poison around. It'd be easy to poison his food. I'll feed him. Just change the water every time you bring him back."

A chill traveled down Rick's back. Carmen's seriousness scared the hell out of him.

Five minutes and several painful scratches later, Quint was secure in his arms, and he and Carmen walked out back and into her cozy little house. Hector and Cody were gone. She shut the door. "He'll be fine. Let him go, he likes it here. We won't let him out."

He took off Quint's leash and collar and was amazed to see the cat immediately start acting like his old self, moving through the house, rubbing, examining, stopping just short of marking his territory, thank God.

"He won't explore the main house," Rick said. "Maybe it's too big."

"He doesn't like it. He knows. Cats know things, Rick. So do dogs." She snorted. "You can't tell it with those inbred rats of Jade's, but a real dog, he knows, just like cats."

"Knows what?"

"In a minute. Sit down." She pointed at a rocking chair nearby and disappeared into the yellow and white kitchen. "Good," she said. "They brought all the food over. I'm gonna heat it up for us."

Rick loved the Zapatas' two-bedroom, one bath cottage. It was a square little Spanish-style bungalow built with arched doorways and ceiling fans like the main house, but much more comfortable and cozy. It had rusty brown carpet, much newer than the stuff in the main house, and the pale eggshell walls served as a background for an assortment of weavings and hangings. Across from the fireplace, an organ took up a short wall, a beautifully bright Mexican blanket hanging behind it to muffle the sound. Ricky had considered the bungalow a haven when he was a child, and he realized now that his feelings hadn't changed.

"Okay, come and eat."

He entered the kitchen and took a seat across from Carmen at the little pine table. They made small talk while they ate. When they were done, Carmen scraped the leftover chili into a bowl and gave it to Quint.

Rick shook his head watching the cat make happy growl

sounds as he devoured the food. "That's the first time he's been really interested in food since we moved."

"It's that house, Ricky. He doesn't like that house." She went to a cupboard next to the refrigerator and withdrew a bottle of tequila and two shot glasses, brought them to the table, then fetched a small plate, a knife, a tub of margarita salt, and a whole lime and brought them also.

"It's kind of early for a drink, isn't it?" Rick asked, thoroughly enjoying the scent of lime zest as she cut into the fruit.

"Yeah, it's early, but we're gonna do it anyway," she told him. "You're never gonna calm down otherwise, and it's time for us to have our talk. I think this is the only way you're gonna sit still for it."

She held him with her eyes, and he found himself nodding agreement. "What about Cody?"

"You should've let me teach you Spanish, Ricky. I told Hector to buy cat food and then take him to the movies. We have all afternoon."

"Swell," he muttered as she poured the shots. "Just great." He should have known Carmen would get her way in the end.

31

The ritual of lime, tequila, and salt was one Carmen found comforting. It was something to do, something to occupy a worried mind, and to return serenity to an anxious one. She hoped it would work on Ricky, because the things she needed to talk to him about, to force him to remember, certainly weren't going to calm him down.

She licked a spot on her hand and shook salt on it, then waited while Ricky copied her. Solemnly they swallowed their shots, then bit into the lime wedges.

"I'm worried about you," she began. "You're wound up tight, like a watch that's gonna break."

He shrugged, and she couldn't help but smile: It was the same gesture that he'd often made as a child.

"I'm okay."

"You will be." She poured two more shots. "Let's do it again."

"I don't want to get sloshed."

"You're not gonna get sloshed, Ricky. You're just gonna relax a little. Drink."

"Yes, boss."

They performed the ritual again. "You gotta calm down, Ricky, or you're gonna do something you shouldn't."

"What do you mean?" he asked defensively.

"You let the old *puta* get under your skin. If you're not gonna send her away, then you better ignore her. You're so

angry right now that I think you're gonna explode soon."
As she spoke, she poured two more. She figured it would
take at least four shots to get him loose enough to really
talk to him.

This time he downed the liquor without protest. "I'm
fine, Carmen, I told you."

"Stop it!" she snapped. "Stop lying to me. Stop lying to
yourself. You lie all the time. You see those little jacks, but
you won't admit it. You'd rather think you're crazy than to
admit you see them, wouldn't you?"

He said nothing.

"Answer me, Ricky."

He slammed the glass down on the table. "What the hell
am I supposed to think, Carmen? Nobody else sees them.
What the fuck am I supposed to think?"

"Watch your mouth. You're a fool. You gotta just accept
that you've been gifted with the sight."

"It's not a gift. It's a curse."

He was hiding so much from himself. "Robin used to tell
you everyone would think you were crazy if you told on
him or if you told other people about the greenjacks."

"How . . . how'd you know?" Obviously he was shocked.
"I didn't tell you . . ."

"No. I heard him threaten you. You were so embarrassed
that I didn't say anything to you. He knew your soft spot. I
thought you'd grow out of it, but all you did was learn to
hide it. You still don't trust yourself at all." *And maybe you
shouldn't,* she thought, watching him. She loved him as if
he were her own, but . . .

His dark blue eyes had glazed over. "So you got me drunk
to tell me I need to trust myself?"

"No. I got you drunk so you wouldn't think I was crazy
when I tell you what I'm gonna tell you." She had the sinking feeling he wouldn't believe anything she said, but she
had to try.

"What do you have to tell me?" He sounded like he was
waiting for his death sentence.

"Ricky, things have been happening in that house ever since you left."

"What do you mean?"

"Jade didn't kill her poodle. She wouldn't do that."

"So who did?" he asked skeptically. "Why did you tell me she put that other dog in the dryer?"

"Because I thought it might stop when you moved in. Sometimes these things work that way. You just never know."

"What would stop?"

"The spirit."

"What?"

"That house is haunted."

"Yeah, right. So a ghost tried to kill my cat but missed and got the poodle instead," he said caustically. "Who's the ghost? My dead brother?"

"Yes."

"And this ghost could pick up a dog, break its neck, and tie a knot around its neck, all after hosing it down so it was nice and wet."

"It could make someone else do it," Carmen said.

"Possession?"

"Probably. I think it's sort of a . . ." She searched in vain for a word. "An *espectro ruidoso*. You know, a noisy ghost."

"A poltergeist?"

"That's it."

"It's really hard to buy, Carmen. Sorry."

"Look at your cat, how he acts here and there."

Ricky said nothing for a long while. When he finally spoke, it was in a soft, beaten voice. "He sees the greenjacks, Carmen."

"What?"

"The cat can see them."

"Good. Then he sees the ghost, too. But why do you believe him, but not yourself?"

Slowly Rick smiled. "I guess I have to. He's not going to try to spare my feelings, is he."

The last comment was a statement, not a question, and Carmen breathed a sigh of relief. Maybe he'd come around.

Then he said, "So who's being possessed, Carmen? Me?"

She swore at him, a long stream of Spanish invective that made him flinch, even though she knew he couldn't understand a word. This wasn't going the way she wanted. *"Madre de Dios,* Ricky," she said after a moment. "You gotta stop feeling sorry for yourself. I told you, things have been going on since you went away. For instance, do you know how many dogs have died in the last fifteen or twenty years?"

"A lot."

"More than what you think. There were some that couldn't be stuffed."

"What happened to them?"

"What didn't?" Carmen threw her hands up. "Want one more?"

"Yeah."

She poured. "One got ground up in the mulching machine. Another was roasted in the oven. A few years ago, one got in one of the passages. *Madre de Dios,* the smell. Rats ate most of it before we found it. Another was run through with knitting needles."

"Good God. How?"

"You name it. Some are honest accidents, I think—chewing electrical cords, choking on toys, and Hector certainly tried to avoid the one that ran under the lawn mower . . ." She grimaced. "But the things like today, that's mostly what happens. Things that can't be accidents."

"Carmen, from what you're telling me, Jade is certifiable."

"She can hardly get up a flight of stairs when she's herself, Ricky. How do you explain the dog we found stuck on the weather vane?"

Ricky's eyes widened. "Well, I guess if I can buy greenjacks, I can buy a ghost." He looked longingly at the empty shot glass, but made no move. "I still think Jade's doing most of this herself—and poltergeists are supposed to be directed by people." He made a silly-looking smile. "I read a book once."

"You're plastered, Ricky," Carmen said, feeling pretty plastered herself. At least the tension had dissipated.

"Carmen, did you know Jade makes sounds at night like she's making love with someone?"

"Puta." Carmen shook her head. "I gotta apologize—I never go over there at night. I knew she used to, but I was hoping she didn't anymore. She's so old."

"That's silly."

"It's unholy." Carmen crossed herself. "Ricky, I think she's having sex with your brother's ghost, that's what I think." She crossed herself.

He looked unconvinced, and at first she was surprised, then she figured it made sense. If he claimed to see green-jacks, but didn't even believe himself, why would he believe her?

"Carmen?"

"What?" She smiled and squeezed his hand again. He was guileless now, once again the little boy she would have given her life for. "What, Ricky?"

"There are things I can't remember."

"Like what?"

"There was something about a baby."

Madre de Dios, she thought, *here it is.* "Yes?"

He raised his eyebrows, then took his hands back and pushed his dark hair away from his face. "There was a baby that died." He paused a long moment. "Evangeline had a baby, didn't she?"

He's starting to remember. Carmen tried to hide her nervousness. *Let him get it on his own,* she prayed. She didn't want to tell him. "No," she said finally. "She was good at getting pregnant, though."

"Oh, God." He looked at Carmen with heavy eyes. "I'd forgotten. You called her 'Our Lady of the Abortion Clinic.' "

"By the time that girl was fifteen, she must've been to the women's clinic half a dozen times to get rid of her mistakes. But she never had a baby," Carmen said harshly. "Remember? She ran off with a Hell's Angel or something, when she was about sixteen."

Rick nodded. "I drank too much."

"Me too. I'll make coffee." She stood and set to work, wondering if he would remember any more on his own.

"Did you know that Robin wanted to get Evangeline pregnant?" Ricky asked. "Jade, too."

She spooned ground beans into the coffeemaker. Good, he was still thinking. "Why?"

"He wanted to make sons who had the sight. For the jacks," Rick shook his head. "He wanted me to. . . . do it too. I guess he thought I'd be more likely to produce children with the gene."

"The gene," she repeated. *Keep him thinking about children.* The coffee burbled as she set two cobalt-blue mugs on the table, then brought the pot over and poured. "You must've been very worried that Cody might have the gene."

"I was, but there was no need." He sipped his coffee. "When he was born I talked Laura into letting his middle name be Thomas. At the time, I didn't know why that meant so much to me. I didn't remember until I came back." He smiled. "Cody's nothing like I was. He's fearless. And he doesn't see things."

"The name fits." She smiled gently. "He's a lot like you, Ricky. Just remember, he didn't have a mean brother teasing him all the time." In truth the boy reminded her very much of Robin when he was very young, before his happy, mischief-making personality soured and turned mean. She watched Ricky, thinking how frightening it was to see Robin's chill anger on his face when he'd confronted Jade. "Ricky," she began slowly. "Speaking of Cody, are you going to take him away Halloween night?"

"I hadn't thought about it." He paused. "I want to be here . . . I want to see Big Jack." He stared into his coffee. "That is, if I didn't imagine him."

"You think you might have?" she asked hopefully.

"I . . . no. I mean, I remember seeing him. But maybe I made it all up because I felt guilty when Robin fell out of the tree. Carmen, I think about it a lot. He *did* change after that."

"Yes, he did," she agreed solemnly.

"Well, he got hit on the head. Maybe he sustained some brain damage."

"Could be."

"I always felt sort of responsible—"

"You shouldn't. You didn't make him climb out there."

"I know I didn't. But I shut the window, then took my sweet time opening it again."

"Ricky, you thought Big Jack was out there."

He made a disgusted sound. "Yeah. And then, when Robin lost his balance and fell while climbing back in, I made up this whole scenario about how Big Jack was trying to get me, and he sacrificed himself for me."

"You could be right," Carmen said soothingly. "But what about the greenjacks? You still see those, and you said your cat sees them."

"There might be a logical explanation." There was hope in his eyes as he spoke. "You know that Audrey's an eye doctor?"

"Yes."

"Well, I told her about a fictitious cousin of mine who sees them, and she said it's possible for eyes to work differently, even that it could be a genetic thing. She said she'd research it."

"Has she found out anything yet?" Carmen asked, pleased that he'd looked for help, even in such a roundabout way.

"I haven't let her talk about it. I—"

"You need to."

"I know."

"What about Big Jack?" Carmen continued. "You're saying that though you see the little ones, you don't believe in him?"

"Yeah." He paused, studying his fingernails. "Maybe I don't. It seemed so real. Emotionally I believe, but intellectually I don't buy it. That's why I want to be here. If it does exist, I want Audrey to see it."

"Maybe you should let Hector and me take Cody up to Madelyn. My sister's having a Halloween party for her grandkids." Despite her love for Ricky, she didn't want his son to be with him. *If Ricky thinks he sees Big Jack, who knows what will happen?* She had to make him remember about the baby, for Cody's sake.

"We'll see, Carmen. I think I'd feel better keeping him with me. We'll see."

They started on their second cups, Ricky silent and thoughtful. Finally he looked up. "You know when I asked you about Evangeline having a baby?"

"Yes?" She could see him struggling to hide from the memory, and decided to prompt him a little. "Maybe you were thinking of Jade's baby."

Ricky's hand shook, slopping coffee over the rim. "Jade." He shook his head. "There's something about Jade's baby, and you said it was our secret. You had on a blue nightgown and it was wet and it smelled liked the koi pond." He shook his head. "You said it was our secret, but I can't remember—"

Carmen realized she was trembling, too. "His name was Paulie," she said, trying to hide her dread. "You loved him very much. Do you remember that?"

32

Waves of blood thundered inside Rick's skull as he stood, deafened and trembling. He tried to see past the black splotches swimming across his vision as he fought down rising nausea and staggered into the bathroom. He fell to his knees and hugged the toilet bowl.

The baby drowned in the koi pond.

He tried to save it and almost drowned too. Carmen was—Carmen was what?

It's our secret, Ricky.

Rick rose slowly, his head aching, his mind clearer, and turned on the cold water, running it into his mouth and over his face.

The laughter began deep in his abdomen, as undeniable and unstoppable as the sickness had been. It burst into his chest, and he grabbed at his throat to stop it, but then it was bubbling out his lips, in fits and snorts, then full-fledged hysterical belly laughs that made him double over.

He tried to stop, but he couldn't. Tears sprang from his eyes, and he made high falsetto noises as he gasped for breath between the giggles that felt so full of hilarity, yet were utterly devoid of it. He felt Carmen take his elbow, and he let her guide him into the living room, sit him on the couch. He laughed as she brought over a box of Kleenex, he laughed as she sat down beside him and said his name once, twice, three times, commanding him to snap out of it.

He couldn't. His sides hurt, but the laughter continued like a roller coaster, up and down, rising to the brink of madness, plunging down into an abyss of despair, but it was all laughter.

If you don't laugh, you cry.

That's what his dad always said. *Words to live by, Rick.* Thinking it now made him laugh all the harder. *If you don't laugh, you cry. If you don't la—*

Carmen slapped him, hard. He put his hand to his stinging cheek and stared at her, hurt. He felt real tears welling up in his eyes, and fiercely he thought, *If you don't laugh, you cry.* The hilarity came back enough to make him laugh slightly.

"Don't do it, Ricky. Don't laugh anymore," Carmen said. "Cry or scream or yell, but don't laugh. You scare me." She reached out to pat his knee as she had a thousand times in the past, but this time he flinched back, not wanting her to touch him. He looked at her and saw that her eyes were solemn and sad.

"I apologize," he said carefully, "for losing control." If it hadn't been for the chili dogs and tequila shooters, he didn't think he would have reacted so badly.

"It was a very bad thing, about the baby."

It's our secret, Ricky. We must take it to our graves.

October 31, 1980

The first time Ricky had seen Robin doing it with Evangeline was a summer day about a year after the Ewebeans had moved in. The twins were only eleven, and Rick didn't even quite know what he was seeing.

Everyone else was gone, and Ricky had ventured down the back stairs to find something to eat. He'd poured a bowl of Cheerios and was about to get the milk out of the fridge when he heard Evangeline giggle and start moaning. There were grunting sounds, too, coming from the family room. He tiptoed through the laundry room, past the bath and

downstairs bedroom, as the noises became louder. At the
edge of the family room, he stopped and peered around the
corner. Evangeline was lying on the old tweed couch that
used to be in the living room, her short skirt hiked up above
her bare hips. Robin was on top of her, grasping her thighs
and thrusting in and out, his body swaying back and forth.
Shocked, Ricky stood there and watched until Robin sensed
his presence and looked up. All he did was grin.

Not long after that, he walked in on Robin and Aunt Jade
doing the same thing in the library upstairs. No one saw him
that time.

Before long, Robin started telling him how much fun it
was to screw the women, actually encouraging him to do it,
too. Ricky was horrified.

Now that he was nearly fifteen and had had his first encounter with Cindy McGuire, a seventeen-year-old cheerleader who seduced him one night and with whom he knew
he would be in love forever, he wasn't so much horrified by
his relatives' behavior as he was disgusted.

Even before Evangeline ran away, most of Robin's atten-
tions went to Jade, who was, Ricky realized, a total nympho.
In the last year, Ricky had grown six inches, his voice had
stopped breaking, and lots of girls called him, either to see
if he'd do homework with them or just to talk. Sometimes
he'd go to matinees with one, though he still avoided going
out at night. He smiled. Cindy said he had great dimples.

The downside was that Jade had tried to seduce him too.
No, he corrected, not seduce. Fuck. That's what she did, she
and Robin, they fucked. It was filthy, disgusting, and nasty.
Sometimes when he passed by Jade, she'd pinch his butt or
make a remark about how nice his pants fit. She made him
want to puke.

Jade and Robin were not careful about where they did it,
and it amazed Rick that Howard had never caught on. But
then his uncle was so far gone into his bottle of Jack Daniel's
most of the time that he wouldn't notice anything.

Rick had heard his aunt and uncle arguing about sex too.
Jade would yell at Howard that he couldn't get it up because

he was drunk, and he'd yell at her that she was a dried-up old cunt. Rick thought they both made valid points. Jade no longer looked like the woman in *American Gothic,* but had taken to coating her long, horsey face with vast amounts of makeup, ratting her dyed brown hair into a big bubble-shaped helmet, and wearing clothes meant for teenage girls. She had the body for it, but not the face. She also had pictures of the Beatles all over the house, especially Paul McCartney. It was completely creepy.

Evangeline had been gone for less than a week when Jade announced she was pregnant. She and Howard got into a screaming match that night after he asked whose it was. "It's yours, of course," she'd maintained, and Ricky couldn't hear exactly what he said, but it had something to do with his preferring a maggoty whore over his wife. After that comment, there was a loud crash. The next day, Howard had a shiner.

Now Paul George Ewebean, a handsome little boy with the midnight blue eyes of the Piper clan, was almost two years old. Jade paid no attention to the child, leaving his care to Carmen. Almost immediately after he was born, Carmen began taking Paulie to her house at night, which made Rick, who found he really liked the child, rest easier.

As much as he could, Rick spent time with Paulie, too, reading him stories out of his old Little Golden Books that Carmen had retrieved from an attic trunk, putting him in a stroller and taking him for walks around town, and even telling him the greenjack stories.

All the while, he wondered if the baby could see them.

He and Carmen tried to keep Robin away from the baby, although sometimes, when Howard wasn't around, Jade would commandeer the child and hand him to Robin straight out, giggling and sniffing and saying, "That's your dada, that's why you're so handsome, not like your ugly pretend dada." Robin would throw the baby up in the air and catch him again. If he tried to take Paul outside, Rick always followed.

Last July Rick became fairly certain that Paul had the

sight. While he and the boy were watching TV one evening—no one else was home—he opened the drapes in the living room. Greenjacks were everywhere, their movement constant and energetic. As always, he looked briefly for the quiet, still one he'd occasionally spotted over the years, but it was nowhere to be seen.

"Here goes," he whispered, turning Paul so that he could see out the window. Immediately the baby cooed and gurgled and began to laugh, his little arms going out, reaching for the glass.

"See them, Paulie?" Rick asked, trying to remain calm. "Do you see the jacks?"

Paulie laughed until several of the creatures merged just outside the window. Then he drew back and sobbed, hiding his face on Rick's shoulder.

"It's okay, Paulie," he murmured, shutting the drapes. "They can't have you. I'm going to tell you a story about your ancestor, Thomas McEnery Piper, and how they almost got him." He rubbed his nose on Paul's, making him giggle happily. "But they didn't. And they won't get you either. I'll make sure."

From that moment on, Rick knew that he had to protect this child, and in many ways, that was the best summer of Rick's life. Having someone else to worry about helped make him strong, gave him purpose. He told Carmen that he'd like to have the toddler move into his room with him, and Carmen soon agreed. Rick became more watchful than ever.

Then, on Halloween night 1980, when Paulie was almost two years old, everything changed.

Since the night Big Jack had claimed Robin, Rick had been very careful not to be alone on the thirty-first. He usually spent the time until midnight, when the physical danger was over, with Carmen or at a friend's. He preferred Carmen because he never had to drum up an excuse to not go out. That other Halloween, over seven years ago, seemed like a vivid dream now, but it still worried him, especially because of Paulie.

This year, as usual, Jade and Howard had gone to the Dew Drop Inn, a sleazy roadhouse just outside of town on Cub Road. The Dew Drop was having a party featuring bobbing for apples (in beer) and a "naughty" costume–cum–wet–T-shirt contest that promised a grand prize of a ten-dollar gift certificate to Frederick's of Hollywood. Since the Dew Drop was where Howard spent a good deal of time with rednecked buddies, he was happy to go drink while Jade flaunted her boobs in competition for the fancy underwear.

Rick watched them leave that night. Howard wore what he always wore: rump-sprung jeans and a short-sleeved plaid shirt. Jade had a butt-length red T-shirt on that she'd drawn a Star Trek insignia on, black panties, no bra, fishnet nylons, old Beatles boots, and Spock ears. She'd put her hair up and drawn her pale eyebrows into Vulcanian shape. Rick had to laugh: With her long-jawed face and squinty eyes, she looked like Mr. Spock in drag, rather than the Vulcan's main squeeze.

Carmen and Hector came over as soon as the Ewebeans left, and Robin was off with some sleazy kids from school traveling around the neighborhood even though they were too old to trick-or-treat. Robin had invited Rick along, goadingly informing him he had to bring his own eggs and toilet paper. As always, Rick declined.

The Zapatas, Rick, and Paulie had dinner, then passed out candy until nine P.M. After that, they turned out the porch light, turned on the TV, and dug into the huge pumpkin pie Carmen had made.

At ten, Hector kissed his wife and went home to bed. Full of pie and candy, Paulie had curled up in the old recliner in the corner. Carmen and Rick sat on the couch nearby and watched television, both glancing often at the baby, both mindful of noises from outside and in, watching for Robin, for Big Jack too.

They were keeping Halloween vigil, as they had for seven years. Before, it was to protect Rick, and now it was to protect the baby, too. Carmen would remain here until after midnight—when Big Jack's power dissipated—then Rick would take Paulie upstairs to his room and lock them in. Paulie slept on the sofa bed, just as Rick had, years before.

But that would come later. Now the fireplace crackled warm, comfortable heat into the living room. Rick's eyes grew heavy and his head would start to droop and he'd jerk awake. He kicked his shoes off and stretched his toes toward the fire. Beside him, Carmen had drifted off and was snoring softly. He wouldn't wake Carmen, he decided; it was less than an hour until midnight, and he could stay awake until then easily. Yawning, he turned his attention back to the Creature Features Halloween marathon. They were showing *The Creature from the Black Lagoon,* which he'd seen about a trillion times. He rubbed his eyes. You'd think they could show something newer tonight of all nights. He yawned again. Something in color.

RICKY! Ricky Ricky Icky Ricky Ricky!

Ricky bolted upright, disoriented and frightened. Beside him, Carmen continued to sleep.

"Ricky!"

Faintly he heard Robin calling him from somewhere outside.

He sat up and glanced at the recliner. The baby wasn't there.

Icky Ricky, come and play, hey, come and play, Ricky, Ricky, Ricky!

Rising, he ignored the little jacks' taunts. "Paul?" he whispered. "Paulie?"

He automatically glanced at the grandfather clock across the room. Quarter to twelve. He'd been asleep for, God, at least half an hour, maybe more. The baby could be anywhere. He turned to wake Carmen, then stopped as he heard the voices.

Out here, icky Ricky, we have your boy toy, boy toy, boy toy!

Ricky didn't like to talk to Carmen about the greenjacks anymore. He didn't want to be a coward.

"Ricky!" came Robin's faraway cry. "Hurry! Ricky! Help!"

He noticed that the front door didn't look right: The heavy black bolt had been pulled back.

With a last glance at Carmen, he raced to the door, determined that for once, he was going to be brave.

"Ricky!" Robin called.

Rick walked out into the night.

Play hey, play, hey, Ricky Ricky Ricky Ricky.

"Shut up," he whispered.

"Ricky!"

The Malibu lights, the filthy few that still worked, cast little light, but as Ricky squinted in the direction of the voice, they served to backlight Robin's legless long-armed form as he waved from near the now-putrefied koi pond. The rocky waterfall bubbled behind him. Glancing around, Rick saw no sign of Big Jack.

"God," Ricky whispered, seeing Paulie's silhouette rise from a squat beside him. The baby waved, and Rick heard his delighted giggle. "No," he whispered.

He started running across the lawn, not even noticing the greenjacks.

Instantly Robin grabbed the little boy and hoisted him above his head like a rag doll. "Come and get him, Icky Ricky!" he screeched.

Paul's gleeful shriek turned into a cry of terror as Robin threw him into the middle of the dank pond.

"No!" he screamed, running faster, his bare feet squishing through the wet grass, his legs feeling the chill caresses as he raced through masses of gibbering jacks.

Icky Ricky, icky Ricky, icky Ricky.

At the edge of the pond, Rick stopped.

"He's drowning!" Robin called from across the fetid water. "He's drowning! Save him!"

A few bubbles rose near a cluster of water lilies in the center of the pond. Rick glared at Robin. His brother could swim; he'd seen him down here frolicking in the water on any number of summer nights. If he wanted to, he could rescue the baby. But why would he want to? He threw him in. The baby was bait, Rick realized as he pulled off his sweater and moved to the water's edge. What Robin wanted most was Rick.

The pond smelled richly of cold water and wet, rotting plants.

The water lilies tugged at his clothes as he swam past them, and then he felt the underwater plants and grasses waving all around him. Rick searched frantically, unable to see anything but small glimmers of moonlight between the lilies, fighting panic each time the water grasses coiled around his ankles like cold, slimy fingers.

He came up for air, then scissored back down. Again.

The third time, at the deepest part of the pool, he blundered blindly into Paulie. Swiftly, he seized the limp body and turned to push himself up from the bottom.

Something wrapped around his ankle, began pulling him back. Wildly Rick twisted to get free, but something sharp twisted around his other ankle now. He strained forward, suddenly felt the slimy plaster pool wall against his arms. Peering up, he could see vague moonlight—he wasn't under the lilies. Frantically he pushed Paul's body upward, up toward the light, blindly shoving him onto the pavement.

He grabbed at the wall with his hands, wishing the rock sides extended farther down to give him purchase.

His lungs felt full of fire, and his legs seemed encased in barbed wire, and suddenly something dragged him across to the other side of the pool. His lungs started to give out as blackness edged Rick's consciousness.

No! Don't let him win!

Water exploded into his throat, choking him, and he began to struggle, fiercely kicking at the bonds restraining him. He grabbed at the side of the pool. Whatever had him—

Big Jack, you know it's Big Jack, he can go anywhere out of doors, of course he can go in the water, there are plants down here, too.

—gave slightly, coming up with him. His head cleared the water, and he coughed, gasping for breath, as water cas-

caded over his skull. He was beneath the waterfall. He
grabbed at the rocks, clung to them, pulling upward, straining, straining harder.

It was so hard, so hard. He coughed again, wanting to
rest, wanting to just give up.

You won't just die, they'll steal your body! He'll win!

At that moment he was yanked under again, and he could
feel the bonelike hands and arms clearly now, embracing
him, squeezing him. His own arms were still free, trying to
grasp at the rocky outcroppings. *You still have a chance.*

His toes connected with the side of the pool. Using every
ounce of strength in his possession, he bent his knees and
shoved off the side.

This time, *it* came up with him, breaking through a net
of lilies and grasses. Rick clutched at the sharp rocks on the
side of the waterfall, higher now, gaining ground.

Gasping, he spit out fetid water. And came face-to-face
with Big Jack himself.

The creature was as he remembered. The jungly green
smell, so like the odor of the pond, the pitch black eyes that
bored into his, the pulsing, twisted vines, the lacework of
thin white roots, all parodies of human physiology. He saw
it all in a millisecond, the bark-chip teeth, the mouth opening
with the obscene vines spewing forth, twining around his
throat, pulling and twisting like tentacles.

"No!" he screamed. Letting go of the rocks, he used his
hands to tear brutally at the Green Man, wrenching the
throbbing jugular vine until it broke, spewing chlorophyll
in his face. He yanked the mouth vines from the creature.
They came away dripping green, attached to a kinked jigsaw
of white roots.

Big Jack faltered, and Rick tore his feet free, pulled his
body up into a ball, then kicked straight out, his feet smash-
ing into the green growing out of the thing. Jack's arm-hold
loosened, and Rick flipped his legs backward to hit the pool-
side, then kicked, shoving off and up, flying out of the water,
tearing the skin off his feet and hands and arms and legs,

banging his cheek into a rock, moving, crawling, staggering, until he was free of the thing.

He crawled onto the pavement, tearing a final vine away from his ankle, crawling toward Paulie's still body. He reached the boy and began artificial respiration, just as he'd been taught in school.

"Icky Ricky, you're so brave." Robin sidled over to him, moving sideways like a crab. "But you're too late. Your precious little baby was under there way too long. He'll come back to life, all right, but he'll be one of us." Robin cackled insanely, staring at something behind Rick.

Rick chanced a quick look back, saw Big Jack lumber out of the water. When it straightened, it stood at least eight feet tall. Paulie coughed. *He's alive!*

Robin's cold hand grasped his arm so hard, he couldn't pull free. "Two for the price of one," his twin whispered in his ear. "That's what I was hoping for. Two for one."

Swaying, scarecrowlike, Big Jack stepped toward them. Robin giggled madly and let go of Rick's arm, backing away from the creature. "Well, little hero, guess it's not quite midnight. Maybe I'll have your body tonight yet. Maybe I'll have your *eyes!*"

"Fuck you," Rick whispered back.

Robin laughed and did a handstand, then, body raised overhead, he fled across the grass and disappeared into the house.

Big Jack stepped closer, vines dripping and snapping in the night wind. Ricky backed up, away from Paulie, thinking he had a better chance of saving both of them if he led the monster on a chase.

Icky Ricky, we've got you now! came Big Jack's powerful voice.

"You have squat!" Rick yelled. "You want me, you have to catch me first!" He leaped sideways and started zigzagging across the lawn, and the church bells began to chime the midnight hour.

It chased him, fueled by long-standing greed and desire. Rick ran, feinting this way and that. Big Jack barely inches from him. Suddenly, on the eighth ring, Rick lost his balance, landing hard and skidding across the dew-damp grass. Big Jack's twig fingers encircled his neck, choking him.

The eleventh bell sounded, and Ricky barely heard it over the ringing in his ears. He couldn't breathe.

The final bell chimed. Slowly Big Jack began to disintegrate, twig fingers dropping off, leaves drying up and scattering. The arms and legs fell into a pile of kindling around him, and then he was surrounded by a tumble of luminescent little jacks as they gave up their Big Jack for the year and swarmed over Rick, screaming and taunting and laughing.

He ignored them to run to Paulie. He fell to his knees and helped the coughing toddler sit up, thunking his hand against his back to help clear his lungs.

"Are you okay, Paulie?" he whispered. "It's all over now."

Paulie coughed violently, then whispered, " 'Kay." It was the best thing he'd ever said.

For just an instant, Rick let himself collapse on the lawn, let himself feel his muscles quiver, became aware of his cuts and bruises, his exhaustion.

Ten feet away, the little jacks watched. He closed his eyes and then opened them again as he felt a cool, feathery touch on his arm. Quickly he looked sideways, saw the faint outline of a single little jack beside him. It touched him again.

Ricky . . .

The voice was so soft, he could barely hear it. The strident jumble of voices from the other jacks assaulted his mind, but he concentrated on this one.

This voice, soft and gentle in his head, was a shimmer on the wind, a solitary sound separate from the others. He knew the inflections of this voice. They were his own.

"Robin?" he whispered. "Robin?"

Ricky . . .

The voice seemed anxious, mournful.

Too late . . .

"What?" he cried desperately.

Changed, he's changed . . .

"No!"

There was no reply, only another sad caress.

Ricky . . .

The sound of his name in his brother's voice made hot tears stream from his eyes.

Remember Thomas . . .

A small voice, faintly riding the wind.

Rick's head ached. "That's all I can remember."

"There's more, Ricky," Carmen said, her eyes boring into his.

The tone of her voice alarmed him. "He died," he said, his eyes burning. God, he'd loved that little kid, and he'd tried to save him, redemption for losing Robin, but that, too, had failed. If he'd only awakened Carmen. "I remember the funeral . . ."

"Ricky, you said he coughed."

"Yes. He did."

"Then why did he die?"

Helplessly, gut twisting, he looked at her. "I don't know! You came out and called the ambulance." *The blue nightgown!* "You were wearing the blue nightgown and you picked him up."

She nodded. "Yes."

Suddenly he heard a key in the lock and then Hector's cheerful voice called out, "Anybody home?"

Rick stood and went to the sink to wash his face. An instant later, Cody was hugging his waist, and grateful to be released from Carmen's prison, he picked up his son. "Your sister's working late tonight. How about you and I getting a pizza?" he asked with false cheerfulness. "Just us guys?"

"Yeah!"

"See you later," he called to the Zapatas as he escaped the cottage.

"What'd you and Carmen do, Daddy? Why's Quint at their house? What kind of pizza do you want?"

He welcomed Cody's endless questions because answering them let him forget about the one Carmen had asked. How *had* Paulie died?

33

October 10

Even native Californians seemed amazed when September turned into the hottest month of the year, but it invariably happened, and was invariably forgotten the following September, when the weathermen and everyone else expressed dismay over the extended dog days of summer.

And so, on the first day of kindergarten, when Cody insisted upon wearing his new fall clothes, Rick hadn't tried too hard to talk him out of it. Taking him to school, Rick was mildly embarrassed until he saw that most of the other kids wore sweaters or jackets even though, at eight in the morning, it was eighty-five degrees, on its way to the hundred mark. Fortunately, his teacher, Miss Cantrell, had instantly charmed the children into shedding a few layers, and since then, everything with Cody had been peaches and cream. The boy had it bad for Miss Cantrell. Lacking apples, he took her a barely ripe orange from the orchard every day.

He'd made some friends besides Bob the Invisible, too, which pleased Rick since Bob had remained fairly important instead of becoming more invisible, as he had expected. But now Bob ranked behind Craig, Matt, and Doug as Cody's priorities. And way behind marrying Miss Cantrell.

Shelly had settled in as well. Late in August, Rick presented her with a little red Bug with only thirty thousand on the speedometer. She hadn't said a word about it not being the coveted PT Cruiser, but instead, became invaluable to Rick and Carmen because she wanted to run everyone's errands for them.

Now that school had started, her life revolved around that and her job. She tried out for and made the cheerleading team—something so incredibly wholesome when compared to her previous goals that Rick still could barely believe it. And even though her phone rang so constantly that Rick bought her an answering machine as a back-to-school present, she was doing reasonably well in school.

For over a month now, Rick had tried not to be alone with Carmen. He hated the dark, serious way she would watch him when she thought he wasn't looking, and though he knew it had something to do with his memory lapse concerning the death of Paulie Ewebean, he'd decided once more that the past was the past and that he would dwell in the present.

Now, in mid-October, the heat had finally ended, and the occasional warmth of a Santa Ana wind had become a pleasant experience instead of a hellish one. As Rick lifted the welding mask from his face and stood back to study his statue, he told himself that life was turning out pretty damned good.

From the tip of Don Quixote's lance, ten feet in the air, down to Rosiante's hooves, his masterpiece was virtually complete. *Semimasterpiece,* he corrected, smiling to himself. Maybe it wasn't great art, but like life, it was pretty damn good.

Except for writing his weekly column, Rick had done nothing but indulge himself in this sculpture, and he'd assuaged his continuing guilt about letting the house go so long by having Hector buy interior paint for the entire house. They'd work on it this winter.

The rat problem seemed to have died down somewhat now, but he still hadn't sealed the rest of the passages, and since Quint had made it obvious that he much preferred to spend his days at the Zapatas' and only come back at night to sleep with Rick, he really saw no need.

Rick lowered the mask and fired up the torch, fixed a small curl on Don Quixote's breastplate.

"That's better," He set the mask aside and put down the torch. He had a lot to do before Audrey arrived.

She'd been wonderful to him, only mentioning in passing that if he wanted the information on vision, she had it. Thus far, he hadn't asked—he'd learned to ignore the greenjacks over the last few months. But he was going to ask her soon, because he needed to be honest with her if their relationship was going to proceed to a more serious level. As it was now, every time it started to, he'd find an excuse to hold off because he didn't want to start something under false circumstances. Fear of rejection, he knew, held him back, even though Audrey seemed more open to the idea of greenjacks than anyone else—even Carmen, who, he'd finally realized, had protected and loved him *despite* his stories about the jacks.

Scratching sounds, faint and annoying, came from the vicinity of the old Rambler. The vermin living in the car were either very smart or very resistant. He'd have to put out yet more bait for these guys.

But not now, he thought as he checked his watch. It was nearly two o'clock already. The piano movers would show up at two-thirty and have Don Quixote moved out to the oval of cement he'd had poured behind the koi pond before Audrey arrived around four o'clock. He smiled to himself. He'd planned on putting the knight out there as a talisman long before he remembered Paulie's drowning. It seemed more fitting than ever, he thought as he locked up and went inside to grab a quick shower.

34

"Hi, sorry I'm late!" Audrey entered the Piper house and sidled away from Rick, so that he couldn't see the package she held behind her back.

"That's okay, I'm running late, too." Rick gestured at his untied tie. "Whatcha got behind your back?" he asked, approaching her.

She smiled. "You'll see soon enough."

"How long are you going to keep me in suspense, evil woman?"

He was like a little boy, practically bouncing with curiosity. She adored that side of him. "I'm going to keep you in suspense as long as I can," she said mischievously.

"Animal, vegetable, or mineral?" he persisted.

"I'll never tell." She grinned at him. Ever since she'd discovered how much Rick loved surprises, she'd been bringing him odd little goodies wrapped up tight as drums so he'd have to really work at them to get them open.

What it was made no difference. He just seemed so pleased and amazed that someone had thought about him—it must have to do with being raised by Ewebeans, she thought wryly—that she loved watching him. Last week she'd given him a pair of little windup sneakers, and they'd walked them back and forth across the table at Scomillo's any number of times before a tall, thin waiter curled his lip and looked disgusted. They'd snickered over that the rest of the evening. The week before, it was a bag of watermelon candy; the week before, a Koosh ball. She had a feeling that a stick of gum would please him as much as tickets to the theater. Well, almost as much.

Watching him watch her as he knotted his tie, she wondered if tonight would be the night; they'd been seeing each other all summer, and nothing but necking had happened yet. When he'd said he wanted to take it slow, she'd been happy, glad to know he wasn't after her for a quick slam bam. But now, even allowing for her ever-present impatience, things seemed to be at a standstill.

Here was a man who was sweet and sensitive, intelligent, and just mysterious enough to drive her crazy. Here was a man with the self-control of a monk. Every time they held each other and kissed good night, it became very obvious he wanted her as much as she wanted him. Last week they went dancing, slow dancing, and his desire was so evident that it took every ounce of self-control she possessed not to let fly with a crude remark to the effect of a hard man was good to find. She didn't know whether he'd take the remark as invitation or insult. He had such strange reactions to things sometimes, and she didn't want to risk the relationship.

Plainly Rick Piper had a lot more willpower than she did. And that just served to intrigue her all the more.

"What are you thinking about, Audrey? You have a funny look on your face." Straightening his tie, he approached her, his smile dimpling the cheeks of that boyish face, the skin around his eyes crinkling just right.

Heat squirmed low in her belly and she blushed. "Here," she said, bringing the gift out from behind her back rather than answering his question. "I was late because I had such a hard time wrapping this."

His eyes lit up. "What is it?" He held his hands out, and she placed the long, thin package in them.

"That's for me to know and you to find out," she told him.

"Let's sit down." He led her to the couch, laid the long

package on the coffee table, and began working on unwrapping it. She'd smothered it in tape and ribbons to prolong the pleasure of watching him as long as possible.

Suddenly she was a little nervous. This was a serious gift, the first one that cost her more—a lot more—than five bucks. It was a sword, an indoor reminder of Rick's sculpture.

She'd purchased it on a whim. While browsing in one of the antique stores on Euclid a few days ago, she'd spotted it in one of the cases. Polished and in perfect condition, it was a beautiful cavalry-style saber with a slightly curved blade and an ornate bronze hilt. The shopkeeper had told her it was of British design, an officer's weapon, most likely used during Wellington's Peninsular campaign against Napoleon near the end of the eighteenth century. Judging by the price, it had probably been used by the general himself. After drawing and quartering her wallet to acquire the weapon, she hoped he'd like it. Her anxiety built as she wondered if he'd like it or if he'd think it was presumptuous of her to give him something so expensive.

"I . . . I can take it back if you don't like it. It might not be right . . ."

He grinned at her, his long-fingered hands dancing among the bows, dutifully untying them instead of cutting because he knew she liked to watch.

"You love torturing me, don't you?" he asked, trying to undo a particularly stubborn piece of ribbon.

She just smiled. Tonight they were going into Los Angeles to see *Les Misérables,* which had just reopened at the Chandler Pavilion. Both had seen it before, but they wanted to see it together. He'd surprised her with the tickets last week; the best seats in the house, he'd told her, obtained by pulling what he called "reporter" strings. So tonight it would be dinner, a play too romantic and schmaltzy for anyone to resist, then home—hers or his, she didn't know or care which—to share the bottle of champagne she'd stashed in a cooler in her car. After that, she intended to try to get him to unwrap *her.* Her patience had run out.

That was the other reason she arrived late; it had taken her forever to get dressed. She'd left the office early and gone to Victoria's Secret, where she invested in a form-fitting beige teddy loaded with tiny silk buttons and matching panties that had multiple ribbon closures. She also bought a garter belt for the first time in her life, specifically because of the snappy things you had to undo to get the nylons off. Her outerwear included hook-laced high-heeled boots, a midcalf black linen skirt which buttoned up the front, and a white high-collared silk blouse with more than thirty miniature button loops for him to undo—and that wasn't even counting the cuff buttons. Finally, she'd pulled her red hair up in a sweep of loose curls, then instead of securing it with a couple of clips, she'd used two dozen bobby pins.

She wanted to be unwrapped in the worst way.

"Audrey?" He was smiling at her. "Earth to Audrey."

"Hmmm?"

"What's on your mind?"

"I'll tell you later."

"I'm ready to open this." He was down to the wrapping paper, all the ribbons piled on the floor next to him.

"Rick, is it hot in here?"

"No," he said, his impatience showing as he plucked' at the paper. "But you look feverish. Are you up for tonight?"

"Oh yes." She smiled. *I hope you are too.*

"Tissue paper," Rick said dryly. "I should have known." He began turning the package over and over until, at last, he uncovered the shining steel blade. "Audrey," he whispered, lifting it away from the wrappings, "it's beautiful." He took hold of the saber's hilt, hefted it, then stood and tried it out, cutting delicate figure eights in the air.

"It's in honor of your sculpture's completion. You're almost done, right?"

"It's beautiful," he told her as he made like a Musketeer. "Wonderful, marvelous. Lord, Audrey, it's incredible! I'll hang it over the fireplace. Thank you."

"You're welcome." She glanced at the clock. "We should get going."

He leaned down and kissed her, then took her hand as she got to her feet. "Thank you so much!" he repeated, his eyes dancing with delight. "For now, I'm going to put this in my room and lock the door." He made a face. "Can you imagine what would happen if Jade got her grubby mitts on it?"

With that, he raced up the stairs. A moment later, he was back. "Before we leave, I have to show you something. It'll just take a minute. Close your eyes," he ordered.

"Rick?"

"Come on, do it. It's my turn to surprise you."

"Okay," she laughed, and shut her eyes.

He led her out the front door, and she waited while he shut and locked it. Then he put one hand around her waist and the other on her elbow and guided her down the front steps.

"Watch out, the grass is wet," he warned. "We're heading toward the old pond. It's pumping out right now, so it kind of stinks. Did I tell you it used to be a swimming pool?"

"No." She laughed. Rarely was he so maniacally happy.

"It was. Hector and I are going to muck it out next week, then the replasterers will come and everything will be refitted, and before you know it, voilà, a swimming pool."

"What will the koi think of that?"

"They've been gone for years," he said, a touch of sadness in his voice. "Ewebean disease, I guess." His voice lightened. "There used to be colored Malibu lights out here. Ultra sixties. My dad installed them. Watch out, the ground dips here. Okay, step up." Her feet encountered a hard smooth surface, and they stopped walking. "Open your eyes."

She did. They stood before the murky, reeking pond. Directly across from them, Don Quixote sat majestically upon his bony steed. "Wow," she murmured. The piece was beautiful and a little frightening at the same time.

"Once Hector installs the new lights," he said, "we'll be able to see his silhouette from the house all the time," he told her proudly. "I'm thinking of changing the landscaping a little so he can be seen from the street too."

"It's wonderful, Rick," she said sincerely.

"Thanks." He looked around, his expression changing slightly, a trace of nervousness showing through his good humor. *Does he see them?* She wondered. *Does he think he sees them?* He hadn't brought up the greenjacks in months and wouldn't even let her talk about the research she'd done—but she was pretty sure he hadn't stopped thinking about them.

"It's getting dark," he. said, his voice suddenly nervous. "We'd better get going now. We're only going to have time for fast food as it is."

She almost tripped trying to keep up with him. He acted like devils were after him, but she said nothing. His strangeness was part of his charm.

35

They ended up at Rick's because Shelly was spending the night at a girlfriend's and he didn't want to make Carmen watch Cody any longer than necessary. That was fine by Audrey. Her apartment was little and cramped, and the people downstairs cooked fish or liver virtually every night, an unromantic aroma at best. She was also convinced the couple across the hall from her both suffered from Tourette's syndrome.

When they came in the house, Carmen eyed the champagne bottle Audrey held, then asked him if he wanted his cat back tonight. He hemmed and hawed for a moment, then Carmen told him that Quint was welcome to stay at her place. He nodded and mumbled something about having to work late anyway.

Audrey was pretty sure Rick blushed when he said it, and hoped work wasn't really what was on his mind. Going to the ladies' room at intermission and maneuvering through all the buttons and bows had been a Herculean task, and she was more intent then ever on making it pay off.

"I'll get the glasses," he said after Carmen left. "You want to watch a movie or something?"

"Sure." *Something sexy.*

"I have lots of tapes. Why don't you pick something out?" He turned to go into the kitchen.

"Rick? Where are the tapes?"

He made a face. "That would help, wouldn't it? I had them there"—he pointed at the bare bookcase to the left of the fireplace—"but that didn't work out." He crooked his finger, and she crossed the room. In a low voice he said, "Jade got into them." He pulled his keys out of his pocket and selected one. "They're in my room," he said. "Do you remember where it is?"

She nodded. She'd seen his room the first time she'd come over, when he'd given her a grand tour of the house.

"They're in my dressing room in a cabinet right beneath my jackets. It's the cabinet without the hanger through the handles."

"Why is that?"

"The cat. He loves to open doors, and there's a passage behind the one with the hanger. I'm afraid he might accidentally push the latch and end up"—he pitched his voice to sound like Peter Lorre—"lost in the bowels of the mansion."

"Gotcha. I'll find it." She smiled at him. "Do you have any apples?"

"Red Delicious, fresh from Oak Glen. You want some with your champagne?"

"Yes. We'll be totally decadent, yet fat-free. Be right back."

After she let herself into his room, she was surprised to see the wire lying on the floor between the two cabinets. Quint's work, she thought, kneeling. She opened the wrong door first, found it empty except for a box of D-Con. Curiously she looked for the interior latch Rick had talked about, but gave up quickly. There were better things to do: champagne to drink, apples to eat, a man to seduce.

She quickly restrung the wire through the cabinet's handles, then opened the other cabinet and, moments later, was overjoyed to find a copy of *Time After Time,* a romantic fantasy filmed in the seventies. The fact that he owned it spoke volumes about the man. As she rose, she glanced around the room, having a brief but uncomfortable feeling that something was watching her. She saw nothing. *Don't be silly. You'll get as nervous as Rick is, and then won't you be the pair!* Reentering the bedroom, she saw a twenty-five-inch TV set and VCR across from the bed. Should she suggest they watch it up here? *No, too forward.*

She walked back down the stairs. The movie concerned Jack the Ripper stealing H. G. Wells's time machine to escape to modern times, and the timid inventor's resulting chase and romance. When Wells fell in love in the movie, the woman who wanted him had to do all the work. She smiled to herself. Old H. G. was a lot like Rick Piper: too shy and retiring for his own good.

But there were good things about that. No doubt because of the sadistic asshole she'd been married to, Audrey was instantly turned off by men who approached her first, no matter how gently; she needed to do the pursuing in order to feel safe. Hence, the attraction to *Time After Time.* Hence the attraction to Rick Piper.

"Find something good?" he asked as he entered the living room and placed a large tray on the coffee table.

"Yes. You're a romantic, aren't you, Piper?" She held up the box for him to see. "No sense denying it. You've been caught."

"Guilty," he said sheepishly. "Have you seen it before?"

"Yes. I never get tired of it." She smiled coyly, thinking that the movie would be great inspiration. She slipped it into the machine.

"Bring the remote," he said, sitting down. He patted the cushion next to him. "And come sit with me."

"Pretty classy, huh?" he asked as she sat. The champagne rested in a silver ice bucket, and four shiny-wet apples were piled in a crystal bowl. Two linen napkins and two champagne flutes also sat on the teak tray.

"Not bad for a Vegas guy," she said.

"Are you implying you expected plastic glasses?" He grinned at her and began to remove the foil from the bottle, Suddenly Jade's obscene moaning began.

"Christ," Rick said. "Jesus Christ. Not now."

She almost suggested they go to her place, then remembered Cody.

"Fuck me!" Jade cried. High-pitched lusty "Oh, oh, ohhs," followed.

Audrey stifled a giggle.

"That's it," Rick said, showing no signs of amusement. "I'm going to tell her to knock it off."

Audrey put her hand on Rick's wrist. "If you do, she'll just cause a scene." She paused. "There's a VCR in your room."

He considered. "There's nowhere to sit, though," he said slowly.

"Fuck me, fuck me, fuck meeee!"

Rick grimaced, obviously interpreting his aunt's behavior as a reflection upon himself.

Audrey snickered. "We can sit on your bed. I mean, that is why you've got that entertainment center on the wall across from the bed. To watch TV, right? You must love movies, with all the equipment you've got."

"Yes, well, that unit used to be in my living room back in Vegas. I put it up there instead of down here because I was afraid I'd spend a lot of my time up there, staying away from Jade." He looked pained. "Besides making those . . . noises, she also goes through other people's belongings and takes whatever she wants—or mangles them, one or the other. She did that with the tapes when I had them down here. Never admitted it, of course." He made a face. "She got sticky stuff all over them. It was disgusting. She must've been eating Twinkies or something."

Audrey smiled demurely. "Are you sure it wasn't Cody's doing?"

"No, he makes little bitty fingerprints. Lord." He rolled his eyes as Jade's lewd noises reached another crescendo.

"At least she's multiorgasmic," Audrey teased lightly. She had to get him out of here before he lost his good mood. "So what do you say? Shall we take this tray and the movie and watch upstairs?"

"You don't feel awkward?" he asked.

"No. Has anyone ever told you you're terribly old-fashioned? Especially for a guy whose best friend is a she-male."

"Your brother's very moral." Rick sniffed dramatically, and placed everything back on the tray. "In his own way."

"I'm teasing you, Rick." She crossed to the TV and ejected the tape.

"I know," he said, gathering everything together on the tray. "I guess I am old-fashioned." They started up the stairs. "Seeing the things my brother did with her"—he nodded back in Jade's direction—"and her daughter, maybe had an effect. They did things animals wouldn't do." Outside his door, he hesitated. "You're sure you're okay with this? I could get some chairs from the kitchen."

"I'm fine with it." She paused. "Are you?"

"I just don't want you to think I'm trying to take advantage."

She laughed; she couldn't help it. "I don't think that at all," she said with utmost sincerity.

"I need to know you, and you need to know me," he added, setting the champagne on the nightstand. "We need to talk more."

"I agree." She put the tape in the machine and brought the remote to the bed. "If there's anything I haven't told you about myself yet, I will when I think of it. I'm out of deep dark secrets, so I hope you feel like you know me. Mind if I take my shoes off?"

"Please." He looked flustered. "I'm only taking the spread off because I paid so much for it—not because I'm trying to—"

"I know," Audrey said quickly. "And I don't blame you, it's gorgeous. In fact, if you don't mind, I'd just as soon we move the blankets, too, and sit on the sheets. They're more comfortable."

He looked at her for an instant. "No problem."

After he was done, she sat on the edge of the high bed and swung her legs up, grateful her skirt was full enough to let her sit cross-legged, a nice innocent position that wouldn't make him so nervous. "So, Rick, do you have any deep dark secrets you haven't told me?" she asked lightly as she hit the remote and started the movie.

He handed her an apple. "Yes."

She studied him a long moment. "Well, you can tell me when and if you want to. I'll take you at face value."

It was his turn to stare at her. "What if you got involved with me and then found out I'm a raving maniac?"

"I'm a big girl, Piper. I'll take my chances. Besides, there's nothing more boring than a really normal person," she added. "Pour the champagne," she ordered as the movie's theme swelled.

They nibbled apples and sipped champagne. About the time Wells got his first kiss, Audrey stretched her legs out in front of her and used a couple pillows to prop herself up against the high headboard. Rick did the same, letting himself move closer to her in the process.

"Is there any champagne left?" she asked a while later.

"Mmm." He poured the last two glassfuls. "To us," he said as they clinked glasses. "You really don't care if I'm a raving maniac?"

"Not in the least." She moved closer to the center of the bed. He did, too, until their legs barely touched. It excited her beyond reason. "You look a little loopy, Rick," she said.

"I'm easy," he said, draining the glass.

"You're anything but easy." She felt tipsy herself.

Quizzically, he looked at her. He took her glass and set it on the nightstand, then took her hand. "This is a great movie." On the screen, Mary Steenburgen had Malcolm McDowall in a clinch.

"It is," she agreed. "So, Rick, do you think women should be that aggressive?"

"The right woman . . ." He got off the bed. "Excuse me a moment." He went into the bathroom, shut the door. She heard water running, then he was back. She smiled when he went to the bedroom door and turned the lock.

He saw her smile and, blushing mumbled something

about not wanting Cody to get the wrong idea. She agreed gently.

She waited for him to climb back on the bed, then pointed at Steenburgen on the screen. "No matter how hard I try, I just can't be that aggressive. You know, to just grab a guy and not let go."

He didn't answer except for a coy smile. He took her hand again.

"Rick?"

"Hmmm?"

"You know what I am good at, though?"

"What?"

"I'm really good at wrapping up presents."

He turned slightly to face her better. "What do you mean?"

"Well," she said, trying to stay calm and cool, "I have another present for you."

"Audrey, you shouldn't give me all these presents."

"I wouldn't if I didn't want to. But this one's special. It's a present for me, too. And I *really* want to give this to you. *Really.*"

"What is it?" He grinned broadly.

"You'll have to find it and unwrap it to see."

Rolling his eyes, he said, "Here we go again. Well, where is it? Are you going to give me a clue?"

"Well, okay. There are a hundred and twenty-two closures on this gift. You have to undo all of them. It's big, weighs better than a hundred pounds."

"Good Lord, Audrey, where is it, in your car? You shouldn't be spending money on me—"

"Hush. Here's another clue." She pulled a single bobby pin from her hair. "Now there are a hundred and twenty-one closures left."

Understanding crossed his features so suddenly and completely that, in the heartbeat that he stared at her, mouth slightly open, she thought: *I've blown it.*

"I just love surprises," he said as he sat up and stared down at her. He touched her hair, her cheek, bent over her and gently kissed her lips. "And I never get tired of unwrapping things." His hand stole up to her hair and removed another pin. "A hundred and twenty. This is going to take a while," he told her. "All night, probably."

"That was the plan," she whispered.

"One hundred nineteen."

36

In the dream, he was making love to Audrey. He lay over her, his head between her breasts. Her skin, milky white but for a light sprinkling of freckles on her arms and legs and across the tops of her breasts where the sun had kissed her, smelled deliciously of female musk.

"Rick," Audrey moaned as he kissed one breast. "Rick," she cried again as he trailed his lips across to the other.

She called his name over and over again as he slowly traced his tongue down the slope of her breast. He moved his mouth down her body, losing himself in her salty-warm taste, in the silky smoothness of her skin, in the rich scent that he'd been addicted to since the first time he'd caught it. He swirled his tongue down and down, past her navel, into the patch of soft reddish hair, pausing to listen as she called his name again, wanting to drive her as mad as she drove him. Her body arched against him, her fingernails digging into his flesh. "Rick, now! Rick!"

"Rick!" Her voice in his ear, urgent, needing him, bruising his biceps with her fingers.

He groaned, reaching for her, wanting her.

"Rick! Wake up!"

"Audrey?" His voice cracked, not wanting to work. He was not below her, but facing her, on his side. She was pressed up against him, her mouth near his ear. His erection was pressed against her thigh. *Oh God, was I humping her like one of Jade's poodles?* Instantly he went soft.

She didn't seem to notice. "Rick! Wake up, please!"

His brain kicked in, discerned the urgency in her voice. "What?"

"Someone's in here. I heard noises."

"I locked the door," he murmured, not wanting to get up.

"I didn't imagine it."

That got his attention. "Of course not. I'm sorry—I was sleeping like the dead."

"I'll say," she whispered. "You're *sure* you locked the door?"

"Positive." He rubbed his eyes. That helped a little. "What did you hear?"

"I thought I heard something moving around. It sounded like it was in the dressing room."

Suddenly goose bumps rose on his arms and neck. "I'll check it out," he said, hoping his voice sounded firm and strong. He sat up and swung out of bed and, not bothering with a robe, crossed to the light switch by the door and flipped it on. He tried the knob.

"Still locked," he said to Audrey, who sat up watching him. Her smile and the locked door made his nervousness go away. "And I've got the only keys."

"Maybe I *was* dreaming," she said without conviction.

"Maybe. I know I was." He smiled, looking at her breasts, thinking about what he was doing in the dream.

She grinned broadly. "You're a friendly fellow."

Looking down, he blushed.

"And you have a gorgeous ass," Audrey snickered. "No wonder Duane wanted you."

He just stood there, dumb and excited.

"And it looks like you're up for seconds," Audrey observed coyly.

Nodding, he took one step toward the bed, then stopped cold.

"Did you hear it?" Audrey's expression had transformed from desire into worry.

He nodded. "I think there are still some rats living in the passages." He stepped toward the dressing room.

"That's probably what I heard," she told him. "A rat. I saw the bait in the cabinet."

"With the tapes?" He glanced back at her.

"No, the empty one. I forgot to tell you. The wire was on the floor when I came up before. I replaced it."

"It was off?" Adrenaline pumped into his bloodstream.

"I'm sure it's nothing," she said quickly. "The doors weren't open or anything. I assumed Quint had played with it and pulled it off."

Snagging up his flashlight, he turned on the dressing room light, crossed to the bathroom, and flicked that light on as well. A little surge of superstitious fear made him check the shower stall, but it was devoid of poodles or other vermin.

Audrey padded into the dressing room as he reentered from the bathroom. "Find anything?"

"Well, the bathroom's safe."

"Good. I have to pee." She held out her finger. "And I brought my traveling toothbrush. Can I use your toothpaste?"

"Be my guest." It was hard to stay nervous when you were looking at a naked woman. As she passed him, he reached out and let his hand stroke the curve of her buttocks.

"I think yours is cuter," she called in a deadpan voice as she shut the bathroom door.

Okay. Let's get it over with, Piper. He squatted and began undoing the wire just as Audrey came out of the bathroom. She knelt beside him.

"Why are your tapes in here when you have that entertainment center in there?" she whispered.

"When the movers brought the furniture in, they left my dresser facing the wall, so I stuffed my clothes in the entertainment center."

"At least you turned the dresser around."

He smiled thinly. Carmen had waited a week, then done it herself. "I just want to take a quick peek in here." Swallowing hard, he opened the cabinet, very aware of Audrey's chin behind his shoulder.

"There's a secret passage in there?" she asked.

"Yeah. They're built so that they stay closed." He shined the light inside, saw nothing unusual.

"Where's the door?"

"You have to hold the latch to open it."

"So let's see."

What the hell. He pushed the lever, and the door slid open, revealing velvet blackness.

"Rick, I swear that's one of the sounds I heard earlier."

"The door opening?" Shocked, he looked at her.

She nodded. "But it's such a soft sound, I doubt that you could hear it from the bedroom."

She nodded. "It was very quiet in there. I really think that's what I heard."

"But . . ." He hesitated.

She crawled forward. "Can I see?" She took the light from his hand. He backed up and waited nervously as she slipped her head and torso into the cabinet.

Rick leaned back, enjoying the view until he realized that she was going to find the knife. He'd left it there in the first place because it seemed dirty and horrible and he didn't want to touch it. God, he wished he'd thrown it out. He waited for her to say something about it.

Instead, she eased her way out of the cabinet and handed him the light. "I don't think I'd want to go crawling around in there. Yuck." She stood up. "Do you think Cody came in and explored while we were out?"

"I locked the door."

"That's right. Could he have come through the tunnel?"

"I blocked the passage in his room, and he doesn't know about any others," he replied as he took the light and quickly examined the interior of the passage.

The knife was gone.

Trembling, he pulled out of the cabinet. "Excuse me," he said, rummaging in a packing box on the dressing room floor. He pulled out an old tie, looped it through the handles several times, then knotted it three times.

"That'll do the trick," Audrey said.

He nodded. "I'll be right back," he said, pulling on his robe. "I'm just going to go down the hall and check on Cody." He tried to sound casual, but inside, he was shaken.

Cody was fast asleep, without a trace of grime on his face. *Maybe Carmen's right about the ghost,* he thought, returning to Audrey.

Wearing his shirt, she waited for him in the doorway.

"That looks better on you than me," he told her. They went back inside, and he noticed that she locked the door behind them.

"How's Cody?" she asked, removing the shirt, then climbing back onto the bed.

"Fast asleep. Angelic." He threw the robe across a chair and joined her. "Maybe I undid it without thinking. Sometimes I don't think my brain works quite right."

She took his hand and traced a circle on his palm. "You want to talk about it?"

He nodded. "I was putting off what we did tonight until I did tell you about it, but you said you didn't care if I was a raving maniac, you still wanted my body . . ."

She looked him in the eye. "I wasn't kidding, Piper."

He hesitated. "I lied about something."

"Your cousin in Scotland?" she asked wryly.

He stared at her in amazement. "Did Dakota tell?"

"Dakota hasn't told me anything. You told me about the greenjacks, you acted antsy outside, and you started talking about your cousin in Scotland, wondering if he was crazy because he claimed to see them. You wanted information." She kissed his lips quickly. "Even if I hadn't caught on then, I would have later, when you refused to talk about it again."

"Oh." He couldn't look at her. "If you already knew, then I guess you really meant it about making love to a madman."

"Christ, you're hard on yourself." She shook her head. "Listen, Rick, I did a lot of research, and it's not at all out of the realm of possibility that you really are seeing some-thing."

Hopefully he looked up. "Really?"

"Really." She smiled at him. "I've delivered lectures be-fore, but never naked."

He chuckled in spite of himself. Audrey certainly had a knack for saying the right thing to relax him. "Believe me, I'll hear every word and never take my eyes off you."

"Better not." She cleared her throat. "There are several possibilities, Rick. You might have an extra set of cones that give you an ability to see colors that other people can't."

"But the jacks are green."

"Because your brain has to put it in a context you can understand. I don't really think that's what's going on, though. Are they only visible at night?"

"Yes. My cat saw them, too."

"Really?"

Quickly he explained. "Does that knock out your theo-ries?"

"No. It makes sense. Let me tell you another one."

"Shoot."

"Well, there's synchronous retinal firing, but I've been looking at your eyes all evening and I think that's out."

"Huh?"

"Jiggling of the eyes—it occasionally happens, and I thought it could possibly put your perception in synch with the greenjacks' frequency. But you don't jiggle."

"Thank God. So, Doc, what *do* you think it is?"

"I think it's one of a couple things, and, Rick, they can't be proven, because the only way to know for sure is to dis-sect the eye."

"Charming."

She smiled. "You see them at night—and Quint sees them, too, so what do you have in common with a cat?"

"I once coughed up a hairball."

She stifled a laugh. "Be serious. Cats see very well in the dark. You might have extremely good low spatial fre-quency perception. It would let you tell the difference between shadows and substance. Like a cat." She paused. "Normally humans only have good high-contrast, high spatial frequency—we can see the black letters on the white eye chart, but the same black letters on a dark gray chart would be very difficult. But I don't think that's it either. I think it's more likely to be pigment migration of your rods and cones."

"That sounds disgusting."

"It's not." She laughed. "It's common to fish, amphibians, and birds."

"Primitive creatures," Rick observed dryly.

"Well, yes, basically. How far back do the stories about greenjacks go in your family?"

"As far back as the family. Grandfather once talked about a Piper in the Crusades who had the sight, but I don't know . . ."

Audrey shrugged. "Let's say a thousand years, then. And that means it goes further back. It has to."

"He said we weren't the only ones, that you only had to look for places all over the world that are overgrown by vegetation, and you'd find a bloodline that carried the gene."

"It all fits, Rick," Audrey said, not bothering to hide her excitement. "Okay, now, listen. You have normal vision in normal light conditions, but at twilight and after dark, pigment migration would come into play. Your cones would retract and the rods move forward.

"Normally cones are useless for night vision, but in pigment migration, you've got retro-directional movement of the cones, which changes their normally angular orientation, thereby enhancing the Stiles-Crawford Effect and making them more sensitive than normal."

"Stiles what?" he asked.

"The Stiles-Crawford Effect says that cones are directionally sensitive to light that hits them head-on, but that their sensitivity falls off rapidly as the light hits them obliquely—like when you look through a paper towel tube. Rods aren't affected—they respond to any light at all. Follow me?"

"Sort of. You're saying that if I had this pigment thing, then it might make sense that I could see things other people can't."

"Yes. And it could very well be inherited, as well as apply to other creatures who see well at night—like cats. It means your eyes work differently—if I'm correct, then you have more visual abilities than most people—and your average man on the street wouldn't—couldn't—comprehend it, and would label you either a charlatan or a madman."

Rick nodded. "So it's a sixth sense? Every time I've ever seen a psychic on television, I always think that person's just out for the money or totally nuts."

"Exactly." She gave him a crooked smile, and made a gentle *tsk-tsk* noise. "Of all people, Rick, you should be willing to believe that at least some of the psychics are on the level." She paused. "But you don't even believe *you're* on the level, do you?"

"No."

"You need to exorcise your brother, Piper. He's still controlling your mind."

"Yeah, I guess." He took her hand and kissed it. "I think you believe me more than I believe myself."

"I think you're right."

"There're just a couple flies in the theory. Things I didn't tell you," he confessed.

"Tell me."

"First, I *hear* them too. In my head. I'm no expert, but I think that makes me schizophrenic."

"Rick, some psychics see things, others hear or feel them, and some do all three, so why not see *and* hear greenjacks?"

Rick thought she sounded slightly less confident now, but decided he had to go the distance. "I've also seen Big Jack."

"Big Jack . . . the one they build out of plant life on Halloween, right? The Green Man?"

He nodded and quickly told her his memories of the night he and Robin fought the monster in the tree. "But," he added, "maybe I never saw it at all. I think maybe I invented all that because I felt like Robin's falling was my fault."

Silently she studied him. "Who have you told this to?"

"Nobody, really. Carmen knows—she always protected me when I was little—but I don't think she believes it much." He shook his head. "She's trying to talk me into letting her take Cody away overnight on Halloween. I think she's more worried about what I might do to him than anything else. Frankly, I don't blame her." He paused, then added, "Of course, she thinks this house is haunted by Robin, so I guess her opinion doesn't mean too much."

"Who's to say that it isn't?" Audrey pushed her hair from her face. "Do you believe in ghosts?"

"Of course not. Do you?"

"I don't *dis*believe any more than I believe. But, Rick, have you been talking to a therapist, or what?"

"No. Only Dakota."

"Of course," she added with a nod. "Has he been giving you advice? Like suggesting that your guilt made you invent that story about Robin in the tree?"

"How'd you know?"

"I know Duane. He loves pop psychology. The therapists he sees are the kind that write the books that are supposed to change your life in thirty days. Not that that's bad for Duane—it's done him a lot of good. But don't let him tell you how *you* think—he'll try to sell you on what works for him."

"I don't know what works for me."

She studied him. "I don't know either, but I'd guess that giving yourself the benefit of the doubt until you have proof one way or the other might be a good way to start."

"So do you want to come over Halloween night and see if we can spot Big Jack together?" His hands were trembling. "If I see him and you don't, we'll know I'm nuts, once and for all."

"And if we both see him, we'll know you're not." Audrey put her hand on his chest and gently pushed him back against the pillows before leaning down and kissing him lingeringly on the lips. Her nipples hardened as her breasts brushed against his chest. "You're going to have to get a lot crazier than this to get rid of me, Piper." She kissed his lips again, then his neck.

She meant what she said, he knew that, but he would not, *could* not, let her ruin her life for him. She pulled one of his nipples into her mouth, biting gently, then moved to the other. As she trailed her tongue down his belly, he prayed that she would see Big Jack too. Then, a moment later, he gave up worrying about anything at all.

37

"Man, Rick, there's some disgusting stuff in this pond." Hector Zapata took off his baseball cap and pushed his fingers through his black hair. "No wonder the pump's been clogging so much, even with that two-inch hose."

"At least there aren't any mosquitoes." Rick squinted at the emptying pond. The sludgy water continued to gurgle into the wide, formerly white hosing, making obscene farting and belching sounds. The smell was so bad on this unseasonably warm day that he wished he had a handkerchief to put over his face.

"No mosquitoes. I don't think anything's lived in there since Howard took to pissing in it." Hector's laugh reeked of disgust. "He dumped other stuff in it too. Antifreeze, that's probably what killed the fish. He bragged about that. Did it to piss off your brother."

"Robin loved those fish," Rick said. They were the only living things he could remember his twin having any fondness for. He knew that Howard urinated in the pool, he'd seen it time after time over the years, but he didn't know about the antifreeze. A chill passed through him despite the warm sunlight. "How many years ago did the fish die?"

Hector put his hat back on. "It was the same year that the carnival came through for the last time. You remember?"

"I remember." A heavy, hard lump suddenly formed in his stomach. That summer was the last time he saw Delia Minuet, the last time he saw Robin.

July 5, 1981

It was Fourth of July weekend, and Rick was sixteen years old. He'd spent all his free time at the Masello Brothers Carnival and Sideshow riding the rides, eating corn dogs and cotton candy, talking to Delia whenever she had a break, and avoiding his brother, who loved the carnival as much as he did, but for very different reasons.

Robin loved to show off, to shock and to steal attention, and racing through the fairgrounds on his hands was a good way to do it. His arms were extremely powerful, and he could execute all sorts of stunts, from his all-time favorite handstand running to using his arms like frog's legs to leap three feet up and six across at a time.

John and Vince, the all-powerful Masello brothers, adored the ground Robin walked on and even seemed pleased when he'd break into regular performers' shows, swinging his little body up a rope or leaping into the middle of the clown show's fire engine act. From the first time he did this—the year following their parents' death—Delia told Rick that the performers didn't like it one little bit, but they couldn't do much about it since the Masellos were so taken by him.

Robin systematically charmed people who mattered, and wasted no time on those who had no power. Watching people fall for his act was frustrating. The sole thing that gave Rick pleasure where his twin was concerned was his lack of success with any of the animals. They hated him, one and all. Where the Ewebean poodles, who also hated him, just whined and pranced nervously around Jade's legs, the circus animals' response to his presence spoke abundantly of their feelings toward him. The elephant trumpeted, and the big cats put their ears back and growled when he approached.

The organ grinder's monkey had strangled itself in its attempt to get away from him.

The animals sensed the truth about Robin Piper.

So did many of the performers, most notably the denizens of the ten-in-one show. These people had certain things in common: physical abnormalities, a strong dislike for the bleeding heart liberals who were trying to take away their livelihood, a camaraderie deeper than most people ever experienced, and the ability to see through the veneer of false personality. They listened to their instincts, and if one didn't sense something himself, he invariably trusted the word of those who did.

That's why Rick was so at home among them; they accepted him from the first time Delia introduced him to her extended family, just as they uniformly shunned his brother. As far as they were concerned, the Masello brothers were the handicapped ones because they were blinded by their own greed, but they accepted this fact as part of life.

Though he only saw her a few days a year, Delia had remained Rick's best friend since that very first summer. He could talk to Carmen, though he rarely did, but Delia was the only person his own age with whom he could share his secrets. He could tell her anything, and she never made fun of him. She had always accepted his stories at face value.

This year he'd looked forward to seeing Delia as much as ever, and when the carnival had arrived three days ago and they met again, things were slightly different between them. She'd looked him up and down and whistled. "You turned into a man this year. Look how tall you are."

"Five seven." He didn't tell her he felt like a shrimp.

The next day she made an observation in her fast-talking, no-bullshit way. "There's a cut on your cheek. Do you have to shave now?"

Finally, today, she'd asked, "Do you have a girlfriend?"

He'd never told her about the cheerleader two years before or about the minor flirtations he'd experienced since. "No girlfriends."

"Come on, Ricky, you must have at least one. You're too cute not to."

He blushed. "My brother has enough for both of us."

Delia made a face. "Stupid girls. They don't see anything but that fake charm. So I bet he screws everything that moves, right? Probably those poodles even have to watch out."

He grinned. Delia knew all about Jade's sexual proclivities, as well as her dogs. "Probably. So do you want to take a walk?"

"You're way too tall," she told him. "We can't talk and walk anymore."

She didn't know she'd hurt his feelings, and he wasn't about to tell her.

Tonight was the last night the carnival was in town, and he wanted to spend all the time he could with her. They needed to find a place where they could sit and talk for hours, and suddenly inspiration hit. "Jade and Howard will be at the carnival tonight, then they'll go to the Dew Drop Inn and not get home before two-thirty in the morning. Want to come over and watch TV?"

Her eyes lit up: Television was a rare luxury for Delia. "Yes! What time?"

"Six?"

"I'll be there. Will *he?*"

She meant Robin. "I hope not. He's hardly ever home on the weekends."

That night Rick and Delia sprawled on the couch and feasted on Swanson TV dinners, Dr. Peppers, and Oreos as they talked and watched TV. By nine P.M. they were holding hands. Delia, despite her abnormal bone structure, was very attractive with thick brown hair that waved halfway down her back and eyes the same color, as deep and rich as liquid chocolate.

At nine-thirty, he kissed her. She climbed into his lap and returned the kiss, putting her arms around his neck, holding him close. And at that moment Rick fell in love for the first time in his life.

They didn't hear Robin come in a few minutes later, didn't know he sat in the shadows and watched them as they whispered and caressed and kissed. They didn't know he was there until he spoke.

"Well, icky Ricky, here you are getting ready to fuck the dwarf. And all this time I thought you were queer."

"Eat shit, Robin," Delia said, boredom in her voice.

"I'm more your size, Delia," Robin said, leering as he slap-slapped his way across the room. Balancing on one hand, he helped himself to an Oreo and pulled it apart. He licked the frosting out, never taking his eyes off Delia. "I bet you'd like me to lick you like I'm licking this cookie, huh, dwarf?"

Rage built in Rick like pressure in a volcano. "Robin—"

"You don't want to fuck him," Robin continued smoothly. "What I lack in legs, I make up for here." He grabbed himself and squeezed, grinning obscenely.

Rick's ears rang as he stood up, dizzy in the fury he felt. "Shut up or I'll—"

"You'll what?" his twin interrupted. "Go whining to Carmen? Lock yourself in your room and cry? What? Huh, icky Ricky? Tell me, I *really* want to know."

He took a step toward his brother. "Oh, my, aren't you a brave dicky Ricky when you've got a dwarf cunt to impress."

Rick said nothing. He extended his arms, intent on his brother's throat, knowing he was going to strangle him with his bare hands.

"Rick, no!" he heard Delia call from behind him.

Robin stayed where he was, moving up and down almost imperceptibly, doing the spider. "Don't worry, dwarfie, he doesn't have the balls!"

His cackle abruptly ceased as Rick's hands encircled his neck and lifted him off the ground. He squeezed harder and harder, feeling a smile spread across his face as a sound like the ocean's echo in a seashell filled his head. In the distance, he heard Delia's high-pitched screams.

"Fuck you," he whispered as he watched Robin's face turn the color of pickled beets. "Fuck you."

Robin's huge arms flailed wildly, ineffectually.

Suddenly Rick realized that he was only supposed to scare his brother, to teach him to leave him and Delia alone. He shouldn't be trying to kill him.

But he wanted to. He *really* wanted to.

He loosened his grip on Robin's neck the tiniest fraction, heard his brother take a strangled, gasping breath. "Don't you ever fuck with Delia again," Rick whispered.

"What about you?" Robin's voice was a hoarse cracking sound. "Can I fuck with you?"

"Rick! Watch out!"

The sudden pain in his groin made him scream and lose his hold on his twin.

Robin continued to squeeze Rick's testicles even after he'd fallen to the ground. Rick, screaming, kicked and flailed at him, but he wouldn't let go. Instead, he twisted them, and even Rick's heavy Levi's provided little protection from Robin's grip. He kicked and punched, but it did no good. Robin laughed and began hopping on one hand, trying to pull him across the room. Rick was jerked a few feet, his brother's marionette, and was ready to give up consciousness to give up and die.

"No!" Delia's scream cut through his agony and suddenly she was there, pushing between them, trying to pry Robin's fingers loose.

Rick moaned. She was making it worse.

"No!" she screamed again, then opened her strong-jawed mouth as wide as she could and sunk her teeth into Robin's forearm.

He let go. Rick doubled up, holding himself, groaning and sobbing, wanting to die. He knew he was vomiting only because he could see it; the sensation was lost entirely to the pain in his groin.

Vaguely, he saw Robin flailing at Delia with his free arm, trying to hit her. Doggedly she kept her teeth sunk into his other arm.

Rick reached toward Delia, wanting to help her, then blackness came and took away the pain.

"Ricky! Ricky!" Slowly he awoke, and the pain began again, less sharp, a horrible aching agony beneath freezing cold. Carmen sat in a chair beside the couch where he lay. She was patting his face with a cold, damp cloth.

"God," he moaned, reaching for his groin, shocked to find his pants were gone. An ice pack sat on his jockey shorts. The cold, he thought, staring at Carmen in shock.

"Hector checked you," she said bluntly. "There was blood. We thought maybe you had to go to the hospital. If the swelling's not down, we'll take you tomorrow. She handed him two aspirin and a glass of water and waited silently while he took the pills.

His hand shook as he handed the glass back to her. "Where's Delia?" he managed.

She looked surprised. "Hector and I got home at ten-thirty. We came in to make sure everything was okay and found you on the floor. No one else was here. What happened, Ricky?"

He tried to sit up so he could see the clock, but he was too sore. "What time is it?"

"Just past eleven. Ricky, tell me what happened."

"Delia was here. We were watching television. Robin came in and . . ."

"And what?" she prompted.

"He said things. About Delia."

"Dirty things?"

Rick nodded. "I got mad. I tried to kill him."

"Madre de Dios."

"I was choking him, I was going to do it, then all of a sudden I realized what I was doing. I started to let go, and that's when he got me."

"I think he did a lot more damage to you than you did to him."

Carefully Rick pulled himself upright. God, it hurt. He set the ice bag on the coffee table. "We have to find Delia."

"Hector already checked the house, but no one was here except you. He's out checking the grounds. We thought maybe you had a run-in with your brother, but Hector thought he should look around and make sure we didn't have any prowlers. Let me help you."

She took his arm as he stood. He felt trembly and light-headed, and oh Lord, did his balls hurt.

"Ricky?"

"I'm okay. Delia was fighting with him when I passed out, Carmen. I'm worried about her."

"Okay. You sit and I'll look again."

"No. I'm going with you."

She looked at him skeptically. "If you insist. You want me to go up and get you a pair of sweatpants?"

He smiled thinly. "Please."

He leaned against the wall until she came 'back. As he gingerly pulled on the pants, he avoided looking at the bloodstains on his shorts.

"I found this, too," Carmen said, handing him a sealed envelope with his name on it. He didn't recognize the handwriting.

He opened it and saw that the note was written on school paper. He scanned the letter quickly, then reread it, not wanting to believe what he saw.

"Dear Rick," it said, "I thought you were a nice person, but if you were, you wouldn't have tried to kill your own brother. Don't come to the carnival. I never want to see you again. Delia."

Stunned, not knowing what else to do, he handed it to Carmen. After she read it she asked, "Ricky, do you know her handwriting?"

"No. I don't think I've ever seen it. Why?"

"I'm thinking this might be your brother's idea of a joke."

Rick looked up hopefully. "Should I go to the carnival and talk to her?"

"I don't think you're in any shape to do that. Where's the carnival going next?"

"The high desert. They're stopping for a few days in Victorville, then they're going to Nevada."

"Tomorrow night you try to call up there. If you can't get through, Hector will drive you, okay?"

"Maybe I could call tonight . . ." he began. Fear rose in his gut. "Or maybe I should wait. I was really weird tonight, Carmen. I . . . I think I went nuts for a few minutes. She probably doesn't want to see me."

"Call, Ricky. Just see if she's there so you can stop worrying about her. I don't believe that letter."

He was about to say he didn't either when there was a knock on the front door. Carmen opened it.

"Robin," she said coldly.

"Hi, baby brother."

Rick's heart skipped a beat.

Robin padded directly up to him. "I walked your girlfriend back to the carnival. She doesn't like you anymore, icky Ricky. She thinks you're a meanie." He feigned a grab toward Rick, who gasped and backed up.

Robin laughed. "Gotcha good, didn't I, little brother? Self-defense. Hope I didn't crack your nuts. Hope you can still make babies."

"Robin!" Carmen said angrily.

"It was self-defense," he said smoothly.

"Did you write this?" Rick asked, brandishing the note.

Robin looked mildly surprised. "No. What is it?"

"You know what it is," Carmen said.

Robin pushed the sleeve up on his shirt and displayed a perfect set of red tooth marks. "She told me she was sorry she did this. She said she got so scared when you tried to kill me that she didn't really know what she was doing."

"Did you write this?" Carmen asked again.

He peered at her. "Nope. She said she was going up to Ricky's room to leave him a nice, private note. I never read it." He slap-slapped to the bookcase and felt for the lever.

A moment later, the case turned, revealing the dark, narrow stairwell. Robin turned and looked directly at Rick.

"You'll be happy to know that I'm running away with the circus, icky Ricky. Just gonna get my things."

"You can't just leave," Carmen began.

"Oh, now, be honest, Carmen. You don't want me here any more than he does. I'm sixteen, I'm leaving. The Masellos made me an offer I can't refuse. My own trailer, star billing, lots of bucks. I'm going." His grin was horrifying. "Nobody's going to miss me but Jade. And she's going to miss me something awful. Dicky Ricky, maybe if your nuts heal up, you can give her what she wants. She's old, but she's got nice tits." He made a face. "And you gotta admit, it's better than fucking a dwarf."

Carmen advanced on him, saying things in Spanish that Rick was happy he didn't understand. Rick himself was too sore and tired to summon up anything but cold disgust. Laughing, his twin disappeared into the stairwell, the bookcase swinging closed behind him.

For fifteen minutes Rick tried to get through to Delia on the phone, but no one answered—the phone was in the office trailer, and no one was there this late at night.

Hector returned, and a moment later, Robin came back. The three watched in silence as Robin, a bulging knapsack strapped to his broad back, hummed to himself and crossed to the front door. "Give my love to Jade, Ricky," he said, opening the door. "Give it to her *good.*"

Rick didn't answer.

No one did.

The door shut.

"Good riddance," Carmen hissed.

July 6, 1981

After midnight, Rick lay in his bed in his locked room, not quite awake, not quite asleep, always in pain. Sometime during the night, he heard Jade and Howard come home.

Drunk and foulmouthed, they argued all the way to their room, their voices fading only after they slammed the door.

A long time later a pair of sonic booms rattled his windows. Soon sirens broke the silence of the night. He thought and dreamed continuously about Delia, worrying, wondering, so unsure of himself that it was yet another physical pain. As dawn approached, he made up his mind to see her before the carnival left for Victorville. He got up.

The swelling wasn't so bad now, but peeing was an exercise in torture. It took him twenty minutes to get dressed, but finally, dressed in sweats and zoris, because he found he couldn't bend over to put on shoes and socks, he slowly made his way down the stairs.

Dawn had arrived. He glanced at his bike by the back door. That was out of the question. He dreaded walking. The Zapatas weren't up yet, so he couldn't ask Hector for a ride.

But Jade and Howard would sleep at least till noon. They had hangovers every time they went to the Dew Drop. He took the car keys from the hook by the back door and went out to the driveway and let himself into their Bulgemobile, a monstrous Impala they'd bought a year ago. Since they'd moved into the Piper house, they'd gone through a series of Bulgemobiles, trading them in every other year for something new to slowly destroy.

This one, parked at a crazy angle, was already missing one headlight and part of a bumper. He slipped the keys into the ignition, and the car started after a couple coughs and a sputter.

He turned it around and slowly pulled out the driveway and onto the street. He'd only driven the driver's ed cars before this monstrosity, but all things considered, he thought he did all right.

He drove down through the circular maze of streets that made up his neighborhood. The air, warm already, was layered with a fine mist. There were no other cars out at five in the morning, and the huge pine trees lining the narrow road loomed ominously, watching and waiting.

Finally he made it down the hill and continued on toward

the fairgrounds. A light turned red at the school corner, and he sat there and waited for no traffic, his stomach nervous, his heart beating too fast. The light changed and he glanced up and saw the low pall of smoke over the fairgrounds.

Numb, not allowing his imagination to run wild—*probably the corn dog stand, an oil fire, that's all*—he drove down the street and pulled to a stop across the street from the entrance.

He got out of the car and started across the street.

He saw nothing unusual at first, except for two police cars and a single fire engine at the inside edge of the vast field that served as the fairground parking lot. There was a faint smell of smoke in the air.

Ducking under the rope that closed the lot, he started across the field. He could see the ticket booths just beyond the police cars and then the square little carnival buildings that should have been dismantled by now. *Maybe they're just a little slow this morning.* Maybe they'd started tearing down from the other side of the carnival, near the trailers where everyone lived.

He couldn't see those from here.

Ignoring the pain, he began to run, then, ducking another set of ropes, he entered the carnival grounds, the smoke acrid and cloying in his nostrils. None of the buildings had been torn down yet, as far as he could see.

"Son?"

He looked at the yellow-coated fireman who called him. "What happened? Where is everyone?"

"Do you have friends here?"

"Yes! Where are they?" Panicked, he shot forward, but the fireman reached his arm out and caught Rick's elbow. "What's your name, son?"

"Rick."

"Rick, do you have relatives here?"

He hesitated. "Robin!" he blurted. "Robin Piper, he's my brother. He's here. I want to go to the trailers, I have a lot of friends here—"

"Hey, Ed," the fireman called over his shoulder.

"Yeah?" called a young cop with dirt smudged on his face.

"Stay here, Rick," the fireman said, and went to talk to the cop. A moment later, the cop came up to him.

"I want to go to the trailers," Rick said.

"There's been a fire." The cop wasn't much older than him, Rick realized. He looked scared, his blue eyes sort of glazed. "There was an explosion. It's bad. There are a lot of fatalities."

"How many?"

"We don't know yet."

"I want to see if Delia's all right."

The cop eyed him. "I thought you were looking for your brother."

"Yes, he's here, but so's Delia and her family. And Clarisse and Omar and—"

The policeman's skin looked too white under the ashes smudged on his cheek. "Rick, most everyone was in their living quarters when the explosion hit. It was very sudden and the fire was so fierce and hot—"

"I thought I heard sonic booms. Was that it?"

The cop nodded. "There's not much left. They had the trailers well away from the carnival. The grounds are so big and all . . ." The young cop looked around him, and Rick thought the guy was trying not to cry.

"What are you saying?"

"I'm saying the carnival wasn't blown up, the living quarters were, and you don't want to see. So far, there are no survivors. A lot of bodies." He shook his head. "They didn't stand a chance. Is your family . . ."

"We live on Via Matanza."

The cop looked relieved. "Maybe you'd better go tell them. We don't even know if we can identify the remains." He pulled out a notebook. "Give me your name and number. We'll be in touch."

Rick did. "I need to see. Just for a moment."

The policeman studied him. "Okay, but not close up. We've got professionals losing their cookies over this."

Rick could tell this man wasn't exaggerating by the sick look in his eyes. "Okay."

They walked together around the rows of buildings until the trailers came into view. There was nothing but charred, blackened ruins dotted with yellow bags. More police cars, fire engines, and a bunch of ambulances sat nearby. As he watched, Rick saw another cop with a handkerchief tied over his mouth and gloves on his hands pick up something long and jointed and put it in a sack.

It was an arm.

"Go on home now," the cop said gently.

38

Rick leaned on a shovel and listened to the pump gurgle. A week after the explosion, they'd held Robin's funeral, and Jade had sobbed histrionically, the poodle in her lap whining along with her. Howard and the Zapatas were there, and some kids from school showed up, but that was all. When they laid the tiny coffin containing a few charred bones in the ground, only Jade cried.

Rick had been glad that his brother was dead, but the loss of Delia hurt him terribly. It still hurt, as did the knowledge that he could never know if Delia really hated him, or if Robin had made it all up. He was sixteen years old and he hated Santo Verde more than ever. He had already started planning to graduate high school a year early and go to UNLV, where he would be surrounded by nothing but sand for four years. There was nothing left in Santo Verde for him. Nothing at all.

The papers, he recalled, had said that police had reason to believe the explosion had been set intentionally, but the perpetrators were never caught.

Rick watched Hector readjust the pump. The only other thing that happened before he left home was Howard's death on Halloween night. Officially it was a heart attack, and the coroner said cirrhosis of the liver would have got him if his heart hadn't.

Evidently he'd been sitting out on the porch as usual,

nursing his Jack Daniels and smoking his Tiparillo, when he decided to take a walk, probably to pee in the pond.

That night, for a reason attributed only to drunkenness, Howard had missed the pond by twenty yards and wandered into the deep front grounds. Hector found him there the next morning, his eyes wide open, his mouth in a rictus of a scream. A cop commented that he looked like he'd been scared to death. The cop wondered about all the grass stains on the clothes and skin, and the leaves in his mouth, and the coroner said he must have thrashed around in the foliage before he died.

What the coroner said was true, Rick had known as he stood there staring coolly at his dead uncle. It was truer than he'd ever know. Uncle Howard had had a little run-in with Big Jack himself.

"Rick?"

Hector's voice startled him out of his reverie. "Yeah?"

"I think we're ready for the dirty work. We can't siphon any more out."

Oh, joy, Rick thought, looking at the greenish black mounds of glop and garbage at the bottom of the pool.

"I'm going to get a couple masks out of the toolshed," Hector announced, pulling off his rubber gloves.

"I guess I should have hired this job out," Rick said.

"It's bad, but we can do it." Hector's lip curled as he studied the muck. "We don't want to get that stuff on us. I'm gonna get some thicker gloves for us, and I think there are a couple pairs of hip boots hanging in the garage. Your grandfather left them here."

"Thanks," Rick called as the other man trudged away. Hector was right—they couldn't climb into that mire unprotected. If they did, they'd both end up on antibiotics from staph infections.

Hector returned a few moments later with the masks, gloves, and dusty but intact waders. They put them on, took garbage sacks and shovels, and climbed down the steps at the shallow end of the pool.

Rick picked his way into the deepest part of the pool,

where the muck reached almost to his knees, and, resigned to his task, began shoveling.

The sludge was mainly liquid compost, probably years-old leaves and grass, and dissolved fish and frogs, though he occasionally found tree limbs, dishes, liquor bottles, and beer cans. There were two oil filters and what might have once been a cowboy hat, all in one corner of the pool. Glancing behind him at Don Quixote, glinting in the midday sun, he wondered what the knight would have pretended this slimy enemy to be.

He moved to the other side of the deep end and began working once more. A few minutes later, his shovel ran into something solid. He pulled back and tried again, and again met resistance. *It's big, whatever it is.* The goop sucked against the shovel, not wanting to give up its prize, but finally he pulled it partway out before it slipped off the shovel and disappeared again.

"Damn." Rick leaned the shovel against the wall and bent over, digging his gloved hands into the mess. He pulled the object out and held it up, trying to see what it was under the dripping goo.

"It's a bone," Hector said, slogging over.

"My God." Hector was right. It was too big to be an animal bone, but it was odd-looking, too. Hector took the bone and set it on the cement edging the pool. Rick dug in again, this time pulling out an oddly shaped rib cage.

"Mother of God," Hector breathed. "It's human."

He didn't offer to take the ribs, so Rick set them aside himself, then grimly he went back to work, pulling more bones from the mire. Finally he extracted the skull, and moaned, his suspicions confirmed by the uniquely ridged brow. "Dear God," he moaned. "It's Delia."

"I'll get Carmen," Hector said.

Numbly Rick nodded and climbed from the pool. He set the skull next to the other bones that dried in the sun, and took the time to study the stunted leg bones. "My God, Delia." Tears ran down his face.

They weren't so much for Delia—he was long used to

the idea of her death—but for himself. Now he knew that his brother was behind the note, behind the death. They were tears of relief.

39

Later that afternoon, Carmen, Hector, and Rick buried Delia's bones beneath a willow tree in the front yard. Hector planted a white rose bush on top of the grave to mark it, and Rick stood by the grave between the couple and said a little prayer to a god he didn't know.

The Zapatas were gone now, leaving him to sit beside Delia's grave. He was thankful for that and for Carmen, who had instantly stopped his knee-jerk intention to inform the police, by pointing out that both Delia and her murderer were officially dead and had been for many years. There was no point in stirring things up.

"Oh, Delia," he whispered. "I wish I could avenge you. I wish I'd known." His voice broke and he let himself sob out his grief.

At last he got to his feet and walked the overgrown path back to the pond, where he stood by Don Quixote and watched Hector working. They'd gotten a lot done before he'd found the bones, far more than he'd realized—the job was near completion.

Staring into the emptying pool, at its slimy green sides, considering the secret that it had held, he had a sudden thought:

Paulie.

Paulie had started to laugh. It was an unholy sound.

"Dear God," Rick whispered, "Oh dear God, no." He grabbed the metal muzzle of the horse to keep from falling.

"Rick?" Hector turned and looked at him. "You okay?"

"I—I—"

"It's bad about Delia," Hector said gently. "And you've been out in the sun too long already. I can finish up here, no problem. Why don't you go to the cottage? Carmen's got a fresh pitcher of lemonade made up."

"Thanks," Rick managed. "I'll do that."

It took all his willpower to make it to the cottage and knock on the door. Carmen opened it a moment later, took one look at him, and insisted he sit in Hector's easy chair while she fetched the lemonade.

Quint poked his head out of the Zapatas' bedroom, then eeled into the room, flirting and rubbing against the furniture as he made his way across the room. He leapt into Rick's lap an instant before Carmen brought in a huge tumbler full of lemonade and ice.

"Thanks." He sipped the juice. "Carmen, about Paulie."

"You remembered," she said. "I can tell by the look in your eyes.

"I killed him."

"Yes, you did," she replied somberly. "You were still holding him under the water when I came out and found you. He was beyond saving."

"I murdered him," Rick whispered.

"How did you know the greenjacks got him? How did you know?"

"His laugh. He was sort of half sitting up when I came back to him after Big Jack came apart at midnight. I squatted down and asked him if he was all right. He started laughing.

"He'd changed, like Robin. He sounded like a demon—it was horrible to hear. And then he said, 'We're gonna getcha, icky Ricky.' He laughed some more, and I remember just staring at him. The greenjacks were everywhere, taunting me, singing their rhymes." Rick rubbed his temples. "Even in the dark, his eyes looked wrong, and then I remembered what Robin—the greenjack that was Robin—said. He said, 'Remember Thomas,' and right then I understood what he meant."

Even as he said the words, he knew they sounded insane, but it was too late now to take them back. "In Grandfather's story about Thomas, he always said that when his parents brought Thomas in, unconscious, his father waited with a sword, ready to run him through if a greenjack had taken his body. That always seemed really horrible, but important, that a father would kill his own son." He paused. "But really his son would have been already dead. He would have been kicked out of his own body and forced to live with the jacks until his stolen body was killed. So really, if Thomas's father had had to kill his body, it would have been the ultimate act of love.

"That's what I thought about while I held him under the water. While I murdered him."

Carmen said nothing for a long time. "Ricky, do you still believe that he was taken by the jacks?"

Rick thought of Audrey telling him to give himself the benefit of the doubt until he had proof. *Do I really believe he'd changed?* Finally he looked Carmen in the eye. "Yes, I still believe he was possessed by a jack. Just as my brother was," he added.

"If that's true, Ricky, then you're no murderer. You committed an act of mercy."

"What do you think, Carmen? Do you believe me?"

"Frankly, Ricky, I don't know. I've never known. Your brother, he changed, that's for sure. But maybe he just went bad. That happens."

"Yes, it does." He took a long swallow of lemonade, but barely felt it go down. "Our secret," he said softly. "The secret we will carry with us to our graves."

"We still will, Ricky. We still will."

He studied her, remembering how she'd coached him on what they would tell the police, and how she'd had him run in the house and call the ambulance while she made a show of resuscitating the lifeless little body. That was their secret.

"You've known that all these years," he said wonderingly.

"Two days after it happened, you forgot the truth. You believed the story we made up, Ricky. Years later, I thought maybe you never came home because you *had* remembered."

"No. Not until now. Carmen, why did you cover up for me?"

"Whether he turned into a greenjack or not, you believed he did. That was the important thing."

"That's more than any person should ever have to do for another."

"I didn't have to, Ricky. I wanted to. When you love someone, that's how it is."

He thought again of Audrey and realized the truth in Carmen's words. "I told Audrey," he said.

Carmen raised her eyebrows.

"She says there are some good scientific reasons why a person could see something like a greenjack."

"Good."

"I told her about Big Jack, too."

"What did she say?"

"She said she's going to stay with me on Halloween and we're going to watch for him together. Carmen, I know it sounds crazy, but at least I'll finally know."

"It's not crazy," Carmen said, smiling gently. "It's brave."

40

October 28

"You sure you don't mind, Dad?"

"As long as Leanne's parents are there somewhere, I think it's a great idea, Shel." He started to swivel his chair back to the computer, then stopped. "No drinking, right?"

Shelly laughed, still shocked that her dad had immediately given her permission to go to an all-night coed Halloween party. "Her parents will be there, and they don't drink or smoke at all." She gave him a crooked smile. "You met them at back-to-school night. I don't think they even have sex."

His expression turned stern. "I hope you're not intending—"

"No, Dad. That was a joke."

"I hope so." His features softened. "They do look like they probably grew Leanne in a test tube." He paused. "You're not going to repeat that, are you?"

"No, Daddy." Was he kidding? She loved it when he talked to her like an equal instead of his little girl. He'd been doing it more and more since they'd moved here, and she loved it. In Vegas he was always asking questions and calling people to see where she was, and now she knew he trusted her a lot more. Of course, he had more reason to; she knew that, too. "Mr. and Mrs. Larson may look like turnips, but they're very nice."

"Is it a costume party?" he asked.

"Uh-huh. I'm going to be a French maid." She couldn't resist tweaking him again. He was so predictable.

"No French maids, dear heart. Promoting a sexist im—"

Oh no, she'd pushed the lecture button. "Daa-dd! I was joking. I'm going as a Supreme Court judge, okay? A Democrat."

He stared at her. "Shel, it's late, I'm tired."

"Okay. I'm going to be a gypsy fortune-teller. I'm going to ask Carmen to help me. Okay?"

"Okay." He smiled faintly. "I'm sorry, kiddo. I just want to finish this last paragraph and get some sleep."

She leaned over and kissed him on the forehead. "I'm sorry I teased. What are you going to do for Halloween? Are you and Audrey going to a party?"

Dad didn't say much about Audrey, but Shelly knew they were getting hot and heavy and was pretty sure they were sleeping together. She was glad: Her dad was much easier to get along with now.

"No parties. We thought we'd take Cody trick-or-treating, then just stay in and watch horror movies."

"That's a good idea. Get scary ones so Audrey will hang on to you!"

"Shelly . . ."

"Sorry." She meant it this time. He really did look tired tonight with those dark smudges under his eyes. "I think Audrey's great, Dad."

It was his turn to stare. "You do?"

"A bunch of us were talking about our parents dating, and some of the kids hate it, like Jenny Morton. Her mom is seeing Bill Manderson's dad, and she's *so* embarrassed. She says her mom never pays any attention to her."

"But you approve of Audrey?"

"Heck, yes. She's Dakota's sister, and he's one of the best guys in the world. He's kind of one of my best friends." She called him every week and told him about school and work.

Dakota also gave great advice: not quite so prudish as a parent, but more like what she thought an older brother might dispense.

"Dakota's a good guy," her dad agreed.

"I know." She really did like Audrey a lot, but there was another reason she wanted them together, one she'd realized on back-to-school night, when Audrey had come along. Her girlfriends didn't try to throw themselves at her dad if he had a woman with him, which was a big relief. Back in Vegas, especially when he had the TV show, she never knew if her girlfriends liked her or just wanted to try to catch his eye.

"Bedtime, Shel," he said.

"When will the pool be ready?" she asked. At dinner the day after he and Hector drained the koi pond, Dad had told her how it used to be a swimming pool back in the thirties. "It's ready as of today," he said, smiling at her. "But do we really want to fill it this time of year?"

"Yes!" She turned puppy-dog eyes on him. "We can heat it, can't we?"

"Sure. Why not?" He smiled. "Don Quixote can be the lifeguard."

He'd said that about a million times too. "What is it with you and Don Quixote, Dad?"

He considered, crossing his arms and tipping back in the chair. Finally he said, "We both tilt at windmills."

Well, *that* made a whole lot of sense. She decided she'd better read the book sometime. "Good night, Daddy." She kissed his forehead once more. "Thank you."

"Night, Shel." He turned back to his computer as she shut the door behind her.

In her room she dressed for bed, did a quick page of English homework, then climbed into bed and read a Stephen King novel until she was sleepy. Between work and school, that never took too long.

She awoke disoriented, knowing it was the middle of the night, and certain that someone was in her room with her. Flicking on the bedside lamp, she looked around the room but saw nothing unusual, and after a few minutes, she turned off the light and lay back in the big bed, still listening, still hearing absolutely nothing. *I must've been dreaming.*

After a few minutes, she closed her eyes. It was silly to worry, because she always locked her bedroom door—at least since those dead poodles had shown up in her room—and only her dad had the extra key.

Right after he finished the sculpture, he'd also gone through the house and nailed a bunch of secret passages shut. She was sorry he'd done it since she'd never had a chance to check them out. Her room had been sealed since her dad was a kid, so he didn't make her drag all her stuff out of her closet. He did all the others, though, telling her how his brother used to use the tunnels to spy on people, but that now they were infested with vermin, maybe even some raccoons and opossums.

She drifted off again and began to have pleasant dreams about Ryan Levine, SVHS's star quarterback and the object of her considerable interest. "Don't open your eyes, Shelly," he whispered, kissing her neck, stroking her bare arms. "Don't open your eyes." She sighed as his fingers slipped under her shirt.

"Ryan," she whispered in her sleep.

Ryan kissed her lips, and she drew his plump lower lip into her mouth, sucking on it as his hands roved lower. He began to pull her panties down her legs.

She raised her buttocks to help him, and as she did, her sleep lightened a little and she passed into a semiconsciousness that allowed her to realize that she was having a very dirty dream. *Safe sex,* she thought, giving herself back to the dream, letting it become a half-waking fantasy as she imagined that Ryan was pushing her legs apart and climbing on top of her. Keeping her eyes closed, she relaxed her legs, her awareness centered on the demanding ache in her crotch. Pushing against him, she felt his erection against her pubis, felt it nudge inward, slowly, gently, deliciously. He would take his time, she told herself, he would take hours if necessary, before he finally and painlessly relieved her of her virginity.

Suddenly there was tremendous pain between her legs. She opened her mouth to scream, but before any sound could escape, a wad of cloth was thrust roughly into her mouth. Choking, she tried vainly to spit it out. Hands pinioned her shoulders, and his penis was like a knife, holding her hips to the bed. She flailed her legs, but that only let him nudge deeper into her. She pulled her legs tightly together, but couldn't push him out. Unmoving, he used his body to hold her prisoner.

This is no dream!

In the dim glow of the night-light, she turned her gaze to her attacker's face.

And recognized it.

Her father's face, twisted and cruel, his eyes boring blackly into hers. He smiled broadly.

Blackness swirled into her ears and eyes. She was going to faint. *No!* She forced herself to stay conscious because if she lost it, her legs would relax and he'd start moving again.

Dazed, disbelieving, she struggled to free her arms.

"Let's be a good little girl," he said in her father's voice. He lowered his face, her father's face, toward her, and stuck his tongue out, played the tip over her lips, teasing them around the gag.

Shelly's mind went coolly calculating. She knew what to do. She moaned. Moaned again.

"If I take the gag out of your mouth, will you be a good girl and not make a sound?" His breath smelled hot and sweet, like candy.

She nodded, and forced herself to moan again as he lowered his mouth to hers and extracted the cloth. He pulled back, eyes glittering, a pair of her panties hanging from his teeth.

Controlling the urge to vomit, she remained silent and hoped her face hadn't betrayed her repulsion.

He dropped the panties and put his mouth back on hers.

This isn't Daddy! It can't be!

His tongue slipped between her lips and thrust against her clenched teeth.

Fighting revulsion, she slowly let her mouth open. Immediately his tongue thrust into it, moving everywhere, along her gums, under her tongue, exploring the soft palate, as if he were tasting her, not kissing her. He tasted of Tootsie Rolls. She forced another moan and slowly drew her tongue to the back of her mouth. He didn't notice. He was moving again, rocking, trying to work his penis in further.

He extended his tongue into a long, narrow dart and thrust it against the inside of her left cheek. She bit down with all her force and held. He groaned.

Suddenly his face snapped back and his hands left her shoulders. Instantly she shoved him off, jabbing at his eyes with her fingers, trying to slam her palm up against his nose.

He hit her on the side of her face. She saw stars and fell back, numb and dumb, expecting him to climb back on and finish his rape before she could regain control.

But he didn't. He said nothing, just made angry little noises that got farther and farther away. Finally there were no sounds. She reached over and flipped on the bedside lamp.

"God," she whispered, starting to tremble uncontrollably. "Oh God." She reached up and touched her face where he'd hit it, felt a knot rising already. She touched her mouth and felt stickiness everywhere. Blood. *Oh, God.*

Then she realized there was something in her mouth. Horrified, sick to her stomach, she spit it out.

A small piece of pink flesh landed on her bare abdomen. The tip of his tongue. The blood belonged to *him.*

Keep your shit together, Shelly! Not letting herself think, not considering anything but the necessity of getting out of there, she slipped on her robe and tiptoed down the hall to the bathroom. In a few minutes she'd cleaned herself up, relieved to find that, not only hadn't he finished his act, but there was no blood. He hadn't even gotten all the way in. Quietly she returned to her room and packed a bag.

As the sun came up, she pulled out of the driveway and

headed for the one place she could be sure she was safe: Dakota O'Keefe's. She didn't think about her father as she drove, nor did she wipe away the hot, silent tears leaking from her eyes.

41

October 29

"Damn!" Inside Dakota O'Keefe's apartment, the phone began to ring, and Dakota, still two doors away, broke into a trot. "Damn!" he cried again as one of his black stiletto heels caught in an old cigarette burn in the hall carpeting. He regained his balance and raced to the door, digging frantically through his purse for the keys and swearing steadily now because he'd counted six rings, and that meant Lil had left the machine off. Again. At last he found the key, stuck it in the dead bolt, found out she hadn't bothered locking it, and, thoroughly pissed, tried the knob. The door swung open. *Magil would forget her own tits if they weren't attached!*

By the time he tackled the receiver, it was halfway through the tenth ring. Though it was unlikely the call would come at seven in the morning, he had his fingers crossed for a plum part in a new show. If he lost it because of a missed call, he'd string Lil up alive. By those firmly attached tits.

"Hello?" He tried not to pant.

"Dakota, thank God."

"Piper?" he asked, disappointed and pleased at the same time. "Is that you? You sound like shit."

"Is Shelly there?"

"Shelly? Why would Shelly be here?"

There was a pause. "Because she's not *here,* Dakota."

"She ran away?"

"I don't know, I think so, but it doesn't make sense. She seemed happy with the move and she was happy last night and now she's gone, and God, Dakota, there's blood on her sheets—"

"Calm down, Piper," Dakota interrupted. "You're talking like a machine gun. Get a grip."

"Yeah, yeah—"

"How much blood?"

"A little."

"Is her car gone?"

"Yes."

"Then she probably wasn't taken by force. Is that what you thought?"

"Y— No. I don't know. She told me she was happy we'd moved, and last night she came to see me. She wanted to go to a party and I said yes and she kissed me good night and now she's gone and it doesn't make sense—"

"Take a deep breath, Ricky. Where's the blood?"

Rick's voice shook. "On her pillow and wiped on the sheet. It wasn't much, but it's still blood and she's gone—"

"A nosebleed, maybe?"

"Maybe."

"Piper, she's hardly ever home, right?"

"But she never gets up early on the weekend."

"Does she tell you every time she goes somewhere?"

"No, but—"

"Calm down. Have you called her friends?"

"Yes. No one's seen her."

"And you probably made a lot of enemies waking them all up, right, Piper?"

No reply.

"Does she have a boyfriend?"

"What are you saying?"

"Lust makes people do strange things, Piper."

"She wouldn't—"

"Maybe, maybe not, but I think you'd better calm down

and give her a chance to come home. It's probably nothing, Piper. Why are you so nervous? You're acting weird, Rick. What gives?"

Piper didn't answer for a long time, and when he finally spoke, there was a different kind of waver in his voice. "The past dies hard, Dakota."

"That's very poetic," he said with brusqueness he didn't feel. "But what the hell does it mean?"

"It means you're right." Rick's voice sounded normal now. "It's probably nothing. I was so tired last night that I didn't hear half of what she said. It's probably something like cheerleading practice. But if it's a boy, once I get her home safely, I'll skin her alive."

"Okay, good," Dakota said, relieved that Piper's voice sounded nearly normal. "Now, how long has she been missing?"

"I, ah, I don't know exactly. She went to bed last night around eleven. That's the last time I saw her."

"So it's been about eight hours. How long ago did you find out she was gone?"

"An hour."

"If I hear from her, I'll call you. But I think she'll show up, safe and sound. Call me the minute she does, but let the phone ring a long time. I'm just going to bed, and Lil's not here." He paused. "How's my sister?"

"Wonderful."

"Good. Give her a call. She'll calm you down."

"I will. Thanks, Dakota."

"No problem." He paused. "Rick? Don't go having a nervous breakdown."

"I'll be fine."

Dakota hung up the phone, and as he got ready for bed, he wondered if Rick Piper wasn't already in the middle of a breakdown.

Two hours later, someone started banging on the door. Dakota tried to ignore it, but the idiot wouldn't go away.

Finally, ready to curse out a Mormon missionary or a magazine salesman, Dakota dragged himself to the door and opened it. "What the hell—" he began, then stopped, shocked to see Shelly Piper. There was a bruised red swelling on the side of her face, and she had a suitcase in her hand.

"What happened?" he cried as he pulled her into the apartment. "Give me the bag, sit down. Did someone hit you?"

She looked up at him, her lip starting to tremble.

"Daddy," she said.

"What?"

"He hit me. He, he tried . . ." She fell into Dakota's arms and cried for at least half an hour before she told him what had happened.

Dakota couldn't believe what he was hearing. He'd known Rick Piper for nearly five years, and he'd always seemed sweet and slightly sad, too intense for his own good, a worrywart, but a hell of a good father. Cody adored the ground he walked on, and even at her worst, Shelly couldn't find anything very awful to say about him. And now this. Dakota studied Shelly's face. She was telling him the truth as she saw it; of that, he was certain. Something had happened, but what?

He had a gift for seeing beyond the packaging into the product. Audrey's husband, for instance; he'd had him pegged from day one. Beneath the Armani suits, twinkly eyes and all, he knew the man was rotten. He'd sensed this about other people, men and women both, and he'd never been wrong. But though there was something undeniably unusual about Piper, something he couldn't quite pinpoint, he sensed none of the corruptness he'd detected in those other people, and he couldn't believe that Rick was capable of what his daughter alleged. But why would she lie?

"Shelly, honey, are you sure it was your dad? Was it dark?"

"The night-light was on."

"So it was almost dark?"

"Kind of. But it looked like him, and sounded like him. He looked crazy."

Don't have a nervous breakdown. That's what he'd said to Rick two hours ago. "Shelly, has your dad been acting funny lately?"

She shook her head. "No. We've been getting along great, and he and Audrey are dating a lot. She's nice." For a moment her voice was normal, then reality—or unreality—set in again. "I mean, he wasn't acting weird or anything." She touched her face, tears threatening.

"Shel, I think we have to solve this now."

"I don't want to go back. I don't want to see him."

"We have to. Tell you what. We'll relax today, then head for L.A. first thing in the morning. If I drive your car and drop you off at a friend's, whatever you want, will that be okay? Then I'll go see your dad. If he's responsible for the attack on you, he needs help."

That undefinable thing about Piper, was it mental illness? O'Keefe wondered after Shelly went into the other room to nap. Certainly some of the things he'd spilled about his childhood—those jack-off things he said he could still see, the sex-crazed aunt, finding his parents murdered . . . Dakota shook his head . . . and that evil twin, for Christ's sake—any one of those things could make for a little instability. Or a lot. *You quiet types, we just never know what you're up to.* How many times had he teased Piper with that line?

For a brief instant it occurred to Dakota that perhaps Rick Piper didn't have a twin brother, that Rick's brother was an alternate personality . . . "No," he said aloud. Who was he going to believe? A man who'd become his best friend or the guy's teenage daughter, who wasn't above manipulation to get what she wanted? He knew that from experience.

Neither, he decided. Shelly wasn't faking, and Rick was stable until proven otherwise. Dakota would do nothing until he saw him in person, not even tell Audrey. The thought of his sister made his heart ache a little: More for her sake than any other reason, he hoped Rick was in the clear. Audrey was falling for him hard, she'd confided, and he wanted her to be happy. For a moment he considered warning her, but decided against it: She'd told him she'd be out of town until tomorrow, attending a small convention. She'd be safe, if there was anything to be safe from.

Clearing his throat, he picked up the phone and called in a couple favors, which resulted in a long overdue week's vacation. Next, he swallowed his nervousness and dialed Piper's number.

Rick answered on the second ring.

"She's here," Dakota said lightly, determined not to show his hand.

"Thank God." The immense relief in Piper's voice gave him hope. "Dakota, do you know why she ran away?"

"All I know is that she's here," Dakota said slowly. "Something frightened her last night."

"Frightened her. What?"

"I don't know," he lied, "but she's not crazy about coming home. She doesn't want to be in the house. I told her I'd drive her back and drop her at a friend's house."

"Which one?"

"I don't know yet. Listen, I'll see what else I can get out of her on the ride." He paused. "She has a bruise on her cheek. It's pretty nasty." He waited for the reaction.

"She's hurt? My God, how? Maybe you should take her to the doctor. Let me give you the insurance number."

If he hurt her, Dakota wondered, *would he want her to be seen by a physician?*

"It's not that bad. Just a bruise," he said. "Rick, maybe you should check around the house, make sure all your windows and doors are bolted."

"Why? Did she—"

"She won't talk," he lied again. "But I get the impression someone broke into her room."

"It wouldn't be the first time," Rick said with sudden firmness.

"It wouldn't?"

"Jade put her stuffed poodles in Shelly's room one night, scared the hell out of her."

Shelly had told Dakota that story, and now it made him suspect that the old bat was somehow involved in things. Shelly disliked Jade, but evidently the old lady absolutely despised the girl. *She's jealous of her youth.* Dakota thought. "Maybe it *is* Jade's doing," he said. "Anyway, I've been wanting to visit you, Piper, and I've got a week's vacation, so I'll see you tomorrow." He hesitated. "I'll be there for Halloween. Do you have a costume or would you like me to bring you one? You'd make a gorgeous Betty Boop."

"I'll pass on the costume, O'Keefe; I'm not much on Halloween." A thrum of tension belied the resignation in his voice. "Just bring me my daughter. Please."

42

October 30

Dakota O'Keefe was fine until he dropped Shelly off at Leanne Larson's house in San Antonio Heights, but as he drove into Rick's neighborhood, he began to sweat and wish he'd remembered his bottle of Di-Gels. Shelly hadn't said much on the ride in, except to reiterate that she couldn't believe what happened. It had been a frustrating conversation because, although she saw some merit in blaming Jade, she rightly pointed out that her attacker was a man.

Almost immediately after dropping her off, he got lost on the curvy streets and screeched to a halt at the curb. After consulting the map, he took off again. *Slow,* he told himself, *slow down.* The trip from Vegas to Santo Verde had been accomplished in just under three and a half hours, a new record for him and, he sincerely hoped, for Shelly's Bug. They'd stopped just once, at the rest stop east of Madelyn, and that had been a disaster because he was so accustomed to wearing drag that he'd walked into the ladies' room wigless and makeupless, dressed in tight jeans and a boxy bomber jacket that hid his bosom. Without the accoutrements of femininity, his strong chin and broad shoulders—not to mention the proud bulge of his one-eyed trouser weasel—betrayed his sexual roots all too easily.

A woman in a tacky plaid jumpsuit had stared at him,

then frantically whispered something through the crack between the door and frame of the nearest stall. Thinking fast,
Dakota unzipped his jacket, putting his thirty-eights on display, and groaned, "My bra is killing me." After that, he was
left to pee in peace.

Leak taken, he'd paused long enough in front of the metal
mirror to fluff his brown hair into a less masculine style and
apply a trace of lipstick and eyeliner. Back in the car, he
took time to consult the map, trying to memorize the off-
ramps and intersections he'd need to find, because he wasn't
too sure Shelly's directions were good and he didn't want to
talk to Piper again until they came face-to-face.

He didn't really want to talk to him at all before he had
a chance to figure out what—if anything—was really going
on between Piper and his daughter. *Either Shelly's on drugs
or Rick's lost it,* he told himself. He didn't want to believe
either theory.

"Damn!" Again he pulled over and dragged out the map.
Santo fucking Verde was made up of a series of illogical,
curvy streets that made no sense whatsoever. *Too rich for
its own good,* he thought, trying to figure out where he was.
Via Matanza, where Piper lived, was a twisted little road at
the north edge of town, close to the mountains, a stone's
throw from the cemetery. Problem was, it was one of a zil-
lion curvy little streets not far from the mountains and the
cemetery. The goddamned map looked more like an English
hedge maze than a street directory.

Okay, he told himself as he tossed the unfolded map care-
lessly over his shoulder, *this is it. I'm going to find it this
time.* He shifted gears and started out, turning left instead
of right and taking a corkscrew street as opposed to the
countercorkscrew.

He passed gnarled pepper trees lining Via Sangre—all
these fucking Spanish names, he thought, annoyed that he
didn't know the meaning. *Via* meant go or way or something.
Something like road. *Sangre* sounded like some kind of
wine, and he wondered if Via Sangre meant "Go Wine. He
could get behind that about now. But he doubted that mean-

ing: By the looks of things, Santo Verde had a proverbial broom up its proverbial ass. Dogs wouldn't dare shit in Santo Verde, and the town must employ half the gardeners in the state. It had to; he'd never seen a place so overflowing with well-coiffed trees and bushes and grass and flowers. Even this time of year.

Maybe it's Spanish for Wino Road, he told himself as he began to believe he'd taken yet another wrong turn. There were several unofficial Wino Roads in Vegas. "Eureka, baby!" he cried as he approached the bazillionth street sign and read it. "I have found it!"

Via Matanza, at long last. He burned a little rubber rounding the corner, then cruised slowly, watching for Piper's house. The address was 667. Neighbor of the Beast. Before, that seemed funny; now it didn't. *God, Piper, did you really do what Shelly said?* No, Rick would never do such a thing, a thing so bad that Dakota couldn't name it, not even in the privacy of his own head. *If he's ill, he might be able to do it,* his subconscious reminded him.

If he was having a nervous breakdown, if he imagined his brother, or hated his parents? *He found their bodies; he could've killed them . . . Would you question him at all if he weren't dating your sister?*

No, he told himself, *probably not.* But he didn't know if that was true or not, all he knew was that he had been compelled to drive to Santo Verde to find out and that his very lack of instinct about Piper worried him immensely.

There it was, 667, painted black on white on the stone curb in front of the most unusual—and only run-down—yard on the block. You could barely see the house for the trees and bushes. Everything else on the street looked like photos from *Better Homes & Gardens* or *Architectural Digest* with their huge, perfect lawns and landscaping. Freeform topiaries, he noticed, seemed to be the in thing in Santo Verde.

But 667 was a mongrel, and a shaggy one at that. In another neighborhood it might have been presentable, but not here in Beamerland, where all good Republicans go to live and everyone wears Dockers and Izods to play golf on Sundays.

He could see that attempts were being made to fix the place up—the lawn was freshly cut, though not nearly short enough, and only half the trees were pruned. As he drove up the long, long driveway toward the house, he noticed something reflecting sunlight between the trees, and a moment later realized it was Rick's metal statue.

At last the house came into full view, and he realized that its being hidden from the street was probably a major blessing. As Rick had said, it needed paint. It also needed a remodel. The place looked like an eccentricity Edward Gorey would draw. *A lunatic must have built it,* Dakota thought, then remembered that Piper had said as much about his ancestor or grandfather or whichever Piper had built it. Said he was as nutty as a nougat bar. He wondered again if Rick had inherited that trait.

"Hmmph." Impatiently he downshifted, grinding the gears as he pulled close to the other cars, Piper's Celica and an older Ford pickup. He almost clipped the Celica when be pulled in next to it, even though the driveway in front of the garage was wide enough to hold six or seven cars parked close together. "Shitty driver, O'Keefe," he muttered. "Shitty."

A minute later he was contemplating the ugly door on the ugly house. As he knocked on it, he thought it looked like the entry to Quasimodo's closet. A dog barked. He knocked again. More barks. And knocked once more. Yippy little barks, closer now. *Poodles from hell,* he remembered as he started pounding. "Come on, Piper, put your dick away and answer the door!"

As he heard his own words, a chill ran down his spine. "Piper!" he called, angry both at himself and his friend. "Piper, open up!"

Within, the floor creaked beneath footsteps so slow, they hurt. Then a wicked-witch voice called out, "Who's there?"

"A friend of Rick's," he replied.

After a long moment of silence, the voice asked sharply, "What do you want?" The poodle yelped a sharp coda.

"To see Rick," he answered, totally pissed. Then he added, more diplomatically, "You must be his aunt Jade. He's told me *so* much about you. He adores you, dear, and I can't wait to meet you."

That did the trick. He could hear chains being removed, then a bolt slid and the big thumb latch clicked up and down. The door opened an inch or two, and an anxious pink dog nose poked out below. Above, a wicked-witch eye to match the voice peered at him. Then it asked, "What the fuck are you?"

"I'm a Vegas show girl, Jade, dear. Ricky's best friend." The door opened wider, barely. Two eyes. The old broad— not as old as he'd expected—was a tall one with puffy skin and full lips held pursed and coated under too much coral lipstick. She might've been a looker, way back when. Still could be if she did something with herself. Nice cheekbones.

"You one of Richard's girlfriends?" she asked suspiciously.

He loved that. "Wish I was," he told her. "But he just thinks of me as a . . . sibling . . ." He let his voice trail off wistfully.

Jade snorted. "What d'you want?"

Old bitch, he thought. He could imagine her skulking through the house with a meat cleaver in hand, but he smiled sweetly. "I'm here to see Rick."

"Why?"

With effort, he held his tongue. "Is he here?"

She harrumphed. "He's in the workshop."

"Could you direct me, dear?"

"Back of the garage. Crazy good-for-nothing boy, he is." She looked down at her dog, and her voice changed to a warm, cracking ooze. "He's a bad boy saying bad things about my wittle lovedottie. Calls him names."

Suddenly the poodle slipped out the door, barked once, then attached itself to Dakota's leg and began humping with a vengeance.

"Shit!" Dakota tried to shake the dog off. "Get off me, you perverted little shit!"

"Don't you talk to my wittle—"

"Get your wittle fucker off me!" he cried, kicking harder. The dog flew off, sailing straight back until it thudded against Jade's leg. Righting itself, it growled at Dakota. Dakota curled his lip and growled right back.

"How dare you!"

Before Dakota could form the perfect response, Jade Ewebean slammed the door in his face.

Clearing his throat, straightening his posture, and regaining his dignity, Dakota turned and walked back to the driveway and up to the garage. He followed the narrow sidewalk around it and suddenly realized that the building behind it, shadowed in trees, was enormous. He continued up the side. "Rick? Where are you? Piper?" he called, not too loudly. From within, he could hear metal on metal, hammering, a high screeching, more hammering. "Piper?" He came to a set of huge closed double doors, the size of garage doors, then saw a normal one, just beyond. The knob turned freely in his grasp. "Piper?" he called again, beginning to push the door open.

The hammering ceased. "Dakota?" Soft, surprised. Then, hopeful, "Dakota? Is that you?"

Heartened, O'Keefe shoved the door the rest of the way. "Piper! My Lord! What in the world are you doing in here?"

Rick stood on a stepladder in front of a large metal *thing*. He wore a welder's mask over his face and hair, tight Levi's, and no shirt. His compact body was looking good, pale skin sheened with sweat, pecs and biceps carved with the weight of the acetelyne torch he held. It was phallic as hell.

"You oughta pose for *Playgirl*, Piper. You look good enough to eat."

"Get a new line, O'Keefe." Rick pushed back the mask, set the torch aside, and climbed off the ladder. "Is Shelly with you? Did she tell you anything else?"

"Piper . . ." he began, then stopped, riveted by the look on Rick's face. He saw the pain and didn't know what to say, saw the pain and knew the answer, and for a moment, was so ashamed of himself for ever doubting Piper's honor or motives that he couldn't look him in the eye. *But if he's crazy,* he reminded himself roughly, *he could be guilty . . . If he's crazy, he could be his own evil twin.*

"Shelly's okay," he said. "She's fine."

Rick took the helmet off and hung it on a hook above a long workbench. "Well, where is she?" he asked eagerly. "Did you drop her off or is she in your car?" He headed toward the door.

Dakota put his hand out and stopped Rick before he could pass. "She's fine, but she's not here."

"When I get my hands on her, I'm going to . . . to hug her, then I'm going to strangle her, then I'm going to ground her until she's thirty . . ."

"I left her at her girlfriend's house. She'll be perfectly safe there. She's just fine. Now, Piper, calm down and tell me about this." He gestured at the metal thing. "What is it?"

"Can't you tell?"

Piper sounded disappointed, and Dakota, suddenly realizing that maybe this was something more than a heap of scrap metal, really looked at it for the first time. "My God, Piper," he blurted. "It's art, isn't it!"

He circled it. "It's a tepee. No? A pyramid?"

"I guess it does look like a pyramid at this point," Rick said. "It's going to be a windmill for Don Quixote. I was climbing the walls waiting for you to show up. I couldn't just sit still and I couldn't concentrate on the column. So here I am."

"It's *so* bizarre," Dakota said, pointing at the pyramid. "Where'd you learn to do this?"

"My dad built cars. He let me play with the scraps."

"I saw Quixote as I pulled up. He's wonderful. I think you should do a whole series of horses and riders. You should sculpt Wilbur and Mr. Ed next. 'Willlbur,' he whinnied, 'what're you doin' back there, Willlbur? Carol's gonna be jealous!' " He saw by the look on Piper's face that he

wasn't improving his frame of mind. "Well, I love your Quixote," he blithered. "Most people have pink flamingos, or
little dwarves."

Rick just stared at him, the ghost of a smile etched in his
eyes, tilting the corners of his mouth. Dakota had an obscene
thought and the good sense to keep it to himself. "We need
to talk about Shelly."

"I'm listening."

"No. We need to sit and talk. There's some weird shit
going on, and we need to figure out where it's coming from"

"You want to go in the house or something?"

"No, Jade hates me. But her poodle loves me. It tried to
fuck me, but it didn't have a condom, so I kicked it." He
smiled coyly. "I was thinking we might go to a drinking
establishment, but I guess you can't leave Cody with the
wicked witch in there?"

"Lord, no! He's with Carmen. They're working on his
Halloween costume." He didn't look very happy about that,
then his expression changed. "Jesus, Dakota. I wouldn't
leave a juvenile delinquent with Jade!"

"Not that I blame you, but you *really* don't like her, do
you?"

"No, I *really* don't. She's as bad as I remembered. Worse
maybe. Come on. There's an overpriced English pub oozing
atmosphere over on Via Pecado. Your sister likes it."

"Sounds great. Stupid street name, though."

"I guess you're not a Southwest native."

"Manhattan, hon."

Rick nodded sagely. "Come on. I'll get cleaned up and
let Carmen know we're leaving."

While Rick showered, Dakota had a short, gleeful reunion
with Cody, during which he promised to bunk in with him,
and met Carmen, whom he adored instantly, primarily because she told him he was gorgeous, and he knew sincerity
when he heard it. She gave him a nickel tour of the house,
and his only disappointment was that Jade's dead poodles
were not on display. The good news was that Jade was nowhere to be seen.

Within a half hour, he and Rick were in Briarwood Tavern, sipping from chill mugs of British ale in a dark corner of an authentically sawdusted room while a couple guys who looked like redneck college grads—if there was such a thing—threw darts badly, at a board just close enough for discomfort.

Vapor curled up from Rick's mug. "What about my daughter? Is she all right? Why won't she come home?'

"She's fine. Now, slow down. This is weird, okay?"

"What's weird?" Piper asked sharply. "You keep saying 'weird.' Has something happened?"

"No. Yes. I don't know."

"Jesus Christ, would you explain already?"

"If you'll shut up for a minute, I will," Dakota said testily. "She says . . . she says she's afraid of you, Piper."

Rick sputtered, sending beer drops spraying. "Afraid of *me?* For God's sake, why?"

"Look, I don't know why or how, but she thinks . . . well, she thinks . . ."

"Just spit it out, for Christ's sake!"

The dart boys looked, and Dakota smiled at them. "Keep your voice down, Piper. If you don't, I won't tell you."

"Okay, okay."

"Promise?"

"Yeah, yeah, I promise. What the hell is going on?"

"That's what I want to know," Dakota said, his voice low and intense. "She says—this is really hard, Rick. She was so upset."

"Go on," Piper said grimly.

Dakota nodded. "Okay. Don't get all excited when I tell you."

Piper nodded impatiently.

"Don't have a shit hemorrhage—"

"Tell me," he growled.

Dakota swallowed. "Shelly believes you attacked her."

"What?"

"Be quiet. She says you tried to rape her."

"Rape her?"

"Shhhh! Shut the hell up."

Piper lowered his voice a tad. "Rape her? My own daughter says *I* tried to rape her?"

"She says she woke up sometime during the night and found you on top of her and that when she fought you, you socked her in the head."

"Enough." Rick slammed his mug down, and beer sloshed across the table. "I've heard enough."

The dart boys gave them another glance, then one shrugged and said something, no doubt derogatory.

"Look, Piper. I know you're upset, but we have to figure out what's wrong, what *really* happened to her."

"Yeah. Oh, Lord, Dakota." He ran his fingers through his hair, the expression on his face so boyish and confounded that Dakota had to resist the urge to take his hand. "She was happy. She told me she liked it here, and then all of a sudden she splits and says—Oh Lord. I'd never, *never*— "

"I know, Ricky. And she does, too, deep inside, but something scared the shit out of her." He paused. "You're white as the driven, Piper."

"My brother's voice," Piper said slowly. "Sometimes I hear old memories. I just heard one. My brother's voice, singing, 'Lay, lay, roll in the hay.' He sang that about Evangeline. That was Jade and Howard's daughter, Evangeline. He claimed they did it in the hay a lot. Old dirty hay that had been in the garage for years."

My brother's voice, Dakota thought. Considering that they had the same voice, the remark seemed odd. "Who did it in the hay?"

"Robin and Evangeline. He liked to screw her. He liked to screw Aunt Jade too. And he talked in rhymes. 'Jade got made, I made Jade. Evangeline lying, lying for me. Wheee,' " he said dryly. "Evangeline was a hard one for him to rhyme. But not to screw." He downed his ale. "He— my brother, my twin—he would have raped his own daughter, just as surely as he raped his aunt and cousin."

"That may be, but you're not your brother."

"I hope not."

"Don't go getting esoteric on me, Piper." Dakota paused. "It doesn't sound like he actually raped them, does it?"

"No. I doubt it. I think he seduced them. He was sort of a Svengali type. All charm."

"Or maybe it was just the freak angle?"

"What?"

"You know. Amputee lust, do it with dwarves, like Snow White. Necrophilia with Sleeping Beauty. Swamp Thing and his lady love. Freaks are very popular," he added. "You wouldn't believe the offers I get. There are a lot of fucked-up people out there."

"You ought to know," Piper added dryly.

"At least *I* admit it," he said, motioning the bartender for another round.

Rick stared at him. "What are you implying?"

"You know exactly what I mean. You're fucked up as hell. You gotta get over this brother thing; you're letting him run your life even though he's been dead for years. You're apologizing for what he did. And I think you're letting Jade run you into the ground."

"No, I'm not."

"The fact that she's in that house speaks volumes. It's your house. I think she's probably behind your problem with Shelly. Get her out of your house, Piper."

"I'm thinking about it. Did Shelly say something about her?"

"Not much. She said you act funny around the old douche-bag, something like that. She was so busy being freaked out over the other thing that I didn't hear much else."

The fresh ale arrived. "Thanks, hon," Dakota said to the barman, who looked O'Keefe up and down, trying to figure out just what he was talking to. He was cute, and Dakota wished he had his blond wig and makeup on. "Look, Piper," he said after the man walked away. "Think. What could have happened to Shelly? A nightmare wouldn't hit her."

"I don't know. I really don't. I went through the house and didn't find anything unlocked or broken. Jade's the only answer, but still, that's not really good enough."

"Jade," Dakota repeated. "It must be."

"I don't think so," Rick said, a hint of finality in his voice. "It's too farfetched. God, this whole thing gives me the creeps." He drank more beer. "You know, two weeks ago I even went through the house and nailed all the hidden passages closed. Shelly keeps her door locked, so I just don't see how—"

"Secret passages?"

Rick nodded. "Robin used to use them to travel all over the house."

"I should've known that mausoleum has secret passages."

"Of course. And Robin loved them. He showed up all over the place. Including on top of me."

Dakota raised his eyebrows. "To frighten, not rape. He put a pillow over my face and tried to smother me on a number of occasions. There's a mark in the wall in Cody's room where he came after me with a knife."

"My God, Piper! You told me he was disgusting, but you didn't say he was murderous." Behind the look of concern he'd plastered on his face, the possibilities horrified him. "Why didn't your parents stop him?"

"Because they didn't know. Robin convinced me that they'd send me to the funny farm if I told. I moved into Carmen's old room when she got married. She gave me a key to the door lock and showed me that she'd nailed the passage to her room closed. That's Shelly's room now."

Carmen, Dakota realized, could verify some of this, if necessary. He smiled at Rick. "You're getting drunk. Let's order some fish and chips."

"Good idea."

"Now, tell me all about your brother."

Two hours passed, dinner was eaten, more ale drunk, and Dakota got further into Piper's mysterious mind than ever before. That was part of the reason he liked the guy so well— you couldn't read him. Piper sat there all suave and handsome and charming in spite of the tenseness he couldn't hide. Piper, Dakota decided, was glib, a good daddy, probably a good lover, sincere as hell, and contained not a drop of snake oil. But there was something else there, hiding just below the surface, that forever eluded Dakota, a secret of some sort. He suspected now that it had to do with the abuse he'd suffered at the hands of his brother. Piper had told him about everything from finding Jade's poodle in his shower to the details of Delia's death and the guilt he felt over it. He'd talked about his wife, Laura, for the first time. She'd been run down by a drunk while on her way to meet Rick for lunch, and he obviously felt responsibility for her death too.

He confessed then that he was falling in love with Audrey and that he was afraid he'd hurt her, too. Dakota, warmly drunk, felt one moment of anxiety before tears sprang to his eyes. He wished he knew how to take Rick Piper's pain away, how to make him understand that Laura's and Delia's deaths weren't his fault.

"Dakota?" Rick said. "Are you crying?"

Dakota wiped a tear from his cheek. "Indulging in romance, Piper. It must be lonely in there."

"Huh?"

"In you."

"No."

"Oh, shut up and listen." He reached across the table and patted Rick's hand before he could draw it away. "You need love, Piper. Don't be afraid."

"I'm flattered, but I'm not into—"

"No, you moron, not me. My sister. She's nuts about you. You are *so* fucked up, Piper. You're so afraid." Even as he said it, he wondered if he meant it. Everything Rick had told him tonight could mean he was a dangerous lunatic who only *thought* he was the victim. He could be throwing his sister to a maniac. Still, Dakota's intuition told him that, no matter how farfetched Piper's stories were, the man was okay, and when push came to shove, Dakota always listened to his intuition.

43

Back at the house, Audrey, just back from her convention, joined them for the evening. Rick insisted on telling her the details about Shelly, and for that, Dakota was glad. He watched his sister carefully, but she showed no signs of mistrusting Rick, only support and puzzlement.

Around eleven, Jade's almost nightly moaning and groaning started up, and to Dakota's disappointment, Rick wouldn't stay for the show, but took them out on the front porch to talk. Rick kept looking out toward the oak tree, trying hard to hide his nervousness.

"I wouldn't have believed it if I hadn't heard it myself," Dakota said. "Maybe she really does have something to do with Shelly's scare, Piper. She's a nympho. A psycho nympho. Hey," he added suddenly, "when you shut off all those secret passages, did you do the ones in her rooms too?"

"No, I didn't, but I guess I should. I'll get Carmen to take her somewhere, and do it." He frowned. "But even if she did have something to do with it, how'd she manage to look like me?"

"I don't know, I just think she might be involved. She's jealous as hell of Shelly, isn't she? She picks on her."

"She picks on everyone."

"Rick," Audrey said. "Duane—I mean Dakota—has a point." She glanced toward the old oak. "Look at those leaves blow. At this rate, the trees will be bare in no time."

"Naked trees," Dakota purred. "How totally kinky. Piper, are there any jack-offs there?"

"Yes," he said slowly. "Lots of them."

"I wish I could see them," Dakota said softly.

Rick looked at him in amazement. "You really mean that, don't you?"

"Yes" He sniffed. "I feel deprived."

"Me, too," Audrey said. Rick shook his head. "I can't believe what I'm hearing."

"Where's Quint?" Dakota suddenly asked. "You said he can see them, too?"

Rick nodded. "Come on inside."

Jade's orgasms were over, thank God. They were hilarious on one hand, Dakota had decided, but horrifying on the other.

"I'll be right back." Rick left them in the living room and headed up the stairs. When he returned a few minutes later, he held his cat—wearing a leash and collar—in his arms. "Quint's been staying at Carmen's since the poodle incident, but she and Hector were going out tonight, so I brought him back early and locked him in my room."

He carried the cat to the covered picture window. "Quint can see them," he explained. Gently but firmly, he gripped the loose skin at the cat's neck with one hand and trapped his body against him, holding the back legs loosely with the other. The cat faced the stairwell.

Rick smiled grimly. "He doesn't like them at all. Open the drapes, please, Audrey."

She did.

"Now, watch the cat," Rick ordered, turning the feline to face the window.

Quint's eyes grew huge, then his ears went flat back and the fur ridged up on his back. Dakota shivered; the cat was scared shitless. A low growl started in its throat, rose to a shriek, and suddenly the animal exploded in Rick's arms, kicking and hissing and biting. One front leg shot free, and claws raked across Rick's cheek. He let go of the cat, and it flopped on the floor in its panic, righted itself, and raced up the stairs, dragging its leash as it disappeared in the direction of Rick's room.

Rick gingerly patted his cheek. "A lot of good the leash did. Do you believe me now?"

"That was incredible," Audrey said.

"Jesus Christ," Dakota breathed. "I've got goose bumps on my balls."

"Please answer my question," Rick said, even more softly.

"I believe you, Piper."

The color had drained from Audrey's face. "Me too. Rick? Your cheek's bleeding—"

"It's okay," he interrupted. "Excuse me. I have to take care of the cat. I'll be right back." He turned and went up the stairs.

Dakota looked at Audrey. "I don't know what the fuck is going on here."

"Me either. You want to come back to my place tonight? You can have the couch."

"No. I promised Cody I'd bunk with him. Besides, I want to keep an eye on things. Until we have an explanation, you know."

Her eyes were sad. "He didn't do what Shelly says he did. He's not capable of it. He's the most gentle man in the world."

"He said he almost killed his brother once."

"Almost. He also said he realized what he was doing and stopped."

"Audrey, be careful. I don't want to think he did it, and my instincts don't believe it, but I'm afraid that could be because he's not stable . . ."

She opened her mouth, but he shushed her.

"I think that if he is responsible, he isn't *responsible,* you know what I mean?"

She shook her head no.

"If he did do it, I don't think he knows he did it. Maybe he's got a split personality or something. All that brother stuff."

Audrey looked stricken. "I don't believe it."

"Then let's find proof."

Audrey nodded. "If you're wondering if Robin existed, I can tell you that he did. Rick showed me some photos taken before their parents died. And Carmen talked about him too. He was horrible. He died in a fire. Carmen has the newspaper clipping. I saw it."

"Christ, I'm glad to hear that. Audrey, I *don't* think he did anything. I'm just playing devil's advocate."

"I know, Duane. You're good at that."

"Besides, you're my sister. What kind of brother would I be if I didn't worry about you?"

Audrey stood on her tiptoes and kissed his cheek. "I know, and I appreciate you very much."

"Boy, was that cat pissed," Rick said as he came back into the room. "Supremely pissed." He had washed the claw marks, and they stood out blatantly against his pale skin. "But I think he's okay now."

"Good. We won't put him through that again." Audrey glanced out the window. "I'm exhausted. I'm going home to bed. Will you fellas see me out?"

They walked her to her car and watched until she was out on the street. Dakota shivered, watching the leaves in the grass. "You know, Piper, it's scary knowing those jack-offs are there and not being able to see them."

"In this case, what you can't see won't hurt you," Rick said dryly. "Believe me, if I could trade you eyes, I would."

"Let's go in."

"Yeah." They went inside, and Rick locked the door, then pulled the drapes closed. "Tomorrow night is the dangerous night, Dakota. Halloween."

"Shelly's going to a party?"

"The overnight," Rick said. "I hope to hell we know what happened before then, but either way, she won't be here."

"What about Cody?"

"Audrey and I were planning on taking Cody trick-or-treating, very early. Do you want to come?"

"Yes." He grinned. "I brought a costume. I love dressing up for Halloween."

"You just love dressing up."

Dakota gave him a shit-eating grin. "Do you have any lines on parties?"

"No. We're coming back before full dark and staying in, where it's safe." He hesitated. "We're planning on watching for Big Jack." He hesitated, obviously trying to make light of something that was deadly serious to him. "If we both see him, we'll know I'm not a raving lunatic."

"It's Big Jack night. If I stick around, do I get to see him, too?"

"I hope so. I'd like you both to see him. That would make me feel . . . less weird." Yawning, he checked his watch. "Let's get some sleep."

A few minutes later, Dakota entered the upstairs bathroom to brush his teeth, then stripped to shorts and T-shirt before quietly letting himself into Cody's room. The boy was fast asleep on the race-car bed by the window. Dakota eased his six-foot-four-inch frame onto the old twin bed near the door. His legs hung over the end, and he knew this wasn't going to be much fun.

He lay quietly on the bed, unable to sleep, his brain going a hundred miles an hour, asking himself questions he had no answers for. As he was about to give up and go take a sleeping pill, he heard a scratching noise emanating from somewhere near the closets. "Cody, Cody!" whispered a voice.

Across the room, the boy sat up.

"Cody!" the voice whispered again.

"Hi, Bob," the little boy said.

"Cody, Cody, let's hit the roady!"

The boy giggled, then shoved his hand over his mouth, looking toward Dakota, who studiously feigned sleep. Quietly, Cody got out of bed and approached the closet. As he opened the door and stepped in, Dakota could hear him giggling. There was a funny sliding sound and the giggling grew faint, then disappeared altogether.

Rising, Dakota turned on the overhead light and crossed to the closet as quietly as he could.

He looked inside.

Cody wasn't there.

A half dozen nails, some slightly bent, were scattered on the floor. He saw empty nail holes around a two-and-a-half-foot square on the wall.

"Shit." With a whole new load of goose bumps rising on his balls, Dakota went to tell Rick.

44

"Piper! Open up!"

Dakota's voice cut through Rick's nightmare, and the pounding on his bedroom door brought him bolt upright. "Hang on," he grunted, extracting Quint's claws from his forearm.

"Piper!"

"Shut up, you're scaring the cat!" The feline suddenly raced painfully across his bare chest and thumped to the floor, heading for the safety of the headboard.

"Hurry up!" Dakota's voice was lower, but he rattled the hell out of the doorknob.

Rick's feet hit the floor, and a moment later, he unlocked the door. Dakota pushed his way inside,

"Christ, O'Keefe," Rick said, shutting the door.

"What is it with you and locks?" Dakota said. "Listen. You know how you can see those greenjacks?"

"Yes."

"Well, I just heard Bob the Invisible Friend."

"What?"

"You heard me. He called Cody's name, Cody answered him, then walked into the closet."

"What?" Rick listened to Dakota's words, hardly able to comprehend what he was hearing. "Cody!" He started for the door, but Dakota grabbed his arm.

"Rick, wait. Cody's not there."

"The passages are blocked; he *has* to be there!"

"Calm down and listen to me. The nails have been driven out from the inside."

"That's impossible!" He tried vainly to pull free of Dakota.

"It must be Jade, Rick," Dakota said. He was breathing fast now, catching Rick's fear. "It has to be Jade. You're here and . . ."

"And what?" Rick asked, his head beginning to throb.

Dakota stared hard at him. "And you're here."

"You mean you thought that *I* might be Bob? That I tried to assault my own daughter?" Furious, he yanked free of O'Keefe and glared at him. "I thought you were supposed to be my friend! You son of a bitch!"

"Rick, you're my best friend and I believe you, but you've been under a lot of stress and, shit, if you were in my place, you'd have to make sure, too."

Stonily Rick nodded. "Well, then, is there anything else I can do to prove to you that I'm not skulking around scaring my children at night? Do you want me to write it in blood?"

"Don't be sarcastic, Piper. You'll just have to apologize to me later, after you've had time to think."

Rick didn't know whether he wanted to cry or commit murder. "You won't tell me where Shelly is because you're not sure I'm not guilty. That's it, isn't it?"

Dakota drew himself to his full towering height and crossed his arms. "We don't have time for bullshit. Yes, Rick, that's right. I don't think you're guilty, but I can't take a chance on Shelly's safety. You'd do the same."

"You fucking bastard." Rick felt his body tense, imagined his hands around O'Keefe's throat. "You fucking—"

"Piper, listen. What if somebody assaulted Cody while I was watching him for you? Wouldn't you be worried about leaving him with me even though you didn't really think I did it? My sexuality is a little strange. Wouldn't you think that maybe, just maybe, I'd branched out into pederasty? You'd worry, wouldn't you? Even though I'm your closest friend, you'd worry."

Fury gave way to grudging understanding, and Rick nodded. 'You've made your point. I have no right to be angry with you for looking out for my kids. I'm sorry." He felt beaten. "God knows, with the stories I've told you about my childhood, you must think I'm completely nuts."

"No. To be blunt, it's a possibility—as you yourself say—but I don't think so. Frankly, I happen to believe you, Piper."

"Thanks. But what do we do now?" Rick asked dully.

"Check passages?"

"This place is a honeycomb. We'd never find him from the inside. Also, you'd never fit, and I'd be a tight squeeze in most of them."

"So let's see if any other ones are missing nails. Where's the one in this room?"

He picked up his flashlight and handed it to Dakota. "In here." He led O'Keefe into the dressing room and pointed. "Look in that cabinet."

Dakota opened the doors, then got down on his hands and knees, shining the light inside. He gasped, pulling back so quickly that he hit the back of his head. He stood up, his eyes boring into Rick's with an intensity he'd never seen before. "We have problems, my friend," he said, his voice shaking.

"The nails are gone?" he asked, thinking, *and proof of my innocence.*

"For a start. Take a look."

Dumbly Rick took the light and squatted. "Dear God," he heard himself say. "Oh, dear God."

Within the cabinet, among the nails, was the filleting knife and Jade's poodle, which lay in a pool of its own blood. Its mouth was taped shut and the hind legs were dismembered and lying several inches from the rest of its body.

"Dear God." Blindly Rick stood and rushed into the bathroom, where he hugged the toilet bowl, violently ill.

Dakota said nothing until Rick had brushed his teeth and splashed his face with water. Then, firmly, he placed his hand on Rick's shoulder. "The dog's body is still warm," he said, his voice cool and businesslike. "We'd better find Cody."

"Yes." Rick walked past Dakota and picked up the phone

"Who are you calling?"

"Carmen. She'll help."

Dakota nodded. "I'm going to get my shoes. Back in a flash."

45

Carmen stood with Dakota, Hector, and Ricky in Cody's
room and stared into the passage within the closet. They'd
called his name for fifteen minutes, but there was no reply,
and now there was talk of going inside the walls to look for
him. Only Rick and Hector were small enough to fit into
the passage, and Carmen did not want either of them to go
in, though Hector appeared more than willing.

"No," she told him. "It's not good to go in there. Something bad will happen."

"All the more reason to go after him," Hector insisted.

"Cody could be anywhere," she said. "Those passages
run all over the house. If we found him, it would be by sheer
luck."

Ricky, who looked pale and ill, nodded. "I should go.
I've been in them before." Nervously he ran his fingers
through his tousled hair. "God, who else is in there?"

"It's a spirit," Carmen said.

"I'll bet it's a kid," Dakota cut in quickly. "Maybe a friend
from school? An older kid. You know, people, he knew exactly what he was doing—he's obviously been in there before—and whoever it was didn't know I heard him, so there's
no reason to think that he won't come back out sooner or
later."

"Dakota has a point," Hector said.

"Yes," Rick agreed. "Except tomorrow's Halloween."

"Here's what we're going to do," Carmen said abruptly "Hector, you go clean up the mess in Ricky's room—"

"Should we leave it for the police?" Dakota asked.

"We don't need police," she said with finality. "Afte that, Hector, please take the cat and put him back at ou house. Make sure you cover his eyes outside so he doesn' see those jacks. Then come back here."

Hector nodded silently, leaving her to eye Ricky and Da kota. "Did either of you check on Jade?" she asked.

They shook their heads.

She pulled a key from her pocket. "Let's go." She bustle toward the stairs, Dakota and Ricky following. "If he's no with her, we'll keep looking until we find him."

Instead of knocking on Jade's door, she inserted the ke in the lock and turned it silently. The door opened on th shadowed room. Putting her finger to her lips to signal si lence, she led them into Jade's living room, crossing hersel as she always did when she saw the murky forms of th stuffed dogs. They seemed to watch her as she move through the room. She paused to whisper to Ricky. "Yo know where the openings are?"

He nodded.

"Check them. Check for dust." Without being told, Da kota remained with his friend. That pleased Carmen, be cause Ricky looked too close to panic to be left alone, an she feared he might fall apart completely. She watched hin tiptoe toward a coat closet that contained an opening, the let herself into Jade's bedroom. The old woman snored i her bed, blissfully unaware that her poodle had been killed The one that died a couple months ago was perched on th night table, fresh from the taxidermist, eternally licking it privates. Carmen crossed herself again, then checked Jade' closet.

Nothing blocked the opening. Jade continued to snore a Carmen pushed the latch. The panel slid open silently, letting cool, stale air waft over her face and making the hairs o her arms and neck stand on end. Involuntarily she shivered then put one hand inside the opening and wiped it across the floor before letting it shut.

Quietly she left the bedroom, then waited for Ricky to finish up. Afterward, she led them out of Jade's quarters, locking the door behind them.

In the living room light, she examined her fingers. No dust. "Ricky? Was there dust?"

"In the one in the closet," he said, wiping his fingers on his sweatpants. "But not in the one by the back stairs."

They heard the back door open, and a moment later, Hector came in. "Everything's taken care of."

"Quint's at your place?" Rick asked.

"Yes. Boy, that cat didn't like it outside." He held up his arm, displaying scratch marks. "He's okay now." He looked at Dakota. "Shelly wants to talk to you," he said.

"Shelly's here?" Ricky interrupted hopefully.

"No. She's on the phone." He turned back to Dakota. "She only wants to talk to you. I told her to call over here, but she wouldn't do it. The front door's not locked; you can go on over."

Dakota touched Ricky on the shoulder. "I'll be right back. Don't worry."

Carmen watched Ricky as Dakota left, and her heart ached for him, he looked so stricken. "Hector," she ordered. "You check the rest of the passage openings down here. If they're open, call Cody." She turned to Ricky. "You and I will check the upstairs. Come on." She grabbed his hand and began to lead him toward the staircase. "We'll find him right away.

She hoped she spoke the truth.

46

Numbly following Carmen into Shelly's room, Rick felt as if he were drowning. He couldn't seem to think anymore, couldn't comprehend what was going on around him. Vaguely humiliated, knowing that she was treating him like a child, coddling him, leading him, he didn't have the strength to take over the search for his son, let alone protest, though he knew he should.

At least he hadn't told Carmen the reason Shelly had run away. Then he'd get the same pitying and nervous questioning glances from her that Dakota had given him since he'd arrived. Rick didn't think he could stand that.

They'll think you're crazy and send you away.

"Shut up," he whispered.

"What?" Carmen looked at him.

"Nothing. Nothing."

"I remember the day I nailed this one shut," she said, her hand on the closet doorknob. "I heard noises in here one night. It scared me so much, I stuck a chair under the knob. The next morning, I looked inside and found one of my dresses was on the floor. It was damp." She shook her head. "I didn't know what was on it, I just threw it away. Then I got a hammer and drove twenty-four nails into the panel. I counted every one."

She glanced at him as she opened the closet door. "Ricky?"

He froze. "Yes?"

"Why did Shelly run away?"

He didn't want to answer, but her expression demanded it. "She says someone attacked her." That was enough truth for now.

"Do you believe her, Ricky?"

"Yes." *I didn't, I couldn't have.*

"So do I. Look." She stepped aside so that he could see inside the closet. Even without a flashlight, he could tell that the panel below Shelly's dresses and shirts had been tampered with. One corner was splintered, the nail next to it bent and only halfway removed. More nails littered the floor. A spray of dark spots that might be blood stained the floor. "I cleaned this room a week ago," she told him. "This wasn't like this then." She bent down and called, "Cody? You in there? Cody?"

"Piper!" Dakota's voice, not Cody's, jolted Rick. He spun toward the door.

"Up here!" Rick yelled.

Immediately he heard O'Keefe's heavy footfalls come up the stairs two at a time. *Seconds are passing,* he thought as he heard him running up the hall, *and they feel like hours.*

Dakota finally appeared in Shelly's doorway, windblown and breathless. He rested against the doorframe, leaning his head back, and took a deep breath. He exhaled noisily.

"What is it?" Rick demanded, impatient with O'Keefe's dramatics. "What did Shelly say?"

"Piper," he said, coming into the room. "Stick your tongue out."

"What?"

"Stick it out. Now."

"No."

In two broad steps Dakota reached him. "Why not? What are you hiding?" He glared down at him.

"I'm not hiding anything," Rick avowed angrily.

"Then stick out your tongue!"

"Why?"

Dakota reached out and grabbed the front of his T-shirt,

twisted it in his fingers, drawing Rick closer, pulling him
up onto his toes until they were nose to nose. Dakota's words
were precise and clipped. "I'll tell you after. Do it."

Rick glanced at Carmen for help, but she was watching
him almost as closely as Dakota. He moved his gaze back
to Dakota and, unable to read the expression in his friend's
eyes, slowly stuck his tongue out. Dakota studied it carefully.
After a long moment, his fingers slowly let go of Rick's
T-shirt. "Okay," he said softly. "I'm sorry."

Rick almost bit it as Dakota grabbed him in a fierce bear
hug, pulling him off the ground again in his enthusiasm.
Rick flailed, his breath cut off by O'Keefe's huge breasts.

Dakota let go. "Sorry. Oh, shit, Piper, when I saw that
dead dog in your room and that knife and all those loose
nails, I started to think—"

"You thought I was crazy," Rick said softly.

"Forgive me?"

"Why did my tongue change your mind?"

"Shelly. She remembered something. She bit the attacker's tongue." He grimaced. "She said she spit out a piece
of it. It's probably on the bed somewhere." So saying, he
crossed to the bed and pulled the sheet straight, examined
it, then did the same to the yellow blanket. "Aha," he said,
pointing at something. "Look at that!"

Rick approached, Carmen following. He leaned over and
saw a tiny red lump, no thicker than a dime.

"That's supposed to be a tongue?" Carmen asked doubtfully.

"The tip," Dakota said impatiently. "The tip."

Rick gingerly poked it with his finger. He couldn't tell
what the hell it was, but in spite of that, he felt a smile creep
across his lips. They knew he wasn't crazy. *You were wrong,
Robin, you bastard, you were wrong.*

"It's all dried up," Dakota was saying. "She took a nice
healthy hunk off the guy." He looked at Rick. "I'll bet we're
dealing with some sort of psycho high school kid with a
crush on Shelly."

If you tell, they'll think you're crazy.

No they won't, he told his brother's voice, *you lied.*

"Piper?"

Blinking, he looked at Dakota. "What?"

"I asked you a question."

"Ask me again."

"Has Shelly been getting any weird phone calls?"

"She has her own line." Rick tilted his head toward the phone on her dresser. "I don't know."

Dakota crossed to the phone and picked up the receiver. He turned his other hand, revealing a phone-number on his palm written in blue ink. He punched it in.

"Shelly?" he said a moment later. "It's okay." He paused, listening. "Yes, he's fine. Listen, do you have any weird guys asking you for dates or anything?" He listened again. "Any obscene phone calls?" He listened, then nodded. "Okay. Hang on." He extended the phone to Rick. "Your daughter wants to talk to you."

Rick's hand trembled as he took the phone. "Shelly."

"Daddy, I'm sorry," she cried.

"It's okay," he said, feeling strength flow back into him. "It's okay, honey."

"I didn't mean to, I mean I didn't really think you'd . . . That man just looked like you, he really did. I'm sorry, I'm so sorry."

"You did the right thing by going to Dakota. I'm just glad you're *safe.*" Sudden fear rushed back into him at those words. "Shel, what do you know about Bob?"

"Cody's pretend friend?" She was silent a moment. "Nothing, really," she said finally. "Why?"

"He's real. He's probably your attacker." Quickly he told her the details.

"Daddy, he looked just like you!"

It can't be—"Shel, are you at Leanne's?"

"Yes. Do you want me to come home?"

"No, kiddo, I want you to stay right where you are. In the morning you can come and get your costume for the party."

"Well, okay," she said doubtfully.

"Thanks, Shel."

"Dad, have you called the police?"

"Not yet, but if we don't find him soon, we will. I'll call you as soon as he turns up."

"I love you, Dad."

"I love you, too. Good night."

He hung up, surreptitiously wiping his eyes before turning to Carmen and Dakota. "Maybe we should call the police."

"Daddy!" Cody's voice carried up the stairwell. Then Hector called out, "I found him!" Rick looked at Dakota, then at Carmen, who was busy shoving a chair under the closed closet doorknob. Without a word, he raced downstairs. Hector and Cody stood in the living room.

"Hector, where was he?" he asked, scooping the smiling child into his arms.

"In the workshop." Hector shook his head. "I went out there to get some wood screws. You didn't need to nail those panels; the levers lock from the outside. Nobody can break through except with a drill if you do that."

Now he tells me. "Cody, what were you doing in the workshop?"

"Bob took me there."

He glanced back as Dakota and Carmen joined them. "How? Did you go outside?"

The little boy shook his head. "Uh-uh. We went in a tunnel."

God, Rick thought, *we're living in an ant farm.* He hadn't even known there was a tunnel to the workshop. *It must go underground,* he thought. "You know the rats in the icky car in the workshop, Daddy?"

"Yes?"

Cody giggled. "It wasn't rats. It was Bob. He was watchin' you."

Rick's stomach knotted itself up, and he took the boy to the couch, set him on it, and knelt in front of him. "Cody? I have to ask you some questions, and I want you to answer the best you can, okay?"

"Okay, Daddy."

"What do you and Bob do at night?"

Cody hesitated, looking at his feet.

"You can tell me, Cody. I won't get mad, I promise."

"He just shows me all the secret places in the house."

"Is that all? Really?"

"Sometimes we sneak food and stuff." Cody finally met Rick's eyes. "I'm sorry."

"It's okay, son. What else do you do?"

"We go outside and play. Daddy?"

"What?"

"Promise you won't get mad?"

"I promise."

"Sometimes Bob likes to spy on people."

"On who?"

"Well, he said he watched Shelly get undressed. He wanted me to watch, too, but I wouldn't."

His stomach filled with lead. "I'm glad you wouldn't look." He glanced at Dakota, saw the loathing on his face. "Cody, is that all?"

"No." The child looked away again.

"What else?"

He didn't answer.

"Did he spy on me, too?"

"Uh-huh," he said, not looking up.

"It's all right. Just say it."

"He likes to watch when you and Audrey have sleep-overs."

Rick was careful not to look at Dakota. "Do you know Bob's whole name, Cody?"

"Uh-huh. But he told me I couldn't tell or he'd hurt you." He met Rick's eyes. "I don't want him to hurt you, Daddy."

"Are you afraid of him?" *It can't be,* he thought. *It's impossible.*

"I wasn't at first. But sometimes now. I don't think he likes you, Daddy."

A pervert was living in his house, corrupting his son, attacking his daughter. Watching everything they did, hearing everything they said. Anger gave Rick strength. He'd kill the son of a bitch, whoever he was. Whatever he was.

"He wanted me to tell you something, Daddy."

"What?" Rick could barely keep from shaking the boy to get his words out faster. "What does he want you to tell me?"

"Well, it's not nice. He called you a name."

"It's okay to tell me, Cody."

"You won't be mad?"

"No. I promise."

"Okay. He said, 'Happy Halloween, icky Ricky.' "

"Holy shit," he heard Dakota say somewhere behind him. Carmen crossed herself.

He couldn't believe it. He wouldn't. *It's some kind of trick.* Outside of the Zapatas and Jade, no one but the O'Keefes knew about that name. He swallowed. "Cody," he said in a strangled voice. "Does Bob have legs?"

"How'd you know? Do you know Bob?"

"Maybe."

"He walks on his hands, Daddy. He does neat tricks and he looks like you, except he's little."

Stunned, Rick stared at his son.

"Madre de Dios," Carmen whispered. "It's his ghost. I knew it."

"Tell me Bob's real name, Cody," Rick said numbly.

Cody shook his head. "He'll hurt you if I do."

"He won't know."

"Yes he will!" Cody spat the words, his fear obvious. "He's listening right now. He always listens. He knows everything you say, Daddy. He says you're crazy, Daddy!"

"Your father's not crazy," Carmen said firmly. She sat next to the child. "But Bob is."

Dakota squatted next to Rick. "Bob's a turkey, Cody," he said, the strain in his voice belying the lightness of his tone. "Gobble, gobble, gobble."

Cody almost laughed, then caught himself. "You shouldn't make fun of Bob. He gets mad."

"Well, where is he right now?" Dakota asked.

Cody shrugged. "I dunno. In the bookcase, probably. That's where he likes to listen from."

Rick glanced back, saw Hector doing something to the lever. "Well, if he's in there, he can't get out anymore."

"Yeah," Dakota added, then raised his voice "Hey, Bob, you're a turkey! Gobble, gobble!"

"Shhh!" Cody was scared now, really scared. "Don't make him mad! He'll hurt you."

"Like he hurt Jade's dog?" Rick asked.

"Uh-huh."

"Cody," Rick said. "Tell me his name, son.

Cody shook his head.

"Then I'm going to guess his name. You tell me when I'm right. Okay?"

Cody thought it over, then nodded once.

"Is his name Robin?"

Cody nodded and began to cry.

Carmen scooped him into her arms. "I'm taking him back to our house and putting him to bed. Dakota, did you lock the door after you used the phone?"

"Uh, I don't know."

She nodded brusquely. "Hector, come on. We've gotta make sure nobody's in our house." She looked at Rick and Dakota. "You two better come along. It's not safe here, not with the *espíritu* loose in the walls."

"It's not a ghost, Carmen. It tried to rape my daughter. It gave her a black eye."

"Ghosts can do that, Ricky." She stared hard at him. "Your brother's dead. He's buried up there in the cemetery. It's his ghost."

"It must be someone who looks like Robin," Dakota said, looking at Rick.

"Who has no legs?" Rick asked grimly. "Who walks on his hands and calls himself Robin, and me icky Ricky? That's too much coincidence for me."

"Robin's dead," Carmen insisted.

"Maybe my brother is," Rick said slowly. "But his body isn't. Take Cody, Carmen. We'll be along soon."

He waited until he heard the back door close, then turned to Dakota. "Are you up for a little visit to Santo Verde Cemetery?"

Dakota regarded him doubtfully. "What for?"

"To see what's in my brother's grave."

"Grave robbing?"

"No. Just looking."

"Jesus X. Christ, Piper. That's crazy."

He flinched at the dreaded word, then composed himself. "No, it's not. I have to know if he's really dead."

"You didn't see him at the funeral?"

"O'Keefe, I told you, he burned in a fire. It was closed casket."

"If he burned, how can you tell if it's him?"

"The bones," he said impatiently.

"I was afraid you'd say that. Look, Piper, can't this wait until morning? We could inquire at the office and—"

"And what? See if we can get a court order to check the grave?" Rick shook his head. "No way. His message was 'Happy Halloween.' Something's going to happen tomorrow. He has plans, and I have to make sure I know what I'm dealing with. We're going to the cemetery. Now."

"Look, Piper. There's an intruder in this house. No matter who he is, he's breaking the law. Let's call the cops."

"What are they going to do? Check every passage in the house? They'd be no match for someone who knows their way around there. They can't do squat."

"Well, we could go sleep at Carmen's, then, first thing in the morning, call the exterminator and have your house tented."

Rick smiled, momentarily tickled by the notion. "That's not a bad idea."

"Good, then it's settled."

"No, Dakota, it's not settled. Just think how bad that body would smell once it started rotting."

Dakota made a face. "You could move back to Vegas."

Rick studied his friend. Even an hour ago, he might have agreed to it, might have jumped at the thought, but there was something so foul and intrusive in the things Cody had told him, combined with the sudden knowledge that he had told and been judged sane, that he couldn't entertain the idea.

"I'm going out to the toolshed for a shovel. I'm going to the cemetery and I'm going to see what's buried in Robin's grave. You can come with me or not. Either way, I'm going."

Dakota gave him a sick grin. "You were easier to get along with when you weren't so macho, Piper."

"Are you coming or not?"

"What are friends for?" he said, and followed Rick to the shed.

Five minutes later, they walked from the house to Rick's car. The greenjacks were going wild, but Rick ignored them.

Five minutes of driving through swirling fog brought them to the cemetery. They'd parked on the lightless street behind it, then hoisted themselves over the wall. It proved easier than expected, especially since the moon had gone down now, and at two in the morning, no one was around to catch them.

Rick had never been here at night. Whereas he found the place soothing and serene in the daytime, the presence of the jacks—not nearly as many as at home, but enough to make him anxious—and the shadowy angles and orbs and crosses poking through the mist made him nervous. He had a second thought, and refused it: He'd finally found some courage, and he was damned if he was going to let go of it now.

They soon found the Piper plots. Rick glanced up at the statue of the piper. "How they hanging, Thomas?" he whispered, then, without allowing himself to think, he began to dig. Soon Dakota fell in alongside. The soil was surprisingly soft, blessedly soft, and before three-thirty, Rick's shovel thunked against wood.

At quarter to four, he sat in the grave on top of the bottom half of the coffin and brushed the dirt off the upper portion. Dakota peered down at him from above, his face a pale moon against the darkness. Rick felt for latches, found one, and worked it until it came undone in his hand. Still the casket wouldn't open. "Hand me the crowbar."

Silently Dakota passed it down.

He worked it along the edge. Suddenly it gave, letting stale air, smelling faintly of charcoal and nothing else, drift into his nostrils. "Turn on the flashlight," he told Dakota. A moment later, a shaky beam of light illuminated the coffin from above.

"Here goes." He pulled the lid up.

At first, the blackened bones contained within told him little. The explosion that had caused the carnival fire had been of tremendous force, and it was obvious that these bones had been close to the center of it. They were unidentifiable: part of a skull, a couple longer bones that might have been arms, and most of a rib cage and the spinal column, whose end he couldn't see. "Give me the light."

Dakota handed it down. Rick held his breath and bent over, shining the light under the lower half of the coffin. He peered below, his face uncomfortably close to the charred skeleton.

He saw an intact pelvis. One hip cavity was empty, but the other contained a ball joint. Following it down, he saw that the leg bone itself extended into the darkness of the casket, out of sight.

"Well?" Dakota hissed.

"Hip bone's connected to the thigh bone," Rick said. "This isn't Robin. They probably just put bones into caskets at random."

"So he's alive?"

"Probably. At least we have no proof that he's dead."

"It's no ghost, Carmen," Rick said an hour later. "He's almost certainly alive."

It was five-thirty in the morning, and he sat at Carmen's

kitchen table, dressed in Hector's robe. He'd already showered the graveyard dirt from his body, and now Dakota was
in the bathroom doing the same.

"Madre Dios," she said. "He's in the house, and Jade, she
knows, doesn't she? All these years, she's known." She
glared. *"Puta."*

"We don't know he's been here the whole time. Chances
are he hasn't been."

"Oh, I think he has. I always thought the ghost was there.
How could I be so stupid?"

"We went to the funeral, Carmen, we thought he was
dead. A ghost makes more sense." It felt good to do the
comforting for a change.

She shook her head. "I was stupid. I saw things. I always
thought Jade ate like a horse. Food disappeared in the night,
but I thought it was her."

Dakota came out of the bathroom dressed in one of Carmen's flannel nightgowns. It ended just above his knees.

"So what are you two talking about?"

"We're wondering if Robin's been living in the house ever
since his alleged death," Rick said sourly. A little voice in
the back of his mind congratulated him on continuing to
keep his door locked after his brother's "death."

Dakota leaned forward. "So do you think that every time
old Jade moans and groans, it's because your brother's sticking it to her?"

Carmen stood up. "I'm going back to bed."

Rick watched her go. "She doesn't like dirty talk."

Dakota ignored him. "So do you think he is?"

"Yes. Let's get some sleep." He gestured at the sofa bed
Carmen had made up for them.

"My dreams come true," Dakota said, batting his eyelashes.

"Try anything and I'll tell your sister on you."

After they lay down on the lumpy mattress, Rick stared
at the ceiling a long time, wishing sleep would come.

"Piper?"

"Hmm?"

"What are you thinking?"

"I'm thinking about my brother. After he changed, Robin became obsessed with leaving his mark on everything. He'd get into other people's clothes, my mother's makeup, the food. Remember, I told you he peed in the lemonade? He'd take my schoolbooks and jerk off on them—I caught him in the act once. After we were twelve or so, he masturbated on anything that moved. And laughed about it. He didn't care if I saw. He used everyone's toothbrushes. I kept mine locked in my room."

"What a fucker."

"Yes," Rick agreed. "His greatest pleasure came from the violation of other people's privacy."

"A rapist in every sense of the word."

"That's right." Memories flooded him, leaving a bitter taste in his mouth. "And now he's doing it again. To my son, my daughter, and to me. I'm going to stop him, Dakota, or die trying. I'm not running anymore. I'm going to take back what's mine."

47

October 31

"I feel like Roddy McDowell standing outside Hell House," Dakota O'Keefe said.

"I know what you mean." Rick raised his hand to shield his eyes from the noontime sun, bright and clear on this chill autumn day. "I don't think anything will happen for a few hours. Not until dark."

"I still think you should tent the place." Dakota smirked. "Exterminate the pests."

"I wish it was that easy." Rick shoved his hands in the pockets of his sweatpants. "Winter's coming."

Dakota nodded, hugging himself. Like Rick, he'd had to put his grave-robbing clothes back on—a pair of shorts, running shoes with no socks, and a sweatshirt, all filthy. "I'm freezing my nuts off. Hey, is the pool water warm yet?" He glanced across the lawn at the sparkling blue water. "That would help."

"No. We only finished filling it yesterday. It'll take days before it's warm enough. Listen, I have jackets upstairs. One's a humongous fleece job. It'll fit you." As he spoke, the cold wind cut through Rick's T-shirt, making him shiver.

"Well, we have to go in, right?"

"Right. It's okay, Carmen's already been inside."

"Then why don't we ask *her* to get the jackets?"

Rick rolled his eyes. "Are you chicken?" he asked, terribly pleased to be the one delivering the words instead of receiving them.

"I'm a hell of a lot more cold than I am scared, Piper." Dakota gave him a wobbly smile. "Let's go for it. Hell, let's get crazy and get an entire change of clothes."

"Good idea." As he unlocked the front door, Rick felt his nerves giving underneath his newfound bravado. *You can't back out now,* he told himself, *not after you called O'Keefe chicken.*

Nothing looked out of place as they moved through the living room. Beyond Jade's closed door, he could hear Maury Povich's voice blaring.

"Hector hasn't finished locking the openings up, has he?" Dakota asked when they reached the kitchen.

"I doubt it." Rick opened the refrigerator and withdrew a carton of milk. He stared at it a moment, then took it to the sink and poured it out.

"Piper? What the hell are you doing?"

"If my brother's really here, you don't want to drink this." Returning to the fridge, he took out a couple apples, examined them, then washed them thoroughly, just in case. He tossed one to Dakota. "Hector's been out in the yard all morning. I don't think he wants to be alone in here any more than we do. And I don't blame him."

"Piper, why don't we just call the cops?"

Rick sighed. "I told you, if someone doesn't want to be found in this house, they won't be found." As true as that was, there was more to it than that, but Rick kept it to himself because he knew O'Keefe would do his best to talk him out of it.

For a long hour at dawn, Rick had lain on the lumpy sofa bed pretending to be asleep while he thought about what he'd told Dakota: that he was going to take back what belonged to him.

When he'd said it, he'd been talking about more than his children, more than his house: He had also been talking about his self-respect. The time had come for him to battle the real monster and leave the windmills behind.

Rick had never stood up for himself, had never ceased to question his own worth. He'd known for years that his lack of fight stemmed from the insecurities that Robin had so carefully instilled in him so long ago, and even now, part of him screamed that if he took a stand, he'd be wrong and everyone would find out how totally inadequate he was.

All his life he had taken the path of least resistance, compromising, making nice, turning the other cheek. His powers of calm persuasion were so considerable that even back in elementary school he could use words to avoid showdowns with school bullies. As an adult, he used them to charm bosses and co-workers, even policemen who wanted to give him speeding tickets. His charm had never failed except where his brother was concerned, but there it had failed miserably, leaving him floundering and helpless to fight back. But now that all had to change.

Returning to Santo Verde and facing the past had been the first step in taking control of his own life. Getting through the last two days without cracking had been the next step. Then, last night, when Dakota and Audrey said they believed he saw the greenjacks and he realized they meant it, the first tingle of real confidence passed through him.

If he called the police now, perhaps they could do something: set a trap, stake out the house, he didn't know what. But chances were, as he told Dakota, they would fail. And if they didn't—if they caught Robin—Rick would again escape the confrontation he had avoided all his life, the final confrontation.

He knew that this was something he had to do on his own, and this morning he began to figure a way to get Carmen to leave for the night. All his life she had been his crutch, and he knew that her presence here tonight might well bring out his old weaknesses. He couldn't take that chance. Instinctively he knew that if he met the confrontation head-on, faced it on his own, with nothing to rely upon but himself, and if he succeeded in overcoming it, he would have control of his own destiny for the first time in his life and would no longer be a prisoner of his own cowardice. He'd been handed a second chance.

And that was something he couldn't explain to Dakota, who lived for confrontations and drama. He would never comprehend how important it was for Rick to fight this battle alone.

"I'm going upstairs," he told Dakota, who had sat down in a kitchen chair. "Do you want your suitcase? It might be a good idea to take some things over to Carmen's for the night." He put his hand on the back stairs rail.

Dakota tossed his apple core in the trash can. "I'll come with you."

The atmosphere in the second-floor hallway seemed as murky as the light filtering in through the windows of the few rooms with open doors. Rick pushed the door to Cody's room wide without allowing himself to indulge the goose bumps rising on his arms.

The closet door stood wide open. Rick saw the closed panel, with the holes where the nails had been, but he ignored it, taking Cody's jacket and the Halloween costume Carmen had helped him make from the hangers. He laid the clothes on his son's bed, then closed the door, using Cody's wooden desk chair to secure the knob.

Across the room, Dakota had hurriedly changed into jeans and a clean shirt, and was now gathering his things and stuffing them in his suitcase. Rick opened Cody's drawers, took underwear, socks, pants, a shirt, and a sweater out, then took the boy's backpack and folded the items and placed them inside it. The costume went on top. A red cape and shorts and blue leotard with a big red *S* sewn on. Rick approved, half wishing he had one just like it.

"Ready?" he asked Dakota.

"Ready."

He went to Shelly's room and repeated the process, then looked around, curious to see if anything had been disturbed. Nothing had. The chair still blocked the closet door, the bed with the spray of bloodstains and the minuscule piece of dried flesh hadn't been touched.

Maybe he's gone, Rick thought. *Maybe it never happened.* His confidence declined the tiniest bit. "Let's get my stuff," he said, heading out the door. Dakota followed quickly.

It was the same here. He extracted the coat for Dakota and another for himself and threw them on the bed. Barely glancing at the closet cabinet in the dressing room, he swiftly changed into fresh clothes, jeans, and a flannel shirt. "Almost done," he called to Dakota, who stood peering out the window onto the orchard below.

A moment later, he'd gathered his toiletries and a brown cable-knit sweater.

Dakota looked at him. "Can we go now?"

"One more stop. I want my laptop. Come on."

The study door was closed, and as he opened it, Rick was surprised to see that the little computer was open and turned on. He had left it plugged in to recharge, he remembered, but as he stared at the starburst screen-saver pattern on the screen, he was fairly sure he hadn't forgotten to turn it off yesterday—or was it the day before? He never forgot. *But the last couple days haven't exactly been normal. You could've forgotten.*

"What's wrong?" Dakota asked from behind.

"Nothing," Rick replied, handing his belongings to O'Keefe. Slowly he walked across the room to the desk. "I just don't remember leaving this on."

If Dakota hadn't been waiting for him, he would have pulled the desk chair out and sat down to check the contents of his article files. As it was, he leaned across the massive desk chair and touched one key, just so that he could make sure everything looked okay on the screen.

The screen bloomed in the dim light, but the desktop didn't appear. Only two white words broke the sea of blue:

ICKY RICKY

He touched my computer. He's probably read my files. "You little fucker. You son of a bitch." He nearly laughed as he realized his outrage had restored his confidence.

"Shit, Piper," Dakota breathed behind him. "Let's get the hell out of here."

"I'm surprised he figured out how to get into the system." Rick leaned farther over the back of the chair and pushed the page down button. Nothing else was on the screen, just the file's end mark. "He's probably never had access to a computer."

"He's here alone with Jade most of the time. He has access to television, magazines, all of that. He could figure it out."

Rick nodded as he scrolled up the screen. "Shit. He *did* get into my files." The words had been written below last week's column. "The little shit." He turned to face O'Keefe. "Maybe he learned how to use this by watching me. He liked to sit in the dressing room and watch our parents make love. He'd be two feet from them, and they didn't know. He could go anywhere, and nobody ever heard him or saw him. Unless he wanted them to. He'd just watch, with this horrible grin plastered across his face." Involuntarily he shivered. "Let me unplug this and we'll leave." *For now,* he added silently.

Rick shut down the computer and pulled the jack from the back. He needed the power pack, too, which was a pain because he had to climb under the desk and reach up behind it to get to the electrical outlet and unplug it. "Shit," he said again, and pulled the chair away from the desk. "This will take a couple minutes."

He could see Dakota's foot tapping impatiently as he got down on his hands and knees. The massive desk was as deep as it was wide, and as he crawled beneath, his body blocked the light. Wishing he'd remembered the flashlight, he began to feel along the cord, intending to follow it to the outlet.

"What the hell?" he muttered as his fingers hit something cold and hard. Feeling along the floor, he realized it was a curved metal object and that the cord lifted off the floor to feed into it. What the hell was it?

"What's taking you so long?" Dakota asked nervously.

"There's something funny down here."

"Swell, just swell. For Christ's sake, be careful, Piper!" Dakota ordered. "He was fucking with your computer. You might get electrocuted or something! You've got the adapter, just get the fuck out of there! You can get another cord at the store."

"You're right." He grasped the cord just where it fed into the metal, thinking that if he couldn't pull it out of the wall socket from here, he'd do exactly what Dakota said. He yanked the cord.

Metal crashed against metal, so close that the wind of its passing blew into his face. He heard himself scream, felt his skull crash painlessly against the underside of the desk as he scrabbled, frantic to get out of the dark hole. Dakota was yelling something behind him, then suddenly his ankles were grabbed out from under him. He flopped onto his belly as O'Keefe dragged him out from under the desk.

"Rick! Are you okay?" Dakota cried.

"Yeah." He still held the cord, and now he saw the metal object he pulled along with it. "Holy Christ!"

It was a bear trap. A big rusty bear trap.

"My God," Dakota whispered as he saw the trap. *"Now* we call the cops."

Rick sat up, rubbing the back of his head as pain started to set in. "No," he said, pulling the trap forward.

"Why the fuck not?" Dakota demanded.

"It belonged to Conlin Piper." The excuse came easily since it held some truth. "It's an heirloom, and I'm not going to let the police take it as evidence. According to family history, he was fond of hunting bear in Holcomb Valley." He pointed to an area of bare wall to the left. "When I was little, there was a bearskin hanging right there. Supposedly it was Conlin's catch, but personally, I think he bought it."

"Piper, why in hell are you talking about frigging bearskins?" Dakota exploded suddenly. "You were almost killed just now, and you're acting like nothing happened!"

He didn't know why he was so calm, so instead of answering, Rick found the catch on the trap and released it, opening the jaws just enough to allow him to pull the cord free. "This thing could use a squirt of WD-40," he told Dakota, letting the jaws close again. The teeth had a quarter-inch gap between them, and he realized that if he'd put his arm in it, as had been intended, it wouldn't have been severed—quite. An unexpected giggle escaped his lips, heralding an impending case of hysterics. He pinched the back of his hand, twisting the skin between his thumb and forefinger until tears sprang to his eyes and the laughter receded.

"Rick?"

"I'm fine," he said. "It looks like the cord is, too." He looked at Dakota. "Sorry. It was a little unsettling having that thing crash down in my face. I'm lucky I still have my nose." He stood up and wrapped the cord around the adapter, then slipped it and the laptop into his computer case and put the strap over his shoulder. "Let's go."

Dakota pointed at the trap. "Are you going to leave *that* here? God knows where you'll find it next."

"Good point." He reached down and retrieved the trap. "This thing weighs a ton. I wonder how he moved it."

They descended the main staircase only to find Jade sitting in his suede recliner, petting one of her stuffed dogs. *Great. This is all I need.* "Aunt Jade?" he said stiffly.

"Stinkums is dead," she announced as she stroked the poodle, a mangy yellowish one with a faded green ribbon around its neck. It was posed so that it appeared to be sleeping, with its nose tucked beneath its tail. "He's dead, isn't he, Luvems?" She scratched Luvems behind its ear, and a clump of fur came off. "Luvems," Jade intoned, sitting up straight, "was a champion!"

"I'm sorry about—" *I can't say "Stinkums"* "—your dog," Rick finished lamely.

"He's so jealous," she said dreamily.

Rick traded glances with Dakota. "Who's jealous, Aunt Jade?"

"Why, my darling little Robin, of course. He's such a good boy. Except when he's jealous."

Jade often spoke of his brother as if he were still living, and Rick had never taken it seriously. How stupid he'd been. "Where's Robin now, Aunt Jade?"

She looked at him sharply. "Why, he's dead, Richard. You know that. He's dead and buried." She laughed, a sound like nails raking a blackboard. She stared pointedly at the bear trap. "That's a dangerous toy, Richard. Don't hurt yourself."

"What do you know about this?" Rick demanded.

"What should I know?"

"How it got under my desk. Do you know that?"

She giggled and scratched her dog's ears. "He's so jealous. And it makes me mad when something happens to my little lovedotties, but he says it means I'm his. His alone, and no one else can have me." She blushed, the cackling giggle growing m intensity.

Dakota tugged his elbow, tilting his head toward the door. Rick nodded and followed him outside.

"She knew about that trap, Piper."

Rick looked at Dakota. "I agree."

"She's psycho." O'Keefe paused. "So's your brother. Anyone who would make love to that dried-up old snatch-cracker would have to be mad."

"I agree." Suddenly the consumer spot on the morning news sounded attractive. "Tomorrow I'll find a place to send her and her lovedotties."

They walked toward Carmen's. "Why not today?"

Rick glanced at his watch. "Well, it's two o'clock already, for one thing. Let her have one more midnight fling." He smiled grimly. "For old times' sake."

48

Dakota was more worried about Rick now that he had acquired the determined, set look to his face and shoulders than he'd even been when the guy had been scared half to death and worried that he was losing his marbles.

Now, as Dakota sat in Carmen's bedroom applying his Marilyn makeup, he didn't know what Piper was up to. Less than an hour ago, Rick had assured him that he had no intention of doing anything, like going back into the house tonight, but Dakota wasn't sure he believed him.

After leaving their things at Carmen's, Rick had insisted on going into the workshop and pushing the old Rambler out of its spot in the corner. The two back side windows were broken out, and there were candy wrappers, apple cores, and white Styrofoam meat trays with bits of dried-up meat still clinging under the edges of the cellophane hidden beneath a blanket in the back of the car. The interior smelled like rotting garbage, dirty skin, and worst of all, an X-rated peep show booth. It was foul.

After that, they explored the area where the car had been stored. There were no openings in the floor, but before long, they found a well-hidden passage built into the paneled wall. Piper hadn't even known it existed. To Dakota's surprise, Piper made no attempt to block it, just stared at it with that new and disturbingly resolute set to his jaw.

Back at the Zapatas', Rick set about convincing Carmen

that she and Hector should go away for the night. Dakota could hear parts of the conversation, low, intense discussion that worried him, but when he opened his mouth to say that in his opinion the Zapatas should go nowhere tonight of all nights, Carmen and Rick stared at him as if he were something from another planet. Then Carmen had squeezed Piper's hand and said solemnly that what had to be, had to be.

Next they talked about removing Cody for the night, but the boy came home from school in the middle of that and insisted he wanted to stay home, and Piper, surprisingly, sided with him. When Carmen objected, he pointed out that three adults would be with him at all times. A few minutes later, he had Cody put on his Superman costume, then took him along with him to see Shelly and deliver her costume for the sleep-over party at the Larsons' tonight.

An hour later, they returned, the visit with Shelly, Piper said, having gone very well.

Makeup complete, Dakota pinned his blond wig on, then slipped off his robe in favor of panty hose, high heels, and one of his retired performance white chiffon dresses.

"Voilà," he said, striking a pursed-lip pose in the mirror. "Marilyn is reborn."

He swept into the living room. "Trick or treat, big boy!"

Cody looked up from the television and laughed with delight. Rick, who sat on the couch silently brooding, smiled thinly.

"Well, is that a Tootsie Roll in your pocket or are you just happy to see me, Piper?"

"Dakota," he said wearily, and glanced at his son.

"Sorry. Where are Carmen and Hector?"

"In their bedroom."

Dakota raised his eyebrows suggestively, but Rick just looked bored.

"They're getting ready to leave for her sister's place in Madelyn."

"Piper, this makes no sense." Dakota asked. "Why do you want them to leave? What's your plan?"

"No plan," Rick said nonchalantly. "It works well for everyone. Since we don't want to stay in the big house, we'll have plenty of room here. Carmen doesn't mind at all, and she really wanted to go visit her sister anyway. After we go trick-or-treating, the four of us can come back here, lock ourselves in, and watch movies till dawn. We'll have our own little Halloween party, right, Cody?"

"Right!" the boy said enthusiastically. "You know what? After we saw Shelly, we rented movies and everything. We got *Blazing Saddles* and *Young Frankenstein* and . . . what else, Daddy?"

"*Love at First Bite*. And *Frankenhooker* for later."

"Well, they're almost horror movies," Dakota said.

"Close enough." Rick's gaze drifted to the clock. "It's almost five. I hope Audrey gets here soon."

Dakota planted himself close to Rick and waited until Cody was lost in cartoons. "Piper," he said softly. "Why do you want your son here?"

"If Big Jack exists, I want him to see it. So he knows that it's a real danger."

The Zapatas came out of their bedroom carrying overnight bags, and the look on Hector's face when he saw Marilyn instantly put Dakota in a better mood. Grabbing his long white scarf, he strutted forth and sang a few breathy bars of "Let Me Entertain You." Carmen laughed and applauded. Hector, grinning and blushing, backed into the wall as Dakota descended upon him, flipping his scarf behind Hector's head and pulling the compact little man forward. He jumped back just before his nose made contact with Dakota's breasts, and O'Keefe let him go, purring, "A hard man is good to find." Hector blushed, smiling uncertainly.

"Ricky?" Carmen asked as Dakota strolled up. "You sure this is okay?"

"I'm sure," he said firmly. "We'll take good care of the place, I promise."

"I brought some extra sheets and towels over from the main house," she said. "They're on the bed."

"Thanks."

A knock on the door made Dakota glance around.

"Audrey's here!" Cody sang, and ran to the door. She stepped inside, wearing jeans and a chambray shirt with a red bandanna in her pocket. On her head she wore a pair of springy antennae topped with blue glittery Styrofoam balls that bounced every time she moved.

"That's not much of a costume, sister dear," Dakota admonished.

"It's a hell of a lot better than Rick's," she countered.

"He's a poop."

"I can see that."

Costumeless Rick remained on the couch, smiling impassively.

"Well, sis, what are you?"

"Hillbilly space alien."

"Lock all the windows tonight, Ricky," Carmen said as she crossed the room, Hector on her tail. "Lock *all* of them. And the doors."

"Don't worry, I will."

"You all be back here before full dark, and don't leave the house until morning," Carmen continued, her voice filled with grave innuendo. "It's Halloween, you know."

"We'll be good," Dakota promised, eyeing Piper. "I'll see to that."

Rick stood as the Zapatas left, crossed to Audrey, and self-consciously pecked her on the cheek. She countered with a solid kiss on his lips.

"So," Rick said. "Let's go trick-or-treating."

"Be ready in a sec. Gotta powder my antennae." Audrey disappeared into the bathroom.

Cody was still staring at the TV, so Dakota pulled Rick aside.

"What are you up to, Piper?"

"What do you mean?"

"You're planning something."

Rick shrugged. "Yeah, right. I plan to make popcorn and watch movies."

"Let me put it another way. Where do you plan to sleep tomorrow night?"

"In my house."

"Why will it be safe tomorrow night?"

"I hope to have Jade moved out by then."

"Besides that. What about . . . the other problem?"

Rick stared at him. "Pest control," he said simply, and turned to Cody. "Let's go, Superboy!"

49

Watching Cody and Dakota, who would never grow up, trick-or-treat while he and Audrey held hands and waited on the sidewalk had been fun, but Rick had been so anxious to get back to the house that he could barely concentrate long enough to make coherent conversation. He told Audrey that it was because he was nervous about seeing Big Jack, and she accepted that, but her brother kept watching him. He knew there was more going on than Rick would admit to, and now Rick worried that O'Keefe would be a problem later. All afternoon O'Keefe had asked him what his plans were, which was actually sort of funny because he truly didn't have any plans. All he knew was that tonight he would confront Robin.

Rick announced that the trick-or-treating was done at six forty-five, and Cody and Dakota, who had collected more candy than Rick had ever seen, both protested, but only mildly. They returned to the car and headed for the house.

The last light of day died as they pulled up the driveway. His stomach in a knot, Rick killed the engine and got out, scooping Cody into his arms.

As they passed the oak, the jacks were as thick and active as Rick had ever seen them, but there was no sign of Big Jack, and he felt so little fear that even the talismanic phrase *I'm Thomas* was unnecessary. Even when they combined and rose right in front of him, he steadfastly ignored them, walking unflinchingly through their greenish forms, feeling the chill wind that went with them and not caring.

He stopped at the front porch and handed Cody to Dakota. "Wait just a second. I promised Carmen I'd look in on Jade."

"Piper—"

Rick ran up the steps. "I'll leave the door open and I'll be right back."

"I'm going with you," Audrey said, trotting after him.

That was fine. He entered the living room and began to cross to Jade's door, intending to do as Carmen asked, just knock politely and tell her good night.

"Fuck me," Jade moaned from within her rooms.

Behind him, Audrey made a strangled sound. Rick turned and grimaced at her, then whispered, "Let's go."

"That was fast," Dakota said as Rick locked the front door.

"She's having her last fling."

"Last fling?" Audrey asked.

"Piper's going to find her a rest home tomorrow," Dakota explained as they quickly walked up the side of the house and around to the Zapata cottage. "Hopefully one well stocked with dirty old men."

The interior of the cottage was warm and cozy, and while Cody spread his booty on the floor and Dakota checked the locks on the house's two entry doors and the latches on all the windows, Rick and Audrey started making popcorn in the microwave.

"We're as tight as bugs in rugs," O'Keefe announced, entering the kitchen. "What have we got to drink?"

"Pepsi or Dos Equis," Rick said.

Dakota opened the fridge, took a beer for himself and a plastic bottle of orange juice for Cody. "What do you two want?"

"Beer," Audrey said absently.

"Pepsi," Rick said, ignoring Dakota's look of surprise. He took a bag of popcorn from the oven, stuck another one in. "Did you want to change clothes, O'Keefe?"

"Piper, dear, I *like* dressing this way." He grinned. "It makes me feel sexy."

"Sorry. I forgot. Watch out for the cat," he added, forcing a grin, trying to act normal. "His claws will shred your frock."

By eight o'clock, halfway into *Young Frankenstein,* Cody had passed out on the floor, the victim of excitement and too much chocolate. While Audrey put him to bed on the little couch in the tiny second bedroom where Carmen kept her sewing machine, Rick stood and sauntered into the kitchen.

"Get me another beer, will you, Piper?" Dakota called.

"I have something better," Rick called back, eyeing the bottle of Sauza Gold on top of the refrigerator.

"Well, bring whatever's better, but bring a beer, too."

"Sure," Rick said. He took the bottle down. A few shooters would make Dakota stop worrying and watching.

Icky Ricky, icky Ricky, come out and play.

He shivered. This was the first time he'd really heard the greenjacks' song all evening. *You heard the voices because you let your guard down.*

"Boo!" Audrey cried, poking his ribs from behind.

He jumped, almost dropping the bottle.

"Oh, Rick, I'm sorry. I didn't mean to scare you!"

"It's okay," he said shakily. "You're allowed on Halloween."

"What are you going to do with that?" she asked, pointing at the bottle.

"Well," he said, opening the fridge and rummaging in the fruit bin until he found a lime, "have you ever had a shooter?"

She made a face. "Yes. Yucko. Is there any margarita mix?"

"Try that cabinet."

Maybe Audrey's was the better idea. After all, he didn't want to get the O'Keefes too plastered to take care of Cody, just relaxed enough not to miss him when he slipped out the back door.

"Eureka," she said, pulling out a green bottle of mix. She set it down. "Glasses?"

"Over there."

He waited until she'd set them beside the mix, then shooed her out of the room. "I'm the host," he said, a tub of margarita salt in his hand. "I'll do the mixing."

"Rick, let me help you——"

"No." He kissed her nose, then led her into the living room, instructing her to sit on the couch by the lovely Marilyn, who demanded his beer.

Rick just smiled. "Forget beer," he told him. "I'm making margaritas. It's better for that girlish figure."

Dakota batted his eyelashes. "I didn't know you cared."

"Slut," giggled Audrey, poking him in the ribs.

Rick left them to their teasing and returned to the kitchen, where he mixed three large drinks, two with double shots of tequila, one with no alcohol.

By nine they were running *Frankenhooker,* and Rick had just delivered a third drink to Dakota. Audrey had stopped at two, saying she'd fall asleep if she had any more, but long, tall Dakota seemed to be a bottomless pit.

"You don't seem very drunk, Piper," he commented as Rick sat down next to Audrey, who was giggling at the movie.

Rick didn't feel capable of anything more than a stupid grin, so he gave Dakota that and said, "I'm just tired." He sipped his drink and grinned again. "I'm a little sleepy."

"This is supposed to be a party," Dakota said, his voice slurring slightly. "Don't go pooping out on me. You either, Audrey."

They sat there for twenty minutes, Dakota engrossed in the movie, Audrey half-asleep. Quietly Rick stood, intending to slip away.

"Where the hell do you think you're going?" Dakota demanded.

Inspiration hit. "I'm going to lie down for a few minutes. I'm really tired, but a nap ought to be enough to keep me up for the rest of the night." His smile, he hoped, was winsome. "Would you do me a favor and wake me up in half an hour?" Judging by Dakota's heavy eyelids, he wouldn't be awake that long himself.

Dakota looked doubtful. "Well, okay. But only a half hour." He glanced at his dozing sister. "You two aren't much fun."

"Sorry," Rick said, heading toward the back of the little house. "I'll be more fun after a nap."

Dakota didn't answer, his attention already back on the TV screen. Rick slipped into the bathroom, and when he came out again, Dakota didn't notice him. He slipped into the room Cody was sleeping in and opened the unobtrusive second door, which led into the kitchen on the far side of the refrigerator.

Picking up the six-inch knife he'd used to cut the lime, he slipped it in his jacket pocket, then let himself out the kitchen door.

In the bedroom, Cody awoke to the closet door creeping open. The sight of his friend scared him at first, but when Bob smiled, the little boy felt much better.

50

Standing on Carmen's side porch in the chill windy night, Rick Piper stared at the back of his house. No lights were on, even though he'd purposely left several burning. Possibly Jade had doused the downstairs lights, but he doubted that she was responsible for the upper floor.

Adrenaline coursing through him, he scanned the yard. The orange trees loomed close around him, and he knew that here, even if Big Jack was standing right beside him, he wouldn't know it. Quickly he walked down the path that led out of the orchard, and as he crossed the small lawn, he could vaguely hear the jacks' taunting calls, though he saw only three or four at the edges of the trees. They were in front, he knew, and many of them were probably busy with Big Jack at the moment.

As he reached the back door and inserted the key in the lock, the wind howled and whistled through the citrus trees behind him. *Big Jack?* he wondered as he fumbled with the lock. "Come on, come on, come on." The whistling sounds grew nearer, then he heard the crunching of footsteps approaching—the familiar sound of Big Jack's tread, like someone walking in a pile of autumn leaves.

Terrified, he jiggled the knob. Nothing happened, and he twisted it harder. "Come on, goddammit!"

Suddenly the lock gave and he swiftly entered the house, pulling the door closed behind him. He didn't bother locking it—greenjacks couldn't leave their natural habitat without donning a human body. Leaves and bark wouldn't do the trick.

Swallowing, he forced himself to turn and look out the window. Something moved among the liquid amber trees, just a flicker at the edge of his vision. *It's nothing,* he told himself, moving deeper into the house.

He didn't want to turn on the lights, and he realized that, as usual, he'd forgotten to bring a flashlight. Trying to move silently, trying not to knock against anything in the dark, he moved through the dining room and into the living room.

Now what? Without a clue, he sat down on the couch so that his back was against the wall and he could see all the corners of the room. He waited a moment, then rose and crossed to the picture window. He drew the drapes wide open. *Might as well see everything you're waiting for.*

The front lawn was a madhouse of activity, and he had to force the jacks' intrusive voices out of his mind, to refuse to acknowledge their attempts to frighten him with their oozing, shifting shapes. He flipped them the bird.

"That's not nice, icky Ricky."

The voice drifted down from the top of the stairs, nearly stopping his heart.

He turned and peered up into the darkness. "Robin?" he called softly.

His brother's laugh was a harsh, ugly sound. "You think you've changed, little brother, but you haven't. You're still a chicken, icky Ricky."

"And you're not my brother." He approached the stairs and stood in the safety of shadows.

"You tell people that, they'll think you're crazy."

"Better get a new line, jack-off. That one doesn't work anymore."

"Oh ho, ho boy, and I thought baby brother was still a scaredy-cat, but he's grown some balls." Robin cackled to himself. "Or maybe he's just really, *really* crazy. Is that it, icky Ricky? Are you crazy?"

The old taunts still worked. Rick's confidence slipped a

notch. *Don't listen to him. This is how he gets you. He's pushing your buttons to get what he wants.*

"Baby brother, are you still there?"

"Go to hell."

Robin only laughed. "You *must* be crazy if your own little girl thinks you tried to fuck her. Have you ever seen your daughter naked, icky Ricky? She's got nice tits and a tight little cunt that—"

"I'm going to kill you, you bastard!" Ricky's cry ricocheted up the stairwell as he stepped onto the bottom riser.

Robin laughed. "You should give your girl a whirl, baby brother. She's hot, she's hot, and she'll beg you for more!"

He's trying to lure you upstairs. In spite of his overwhelming fury, Rick forced himself to remain where he was. "I'm going to kill you tonight," he said, his voice shaking with unleashed anger. "You can count on it."

"Oh boy, icky Ricky really does have balls." Peals of maniacal laughter floated down. "Your daughter's snatch smells good, did you know that, icky Ricky?"

I will not react, I will not react, I will not react. But his other foot moved onto the steps of its own accord.

"I watched you fuck your girlfriend. Remember when we watched good old Mom and Dad fuck, dicky Ricky? Remember that?"

Rick didn't reply. Slowly he continued up the stairs, keeping to the shadowy edges, his hand gripping the hilt of the knife.

"Hey, I read your stories, icky Ricky. I guess you think you're a big hotshot, don'tcha, pricky Ricky? Did you like the surprise I left for you under the desk?" He paused. "Jade helped me move it. She's all the snatch I got these days, baby brother. I think you'd better start sharing your daughter *and* your girlfriend." He cackled evilly. "It's the brotherly thing to do. You with all that nooky, and all I have is that dried-up old douche-bag. I did it to her in your water bed tonight, icky Ricky. It was fun." He cleared his throat. "Your cock's almost as big as mine, little brother, but you need some lessons. I can show you how to *really* fuck your girlfriend. How about I show you how to fuck your daughter, too?"

"No!" He couldn't stand it any longer, and suddenly he was tearing blindly up the staircase, the knife out, intent on murder.

Something sharp and cold sliced across his shinbone as he reached the landing. It withdrew, then came again, and this time he could feel the chill of it inside the meat of his calf. The coldness pulled free, and Rick whirled in the dark, stabbing the knife in front of him.

Metal hit metal, the knife deflecting Robin's next thrust, and Rick backed up, feeling for the light switch on the wall. His brother laughed again, then something whizzed through the air, grazing his midriff and clattering to the floor somewhere beyond.

"I'm gonna go play outside, icky Ricky. Why don't you come and play with me?"

slap-slap slap-slap slap-slap

The sound of hand-slaps descending the stairs chilled him. His fingers finally found the light switch, flipped it on.

He stepped forward, nearly tripping over his left leg, grabbing the railing for balance. Looking down, he saw that his brother was gone. The front door hung open. "Jesus," he whispered as the pain hit him. Clutching his leg, he dropped to the floor.

"Sweet Jesus," he breathed. The side of his leg was sheathed in blood. He couldn't see the wounds, but blood was pumping out of him rapidly, and he had to stop it now. Using the railing for leverage, he pulled himself up and started for his bedroom. Then, a moment later, his foot hit something. He looked down.

The sword Audrey had given him lay on the floor, the blade coated with his own blood.

Grimly he grabbed it by the hilt and took it with him. His brother had managed to climb all the way to the shelf in the dressing room, seven feet off the ground, to get to it. *So what else is new?*

Safely inside the bedroom, Rick turned on the light and

locked the door behind him, then limped through the dressing room, pausing only to slide the sword through the cabinet doors to ensure that his brother couldn't get in. Entering the bathroom, he flipped the toilet lid down and sat heavily, dizzy from shock and, perhaps, blood loss.

He pulled open the vanity, found the scissors, cut his pant leg off at the knee, then began to pull the material, but it was stuck in his flesh. Gritting his teeth, he pulled it free.

Both wounds were in his lower leg. The saber had run clean through the fleshy part of his calf, and it hurt like hell. The other was near his knee. The blade had glanced off his shinbone, and his stomach turned as he saw the white bone under the meat. *Dakota will be pleased. I'll consent to stitches this time.*

Resolutely he pulled a clean towel from the cabinet and began wrapping the leg. As he worked, he purposefully set about building his anger, thinking about the things Robin had said about his daughter, so that by the time he grabbed a roll of adhesive tape and began wrapping it tightly around the towel, his outrage outweighed his pain. "You little fucker," he whispered, limping into the dressing room. He pulled the sword free. "You're dead, you're dead, you're dead."

Using the sword as a cane, he entered the bedroom and eyed the phone on the side of the bed. Maybe he should call Dakota or Audrey and let them call the police.

He reached for the phone and stopped as he realized his expensive bedspread was soaking wet. *What the hell?* He grabbed the edge of the comforter and pulled it back, revealing sodden bunched blankets. He pulled those away, too.

"Dear God," he whispered.

Jade was in the mattress. Not on it, in it, floating in the water and air baffles, her sightless eyes staring at him through a thin covering of water.

I did it to her in your water bed.

He saw the X-shaped slit in the mattress and knew that Robin must have lured her up here onto the bed, then killed her and sliced the mattress open with the sword. The plastic liner and high sides had kept any water from escaping.

He picked up the phone, heard no dial tone, then saw that the cord had been cut. "Shit."

The lights went out.

Ordering himself to remain calm, he felt for the nightstand, opened the drawer, and grabbed the flashlight. He switched it on, and found that there were only minutes of dim glow left before the batteries failed altogether. Leaning on the sword, holding the light, he hobbled toward the staircase.

"Daddy! Are you okay? Bob said you were hurt."

The sound of Cody's voice turned Rick's gut to ice. *Don't panic.* He halted and shined the light down the long hallway. His son stood partially visible in the open doorway of his room. "Cody!"

"Daddy! Bob said I had to come!"

"Come here, Cody! Run! Now!"

"Daddy!" the child cried, then Robin's laugh boomed down the corridor as a huge arm thrust Cody farther out into the hallway. Robin's head appeared in the doorway, his silhouette only slightly shorter than Cody's.

"Come and get him, icky Ricky!" Cackling, he yanked the boy back into the room. "Catch him if you can!"

Robin's going for the oak tree! Swearing, he tried to run. He had to get there before Robin opened the window. "Christ." His leg twisted painfully and he fell. Biting back a scream, he pulled himself up and continued on, dragging his leg behind him. It seemed to take forever.

Cody screamed. Robin laughed.

"I'll kill you, you son of a bitch," Rick yelled as he stumbled toward the room. Angrily he shook tears of pain from his eyes.

He made the doorway, only to see that, across the room, the window was already open. "Cody?"

"We're out here, icky Ricky. We're having a little monkey climb."

Robin rested his short body in the thick crotch of the tree, Cody trapped in his bulging arms.

"Cody!" Rick staggered forward.

"Daddy!"

"Come and get him, icky Ricky!" Robin taunted. "Come out and play!"

Rick made it to the window and pulled himself onto the ledge, memories of that other night so long ago flooding his mind. That night Robin had given up his life to save Rick's.

Tonight Rick had to save his son. "Hold on, Cody. I'm coming."

"Balls, balls, icky Ricky has balls." Robin turned to Cody. "Your daddy was a coward, did you know that? Oh yes, we all thought he was crazy. Crazy, crazy, crazy! He had no balls, no balls at all. But now he does. He thinks he does! Look at him coming out here with his sword, just to save little old you."

Rick edged into the tree, leaving the flashlight behind. The full moon cast plenty of light, and for the first time, he saw his twin's face.

It was like looking in a distorted mirror at a carnival. It was him, but not him, a twisted ugly vision of himself, paper white from living in the tunnels, and warped with anger and hatred. He remembered his grandfather saying that when greenjacks can't communicate with their own kind, their frustration and loneliness overwhelm them and turn them from mischievous, selfish creatures to twisted, evil things. *He's insane, not me.* A tiny thread of pity twisted through him, and was gone.

"You going to stick me with that sword, icky Ricky?" Robin sang as Rick edged closer. "If you do, I'll drop your little baby boy right on the ground, head first, and his head will break open and all his brains will goosh out."

Cody began to cry.

"Let him go," Rick said softly. "He can't see them."

"I know that, you asshole."

"You want *my* body."

"Of course I do, and if I let your baby boy go, you're just going to hand it over, right?"

"No. Let him go and I'll fight you for it."

Robin regarded him, then looked down as a windy whistling sound began below. Foliage crunched.

"He's here, icky Ricky, he's here."

A skeletal hand appeared on the branch where Robin sat. A second appeared.

Rick stood paralyzed, his pain forgotten.

Big Jack's face appeared, just as he remembered it, brown and green, with huge, leering, fathomless black pits for eyes, and vines growing out from between the bark-chip teeth.

It opened its mouth, and he heard the whistling sound again, like wind hissing. In its neck the jugular vine pulsed with life; in the torso, obscenely green growth glistened and throbbed among the white net of tiny roots.

One long leg bent, and it placed its twig-and-stick foot on the limb next to Robin. An instant later, it pulled itself up.

To Rick's horror, Robin handed Cody to Big Jack.

"Save him, save him, icky Ricky!" Robin screeched before descending the tree, swinging down like a monkey.

Rick stepped forward, raising the sword. Big Jack hissed, sibilant, snakelike, and Cody cried, squirming in its grasp.

"Cody," Rick called softly. "Cody, you can hurt it. It's just leaves, son. Pull the leaves, hard."

The boy did nothing for a moment, then suddenly yanked on one vine, then another. With a cry, he plunged both hands into the heart of the thing and began yanking with all his might.

Rick sliced the sword through the air but hit nothing, but Big Jack was fending off Cody's attack and didn't appear to notice. Rick sent the blade whickering through the air again, and this time it struck the heavy branch that made the monster's thighbone.

It cracked. Big Jack wavered.

"Cody, grab the tree!" Rick ordered as he struck again.

"Piper!" Dimly he heard Dakota calling him from somewhere below. "Piper! Where the hell are you?"

The thigh snapped and Big Jack fell, taking Cody with him. The boy's thin scream cut through Rick like a knife.

They seemed to fall forever. Out of the corner of his eye, he saw Dakota, still in drag, and Audrey, running across the lawn.

Big Jack caught a limb halfway down and held on. Cody clung to its torso. "Climb down," Rick called. "Climb down its leg and you can jump from there. Go to Dakota."

"Piper! Cody!" Dakota called.

"Here!" Rick screamed as loud as he could. "The oak tree!"

Cody had slithered almost the entire length of Big Jack's body when Dakota appeared below. He reached up and snatched the child into his arms, then Audrey took Cody from him and retreated, moving toward the house.

Dakota remained where he was, staring upward. "Shit, Piper," he cried. "That's the damned Big Jack, isn't it?"

"Yeah," Rick called. "And it's pissed." He paused. "Dakota, be careful."

Dakota yanked on the remaining leg, once, twice, then the creature fell. Almost instantly it was upright, balancing on one foot. "Piper, its other leg's growing back!" Dakota backed away. "What the hell do I do now?"

"Run! Lock yourselves in the cottage! Now!"

"Piper!"

"Get my son and your sister in that cottage! *Now!*"

Before Dakota could move, Big Jack lurched forward, its arms out. It grabbed at O'Keefe, snagging the hem of his chiffon skirt.

"You fucker!" Dakota cried. He brought his high-heeled foot up and kicked it, but Big Jack caught his ankle, and then Dakota was down on his ass, the Green Man all over him.

"Duane!" Audrey cried from the walk near the house. She stepped forward, Cody in her arms.

"No!" Rick yelled. "Get Cody inside!"

She looked up, her face stricken.

"Go! He'll be okay."

Audrey didn't move, forward or backward, and directly below, he could see flashes of Dakota's white dress as he grappled with Big Jack. The thing was probably trying to strangle him. *I have to do something now!*

Painfully he climbed back into the house, then hobbled down the hall to the back stairs. There had to be a way to stop the thing. The sword would do it, if he could get there in time.

By the time he made the bottom of the stairs, his leg felt numb. He limped out the kitchen door and moved toward the workshop, expecting every moment to run into Robin, every second to hear Cody scream.

Then he saw the garage. "Don't be locked," he whispered as he went around to the big door to check. It wasn't even latched, thank God, and he quickly pulled the door up. Even before it thunked against its springs, he was inside the dark building, frantically trying to see where he was going.

In a glint of moonlight, he found it. Hector's riding lawn mower.

Its engine started on the second try, and he rode it out, past his car, toward the front lawn, the smell of fresh-cut grass clear in his nostrils.

As he rounded the bend, he saw Audrey and Cody still standing in the glow of the front porch light. Dakota was on his feet, but still struggling with Big Jack.

"O'Keefe," Rick yelled, "get your ass out of there!" Revving the engine, he punched the gas, and the mower trundled forward. Audrey saw him and set Cody down by the steps, then ran to Dakota and grabbed at the white material floating around him. Suddenly Rick saw the cloth give, then Dakota was loose. Audrey yanked him toward the front steps, scooped up Cody, then pointed. Dakota looked, and Rick could see his grin even from here.

"Gotcha now, Jack," he said as he aimed the machine at the creature. It turned and looked at him, then, with the combined roar of a dozen greenjacks, moved toward him.

"You're a stupid Big Jack, aren't you!"

The mower hit the monster in a shower of twigs and leaves, and the sound of a thousand snakes hissing rent the air as Rick watched the little jacks leaping from the mangled body. He backed up and ran over it again.

O'Keefe ran up as Rick took the engine down to an idling purr. "What the hell do you think you're doing out here by yourself?"

"Don't talk, O'Keefe. Get them in the cottage. Make sure it's empty, then lock yourselves in, and don't come out until I tell you."

"What? And leave you out here?"

Audrey, carrying Cody, approached. "What's going on?"

"All of you, get in that cottage now!"

"You're hurt," she said.

"I'm fine. Get inside."

"And just leave you out here?" she cried.

"I know what I'm doing."

"Where's Robin?" Dakota asked.

"We're having a meeting just as soon as you three get out of here."

"Piper, there's no way in hell that I'm going to leave you out here by yourself," O'Keefe declared.

Rick stared at him. "Yes, you are. This doesn't concern you."

Audrey kept her eyes on Rick as she handed Cody to her brother. "Duane, he has to do this by himself."

"What? Audrey, don't tell me you're buying that macho shit."

"Macho shit has nothing to do with it," Rick said grimly.

"No—"

"Duane, do you think I want him out here by himself any more than you do?" Audrey demanded. "Do you?"

Dakota shrugged.

"I don't. But he has to!"

"Okay." He punched Rick's arm. "Win one for the gipper," he said, "whatever that is."

"Thanks." Quickly he kissed Cody, then Audrey, and

watched as they disappeared around the corner of the house. A moment later, the pool lights came on, illuminating the blue water, highlighting Don Quixote as he sat on his horse, holding his lance.

Another figure sat just behind the knight.

"Robin," Rick whispered, turning the machine and riding toward the pool.

Robin waved at him as he parked the mower across the pool from the statue.

"Icky Ricky, didja come out to play?" Robin called.

As Rick turned off the motor and dismounted, Robin climbed down the statue, calling, "Icky Ricky's an artist, too, whoop-de-do."

He showed off, turning upside down and walking toward Rick in a handstand, his hands slap-slapping against the white pavement. Rick stood there, leaning on the sword, waiting. The church bells struck midnight.

Robin halted three feet from him. "A fight for possession of your body? Wasn't that your offer?"

"It doesn't count now. That was if you handed over my son. You didn't. Now I just get to kill you."

"You don't have the guts."

"Try me."

Robin's face twisted into a malignant smile. "Remember the last time you tried to kill me? You didn't have the nerve then, either." He put his callused hand out, palm upward, and slowly closed the fingers with a hard, twisting motion. "I'm surprised you could father children after I got through with you."

"You murdered Delia."

His grin was malicious. "You pissed me off, trying to strangle me like that. It's all your fault."

Rick hesitated, caught by the words. *It's not your fault,* he told himself sternly. *Don't listen to him.*

"Of course, I screwed her brains out before I killed her," his twin taunted.

Don't take the bait. Rick held his ground. "You killed Mom and Dad because they were going to send you away."

Robin nodded. "All your fault, Ricky."

"And you set the explosion at the carnival to stage your own death."

"You catch on quick, icky Ricky."

His leg throbbed, and a lead weight filled his stomach. "Do you even know how many people you killed that night?"

Robin laughed. "Nope. Who cares?"

Rick lifted the sword from the ground and stepped toward his twin. His leg almost twisted out from under him, but he managed to keep his balance. "This is for my parents and Delia and for all the carnival people you killed." He aimed the saber. "This is for my children. And this is for *me.*"

"You can't kill me," Robin said, undaunted. "They'll put you in jail."

"No. You're already dead. If you hadn't killed Jade, I'd just kill you for good and bury you out in the yard among your friends. But you committed murder and left mountains of evidence, so I'll just kill you in self-defense and tell the police all about it. No problem."

For the first time, Robin showed concern. His gaze traveled toward the left side of the house. Rick knew what he was thinking. "They won't call the police until I tell them to. It's just you and me."

On the grass at the edge of the cement, several jacks appeared to be watching. One, dimmer than the rest, waited unmoving.

"Robin," Rick said softly.

"Robin?" his twin mimicked immediately. "I told you you couldn't kill me, you sentimental asshole."

Ricky . . . The voice strained with effort to be heard. *Help me.*

Rick nodded at the quiet little jack, then turned his attention back to Robin. "My brother's here. He's here and he's watching. He's waiting for you to die so that he can go free."

Robin had been resting on his hands, doing the spider as he spoke. Suddenly, before Rick could react, his twin bent his elbows into a crouch, swung his body back, and propelled himself at his legs. The sword flew out of Rick's hands and clattered to the cement and his leg exploded with pain as he fell backwards into the cold pool water, Robin attached. He tried to kick his way to the surface, but Robin held his legs together, a lead weight pulling him down, deeper and deeper.

Fresh blood seeped redly into the clean water.

The world moved in slow motion. His lungs burned. *He's going to hold me under until I pass out, then he'll drag me out and move in.* Robin would kill the old body and assume his identity. *What am I going to do?* Black spots filled Rick's vision. He was almost out of time.

Frantically he reached down and grabbed Robin's hair, yanking his head up. His twin glared at him, and started to climb up Rick's body.

No! Rick pushed his free hand through the water and smashed it against Robin's nose, but the fluid resistance was too strong. His twin's hands dug into his thighs, crawling toward his groin, and Rick let go of his brother's hair and immediately shoved one thumb into each eye as deeply as he could.

One second. Two. Robin's hands let go of Rick's legs and flew to his wrists, trying to yank them free. Rick kicked frantically toward the surface.

His head broke water and he gulped fresh, cold air. It gave him the strength to hang on to Robin, to keep his thumbs pressed against his eyes. He winced as his twin bit into his wrist, once, then again, but he managed to keep his head above water, and Robin's below.

"Rick!"

Dimly he heard Dakota's cry. "Go!" he screamed. "Leave!" He had to concentrate on what he was doing or Robin's powerful arms would pull him free.

Long seconds passed, and finally his brother's hands loosened, then fell away. Rick grabbed one limp arm and swam to the edge of the pool. Wearily he climbed out. He turned and pulled Robin's body from the water and laid it on the cement near the grass.

The dim greenjack hovered next to it. Rick glanced

around, saw Dakota watching from the front porch. Relieved, he said, "He's dead."

Ricky!

"Trick or treat, little brother!" Robin sat up, the flesh around his eyes looking puffy and bruised. "Fooled you, didn't I?" He lunged.

Rick rolled backwards out of the way, felt the sword under his arm and grabbed its hilt. He brought it around and held it out as Robin flew at him.

Robin's eyes grew huge as he saw the sword, but it was too late. He couldn't stop, and the saber drove straight into his chest.

Screaming, he fell back on the grass, and the sword pinned him to the ground below. Rick knelt beside him and saw that it had run him through just below the heart.

Robin breathed rapidly, his eyes open and furious as the little greenjack approached. "I hate you," he snarled.

Then, for a brief second, the face went blank, and at the same time the little jack flared with bright color and its face vaguely resembled Robin's.

Icky Ricky icky Ricky icky Ricky icky Ricky.

The words faded as the ousted jack sped away toward the oak.

"Ricky."

"Robin."

His brother's face looked like his own now, open and youthful. "Robin? It's you, isn't it?"

"It's me." Robin coughed. Rick gently lifted his brother's head, letting it rest on his uninjured leg. He wiped flecks of blood from Robin's mouth and pushed the dark, wet hair from his eyes. He looked at the sword piercing the body, back at Robin.

"Leave it," his brother said.

"Okay." Rick looked toward the house. Dakota was gone, thank God.

"Every night I came out and watched you, wishing I could talk to you. But I couldn't." Robin coughed a little more blood. "I wasn't strong enough. Sometimes you heard me, though, didn't you?"

"I did."

"I thought you did. I thought I heard you answer." He reached up one trembling hand and felt the contours of Rick's face. A corner of his mouth crooked up. "We're good-looking, aren't we?"

Rick smiled. "Yes, we are. Robin, were you happy with the jacks?"

Almost imperceptibly he shook his head. "It was fun running and moving, but there was nothing else. I wasn't one of them. Their senses are different. There's no taste or smell. You can't touch anything." As he spoke he took Rick's hand. "I should have listened to you, Ricky. I shouldn't have teased you. I should have believed you."

"We were kids, Robin. Just kids."

"Yeah." Robin's voice broke. "Just kids."

"Yeah," Rick repeated, cradling his twin closer. His tears splashed down on his brother's cheek.

Robin reached up and touched a tear with his finger. "It's hot. I can feel it." He started to cry, until coughing stopped the tears. "Oh, Ricky, I missed you."

"I missed you, brother."

Robin's breath hitched a little and the color began to drain from his face. Rick took his hand again and held it against his own beating heart, barely able to see his brother, his eyes were so full. "Thank you for saving my life that night in the oak tree."

"You're welcome," Robin said softly. For an instant his eyes drifted, then he seemed to force them to focus on Rick. "Thank you for saving *my* life tonight."

Rick wiped a bubble of blood from Robin's pale lips. "I'm a little late."

"Better late than never." Robin gave him a small smile and coughed up more blood.

Rick wiped it away. "I'm sorry."

"No, don't be. Wow, this is weird." Robin seemed to be looking at something beyond Rick.

Rick glanced behind him, saw nothing. "What?"

"I can see some pretty light. I hear Mom and Dad. Do you?"

"No, I don't. Robin?"

Robin pulled his gaze back to his brother.

"People you love are coming for you. They come in the light. The light's good."

Robin coughed. "I believe you this time." He smiled slightly. "For once, I can see something you can't. Ricky, thank you. I guess we can talk more later."

"In another place," Rick said gently. "Or time."

Robin said something Rick couldn't understand. His respiration had slowed to a faint hitch that came at longer intervals.

Suddenly Robin squeezed his hand. "Ricky, I love you. I've always loved you." His hand went limp and his gaze drifted to the beyond.

"And I love you." Rick bent and kissed Robin's forehead. "Never forget," he whispered as his brother sighed and set free his final breath. "I love you."

He closed his brother's eyes and held him, and after a time, he didn't know how long, he carefully eased Robin's head down against the grass. Then, wiping his eyes, he rose and took the pool net from its holder to use as a staff.

He limped around the pool, then paused to look back across it at his brother's still form, then up at Don Quixote, who stared heroically into the night. Rick saluted him, before turning to make his way painfully across the lawn and into the backyard.

Limping up the little walkway to Carmen's cottage, he saw the warm yellow light glowing in the windows. He rapped on the door, and Audrey opened it immediately, kissing him frantically as she and Dakota put their arms around him and helped him inside, exclaiming, loving, accepting him. Berating him, too, he realized happily. Cody, asleep on the couch, woke and tried to climb into his wet lap, but Dakota gently pulled him away, telling him later, there would be plenty of time later.

"You can call the cavalry now, O'Keefe," Rick said. He suddenly felt so tired that he could barely keep his eyes open.

"Cavalry hell," Dakota said as Audrey wrapped a fresh dry towel around his leg. "I'm just calling the cleanup crew." He looked Rick up and down as Audrey draped a blanket around his shoulders. "Piper, dear, *you* are the cavalry."

Dear Readers:

I hope you've enjoyed BAD THINGS. I had a lot of fun writing it. The greenjacks (and Big Jack) are a type of element that ties into the lore of the Green Man. He is an archetypical nature god dating to the earliest humans. The most famous variation is Pan, and it was his horns and cloven hooves that the European invaders assigned to Satan. As usual, the god of the old became the devil of the new.

Sometimes called Jack O' the Green, the nature deity was banished by church of Rome missionaries sent to the British Isles by Pope Gregory the Great in 600 A.D. Pagan artists forced to adorn the churches quickly began sculpting many of their nature deities (primarily the Green Man) into the ornamentation of these buildings. That way the people could secretly worship their own gods.

My next novel is an unusual ghost story. Psychologist Will Banning is haunted by a just-out-of-reach memory from his childhood. Trying to uncover this forbidden secret dominates his thoughts until his attention is diverted by lifelong friend (and should-be lover) Maggie Maewood, who tells him about the strange behavior of animals in her veterinary clinic. Will, having already noticed strange avian behavior, is fascinated.

Then people begin acting strangely too. His office is filled with patients, old and new, exhibiting sudden signs of schizophrenia, seeing ghosts, hearing voices. After one patient tells him something that, on the surface, seems outrageous but has a ring of truth, Will delves deeper and deeper, unconcerned with the danger of asking too many questions.

As always, I look forward to hearing from my readers. You can visit my Web site at www.tamarathorne.com.

Best,
Tamara

Nail-Biting Romantic Suspense
from Your Favorite Authors

Thrilling Suspense From
Wendy Corsi Staub

__All the Way Home	0-7860-1092-4	$6.99US/$8.99CAN
__The Last to Know	0-7860-1196-3	$6.99US/$8.99CAN
__Fade to Black	0-7860-1488-1	$6.99US/$9.99CAN
__In the Blink of an Eye	0-7860-1423-7	$6.99US/$9.99CAN
__She Loves Me Not	0-7860-1768-6	$4.99US/$6.99CAN
__Dearly Beloved	0-7860-1489-X	$6.99US/$9.99CAN
__Kiss Her Goodbye	0-7860-1641-8	$6.99US/$9.99CAN
__Lullaby and Goodnight	0-7860-1642-6	$6.99US/$9.99CAN
__The Final Victim	0-8217-7971-0	$6.99US/$9.99CAN

Available Wherever Books Are Sold!

Visit our website at **www.kensingtonbooks.com**